Elisabeth Engberg-Pedersen
Space in Danish Sign Language

**International Studies on Sign Language
and Communication of the Deaf**

Volume 19

Elisabeth Engberg-Pedersen

Space in Danish Sign Language

The Semantics and Morphosyntax of the Use of Space in a Visual Language

SIGNUM

International Studies on
Sign Language and Communication of the Deaf
edited by Siegmund Prillwitz

on behalf of the *Society* and the *Center*
for German Sign Language and Communication of the Deaf
University of Hamburg

Volume 19

This thesis has been accepted, on December the 3rd 1991, by the Faculty of the Arts, University of Copenhagen, for public defence for the degree of doctor of philosophy.

Denne afhandling er den 3. december 1991 af Det humanistiske Fakultet ved Københavns Universitet antaget til offentligt at forsvares for den filosofiske doktorgrad.

9. december 1991   *Jan Riis Flor*, dekan

Forsvaret finder sted den 10. september 1993 kl. 13.00 i lokale 15.1.30A, Københavns Universitet, Amager, Njalsgade 80.

Die Deutsche Bibliothek - CIP-Einheitsaufnahme
Engberg-Pedersen, Elisabeth:
Space in Danish sign language : the semantics and
morphosyntax of the use of space in a visual language /
Elisabeth Engberg-Pedersen. - Hamburg : Signum-Verl., 1993
   (International Studies on sign language and communication of the
   deaf ; Vol. 19)
   Zugl.: Kopenhagen, Univ., Diss., 1993
   ISBN 3-927731-45-5
NE: Internationale Arbeiten zur Gebärdensprache und Kommunikation
   Gehörloser

© 1993 SIGNUM-Verlag
Hans-Albers-Platz 2, (2000) HAMBURG 36
Tel. (040) 319 21 40 • Fax (040) 319 62 05

Coverpainting: Paul Klee *Schwarzer Fürst*, 1927. Staatliche Kunstsammlung Düsseldorf
Herstellung: Poppdruck Langenhagen
Printed in Germany
ISBN 3-927731-45-5

Acknowledgements

In 1976 Inger Ahlgren told me about her work with deaf children and her study of their acquisition of Swedish Sign Language. I was attracted by the idea of a language expressed in a different medium and later wrote to Britta Hansen at the Centre for Total Communication in Copenhagen to enquire if there was any possibility for me to get involved in research on Danish Sign Language. Britta immediately invited me to take part in projects at the centre.

Compared with many signed language researchers who have had to start from scratch in their respective countries, I have had the advantage of being welcomed by deaf and hearing people eager to contribute to my research. I would like to take this opportunity of expressing my gratitude to all the people, deaf and hearing, who have supported and encouraged my work by contributing their language and intuitions and by wanting to learn from the results. In particular, I wish to thank the people from whose language the examples in the book have been taken, namely Eva Abildgaard, Asger Bergmann, Ritva Bergmann, Jane Brøndum, Leif Frederiksen, Anne Skov Hårdell, Jørgen "Rødtop" Nielsen, Ketty Nielsen, Annegrethe Pedersen, Inga Pedersen, Birthe Petersen, and Sussi Toft.

For this work, I have benefitted from discussions with many linguists. I would like to thank in particular Inger Ahlgren, Karen Albertsen, Brita Bergman, Una Canger (the Aztec material), Michael Fortescue (the Koyukon material), Robert E. Johnson, and Scott K. Liddell. *Space in Danish Sign Language* was presented for evaluation as a doctoral thesis at the University of Copenhagen. The evaluation committee, consisting of Penny Boyes Braem, Jørgen Rischel, and Henning Spang-Hanssen, wrote a very penetrating and thorough criticism for which I am also grateful.

Marina McIntire took on the extensive and tedious work of correcting my English and improving the style of the text.

Needless to say, I am responsible for all errors and shortcomings.

I worked on this book at the Department of General and Applied Linguistics, University of Copenhagen, the Department of Linguistics and Interpreting, Gallaudet University, and the Centre for Total Communication, Copenhagen.

The work was supported by the Danish Research Council for the Humanities and, through a grant to the Centre for Total Communication, by the Egmont Foundation. The photos were taken by Gerda K. Nielsen; the model is Eva Abildgaard; the drawings were made by Hanna Orlof, the cover was designed by Tomas Vollhaber. The publication of the book was supported by the Danish Research Council for the Humanities and Lillian and Dan Fink's Foundation.

Roskilde, November 1992
Elisabeth Engberg-Pedersen

Contents

I Introduction

1	Linguistic analysis of signed languages and language universals	13
2	Traditional analyses of the use of space in signed languages and localist linguistic theories	16
3	The aims of the present analysis	18
4	The composition of the book	20
5	Characterisation of the data	23
5.1	Expectations of iconicity	23
5.2	Judgements of grammaticality	25
5.3	Different language varieties	30
5.4	The informants and the data of this study	33
6	Form analysis of signs	35
6.1	The articulatory means of signed languages	35
6.2	The manual alphabets, the Mouth-Hand System, and names	43
6.3	Liddell and Johnson's sequential form analysis of signs	45
6.4	The term *locus*	52
6.5	Formal description of some different verb types	57
6.6	The morphological type of signed languages	60

II Discourse and Space

1	Introduction	69
2	The frame of reference	71
3	Time lines	80
3.1	The time lines	80
3.2	A comparison with time lines in spoken languages	90
3.3	Conclusion	95
4	Loci and referentiality	97
5	Shifted reference, shifted attribution of expressive elements, and shifted locus	103
6	Pointing signs	117
6.1	Types of pointing signs	117
6.2	The pronoun, the determiner, and information-packaging	128
6.3	Person, place, and shifters	131
7	Discourse and space: Conclusion	140

III Verbs and Space

1	Localism and transitivity	147
2	Different types of modifications: An overview	151
3	Earlier verb classifications	157
4	Plain signs	162
5	Modifications for distribution	165
6	Semantic agreement and marking for a specific point of view	173
6.1	Alternative descriptions	173
6.2	Agreement features, direction, and domain	183
6.3	The many uses of the *c*–form	194
6.4	First person, point of view, and agentivity	208
7	Pragmatic agreement	214
7.1	Pragmatic agreement, semantic agreement, and point-of-view marking	214
7.2	Other treatments of phenomena like pragmatic agreement	221
7.3	Equivalents to pragmatic agreement in spoken languages	224
8	Polymorphemic verbs	227
8.1	Introduction	227

8.2	Predicate classifiers and classificatory verbs in spoken languages	235
8.3	Classifiers or verb stems in Danish Sign Language?	243
8.4	Movement morphemes in polymorphemic verbs	254
8.5	Categories of stems in polymorphemic verbs	273
8.6	Polymorphemic verbs and space	283

IV Space in Danish Sign Language 307

Appendix A: Signed language in Denmark	319
Appendix B: Guide to the transcriptions	321
References	327
Subject index	341
Name index	345
Index of signs in the illustrations	349
List of figures	350
Summary in Danish / resumé på dansk	351
Illustrations	359

I
Introduction

1 Linguistic analysis of signed languages and language universals

What can we learn from the study of signed languages? Earlier the study of these languages was clearly seen as relevant primarily to the teaching of deaf children. The earliest description of Danish Sign Language was three pamphlets by the medical doctor P. A. Castberg, who founded the first school for the deaf in Copenhagen in 1807. They were entitled *Om Tegn- eller Gebærde-Sproget med Hensyn på dets Brug af Døvstumme og dets Anvendelighed ved deres Undervisning* ('Of the Sign or Gesture Language with Regard to Its Use by the Deaf-and-Dumb and Its Usefulness in the Teaching of Them') (1809-1811).[1] But since the first modern linguistic analysis of a signed language, William Stokoe's description of American Sign Language (ASL) in 1960 (revised edition from 1978), which focused on the structure of individual signs, but covered also parts of the grammar, signed language research has spread to all areas of linguistic analysis. (For an overview of the research on ASL, see Wilbur 1987.) Today there are partial linguistic analyses of signed languages from many parts of the world.

The linguistic analyses of signed languages seek to find their characteristics as languages and to test universal claims about language structure. Sign linguists take as their point of departure that signed languages are natural languages, in the sense that they are the primary means of communication among human beings in everyday situation of life and that they are not parasitic on any other means of communication. Signed languages make use of different means of expression than spoken languages. To the extent that claims about linguistic universals are based on theories about human linguistic and cognitive skills or about the necessity of specific structural distinctions in a communication system as rich as any natural language, we must examine whether the universal claims are also true of signed languages irrespective of differences in expressive means. As the research on signed languages has progressed and it has become clear that such languages can be described as natural languages, the focus has shifted: if the universals claimed for other natural languages are true as well of signed languages, despite any differences in means of expression, the universals are corroborated. Otherwise, it must be examined whether the universals can be explained as dependent on specific means of expression.

It is natural to ask whether the difference in means of expression makes the structure of signed languages different from that of spoken languages. In this book, I focus on an aspect of signed languages that makes them appear very different from spoken languages, namely the use of space in morphosyntax and discourse structure. Since the use of space as a means of expression is unique to signed languages, we may expect to find structural differences from spoken languages in this area.

The use of space in signed languages and language universals
Signers may refer anaphorically to nonpresent referents by means of directions from

---

[1] Appendix A is an overview of the use of Danish Sign Language in Denmark and Danish deaf people's situation

their bodies or points within the space in front of their body. They keep referents apart in anaphoric pronominal reference by modifying the pronoun PRON for the appropriate direction or point (the modified form of PRON looks like a pointing gesture in the direction in question). I use the term *locus* (pl. *loci*) for a direction from the signer or a point in the signing space by which a referent is represented. A locus can be expressed in modifications of signs such as PRON and in gaze directions and head and body movements.

Loci seem to occur in all signed languages (see, however, Washabaugh 1986, 36-42). There do not seem to be any limitations as to which directions from the signer in the signing space can be used to express loci. Thus Lillo-Martin and Klima (1990) find that 'from the point of view of grammar, as opposed to performance, there seem to be an indefinite number of distinct pronominal forms (and thus potentially an infinite number of distinct pronominal forms)' (194). No spoken language has an indefinite, or infinite, number of pronouns, but Lillo-Martin and Klima do away with this structural difference (and introduce a new one) between signed and spoken languages by analysing all pronominal forms as manifestations of one pronoun. In the description of both spoken and signed languages we need to indicate which nominals are intended to co-refer. In linguistic descriptions this is often done by means of indices in the form of subscript letters. Thus, according to Lillo-Martin and Klima, the difference between the signed language, ASL, and the spoken language, English, is that 'what are unspoken referential indices in English are overtly manifested in ASL' (ibid., 198). In the signed language pronoun, distinct referential indices are expressed by distinct loci, and Lillo-Martin and Klima predict that 'there will be fewer ambiguities in the assignment of discourse referents for ASL pronouns than there are for English' (ibid., 199).

In other words, signed languages manifest semantic features that we already know from the analyses of spoken languages, namely referential indices; but the way these features are expressed differ in the two types of language. Thus, according to Lillo-Martin and Klima's analysis, we find a higher degree of differentiation in the signed pronoun than in spoken language pronouns. At the same time, signed languages, by not distinguishing three or more persons in the pronouns, are less differentiated than spoken languages.

The conclusion of the analysis of the pronominal "pointing" signs in Danish Sign Language that I present in II.6.3 is that there is a two-way distinction between first person and non-first person in these signs. Greenberg's (1966) universal 43 states: 'All languages have pronominal categories involving at least three persons and two numbers' (113). Does that mean that the universal is invalid, or that signed languages are not languages? Rather than trying to answer that question, a more fruitful approach is to examine what distinctions are made in individual signed languages, to compare the results of such analyses with what is known about other signed languages and about spoken languages, and to look for explanations of differences between signed and spoken languages in their different means of expression. Then we can specify the universals as being true of either signed or spoken languages or true of languages irrespective of their means of expression.

2 Traditional analyses of the use of space in signed languages and localist linguistic theories

In signed language research, there is a tradition of distinguishing between two different uses of space. They have been most strongly contrasted by Poizner, Klima, and Bellugi (1987, chapter 8), in a study of four American deaf aphasics, as a difference between 'spatial mapping' and 'spatialized syntax'. Spatial mapping is a more or less iconic use of space to represent location, i.e. a spatial mapping relation between content and form. In spatialized syntax, space serves syntactic purposes and discourse purposes and loci have an 'arbitrary, abstract nature' (ibid., 206).

The two uses of space in signing have been distinguished in signed language research especially in relation to two kinds of verbs or predicates. The verbs associated with the syntactic use of space have been claimed to show agreement. These verbs are modified for loci in space to show the syntactic or semantic relations between the verb and its arguments. In (1) from Danish Sign Language, the verb ANSWER is modified for the locus of its agent and for the locus of its recipient:[2]

```
(1)           t         bekræfte
       LF DET+fh  /  fh+SVARE+c  /

              t          affirm
       LF DET+fr  /  fr+ANSWER+c  /

       (Ill. 1)

       LF [The Danish National Association of the Deaf] has
       answered me.
```

The modification can be described loosely as follows: the verb is made with a linear movement and in the modified form the hand is first placed at a certain distance from the signer in the direction of the locus of the agent referent; then it moves toward the signer, the locus of the recipient referent.

It has been claimed that in spatial mapping or locative constructions verbs do not manifest the syntactic relationship between the verb and its arguments, but show a semantic locative relation (see in particular Padden 1988b, 40ff.). Liddell (1980, 95ff.) describes the difference between what he calls SVO constructions, i.e. constructions with a syntactic verb-argument relation between the constituents, on the

---

[2] Signed languages are traditionally transcribed by means of a score system in which the individual lines represent the activities of each articulator: each hand, the mouth, the eyes, the head, etc. (See also Appendix B.) Manual signs are transcribed by means of spoken language glosses usually chosen as a mnemonic to the sign's meaning. This practice, however, introduces a serious risk of confusing the sign with the spoken language word with respect to meaning, word class, etc. In this book, there is furthermore a risk that readers who are used to seeing English glosses used for signs from other signed languages, in particular American Sign Language (ASL), will misinterpret the gloss as representing a sign from another signed language. As a warning, I have transcribed example (1) first as it would look in a text in Danish.

one hand, and locative constructions, on the other. He discusses an example where a signer uses a locus for a fence on her right and a locus for a man on her left. In ASL, the signer can then make the sign BUY in the direction of the locus right:

(2) MAN BUY+fr /   (after Lidell 1980, 96)
     The man bought the fence.

In different versions of the same sentence the signer will sign the verb toward slightly different points in space; this does not change the meaning of the sentence. But if the sign BUY+fr is not made sufficiently close to the locus, the sentence becomes ungrammatical. It cannot mean something like 'the man missed buying the fence by six inches' or 'the man bought something six inches from the fence'. By contrast, if the signer uses a locative verb, there is always a locative relationship holding between the verb and the locus. For instance, if the signer uses a locative verb of a cat in relation to the locus for the fence, she says something about the cat's relation to the fence: that it was on the fence, a little to the right of the fence, behind the fence, etc.

The claim is that in spatial mapping the association of a referent with one point invests the entire signing space with meaning; all other points will be seen as related to the first one and to each other in terms of location. In spatialized syntax, the association of a referent with a locus is only relevant to that one referent and is manifested only in signs that refer to that referent or, in the case of verbs, in signs that are cross-referenced for that referent.

If one of the most conspicuous differences between signed languages and spoken languages is that signed languages make use of space and we find that signed languages make a sharp distinction between two uses of space, spatial mapping and spatialized syntax, this will weaken localist theories of spoken languages seriously. Lyons (1977) defines localism as

> the hypothesis that spatial expressions are more basic, grammatically and semantically, than various kinds of non-spatial expressions ... Spatial expressions are linguistically more basic, according to the localists, in that they serve as structural templates, as it were, for other expressions; and the reason why this should be so, it is plausibly suggested by psychologists, is that spatial organisation is of central importance in human cognition ... (Lyons 1977, 718)

If languages that manifest relations between constituents spatially contrast locative constructions and other kinds of syntactic constructions, localist theories lose credibility.

3 The aims of the present analysis

What I want to show is that the two uses of space, spatial mapping and spatialized syntax, are related, but do represent extremes on a continuum. Factors other than localism influence the way Danish Sign Language is structured. Cognitive and social factors work against the iconicity of locative constructions. In III.8 Polymorphemic verbs, I show how signers, during discourse, reduce more complex and more iconic descriptions of a locative event to verbs resembling single conventional signs. Moreover, there are several ways of viewing a situation that consists of a transfer from one location to another. It can be conceived as a process of transfer from one location to another, but also as an event where an agent brings about a certain effect in relation to an entity, i.e. it can be described by a transitive construction. Two semantic features connect locative constructions and transitive constructions; one of them is transfer, the other is point of view. Transfer is clearly part of the semantic basis for the expression of locative as well as transitive constructions in signed languages. The expression of a specific point of view in signed languages has been studied much less; it involves a factor which is so obvious that it is easily overlooked, namely the signer's centre in the signing space.

The signer's body and the area near the signer are part of the expressive means of signed languages and they are used for expressing a specific point of view. In describing the use of the signer's body and the signer's locus as the sender locus, I use two concepts known from the analysis of spoken languages. The first one is shifted reference, which means the use of pronouns and nominals from a quoted sender's point of view, in particular the use of the first person pronoun for a quoted sender. The second concept is shifted attribution of expressive elements. The term is meant to cover cases where the emotions and attitudes expressed by the signer (or speaker) should not be attributed to the sender in the context of utterance, but to somebody else. A third concept is needed: shifted locus, which is special to signed languages. Shifted locus is the use of the sender locus for a referent other than the signer and, less frequently, the use of another locus than the sender locus for the signer. Shifted locus is crucial to the expression of a specific point of view in Danish Sign Language, and it should be distinguished from shifted reference and shifted attribution of expressive elements.

One of my main points in writing this book has been to find out what loci are. They are intrinsic to signed languages and, as they totally depend on the use of space, they are unknown from analyses of spoken languages. Loci are expressed through locus markers by means of directions or points in space that determine the position and/or orientation of the hand(s) in the production of signs. Loci are what I call *referent projections,* also a concept that is unique to signed languages. There are three types of referent projections in signed language: loci (including the sender locus), the signer's head and body, and the stems of certain verbs, i.e. polymorphemic verbs of motion and location. Referent projections contribute to what Lehmann (1982), in an analysis of agreement in spoken languages, describes as keeping a linguistic object (i.e. a referent) constant. This is the reference-tracking function of referent projections. But as mentioned above, the sender locus is used for expressing a specific point of view in constructions with shifted locus, where the sender locus is used for a referent other than the signer. This phenomenon interferes with the reference-tracking function of loci as the referent in a shifted locus construction is no longer associated with the same locus as it may have been earlier in the discourse. Moreover, loci have functions other than reference-tracking: they express high referentiality and such semantic affinities between referents as possession, empathy, mental distance, comparison, point of view, locative configurations, and temporal relations. Loci are relevant both at the clausal level and the discourse level. This has led me to organise the book into two main parts: Part II, Discourse and Space, and Part III, Verbs and Space.

4 The composition of the book

Discourse and space
In Part II, Discourse and Space, I show that the choice of anaphoric loci is not a free one, but is influenced by semantic-pragmatic notions known from the analysis of spoken languages, and that a change in the locus of the same referent may signal different discourse layers (II.2 The frame of reference). One particularly clear demonstration that the choice of loci is not free is the association of time referents with loci in the signing space. These loci have different meanings and thus assign particular relational meanings to time referents (II.3 Time lines).

Only some referents are represented by loci. They are referents with high referentiality or high discourse value (II.4 Loci and referentiality). Some referents that rank high on the referentiality scale are represented by the sender locus in what I call constructions with shifted locus (II.5 Shifted reference, shifted locus, and shifted attribution of expressive elements).

Loci are also relevant to pronominal reference. In II.6 Pointing signs, I examine different kinds of pointing signs that can be analysed as verbs, a pronoun, a determiner, and a proform that carries spatial morphology under special circumstances. Different forms of the pronoun and the determiner manifest differences in information-packaging, such as assumed familiarity and salience in terms of the sender's assumptions about which entity the receiver is focusing on at the time of the utterance (II.6.2 The pronoun, the determiner, and information-packaging). In II.6.3 Person, place, and shifters, I argue for an analysis of pronominal pointing signs in Danish Sign Language as distinguishing two persons, first and non-first person. The non-first person pronoun can be used to refer to all kinds of referents, such as places, time referents, and human beings. In the conclusion to Part II, I compare the role of loci in signed discourse with reference-tracking mechanisms in spoken languages, especially gender.

Verbs and space
In Part III, Verbs and Space, I first present an analysis of the spatial morphology that occurs with signs having a base form, in contrast to the verbs that I describe as polymorphemic. Signs, and in particular verbs, having a base form can take three kinds of spatial morphology: distribution, agreement, and marking for a specific point of view.

Modifications for distribution denote the distribution of a state, a process, or an event over points or periods in time or over entities or locations. They can be expressed in signs of all kinds having predicative function, provided that they have a phonological form that permits spatial modification (III.5 Modifications for distribution).

Agreement between particular verbs and their arguments and the difference in agreement patterns with different generations of Danish Sign Language users cannot be analysed independent of marking for a specific point of view and the encoding of agentivity in the sender locus (III.6 Semantic agreement and marking for a specific point of view). Verbs of one particular group, traditionally called agreement verbs, agree with arguments with which they have semantically unambiguous relations. This kind of agreement is called *semantic agreement*, but it only represents one kind of agreement in Danish Sign Language. The other kind, *pragmatic agreement*, is found with many more signs than is semantic agreement. Before I describe pragmatic agreement, I analyse the concept of agreement in relation to the modification of signs for loci in terms of agreement feature, direction, and domain (III.6.2 Agreement features, direction, and domain), and I discuss the difference between marking for a specific point of view and agreement omission (III.6.3 The many uses of the *c*-form). In III.6.4 First person, point of view, and agentivity, I compare the interrelations of first person agreement, agentivity, and marking for a specific point of view in Danish Sign Language with similar phenomena in spoken languages.

A very large group of signs in Danish Sign Language can show what I call *pragmatic agreement* (III.7 Pragmatic agreement). Pragmatic agreement also involves loci, but it differs from semantic agreement in that the relation between the agreeing constituents is not unambiguous. The so-called agreement verbs, which can show semantic as well as pragmatic agreement, have different modified forms for the two kinds of agreement. Moreover, in pragmatic agreement all signs of a predicate show agreement provided that they can be modified for a locus. Pragmatic agreement underlines the relationship between the predicate and the topic and manifests such semantic-pragmatic phenomena as comparison, mental distance and persuasion.

In III.8 Polymorphemic verbs, I present an analysis of a special category of verbs, polymorphemic verbs. It is an alternative to the widespread analysis of similar verbs in other signed languages as classifier verbs. These verbs have been compared with classificatory verbs in Athapaskan languages, especially Navaho, and through Allan's (1977) characterisation of Athapaskan languages as predicate classifier languages, the term *classifier* has been introduced in signed language research. By means of a description of the classificatory verbs in the Athapaskan language Koyukon, I show that Allan's use of the term *classifier* in relation to such verbs is unwarranted (III.8.2 Predicate classifiers and classificatory verbs in spoken languages). The verbs of Danish Sign Language cannot be described as classificatory in the strict sense, but they resemble the Koyukon verbs by conflating Figure and Motion (Talmy 1985) in their stems (III.8.3 Classifiers or verb stems in Danish Sign Language).

The polymorphemic verbs differ from the verbs treated in III.4-7 in that their stems can combine with a sequence of different morphemes expressed by movement and denoting motion or location. Other morphemes with which the stems can combine express manner, distribution, extension, and aspect (III.8.4 Movement morphemes in polymorphemic verbs). The stems can be categorised into different types on semantic and morphological criteria (III.8.5 Categories of stems in polymorphemic verbs). In III.8.6 Polymorphemic verbs and space, I finally discuss the analysis of simultaneous constructions where two verbs are articulated simultaneously by the two hands. Such constructions are compared to constructions of backgrounding and foregrounding in spoken languages. In Danish Sign Language backgrounded constructions are used in expressions of locative configurations, but can also be used to express discourse coherence. In III.8.6 Polymorphemic verbs and space, I also develop the analysis of referent projections and show that it is necessary to distinguish the sender locus from the signer's head and body in relation to some polymorphemic verbs. Finally, I describe how polymorphemic verbs are used to express a specific point of view.

Methodological problems and form analysis of signs
Some methodological problems are common to all linguistic analysis and some are special to analyses of signed languages. The discussion of iconicity as a methodological problem, judgements of grammaticality, and linguistic variation in I.5.1-3 leads to a characterisation of the informants and the data used for this study (I.5.4 The informants and the data for this study). In I.6 Form analysis of signs, I first give an elementary description of the articulatory means of signed languages and of different form types of signs, and I introduce some terms that are the necessary equipment of signed language linguistics. In I.6.3-5, I present one suggestion for a form analysis of signs, Liddell and Johnson's (1989) sequential analysis of signs. Their analysis is particularly suited to illuminating the notion locus from a formal point of view (I.6.4 The term *locus*) and to describing verb agreement formally (I.6.5 Formal description of some different verb types). Except for I.6.4 and I.6.5, section I.6 is intended as an introduction to signed language research. Therefore, some of the topics that are taken up later in the book appear here without any discussion. It is my hope that the section will familiarise readers who have no knowledge of a signed language sufficiently with the way these languages "look" and the ways sign linguists talk about signed languages that they will be able to read the rest of the book.

Here I would also like to mention an area that I do not touch upon, but which is very close to the discussion in especially the two sections on agreement, III.6 Semantic agreement and marking for a specific point of view, and III.7 Pragmatic agreement. It is the syntactic analysis of the arguments of the verb. I avoid using the syntactic terms *subject* and *object* except when I refer to other linguists' analyses. The reason is that a syntactic analysis must draw on other criteria than merely agreement, notably constituent order and systematic relations between clauses with the same verb and different numbers of constituents or different markings of the constituents; however, the analysis of such phenomena in Danish Sign Language still lies ahead.

5 Characterisation of the data

5.1 Expectations of iconicity
In signed languages, individual signs and much of the morphosyntax manifest iconic relations between content and expression (see, among others, Frishberg 1975; Bergman 1977; DeMatteo 1977; Mandel 1977; Klima & Bellugi 1979, Chapter 1; Wilbur 1987, 161-169). Iconicity is, therefore, an analytical and conceptual challenge to the signed language researcher; but it also represents a methodological danger. Both linguists and informants may be tempted to see iconicity where there is none and to expect constructions in signed languages to be more iconic than they are.[1] I shall demonstrate this danger by examples from my own work with Danish signers.

In order to examine how specific nonmanual features are used to mark information as given or new or having high discourse relevance, I made a tape with single sentence excerpts from signed monologues. The nonmanual features were: raised brows, lowered or pulled back chin, and squinted eyes (i.e. the signer contracts the muscles of the lids so that the eyes appear as narrow slits). I presented the tape to native signers and asked them questions like *Do you think that the person the signer is talking about has been mentioned earlier in the monologue?* and *What do you think the signer will go on talking about, x or y?* It turned out that most signers found it very difficult to answer such questions.[2] When I told them that I was interested in the function of specific facial expressions, they began to point out facial expressions signalling emotions such as surprise, anger, and sorrow. Signals of emotions are part of deaf people's language awareness: *If you use the sign HAPPY, you should look happy.* This is clearly false since signers do not look happy while uttering the equivalent of *Are you not happy?*

The reason that informants were not able to identify the features that I was interested in might of course be that they are not relevant to signing. That is not the case, however. Squinted eyes are used with referential expressions to check the receiver's understanding of the reference: the sender believes that the receiver knows the referent (givenness), but may have problems identifying it at the moment (accessibility) (Engberg-Pedersen 1990). Squinted eyes serve as an appeal: 'I believe that you already know this referent, but if you need help to identify it, tell me so. Then I'll give you more information about the referent.' A clear signal that squinted eyes have a function in Danish Sign Language is that receivers nod or look puzzled in response to squinted eyes.

---
1 Corbett (1988) mentions similar problems from the analysis of spoken languages. Here informants are not misled by iconicity, but by "logic". Confronted with examples of alternative agreement possibilities in Russian, 'Informants sometimes claim that there is a semantic difference between certain agreement options. In some cases it appears that they are imposing a logical interpretation on surprising and troublesome facts about their own language.' (47).

2 One signer, however, gave a very precise description of her own use of the signal squinted eyes.

When I presented my analysis of the three nonmanual features to a group of deaf persons, they accepted it. But in one case they denied that squinted eyes are used with the above-mentioned function:

```
(1)  brows:   raised------    furrowed------
     eyes:    squinted----
              PRON+fr HOME / ANGRY  PRON+fr  /

     When he comes home, he is mad.
```

Everyone agreed that the proper translation of (1) is with an adverbial clause, i.e. *When he comes home.* Squinted eyes are used on other occasions with time adverbials such as MONDAY MORNING. Earlier in the monologue, the signer says that the individual in (1) comes home. That is, the first part of (1) is an adverbial clause expressing given information. Therefore, it fits the analysis that the clause should be marked by squinted eyes. But the informants insisted that the facial expression in this case indicates anger, even though the contraction of the eye muscles ceases before the sign ANGRY. There is no doubt that the signer also expresses negative feelings during the first part of the sentence, as informants who only saw this part found that the signer expressed sadness. But the example demonstrates many signers' notion of their own language: facial expressions signal emotions (see also Klima & Bellugi 1979, 246). This view of nonmanual signals is not surprising when you consider both the extent to which facial expressions do signal feelings in signed languages, and the abstract nature of the function that squinted eyes fulfil (referent accessibility).

The use of emotional facial expression for linguistic purposes in signed languages is an example of the kind of iconicity in which linguistic expression mirrors content. This is the type that Haiman (1985b, 10) describes as an image. Another type of iconicity is diagrammatic iconicity with the subtype isomorphism, i.e. the principle of one meaning, one form (ibid., 11, 14). In relation to signed languages, this type is relevant in an area that has to do with space; it is often described in a way that feigns isomorphism. Space is used, among other things, for keeping track of reference. A referent may be represented by a locus in space, and many signs that refer to it or imply reference to it are made in relation to the same locus. The choice of locus for any individual referent is generally not predetermined in signed languages. Therefore, we might expect that signers would explicitly assign new referents to loci when they introduce them or, put differently, that they would explicitly establish a locus – or an index, as it is often described – for a referent (Mandel 1977, 76; Baker & Cokely 1980, 223; Newport & Meier 1985, 916; Wilbur 1987, 153). That is, we might expect there to be a formal difference between assigning referents to loci (or establishing loci for referents) and using a locus once it was established. A pointing sign could, for instance, be an obligatory part of the nominal that introduces the referent. Or the first pointing sign manifesting the locus could be longer (be held for a while or have repeated movements in the direction of the locus) compared with later pointing signs which "only" make use of the locus, once it is established. But no such formal difference exists between the two uses of loci in Danish Sign Language, i.e. the language does not distinguish 'establishing a locus for a referent' from later anaphoric reference by means of the same locus.

Iconicity, especially of the image type, is a reality to deaf people. Therefore, there is a danger that informants will not only interpret examples iconically, but also will present linguists with signing that is more iconic than their everyday signing and accept such examples from the linguist. That is one reason why I have preferred to use primarily signed monologues and dialogues and not elicited sentences or judgements of grammaticality of such sentences as data.

5.2 Judgements of grammaticality

Since the structuralist separation of language structure and language use, judgements of grammaticality have been considered an important way of procuring valid data for linguistic analysis. Judgements of grammaticality are seen as a way of getting around the "shortcomings" of naturalistic data in the form of processing problems such as faulty memory. We can, however, only rely on grammaticality judgements if we know that they are not subject to other kinds of shortcomings.

Judgements of grammaticality and prototype theory
Since cognitive psychologists showed that many concepts are better described in terms of prototypes than as having clear boundaries (Rosch 1977), a number of linguists have shown that grammatical categories can have the same character (Dahl 1985; Hopper & Thompson 1980, 1985; Bybee & Moder 1983; Taylor 1989, Chapters 10-11). If linguistic categories do not have clear boundaries, native speakers naturally hesitate when asked to evaluate the acceptability of constructions that are not close to the prototype. I will demonstrate this by means of judgements of the Danish construction sentence intertwining.

Sentence intertwining ('sætningsknude') is typical of spoken Danish and its characteristic is that a constituent that syntactically belongs to a subordinate clause appears at the head of the main clause as in (1) and (2):

```
(1)  ham ved jeg du    kender
     him know I  you   know
     That one, I know you know him.

(2)  ham ved jeg i grunden ikke om        jeg har  hørt om    før
     him know I actually   not whether I  have heard about before
     Actually, I don't know whether I have heard about him before.
```

To illuminate the problems of judgements of grammaticality, I asked a number of native speakers of Danish to evaluate examples of sentence intertwining. Out of 35 informants, 16 said that (3) was acceptable, 13 that it was unacceptable, and 6 were in doubt.

(3) den bil er det din   egen skyld hvis du   ikke får   solgt
     that car is it your own   fault if   you   not   get   sold
     That car, it's your own fault if you don't manage to sell it.

Creider (1986) made a study of similar sentences in Norwegian. He asked a number of speakers of Norwegian to rate the sentences with respect to grammaticality on a scale from 1 (least grammatical) to 4 (most grammatical) and found significant differences in means of judgements between different types of complements.[3] Creider concludes:

> In sum, although research of the type reported here is not substitute for the sensitive judgements of native-speaker-linguist, I hope I have shown that quantitative study of acceptability judgements can reveal interesting and sometimes unsuspected patterns and can thus serve as a useful adjunct to the individual judgements that provide the bulk of the data on which linguistic research is based. (Creider 1986, 421-22)

But do we really know what we are doing when we make judgements of grammaticality? Even people with some linguistic training, when asked to evaluate whether (3) is acceptable or unacceptable as a Danish sentence, asked whether I meant 'intelligible' or 'correct'. *Grammatically acceptable* is supposed to mean neither.

Fuzzy set theory
The sentence in (3) is not close to prototypical sentence intertwining. It deviates from the prototype in ways that result in indeterminacy. One way to illuminate what this means is to show what it does not mean. It does not mean that the boundaries of the category sentence intertwining are fuzzy and that membership of this category is gradual, that membership is a question of degree and can be fixed at some more or less arbitrary number. If membership of the category were gradual, it could be described by fuzzy set theory which imposes linearity on the relation between an item and a prototype: the higher on the scale an item is rated, the closer it is to the prototype, or the more representative of the category.

Set theory is concerned with sets within a certain domain, while a theory of concepts is concerned with classes in a context. The difference between domain and context is inadvertently brought out by Osherson and Smith's (1981) demonstration that prototype theory as a theory of concepts combined with fuzzy set theory leads to contradictions and counterintuitive predictions. For that reason, they reject prototype theory as a theory of concepts. But Osherson and Smith explicitly disregard con-

---
3 I conducted a similar test with 16 Danes who evaluated Danish translations of Creider's sentences, and got very similar results.

text. One of their examples is the set of striped apples in the domain of fruit. According to set theory, the set of striped apples in the domain of fruit consists of all the members of the intersection of the set of striped fruit and the set of apples. Membership in an intersection is the minimal value of membership of either of the intersecting sets. Therefore, a striped apple is more typical of either striped fruit or of apples than it is of the intersection, striped apples; but intuitively, a striped apple is, of course, more typical of striped apples than of either apples or of striped fruit.

What Osherson and Smith do not see is that the contradiction arises because fuzzy set theory disregards a natural context and operates with sets of equal status: striped fruit and apples. In the context of a society where apples are a common kind of fruit, a striped apple is not something that is both striped and an apple, it is an apple that is striped. If we want to evaluate the typicality of a striped apple, we do it within a particular context. That is also why a guppy (another of Osherson and Smith's examples) can be a typical pet fish without being a typical fish. What is a typical member of the "intersection" is not necessarily a typical member of either of the original sets (the set of pets and the set of fish), because members of the "intersection" are not simply items that belong to both sets. (For a more extended criticism of Osherson and Smith's article, see Lakoff 1987, 139-145.)

The use of fuzzy set theory to explain the imprecision of categories with prototypes 'confuses indeterminacy with graduality' (Dahl 1985, 9). It is an attempt to create precision where there is none and to impose linearity on multidimensionality. Lakoff (1986, 41, 50) argues that linear structures such as representativeness structures ('closeness to the prototypical case') hide the richness of structure that is characteristic of categories with prototypes. Fuzziness arises when category membership is a matter of degree, and it results in prototype effects. But prototype effects may have other sources than fuzziness. The concept 'mother' is an example of what Lakoff calls an experiential cluster: a number of base models converge so that the prototypical mother is the person giving birth and having contributed the genetic material, who nurtures and raises the child, is married to the child's father, and is the female of the first ascending generation. If a mother deviates from this prototype, it is impossible to describe the deviation as a matter of degree (Lakoff 1986, 43-45; 1987, 74-76).

Multidimensionality of grammatical constructions
Prototype theory as a theory of linguistic categories implies that we cannot make rules of grammar that clearly define the boundary between acceptable and unacceptable constructions of a language. One sort of imprecision is multidimensionality of grammatical constructions: a construction may share a number of properties with a specific type of construction, but deviate from it in other respects. Whether it is grammatical or not may be impossible to determine, and whether it will actually occur may depend on whether an appropriate context makes it possible.

Creider's (1986) study of what he calls constituent-gap dependencies in Norwegian, as well as my own study of the Danish translations, showed that topicalization from a complement clause of a declarative verb as in (4) is rated highest on the acceptability scale, and topicalization from a relative clause as in (5) lowest on the scale (the examples and the results are from my own study):

(4) de   blomster sagde Ulla at   Peter havde fundet på   marken
    those flowers said Ulla that Peter had   found in the-field
    related to the Danish equivalent of *Ulla said that Peter had found those flowers in the field.*
    [rated highest on the acceptability scale by 9, and next highest by 7]

(5) den mand kender jeg damen   der så
    that man know   I   the-lady who saw
    related to the Danish equivalent of *I know the lady who saw that man.*
    [rated lowest on the acceptability scale by 16 out of 16]

This means that clause type influences judgements of acceptability. But the issue is more complex. Topicalization from a conditional such as (6) (not in Creider's study) was rejected by 34 informants and accepted by 1:

(6) den bil vinder jeg et ur   hvis jeg får solgt
    that car win   I   a   watch if   I   get sold
    related to the Danish equivalent of *I'll win a watch if I manage to sell that car.*

In (6), there is a contingent relation between the two propositions. Example (7), also with a conditional, was accepted by 14 informants and rejected by 5:

(7) det bliver jeg sur over hvis jeg hører
    that become I   mad PREP if   I   hear
    related to the Danish equivalent of *I'll get mad if I hear that.*

and (8) was accepted by 4 and rejected by 8:

(8) den bliver jeg glad hvis du tager med
    that become I   happy if   you take PREP
    related to the Danish equivalent of *I'll be happy if you bring that.*

In both (7) and (8), there is a causal relation between the main predicate and the conditional: the conditionals express the events that cause the reactions expressed by the main predicates. In (7), the topicalized constituent can be understood as being the object of the main verb (*bliver sur over*) as well as of the verb of the subordinate clause, whereas the topicalized constituent of (8) can only be the object of the verb of the subordinate clause. Some informants claimed that the acceptability of (8) increases if you insert a preposition (*for*) before the conditional. Such a preposition would both reinforce the causal relation between the main verb and the conditional and make the topicalized constituent a constituent of the main clause (*den bliver jeg glad for* is a completely acceptable independent sentence).

Thus, sentences can deviate from the prototypical sentence intertwining along several dimensions. The parameters mentioned here are the syntactic type of the subordinate clause, the semantic relation between the main clause and the subordinate clause, and whether the topicalized constituent can be interpreted as a syntactic constituent of the main clause. (For a similar discussion of English transitive clauses, see Taylor 1989, 210-217; DeLancey 1987.) But we cannot predict which dimensions language users will consider relevant when they extend the use of linguistic constructions. Neither can language users in a test situation. Have they heard a particular extension before? How often? Can they imagine a context where it would be appropriate? In fortunate cases, what the language users do is evaluate what they feel comfortable about, either because they manage to create a context for the sentence or because they find that the sentence is within the limits of some norm of correctness. The result in terms of "grammaticality judgements" reflects the language users' (lack of) linguistic creativity or openmindedness, but that is not what grammar writing is supposed to be based on.

Prototypicality and frequency
One source of prototypicality is frequency. That became particularly clear in my study of three verb stems of polymorphemic verbs used to describe the motion and location of human beings in Danish Sign Language (see III.8.3 Classifiers or verb stems in Danish Sign Language?). Informants agreed on which stems could be used in verbs to describe someone approaching the holder of the point of view; but they were either uncertain about or disagreed on which stems could be used in verbs for someone passing by the side of the holder of the point of view. We talk much more often about someone coming toward us than about someone passing us.

Indeterminacy of linguistic categories
To accept prototype theory as a theory of linguistic categories does not mean, of course, that the notion of grammaticality should be abandoned. All native speakers have an intuitive feeling that some constructions are completely unacceptable in their language. But when linguists ask native speakers to judge the grammaticality of certain constructions (or when linguists as native speakers make such judgements), they are seldom interested in completely unacceptable constructions. Rather they start with a certain kind of construction and try to find its boundaries by inventing new constructions along specific dimensions relevant to a delineation of the construction in the language in question. These constructions may extend from the

prototype in such a way that native speakers are unable to say when the boundary between acceptable and unacceptable constructions is reached. The boundary does not exist as a sharp line.

Distrust in grammaticality judgements of borderline cases should not, of course, lead to a complete lack of interest in possible extensions of a prototype. We must, in Taylor's words:

> specify, not only the prototype, but also the manner and the extent of permitted deviation from the prototype. In other words, the degree of productivity of a construction needs to be stated as part of its characterisation. (Taylor 1989, 200)

But we should also be aware of the danger of making linguistic descriptions more determinate than the language.

The sources of indeterminacy of linguistic categories in spoken languages also play a part in signed languages. Moreover, besides being influenced by the indeterminacy of categories and constructions and by iconicity, judgements of grammaticality in signed languages are also influenced by the existence of a number of language varieties in the signing community and by deaf people's attitudes to their language (see I.5.3).

5.3 Different language varieties

The signs DEAF and HEARING are used not only to refer to the (lack of) ability to hear, but also to a spectrum of attitudes and to competence in Danish Sign Language. Some persons with normal hearing ability are closer to the deaf community than some persons with a severe hearing loss. Moreover, deaf persons are integrated in the deaf community to different degrees. The sign ÆGTE ('genuine') in Danish Sign Language is used to qualify DØV ('deaf') when deaf people want to characterise a deaf person as belonging to the deaf community (Widell 1988, 208). The expression does not characterise degrees of hearing loss, but signifies that the person in question is a core member of the deaf community in attitudes as well as language. It can also be used about the signing of a hearing person (he signs like an ÆGTE DØV), but cannot be used to describe a hearing person as such, no matter his attitudes and signing skills.

Among signed language researchers writing in English, it has become customary to distinguish between *deaf*, about a person with a hearing loss, and *Deaf*, indicating membership of a particular subculture (Padden & Humphries 1988, 2). As I do not feel competent or entitled to decide who is what, I shall not follow this practice.

The deaf community
Baker and Cokely (1980) see four possible entries to membership in the deaf community in the United States. One of them is hearing loss, but this factor by itself is not sufficient to become a core member of the community. It interacts with three

other factors. The first is fluency in ASL. The second is 'the ability to satisfactorily participate in social functions of the Deaf Community. This means being invited to such functions, feeling at ease while attending, and having friends who are themselves members of the Deaf Community' (ibid., 56). The fourth factor mentioned by Baker and Cokely is political, i.e. 'the potential ability to exert influence on matters which directly affect the Deaf Community on a local, state, or national level' (ibid., 56). The purpose of Baker and Cokely's model is to describe avenues to the deaf community. As a byproduct, however, it describes core members of the community as persons who have a hearing loss, are fluent in the signed language, have political influence within the community and in relations between the community and the environment, and who are socially at ease and active in the community.

Active participation in deaf political issues may be an avenue to membership in the deaf community for hearing persons, but it would be wrong to claim that being politically active in the community is a prerequisite to becoming a core member of the community in Denmark. The same is true about fluency in Danish Sign Language. That is, some deaf persons are accepted as core members of the deaf community even though their signing is strongly influenced by Danish. These persons are, however, able to understand, without any problem, Danish Sign Language as it is used among deaf persons having deaf parents. There are no thorough studies of criteria for membership of the deaf community in either the United States or Denmark, but the presumed differences may be due to the difference in size. As the deaf population in Denmark is very small, individual attitudes may become more important in determining membership than language.

Social stratification
It has been shown that it is necessary to recognise social stratification within the deaf community of the United States (Stokoe, Bernard & Padden 1976 (1980); Woodward 1983). As yet, we know very little about the social varieties of Danish Sign Language, but many elderly deaf persons are said to sign differently than younger people. For instance, many elderly deaf persons use the Mouth-Hand System (see I.6.2 The manual alphabets, the Mouth-Hand System, and names) more than younger people. There are also regional differences, especially at the lexical level. These differences are linked to different schools for the deaf.

Sign-supported Danish, interlanguage, and contact signing
The fact that there are many noncore members of the deaf community is one source of variation in signing. Very few noncore members become fluent in Danish Sign Language. For educational or practical reasons, many hearing persons prefer to use spoken Danish accompanied by signs (sign-supported Danish). Some simply fail to learn Danish Sign Language properly because of their marginal relation to the

community. Instead, they use an interlanguage that may be, but not necessarily is, influenced by Danish. Many core members switch between different varieties depending on the receiver. They use Danish Sign Language with their deaf friends and what Lucas and Valli (1989), in an American context, call a form of *contact signing* with hearing persons who know some signed language.

Another source of variation is the recruitment of language users. Most deaf children (between 90 and 95%) have hearing parents who, at first, know no signed language. The parents are offered courses, but rarely reach an advanced level of signing unless they actively seek the company of deaf adults. Some children attend kindergartens with other deaf children, but other deaf children see very little signing before they start school. Here they learn Danish Sign Language from the deaf children who have deaf parents, from older children, from the deaf adults at the schools, and from an increasing number of hearing teachers who master Danish Sign Language as a foreign language. But many hearing teachers still use sign-supported Danish. This means that most deaf children are surrounded by people who use either sign-supported Danish or an interlanguage form of Danish Sign Language.

A study of some deaf children's signed language (Kjær Sørensen & Hansen 1976) revealed that deaf children of deaf parents used a linearisation rule in describing a drawing: they mentioned first the items that were closest to the picture's foreground. Deaf children of hearing parents did not use such a rule. My own experience from summer camps with deaf children is that many children below the age of 12 neither use nor understand signs that are normally only used in interactions between deaf persons (Engberg-Pedersen & Pedersen 1985b; Engberg-Pedersen & Hansen 1986). But many deaf children's language has changed considerably in recent years because of their parents' increased use of Danish Sign Language and the parents' insistence that the children attend kindergarten with other deaf children and the schools for the deaf rather than be mainstreamed into classes with hearing children.

Attitudes to Danish Sign Language
Especially earlier, many teachers and administrators in the educational system regarded Danish Sign Language as the last resort when a deaf child failed to learn to speak and understand Danish, and this attitude has inevitably influenced many deaf persons' attitude to Danish Sign Language. Many still feel that Danish Sign Language is more "primitive" than Danish; they attribute a higher status to deaf persons who can speak Danish (Faustrup 1980; Christensen 1989; Vikkelsø 1989). When hearing persons say about a deaf person, *He has very good language*, they almost always mean 'He speaks Danish well'. They forget that a deaf individual may be fluent in Danish Sign Language besides knowing some Danish. For many years, the language used in the news programmes produced specially for deaf people was sign-supported Danish, and many deaf persons still doubt that it is possible to talk about many subjects in Danish Sign Language even though they do so regularly in the

deaf clubs (Hansen 1986). Because such attitudes are widespread, it is still difficult, when videorecording deaf persons for the first time, to elicit Danish Sign Language rather than a variant of signing that is closer to Danish.

5.4 The informants and the data of this study

The main body of data for this study is about 3 1/2 hours of videorecorded monologues and dialogues by twelve native deaf signers, as well as observations of deaf persons' signing in natural settings, in particular at the Centre for Total Communication in Copenhagen. The data are about the informants' everyday life: work, meetings, holidays, problems with day care institutions, and the like. The signers are between 18 and 60 years of age, most of them between 30 and 45. Two have hearing parents, the rest all have deaf parents. Many of them have deaf children and their spouses are deaf. One of the informants is a native signer of another signed language and near-native in Danish Sign Language. The main informants are accustomed to being videorecorded. Several of them are employed by the Centre for Total Communication.

All of the informants are core members of the Danish deaf community in the sense that they use Danish Sign Language in their daily life and they socialise with deaf people. Many of them are exceptional in the sense that they use Danish Sign Language also in their work. The employees of the Centre for Total Communication are politically influential in the deaf community as a consequence of their work, and some of them hold other offices in the deaf community. Most of the informants are well-educated compared with the deaf population at large, and their signing is more influenced by Danish than the signing of some members of the deaf community.

The data have been supplemented with the outcome of discussions of my analyses. I have known the informants for between 5 and 14 years, and I often discuss my analyses with them and with other deaf persons. It has turned out that the discussions are most fruitful when several signers take part and when we discuss examples from the monologues, i.e. examples in a context. In such cases, the signers at times reach an agreement on grammaticality judgements; but even when this is not the case, the discussions bring about new examples and intuitions about the language.

Another kind of data is translations of sentences that focus on specific grammatical problems. Such sentences were presented to the informants with a context in written Danish or I explained the content and the context to the signers. Informants read the sentences, made sure they understood them, and tried to remember the content. Some time later they were videorecorded while they signed to another deaf person. Very few of the examples in this book come from this kind of sampling. One reason for repeatedly emphasising the textual and situational context is that the categories that I focus on in this study are context-dependent to a large extent, as I will show.

All transcriptions and translations of examples in the text have been checked with at least one native signer.

Throughout the book, when I talk about *Danish Sign Language* I mean the body of data that I have just described. In a few places, I comment on different varieties that appear in the data. What I have wanted to do in this study is not to formulate rigid grammatical rules, but to examine the different areas of the language where space is used: what are the morphosyntactic functions of the uses of space? For what discourse purposes is space used? How do the different linguistic areas interrelate?

6 Form Analysis of Signs

6.1 The articulatory means of signed languages

In this section, I will give a short introduction to the articulatory means of signed languages and the ways in which signed language researchers talk about the form of manual signs. The introduction is meant as a help to readers without prior knowledge of a signed language. I will also describe ways in which morphological modifications are expressed through changes of a sign's base form. In I.6.2 The manual alphabets, the Mouth-Hand System, and names, I describe the main principles of the Mouth-Hand System and the use of this system and the manual alphabet in Danish Sign Language. I.6.3 Liddell and Johnson's sequential form analysis of signs, is an introduction to one sequential analysis of signs, the one developed by Liddell and Johnson (Johnson & Liddell 1984; Liddell 1984a, 1990b; Liddell & Johnson 1986, 1989). The model is particularly suited to the analysis of modifications of signs for agreement. A central notion of agreement is locus, which is discussed from a formal point of view in I.6.4 The term *locus*. In I.6.5 Formal description of some different verb types, I present different types of verbs showing agreement. Finally, in I.6.6 The morphological type of signed languages, I briefly discuss how signed languages can be classified typologically, and I question the widespread use of *inflection* in the analysis of these languages.

The hands
The most obvious, but by far not the only, articulatory means of signed languages is the hands. Many manual signs can be modified in meaningful ways, often depending on their form. Some of the important form distinctions of the base forms of signs have turned out to be:
— whether the sign is made with both hands or with only one hand;
— whether the hand(s) is/are close to or make(s) contact with an area on the head, face, body, or the other hand, or move(s) freely in space;
— whether both hands in two-handed signs are active, or one is active, the other passive;
— whether the handshapes in two-handed signs are different or alike;
— whether the movement of the hands in two-handed signs with both hands active is simultaneous or alternating (in the latter case, one hand moves in one direction while the other hand moves in the opposite direction, and then vice versa);
— whether the movement of signs with reduplicated movement is unidirectional (movement in only one direction with a transitional movement back to the initial position) or bidirectional (movement back and forth).

Most human beings are either right- or left-dominant, which means that they prefer to use either their right hand or their left hand for most motor tasks. Signing can be right-dominant or left-dominant, but as the form criteria mentioned above make clear, we also need to distinguish between the active and the passive hand, or the *strong* and the *weak* hand (Padden & Perlmutter 1987). The strong hand is the active hand in a two-handed sign. A right-dominant signer generally uses her right hand as the strong hand and her left hand as the weak hand, but she may switch to using her left hand as the strong hand. Left-dominant signers may use their left hand as the strong hand and switch occasionally like right-dominant signers, but there is much individual variation in the extent to which different signers switch hands. Some signing styles, especially those having many complex predicates of motion and location (see III.8 Polymorphemic verbs), also seem to call for more switching than other styles (Engberg-Pedersen 1988; see also Frishberg 1985).

Because all my language consultants are right-dominant and predominantly use their right hand as their strong hand, I use the top line of the "hand" lines of the transcriptions for glosses of signs made with both hands as strong hands or the right hand as the strong hand. The lower line is for glosses of signs made with the left hand as the strong hand. I also indicate in the lower line that the left hand contributes to a two-handed sign when its activity is crucial to an understanding of the example.

"Phonological" analyses of signed languages
The first submorphemic analysis of the manual signs of any signed language was Stokoe's (1960, revised edition 1978) analysis of American Sign Language (ASL). Stokoe talked about the 'cherology' of ASL, using a word based on the Greek word meaning 'hand'. In spite of the etymology of the word *phonology*, it has, since then, become customary to talk about the phonology of signed languages (a term also accepted by Stokoe (1978, 81)) as a parallel to the submorphemic level of analysis in descriptions of spoken languages. Signed language researchers find an approach parallel to the phonological analyses of spoken languages fruitful in descriptions of, for instance, stress (Coulter 1990), syllables (Wilbur 1990), and ordered rules (Supalla & Newport 1978). (See also Brentari 1992.) I shall follow the practice of talking about the *phonology* and *phonetics* of signed languages.

The parameter model
What are now regarded as traditional phonological analyses of signs describe the sign as a simultaneous unit of items from different *parameters* (Friedman 1977; Battison 1978; Klima & Bellugi 1979; Brennan, Colville & Lawson 1984; Wilbur 1987). The sign pair THINK (Ill. 2a) and HAPPY (Ill. 2b) from Danish Sign Language demonstrates a difference in one parameter: *place of articulation*. The two signs are both one-handed signs; they are made with the same handshape and the same movement. In THINK, however, the hand is moved outside the forehead, while in HAPPY it is moved outside the mouth. Some other possible places of articulation are the side of the face, the nose, the side of the neck, the sternum, the contralateral arm, and neutral space. *Neutral space* is an area from a little above the signer's waist

to her throat. Signs that have neutral space as their place of articulation are made at lexically determined heights. Two-handed signs are usually made in the space at the middle of the signer's body; one-handed signs usually displace the hand a little to the ipsilateral side. Neutral space should be kept distinct from the *signing space*, which is an area from a little above the signer's head to a little below her waist; its depth corresponds approximately to the length of the lower arm to the sides and forward from the body. Signs which have neutral space as their place of articulation can change meaningfully so that they are no longer made with the hands in neutral space, but the hands stay inside the signing space in unmarked signing.

The second parameter is the *handshape*. Signs can be identical for all parameters except for the handshape. An example of a minimal pair that differs only with respect to handshape is DANGEROUS (Ill. 3a) and STRANGE (Ill. 3b).

The third parameter is the *movement* of the hand or hands. Here SUMMER (Ill. 4a) and BAD (Ill. 4b) constitute a minimal pair. The movements can be local or nonlocal. A local movement is a movement of the fingers like wiggling; a nonlocal movement is a movement of the whole hand. A nonlocal movement can be characterised as to its direction, shape, and intensity. The signs THINK (Ill. 2a) and HAPPY (Ill. 2b) are made with both nonlocal movement (a straight, horizontal movement) and local movement (wiggling).

The fourth parameter is the *orientation* of the hand(s). The signs ALL-RIGHT (Ill. 5a) and DAY (Ill. 5b) are an example of a pair of signs that are only distinguished in terms of the orientation of the hands. The orientation of the hands was not distinguished as an independent parameter of the sign in Stokoe's first form analysis of ASL signs, i.e. in what is called the aspectual model of the sign.

The aspectual model
In his analysis of signs in ASL, Stokoe (1960) did not separate the hand's orientation from its shape (see also Bergman 1977), and he did not talk about the parameters of the sign, but about the three aspects of the sign. His *aspectual model* is markedly different from the parameter model. Whereas the parameter model is an attempt at a phonological analysis of signed morphemes parallel to phonological analyses of spoken language morphemes, Stokoe based his analysis of sign forms on a recognition of the difference between a spoken and a signed morpheme:

> Analysis of morphemes in a spoken language requires recognition that speech sounds are produced and processed in sequence, one after the other. But morphemes in a signed language are made and perceived as unitary acts. To analyse them requires the recognition that what composes a sign morpheme must be different aspects of the same act.
> These aspects appear only when a conscious analysis picks out different simultaneous components for special focus of attention. They are not physiologically or physically separate or separable. They cannot be performed in isolation and in different orders, as for example the segments /æ/, /k/, and /t/ of cat and tack. The aspects of a sign morpheme make sense only in terms of each other. (Stokoe 1978, 82 – emphasis in the original)

Stokoe found that a sign could be analysed in terms of 'what acts', its action, and its action's location. Such an analysis gives priority to the articulator, i.e. the hand or hands with a particular handshape including the rotation and extension of the arm[1] (for an even more radical emphasis of analysing signs as constituted by 'what acts' and its action, see Stokoe 1991). The aspectual model underlines the simultaneity of the three aspects. Each aspect is a different way of focusing on the unit that is the sign.

To characterise the orientation of the hand(s) Stokoe uses the terms supination and pronation. If a person stands with his arms hanging at his side, he can rotate his arms so that his palms face forward. This is the supinating rotation. If his palms face backward, his arms are in the pronating position. When his palms face inward, the forearm rotation is neutral.

The parameter model arose out of a focus on minimal pairs and especially minimal pairs of signs such as ALL-RIGHT (Ill. 5a) and DAY (Ill. 5b) in Danish Sign Language. There are few minimal pairs like ALL-RIGHT and DAY in which palm orientation is independent of the other parameters of the sign. Palm orientation is a result of forearm rotation or wrist bend, and it is unlikely, Stokoe claims, that sign receivers 'read palm direction and angle as a kind of instant problem solving in solid geometry' (1978, 84). Rather they perceive 'what acts' as a complex of muscle activities including forearm rotation and wrist bend. It is this view of the sign as a simultaneous unit that can be regarded under three aspects which underlies Stokoe's aspectual model. The two signs ALL-RIGHT and DAY can be distinguished in terms of what acts: a particular handshape with the forearm held in pronation (ALL-RIGHT) or in supination (DAY).

Stokoe suggests that if the aspectual model is abandoned, an alternative model should be a sequential analysis of signs as forms extended in time instead of the parameter model. Such models have been suggested within the last ten years and an example is presented here in I.6.3 Liddell and Johnson's sequential form analysis of signs (for an alternative sequential analysis, see Sandler 1990a, 1990b; for an overview, see Wilbur 1987, Chapter 3; for a critical view of temporal, segmental models of signed morphemes, see Edmondson 1990b). Stokoe's own model stresses the view that signing is muscle activity. By contrast to the muscle activity that produces speech, the muscle activity that produces signing can be observed, either as an action (what the muscles are effecting) or as a result (what the muscles have effected). There is complementarity between what acts and the action of a sign; a handshape with a particular forearm rotation may occur at the starting point of the sign or may be the result of the action of the sign, i.e. its movement. But the parameter model describes the four parameters as being independent of each other.

---

1 *Articulator* is defined as including the handshape and the arm rotation and extension. But as many signs have a nonmanual component, a particular mouth pattern, we must distinguish the *manual* from the *nonmanual articulator*. I use *hand* and *manual articulator* interchangeably in the sense of *manual articulator*.

Modifications of signs
Neither the aspectual model nor the parameter model, however, is suitable for describing the fact that the movement and place of articulation of a sign have a fundamentally different status from its handshape. Many base forms of signs can be modified to express particular meanings and such modifications affect the base form's movement, its place of articulation, or the orientation of the hand(s). For ASL it has been found that meaningful modifications of signs involve kinds of movement and changes in space that are not found in unmodified signs (Klima & Bellugi 1979, 264; Wilbur 1987, 135-137). For Danish Sign Language this is true of at least meaningful modifications in which different directions from the signer's body are distinguished morphologically. Direction differences are not distinctive at the submorphemic level. Moreover, the following pair of sign forms demonstrate the inadequacy of a purely simultaneous analysis of modified signs. The modified form c+GIVE+multiple+fr ('I give to many/all of them') (Ill. 6a) can be described loosely as follows: the hand moves from near the signer's body forward right and then makes a sideways sweeping movement. In the form c+GIVE+fr ('I give to him') (Ill. 6b) the hand also starts from near the signer's body and moves forward right, but there is no final sweeping movement. That is, the beginning of the two signs is identical, and, morphophonologically, we need to separate out a final segment that distinguishes the two signs.

The base form of a sign is its dictionary form, the form of the sign where it has not been modified in any way that adds meaning to or changes the meaning of the sign. A base form is rarely modified by having new phonological material comprising all the parameters of a sign affixed to the stem. Rather, modifications affect one or more of the parameters of the base form. It is not always a simple matter to decide whether a certain modification is expressed spatially or through movement. Movement and space are intrinsically related in the sign; we cannot perceive one without the other. In this sense they are both aspects of the entire activity that constitutes the sign, as claimed by Stokoe.

Loosely, we can distinguish five types of form changes, which may, however, be combined in individual modifications of signs (see also Klima & Bellugi 1979, 300-302). The five types, which are described in a little more detail below, are:
1. the *intensity* of the sign's movement is changed;
2. the sign is *reduplicated*;
3. the sign undergoes *spatial* change, i.e. a change in the position or orientation of the hand(s);
4. the sign is *embedded in a movement* of the hand(s) or an *extra movement* of the hand(s) is *added*;
5. one-handed signs become two-handed with both hands moving either alternately or simultaneously.

A change in the intensity of the movement of a sign is often accompanied by other changes. An example of this is the modified form BAD+intensive ('very bad') (Ill. 7). The base form BAD (Ill. 4b) is made with a downward movement of the hand held in supination from outside the signer's mouth. In the modified form, the hand starts from a slightly higher position, the arm is pronated, and the initial position is prolonged. Then the hand moves downward while the arm is rotated to supination, the movement being faster and longer than the movement of the base form. I describe this modification as primarily expressed by a change in the intensity of the sign's movement despite the change in orientation of the manual articulator. The reason is that in all signs that are modified for (semantic) intensity, the modification is expressed by a prolongation of the initial position followed by a movement that is faster and longer than the movement of the sign's base form. Not all signs show a change in orientation of the manual articulator.

Base forms can be *reduplicated*, with or without changes in the intensity (speed) and shape of their movement. The verb GO-TO (Ill. 8) can be reduplicated to mean 'go somewhere regularly'. Then the base form of the sign is repeated, which is, of course, only possible if the hand is moved back to its original position between each new cycle.

Base forms can also change in ways that do not alter the intensity or shape of their movement. Instead, the signer changes the position or orientation of her hand(s) in relation to the base form of the sign. This change of the base form affects the place of articulation of the sign and I describe it as a *spatial* change. I present several examples of that in I.6.3 Liddell and Johnson's sequential form analysis, and I.6.5 Formal description of some different verb types.

A number of modifications are expressed in the way that the base form of the sign is *embedded in a movement* of the hand(s) or an *extra movement* of the hand(s) is *added* to a part of the sign form. For instance, the sign BECKON (Ill. 9a), whose base form is made with a local movement only, may be reduplicated while the hand moves sideways ('beckon many/all of them') (Ill. 9b), and, as mentioned, c+GIVE+multiple+fr (Ill. 6a) is made with an added sideways movement of the hand in the final part of the sign. In some cases of embedding of a base form in a particular movement, the movement of the base form is eliminated, e.g. in TEACH+multiple. Morphologically relevant changes of a base form through embedding of the sign in a movement or adding of an extra movement affect both the movement contour and the place of articulation of a sign. With respect to the latter parameter these modifications are also expressed *spatially*.

Finally, one-handed signs may become two-handed with both hands moving either alternately or simultaneously.

In this book, *modification* is used both for a category with a particular meaning (e.g. modifications for distribution) and as a cover term for different kinds of changes of sign forms which express such a category parallel to different kinds of affixation and reduplication in spoken languages. That is, I will say both that a particular sign is modified for distribution and that the sign is modified by being reduplicated. But *modification* is only used for morphologically relevant changes of sign forms, not in relation to, for instance, assimilation.

Space and *movement* are specific expressive means of signed languages and should be kept distinct from *location* and *motion*, which are semantic notions relevant to all languages. In this book, I will focus on modification of types three and four above, i.e. changes in the position or orientation of the hand(s) compared with the base form and embedding of the base form in a movement of the hand(s) or addition of an extra movement of the hand(s) to a part of the sign form.

Nonmanual articulators

The *nonmanual* means of articulation of signed languages is movements of the head or body, mouth patterns, movements of the eyes (gaze directions), eye blink, and other facial expressions consisting of contractions of the muscles of the face.

Some *mouth patterns* are silent imitations of the visible articulation of Danish words. They are usually linked with manual signs, but sometimes a signer uses the mouth pattern of, for instance, a Danish preposition without a manual sign in the middle of a sentence. Some signs are almost always accompanied by a Danish mouth pattern, while others never are. Under certain circumstances, e.g. when eating, signers may leave out a Danish mouth pattern that is otherwise part of a sign; on the other hand, a Danish mouth pattern may in some cases replace a sign, e.g. in answers consisting of a single word.

That Danish mouth patterns are an integral part of the language appears from the fact that signs having Danish mouth patterns cannot always be translated by the Danish word in question. When the sign verb STEAL includes a Danish mouth pattern, it is the mouth pattern of the Danish word *tyv* ('thief'), which is a noun. Even though STEAL functions as a verb in signed clauses, it includes the mouth pattern of the noun *tyv*. The Danish verb meaning 'steal' is *stjæle*, which has quite a different mouth pattern (unrounded versus rounded vowel). Another example is the negative existential which also has a manual and a nonmanual component. The latter is the mouth pattern of the Danish word *tom* ('empty'). The negative existential can be used in negations where the word *tom* is excluded in a sentence in Danish, e.g. as an answer to the question in (1):

```
(1) A:    _____?
          TODAY ANNE EXISTENTIAL /
          Is Anne here today?

    B:    NEG-EXISTENTIAL /
          tom ['empty']
          No.
```

Signers vary much with respect to how much they use Danish mouth patterns. Spoken language mouth patterns have been investigated in particular in some European signed languages (Vogt-Svendsen 1983, 1984; Schermer 1985, 1990; Schröder 1985; Ebbinghaus & Hessmann 1990; Pimiä 1990) .

Mouth patterns that do not imitate Danish words may be parts of lexemes. A verb that means 'be very curious, be very eager' has a mouth pattern that can be described approximately as pursed lips (as for a long rounded vowel) followed by extended lips (as for a long unrounded vowel). Other mouth patterns express modifications of signs. Some action verbs can take a modification which is expressed by a mouth pattern that consists of slightly extended and protruding lips. The meaning is that the action takes place as expected, without any problems. Finally, mouth patterns can express emotions such as anger or sorrow, usually coordinated with other features of facial expression.

Facial expressions involving raised brows, widened eyes, contraction of the muscles of the eye lids, and the like have been identified as components of the marking of questions, relative clauses, conditionals, and topicalizations in several signed languages (see among others Baker & Padden 1978; Liddell 1978, 1980; Coulter 1983; Engberg-Pedersen 1990). The position and movement of the head are also relevant to some of these constructions.

When a constituent is *topicalized* in Danish Sign Language, it is marked by the following nonmanual features: the chin is pulled back or lowered, the eyes are squinted (i.e. the muscles of the eye lids are contracted) *or* the brows are raised or both features co-occur, the muscles of the upper lip may be contracted, and at the end of the topicalized constituent, there may be a head nod. An example of topicalization is seen in Ill. 27. Two constituents can be topicalized one after another. Then there is a slight change in head position and in the facial expression between the two constituents.

Squinting, i.e. contraction of the muscles of the eye lids, can be used with a referential constituent in the middle of a clause. Then the constituent is not accompanied by the other nonmanual features mentioned above, but there may be slight changes in the position of the head just before and after the constituent. Squinting of the eyes signals *reference check*: the sender wants the receiver to indicate whether he can identify the referent (Engberg-Pedersen 1990).

Eye blink is one of the most frequent (although involuntary) indicators of a major constituent boundary. Clause boundaries are usually also accompanied by changes in head or body position (Engberg-Pedersen, Hansen & Kjær Sørensen 1981; see also Baker & Padden 1978), but movements of the head or the body may also occur within a clause or a major clause constituent.

Gaze directions and head and body orientation and posture are also relevant at the discourse level (see especially II.5 Shifted reference, shifted attribution of expressive elements, and shifted locus).

6.2 The manual alphabets, the Mouth-Hand System, and names
The manual alphabets
Manual alphabets consist of signs for each letter of an alphabet. The signs of the two manual alphabets used in Denmark are one-handed signs. Most of the letter signs have a distinctive handshape, a few are distinguished by the movement or the orientation of the hand. In the signs' base forms the hand is held at a distance of approximately 10 centimetres (4 inches) from the ipsilateral shoulder. The signs are nouns (as in a sentence meaning 'Is København spelt with a *k*?') and can be used for spelling words of written languages.

Two manual alphabets are in use in Denmark: an alphabet that has been used since the foundation of the first school for the deaf (the "old manual alphabet"), and the so-called international manual alphabet, which was introduced in Denmark in 1977 with the addition of three signs for the three last letters of the Danish alphabet, Æ, Ø, and Å.

Some of the handshapes of letter signs are also used in underived (see below) signs, e.g. the handshapes of the letter signs S (in WORK), O (in one version of HOTEL), V (in ASK), and G (in IN-A-LITTLE-WHILE) of the new manual alphabet. The use of the same handshape in these signs as in the letter signs is accidental; it is not influenced by the signs' meaning. Other handshapes of the letter signs do not occur in underived signs, e.g. E of the new manual alphabet. Conversely, there are handshapes that do occur in underived signs, but not in the manual alphabets, e.g. a fist with extended, slightly spread index and middle fingers bent at the outer joints. In a few places in this book, I use a letter name as a symbol for a handshape; it is only a mnemonic device and does not imply any semantic relation between the letter sign (or a Danish word) and the sign in which the handshape occurs.

The manual alphabets are used for spelling Danish words and names when the signer does not know an equivalent sign or does not expect the receiver to know the sign, or when she wants to draw the receiver's attention to a Danish word. They are also used by children for playing just as spoken language alphabets are used by hearing children. Moreover, single letters are used for some Danish affixes, e.g. *u-* in the compound U^PATIENT (Danish: *u-tålmodig* 'impatient').

Some signs are derived from fingerspelled versions of Danish words. A sign derived from a fingerspelled version of a word differs from the full fingerspelled version in several ways (Engberg-Pedersen, Hansen & Kjær Sørensen 1981, 92-109; for an analysis of ASL signs derived from the signs of the American manual alphabet, see Battison 1978). The fingerspelled version is made with the hand held a little outside the ipsilateral shoulder, while the derived form may be made in other positions. The derived sign may consist of only the initial letter of the word. The movement of the hand in the derived sign is normally different from the movement of the letter sign. For instance, the sign DAUGHTER is made with the handshape and orientation of the letter D from the old manual alphabet, but the hand is held at a much lower level than in the letter sign and the sign is made with a repeated movement. Fingerspelling can be modified to signify the location of a text or written word (on a sweatshirt, a wall, etc.), but a derived sign can take a modification which is expressed spatially, but does not have any locative sense. LF is the Danish abbreviation of the Danish National Association of the Deaf (from *Landsforbundet*), the sign name of the association consists of the letters L and F from the manual alphabet. This sign, LF, can be modified in relation to the frame of reference (see II.2 The frame of reference) as many other noun signs.

The Mouth-Hand System
The Mouth-Hand System was invented in the beginning of this century as a means of showing the articulation of Danish words manually (Birch-Rasmussen 1982). It consists of 15 handshapes with particular orientations that roughly signify the articulation of Danish consonants. The hand is held just below the chin and the receiver is expected to decode the articulation of the Danish word by combining the handshapes and the mouth pattern. I transcribe words and affixes rendered in the Mouth-Hand System by means of a Danish gloss in small letters followed by a capital M in parentheses and by an English translation or, if needed, explanation in parentheses: var(M)('was/were') or Vibely(M)(name).

The Mouth-Hand System is used for teaching articulation in the schools for the deaf. As with the manual alphabets, it is also used in signing when the signer does not have a signed equivalent of a word, does not expect the receiver to know the sign, or wants to draw the receiver's attention to the Danish word and possibly its pronunciation. Moreover, many lexemes are made by the Mouth-Hand System, e.g. duks(M) (a student being in charge of keeping order in the classroom), giro(M) (a way of postal payment), juli(M) ('July'). The Mouth-Hand System is also used for particles in combination with signs in translation loans from Danish. For instance, the verb FIND ('finde') is combined with the particle *af*, FIND^af(M), corresponding to Danish *finde ud af* ('find out'), and as an equivalent to Danish *have brug for* ('need') we find the combination of the verb USE ('use', Danish: *bruge*) and the particle for(M), USE^for(M), meaning 'need'. There are also compounds with Danish affixes rendered by the Mouth-Hand System, e.g. the suffix *-hed* for deriving nouns is used in a compound meaning 'love (noun)', LOVE^hed(M), corresponding to Danish *kærlighed*. Such forms are not typical of the varieties of signing that are much influenced by Danish; on the contrary, they are typical of communication among deaf people only.

Just as there are signs that have been derived from fingerspelled versions of spoken language words, there are also signs derived from versions of words in the Mouth-Hand System. Such derived signs often leave out some of the handshapes compared with the full versions. There are, for example, seven handshapes in the complete Mouth-Hand System version of the Danish word *selvfølgelig* ('of course'), but the sign OF-COURSE (Ill. 10) is made with only the first and the last of these handshapes. Moreover, in the sign, the forearm is in the neutral position (the palm of the right hand facing left) instead of being pronated as for the Mouth-Hand System (the palm facing the signer's sternum).

Name signs
Names may be fingerspelled or rendered by the Mouth-Hand System, and name signs may be derived from either a fingerspelled or a Mouth-Hand System version of the name. But a person's name sign may also be a sign that characterises some aspect of the individual. If a person has wavy hair, his name sign may be WAVY-HAIR, accompanied by the mouth movements of his Danish name. A name sign may also imitate a movement that an individual typically makes such as rubbing her nose with an index finger. Some names have fixed name signs independent of the individual. The name sign for the Danish name *Morten* is HARE because hares are typically called Morten in Danish children's books. Likewise, the name sign for the Danish name *Vibeke* is the sign LAPWING because of the similarity between the Danish word for lapwing, *vibe*, and the name. In many cases, a modified version of the letter sign corresponding to the first letter of the individual's name is used to identify the individual: the appropriate handshape is used with a repeated straight or a circular movement with the hand held in the position of the letter sign (outside the ipsilateral shoulder). The Danish mouth pattern of the name is part of name signs and letter signs used with a naming function.

I transcribe name signs proper (not fingerspelled versions or versions made by means of the Mouth-Hand System) as other signs, i.e. with a gloss written in capital letters: ASGER.

6.3 Liddell and Johnson's sequential form analysis of signs

Sequentiality
Within the framework of autosegmental phonology, Liddell and Johnson (Johnson & Liddell 1984; Liddell 1984a, 1990b; Liddell & Johnson 1986, 1989) have developed an analysis of signs in ASL that is based on the notion that signs have sequential structure. Earlier descriptions of signs (especially Stokoe 1960, 1978) also involved sequentiality, but sequentiality was not seen as phonologically relevant. Liddell and Johnson argue that there is evidence for a phonological analysis of signs as sequences of segments. One of their arguments (see in particular Liddell 1990b, 46ff.) draws on ASL pairs of signs similar to the sign pair TO-TOWN (Ill. 11a) and OUT (Ill. 11b) in Danish Sign Language. These two signs are derived from the Mouth-Hand System, but are integrated in Danish Sign Language as verbs that can be modified. Phonologically, they have the same initial handshape, a fist; TO-TOWN, however, ends with an

index hand, OUT with a fist with extended index and middle finger. That is, the two signs are only phonologically distinct in their final segment.

Another argument for a sequential analysis presented by Liddell and Johnson involves the morphophonological description of verbs that show agreement. Because I find it to be as yet the most developed model of how to conceptualise the morphological structure of a modified sign, and in particular a sign showing agreement, I will present the overall structure of the model and the features of it that are directly relevant to the description of agreement.

Movements and holds

Periods in the production of a sign during which some aspect of the articulation is in transition are called *movements* (Ms), while *holds* (Hs) are periods during which there is no such transition of any aspect of the articulation. Signs can consist of different sequences of movements and holds. The sign THINK in Danish Sign Language (Ill. 2a) consists of the sequence MH, while DANGEROUS (Ill. 3a) consists of the sequence MMH.[2]

Segmental and articulatory features

Each segment of a sign is composed of two major types of features: the segmental features and the articulatory features. The segmental features specify the activity of the hand (i.e. whether the segment is a movement or a hold) and the contour of movements, any local movement of the fingers, and timing information such as duration. The articulatory features specify the hand configuration (handshape), the position and orientation of the hand, and nonmanual signals. The articulatory features cluster in six groups, so that the notation of each segment of a sign consists of seven clusters as in Fig. 1.

Segmental Features (a *movement* or a *hold*)

Articulatory Features:
- Hand Configuration Features
- First Location Features
- Placement Features
- Second Location Features
- Orientation Features
- Nonmanual Signal Features

Fig. 1. The seven feature bundles of a segment

As all aspects of the articulation are in a steady state during a hold, a hold can be described with a single matrix of features. A movement, in contrast, is defined as a period during which there is a transition between two states. Thus it requires the specification of an initial and a final bundle of articulatory features. Fig. 2a presents

---

[2] Liddell and Johnson's model has been criticised for being difficult to apply: it is not always easy to make the segmentation into movements and holds (Sandler 1990b, 29). It is not clear to me how to decide when a sign has an initial hold segment.

the three segments of the ASL sign GOOD, which has a HMH structure. The segmental features of the middle segment (i.e. the top, middle square) are attached to two sets of articulatory features, one set for the initial state of the segment and another set for its final state.

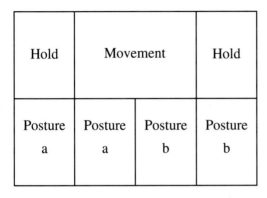

Fig. 2a. Representation of the feature matrix of the sign GOOD (ASL) (Liddell & Johnson 1989, 213)

The specification of the initial articulatory features of any segment in a string is identical with the specification of the final articulatory features of the preceding segment. Thus it is uneconomical to notate the articulatory bundles for every movement and hold segment. Liddell and Johnson use an autosegmental representation 'which permits the attachment of single clusters of features of one sort to single clusters of features of another sort' (1989, 213), in the case of signs, the attachment of clusters of articulatory features to clusters of segmental features. Such a notation reduces the notation of GOOD in Fig. 2a to the notation in Fig. 2b.

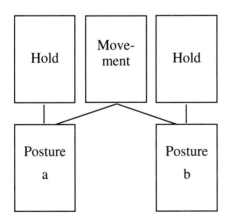

Fig. 2b. Representation of autosegmental attachment of feature bundles for the sign GOOD (ASL) (Liddell & Johnson 1989, 214)

In the list of articulatory features (see Fig. 1), the hand configuration, or handshape, features describe the shape of the fingers and the thumb, and the nonmanual signal features specify nonmanual behaviours that are lexically relevant, such as specific lip movements. The other four clusters of articulatory features combine to describe the orientation and position of the hand, as well as whether the hand or some part of the hand makes contact with the other hand or a place on the body or head. The way these four clusters interact can best be understood by means of an example of a verb that can show agreement.

Orientation and position of the hand(s)
The verb ANSWER in Danish Sign Language is a verb that can show agreement. Ills 1, 12a and 12b show three forms of the verb which can be translated as 'he$_i$ answers me', 'I answer him$_i$' and 'he$_i$ answers him$_j$'. The direction of the hand's movement is reversed in the form in Ill. 12a compared with the form in Ill. 1.

The sign is composed of the sequence HMH, and the form in Ill. 1 is made in relation to two positions in space, a position on the signer's right and the position of the signer's body. At the beginning of the form in Ill. 1, the hand is at or near a position that we shall call x, with the palm facing the signer. The movement is straight and takes the hand along a line between x and the signer. To describe the hand's position at the beginning and at the end of the sign, we specify two position features at two different moments in time: placement (where is the hand?) and facing (which part of the hand faces where?). The position features are specified for both the first and the second hold.

The relationship between facing and placement is brought out by the three clusters First Location Features Bundle, Second Location Features Bundle, and Placement Features Bundle. The two Location Features Bundles specify the two positions relevant to placement (where is the hand?) and to facing (what does the hand face?). The Placement Features Bundle indicates which of the two Location Features Bundles specifies placement. By inference, the other Location Features Bundle specifies facing.

In a full description of the hand's position and orientation in space, we need to specify its orientation in relation to one more plane. That is done in the Orientation Features Bundle.

A simplified notation of the form of ANSWER in Ill. 1 ('he$_i$ answers me') is shown in Fig. 3. The sign has three segments: a hold, a movement, and a hold. The movement is a straight line (*str* in the Segmental Features Bundle). The hand configuration at the beginning of the sign is like the handshape of the letter K; during the sign, it changes to approximately the handshape of the letter V. In the first segment, the back of the fingers (BKFI in the First Location Features Bundle) are proximal (*p* in the Placement Features Bundle) to the position x, and are positioned at sternum level (ST in the First Location Features Bundle), in line with this position (the term *in line* is explained below). The inside of the fingers (INFI in the Second Location Features Bundle) faces position c, the signer's position, at sternum level (ST in the Second Location Features Bundle). The ulnar side of the hand (UL in the Orientation

Features Bundle) faces the horizontal plane (HP) in the first segment. In the final segment, the palm (PA) faces the horizontal plane.

Any values of the first hold segment which are not explicitly changed in the last hold segment are transferred automatically from the first to the last segment. In Fig. 3, I have left them out to reduce redundancy.

At the end of the sign, the relationship between facing and placement has been reversed. We indicate this in the Placement Features Bundle, by changing 1 (for First Location) to 2 (for Second Location). That is, now the radial side of the hand (RA in the Second Location Features Bundle) is proximal (p in the Placement Features Bundle) to c at sternum level (c and ST in the Second Location Features Bundle), while the ulnar side of the hand (UL in the First Location Features Bundle) faces the position x at sternum level (x and ST in the First Location Features Bundle). The Location Features Bundle that is not specified as placement in the Placement Features Bundle is understood as determining facing in the final segment, i.e. the ulnar side of the hand (UL) faces x during the final hold.

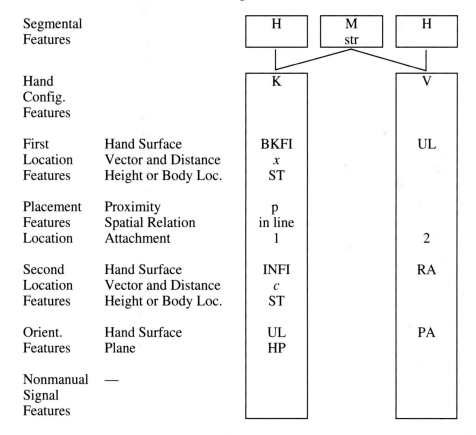

Segmental Features		H	M str	H
Hand Config. Features		K		V
First Location Features	Hand Surface Vector and Distance Height or Body Loc.	BKFI x ST		UL
Placement Features Location	Proximity Spatial Relation Attachment	p in line 1		2
Second Location Features	Hand Surface Vector and Distance Height or Body Loc.	INFI c ST		RA
Orient. Features	Hand Surface Plane	UL HP		PA
Nonmanual Signal Features	—			

Fig. 3. A simplified notation of the form of ANSWER in Ill. 1 ('he$_i$ answers me')[3]

In order to describe the form of ANSWER in Ill. 12b ('he$_i$ answers him$_j$'), all that is needed is to change c in the Second Location Features Bundle to y (a symbol for a position on the signer's left). The notation then correctly indicates that, at the beginning of the sign, the back of the fingers are proximal to the position x and that the inside of the fingers face y, and that, during the last hold, the radial side of the hand is proximal to y and the ulnar side faces x. Note that the form of ANSWER in Ill. 12a differs from the forms in Ills 1 and 12b by having a handshape closer to the handshape of the letter sign V in its first segment and a handshape closer to the handshape of the letter sign K in its last segment. That is, there are (at least) two allomorphs of the root morpheme ANSWER.

The positions that are notated as c, x, and y are morphologically and syntactically relevant. They represent the arguments of the verb, and their nature will be discussed in later parts of this book. In the verb in Fig. 3 (Ill. 1), x is a marker for the verb's A argument and c for its IO argument.[4] What the notation of a verb such as ANSWER in Liddell and Johnson's model brings out is that the verb has two cells that can take a marker for the verb's A argument and its IO argument, respectively. The A cell of ANSWER is in the Vector and Distance tier of the First Location Features Bundle, while its IO cell is in the Vector and Distance tier of the Second Location Features Bundle. The root ANSWER is unspecified as to its A and IO arguments, so the A and IO cells are empty. The root ANSWER is therefore what Liddell and Johnson call an *incomplete s-morph*. Its representation is *s*egmental, but incomplete. The specifications that can be inserted into the A and IO cells are called *p-morphs*; they do not contain segmental information, but provide *p*aradigmatic contrast. ANSWER represents only one morphophonological and morphosyntactic verb type out of many in Danish Sign Language (for other morphosyntactic types, see I.6.5 Formal description of some different verb types).

Vector, Distance, and Height or Body Location
The Vector and Distance tiers and the Height or Body Location tiers require elaboration. The position of the hand in space can be determined in relation to areas on the signer's body. For example, it is possible to specify a position a few inches outside the signer's right shoulder. Liddell and Johnson have found, however, that with verbs showing agreement, the position of the hand(s) in space is most easily

---

3 Fig. 3 presents a later version of the model than the one presented in Lidell and Johnson (1989). The organisation of the articulory features has been changed somewhat (Scott Lidell & Robert Johnson - personal communication).

4 I use Comrie's symbols A of the argument of a transitive construction that correlates most highly with agent, and P of the argument that correlates most highly with patient (Comrie 1981, 64). I use A also of the argument of intransitive verbs in unergative constructions and P of the argument of intransitive verbs in unaccusative constructions (Perlmutter 1978). With ditransitive verbs, I use IO of the third argument. In relation to utterance verbs such as ANSWER and ASK, the receiver argument is characterised as an IO argument even though it is probably not possible to analyse reported speech as an argument of the verb in Danish Sign Language.

described in relation to positions that are imagined as situated on what they call vectors radiating from the signer's body (Liddell & Johnson 1989, 232). They describe seven such vectors in ASL verb agreement. On each vector there are positions, or loci as Liddell and Johnson call them,[5] at four distances from the signer's centre. But in ASL verbs showing agreement, the hands do not move from one locus to another, but between loci along the vectors. That is what is notated as *proximal* and *in line* in the Proximity and Spatial Relation tiers of the Placement Features Bundle in Fig. 3. In other signs, the relationship between the hand and the locus may be *over, under, ahead*, and the like.

The position of the hand is specified for height in the Height or Body Location tiers. In the ASL clause meaning 'I tell you no', the hand making the verb SAY-NO-TO is directed at the receiver's nose, while the hand in the verb ASK in a clause meaning 'I ask you' is directed at the receiver's chin. Similarly, the hand making the verb GIVE in the clause meaning 'I give you' is directed at the receiver's trunk (Liddell 1990a, 182ff.). If the signer uses ASK with an IO argument used to refer to a person who is taller than herself, or somebody who is at a higher level, the sign is made upward toward the receiver's chin. When referents are not present and the signer uses loci on vectors to represent the referents, the heights are still relevant. If the signer uses ASK with an IO argument that is used to refer to a giant, the hand making ASK is directed at the imaginary giant's chin, i.e. upward from the signer. When the height or position of the IO argument's referent is not specified, the default value for height specification is the signer's own body, i.e. the hand making ASK is directed at a locus at the height of the signer's chin.

In Danish Sign Language, verbs also differ lexically with respect to height. For example, TEACH is made at throat level, the final segment of DECEIVE at sternum level, and GIVE at chest level. The lexically specified height differences need not be indicated in the gloss transcriptions. But as pointed out by Liddell, height differences also reflect the height or level of the imagined referent; height differences are cues to the signer's conception of the referents' heights or levels in relation to the holder of the point of view. Ill's 13a and 13b show the difference between two versions of EXPLAIN. The first has the default value for height specifications, the second a low value for height specification as, for instance, in a clause meaning 'I explained it to him (a child)'. Such height differences must be notated in the transcriptions as the difference between +*sr* for sideward-right and +*srd* for sideward-right-downward (see further I.6.4 The term *locus*).

In Liddell and Johnson's analysis, loci in verb agreement are points on vectors. As verbs are made at lexically different heights, phonetically different points in space may have the same morphological value. In the ASL clauses meaning 'I tell him no' and 'I ask him' where the two objects are co-referential, the P cell of SAY-NO-TO and

---

5 In order to preclude misunderstanding, I want to emphasise that Liddell and Johnson's use of the term *locus* is different from mine. The difference will become clear especially in I.6.4 The term *locus*.

the IO cell of ASK are filled with a p-morph specifying the same vector locus. But the two verbs differ lexically in height. The verb SAY-NO-TO is specified for the nose (NS) in the Height or Body Location tier, whereas ASK is specified for the chin (CN). The two kinds of location information, vector locus and height, differ: the vector locus depends on the verbs' arguments, while height is lexically determined. This is brought out clearly by the notation where the Vector tier is empty in the notation of the root, whereas the Height tier is filled with NS for nose in SAY-NO-TO and CN for chin in ASK. If the verbs are used with arguments that refer to real or imagined referents that are not at the neutral height level, the notation for height (CN or NS) is understood as the chin or nose level of the real or imagined referent.

6.4 The term *locus*

Locus in Liddell and Johnson's model

For a verb showing agreement, Liddell and Johnson's notation system specifies three different positions in space in relation to the placement or facing of the hand. The first position is the locus specified in the Vector and Distance tier. This position is one of the loci on the vectors. In the notation of x+ANSWER+c (see Fig. 3, earlier), the vector locus that defines placement in the first segment is x. It combines with the notation in the Height and Body Location tier to specify a position at a particular height level, in Fig. 3 the sternum level for ANSWER. But the hand is not necessarily at this position; it may be proximal to it, rather than at it. The actual position of a part of the hand in relation to the position determined by the Vector and Distance tier and the Height and Body Location tier is specified by the Placement Features Bundle. In Fig. 3, the back of the fingers are *in line proximal* to the locus x (at sternum level).

Thus the three positions that combine in describing the actual position of the hand during the first hold of x+ANSWER+c are:
1. one on the vector (specified in the Vector and Distance cell);
2. one at the lexically specified height level (specified by a combination of the Vector and Distance cell and the Height and Body Location cell); and
3. one where the hand actually is (specified by a combination of the Vector and Distance cell, the Height and Body Location cell, and the Placement Features Bundle).

If two verbs, e.g. the ASL verbs SAY-NO-TO and ASK, have co-referential arguments, they may have the same specification in the Vector and Distance tier, but their level specifications differ: SAY-NO-TO is made at nose level, ASK at chin level. As vectors define semantically relevant directions from the signer, and as SAY-NO-TO and ASK are made in relation to semantically the same locus on one of the vectors, but at different heights, it is not possible to uphold a definition of *locus* as 'a *point* on the body or in the signing space that serves an articulatory function' (Liddell 1990a, 176 – emphasis added). Vectors in Liddell and Johnson's model must be vertical planes radiating from the signer and loci must be vertical lines on these planes at different distances from the signer.

Locus in Danish Sign Language
An anaphoric locus is a projection of the referent into space in the absence of the entities in the situational context of utterance. In Danish Sign Language, it is generally impossible to determine a locus's distance from the signer's body or the hands' distance from the locus in the way presupposed by Liddell and Johnson's model (the Proximity tier in the Placement Features Bundle). The movements of the hand(s) in verbs showing agreement differ lexically in length: a verb such as TEACH has a very short movement, while ANSWER has a longer movement, but the two verbs can be modified grammatically for the same locus. Some verbs have first person agreement forms where the hand makes contact with the signer's body. For instance, the verbs DECEIVE, COMFORT, BURDEN, NOTIFY, and INFORM are lexically specified to have contact with the signer's body when the first person agreement marker is inserted in their P/IO cell. When these verbs take a P/IO argument, however, which refers to others who are present in the context of utterance, the hands in the verb forms do not normally make contact with the persons in question. Therefore, such verb forms cannot be used as a criterion of the locus's distance from the signer in the case of anaphoric reference.

Some loci seem to be expressed closer to the signer than other loci, i.e. some referents are, so to speak, "imagined" as being closer to the signer's centre than other referents. That is particularly the case with loci that represent referents with which the signer empathises (see II.2 The frame of reference). Loci of the time lines also seem to be expressed by points or areas in the signing space at variable, but specific distances from the signer's body. Otherwise, there need not be any difference in the signing used to represent a conversation with, for instance, someone lying in the upper berth of a bunk bed and an angel in the sky. The locus's distance from the signer cannot be seen on the verb and it is not necessarily made explicit in any other way. Moreover, it seems that what is morphophonologically relevant in Danish Sign Language are larger areas in different directions from the signer rather than specific points, or vertical lines, on vectors. The hands in two tokens of the same verb which are morphologically specified for the same locus may be at different positions in space, as long as the direction is perceptually different from other morphologically relevant directions in the context. The signing hand is moved and oriented in a certain direction and there is no indication of a point or line "out there".

Except in a phonetic description, it is unsatisfactory to talk only about the actual positions of the hands, as the articulators of different lexemes are at different heights and different distances from the signer, even though they are modified in the same way semantically. If we only talk about the positions of the hands in space, we miss the generalisation that the verbs all take the same morphological modification. As it is impossible to determine many loci as positions or lines on planes radiating from the signer's body, it is preferable to do away with the idea of loci as *points* on the body or in the signing space that serve an *articulatory* function (Liddell 1990a, 176). Instead, I suggest a definition of *locus* as follows: a category whose members are specific loci in paradigmatic contrast. The meaning of the category has to do with reference and will be further investigated in this book. A locus marker is a morpheme that is expressed in the way it influences the position and/or orientation of the hand(s) in the production of a sign. The locus as such can only be expressed linguistically through the locus marker, but a locus can be thought of as a meaningful direction from the signer or, in the case of loci of the time lines (see II.3.1 The time lines) and some constructions with polymorphemic verbs (see III.8.6 Polymorphemic verbs and space), as a meaningful point or area within the signing space. When the locus is used anaphorically to represent a specific referent, the direction or point can be seen as a projection of the referent as a cognitive entity, corresponding to real-world entities in deictic reference (see further *Referent projection* in III.8.6 Polymorphemic verbs and space).

One of the reasons we need to talk about both the locus and the locus marker is that a locus has meaning independent of the referent it represents in a specific discourse. But the locus also acquires meaning from the referent it represents in a specific discourse (see II.2 The frame of reference, and II.3 Time lines); and the locus marker is only used when the locus represents a specific referent.

As loci are expressed only through locus markers that influence the production of signs by changing the orientation of the hands and/or the place of articulation, the term *locus* 'place' may seem unsatisfactory. I do, however, use this term, both because it is already current in sign linguistics and because of its relatedness to *location*. There is no doubt that what lies behind the anaphoric use of loci in signed languages is deictic reference by pointing gestures to items in the context of utterance, and such items are in certain locations. An anaphoric locus is a referent projection, an imagined referent, but it is not *expressed* in signing by a point, plane, direction or anything else within the signing space; it is only expressed through a locus marker which influences the production of individual signs.[6]

Muscle activity or geometry
In an article on marking tense on verbs in ASL, Jacobowitz and Stokoe criticise the use of terms from 'the classical mathematics of three-dimensional space' (1988, 334) to describe signed languages, in particular in descriptions of what has been called

---

6 The term *locus* also relates to the use of the term in cognitively oriented descriptions of anaphoric reference. Givón, for instance, puts forward a hypothesis of the function of old information in which he uses *locus* of a cognitive phenomenon: 'The chunks of old, redundant ('topical') information in the clause serve to *ground* the new information to the already-stored old information. Cognitively, they furnish the *address* or *label* for the *storage locus* ('file') in the episodic memory' (Givón 1990, 899 – emphasis in the original). In Part II, Discourse and space, I will show how loci are used to keep track of reference in signing.

time lines in these languages. (I will return to this criticism in relation to time lines in II.3.) They find that such terms are failed, or inverse, metaphors, as they liken 'something fairly complex to something even more abstract' (ibid., 334). As an alternative they encourage an investigation of the physical structure of the system under study (see also Stokoe 1991). They find, for example, that 'all else remaining unchanged in a sign verb of ASL, extension (of the hand) at the wrist, (of the forearm) at the elbow, or (of the upper arm) at the shoulder, or two or more of these, will denote future time' (ibid., 337).

This criticism is in line with Stokoe's criticism of the parameter model of signs (see I.6.1 The articulatory means of signed languages). In both cases, what is stressed is the necessity to describe signing as muscle activity instead of imposing an abstract model on it. The criticism is also relevant in relation to the use of terms such as *vector* and *locus*. All that is described as spatial in signed languages is manifested through muscle activity. That is, when we talk about a particular verb sign being modified for a locus, what we see is extension of the hands and arms in a certain direction in relation to the signer's centre.

The term *locus*, however, can be justified at another linguistic level. A one-handed sign such as the verb form x+ANSWER+c (Ill. 1) can be made either with the signer's left or right hand. If the signer makes the sign with her left hand, she must, among other things, raise her arm more at the shoulder level than if she makes it with her right hand; but the two different versions of the sign, however they are to be described formally, would have the same meaning. The two forms manifest the same combination of morphemes. Whether the two forms should be described as different allomorphs of the same morpheme or as phonetic variants of the same morph is still unclear. It depends among other things on the results of an analysis of the functions of shift in strong hand in signing. But at some level, a number of different muscle activities must be described as phonetic variants of the same allomorph, and different allomorphs must be described as belonging to the same morpheme.

An ideal linguistic description would start by identifying the sequences of meaningful units in some phonetic transcription and from there move on to an analysis grouping morphs as allomorphs of the same morphemes. But the phonetic description of signs is still far from being so developed that we can describe the physical aspects of signs, including body and head movements and the movements of the facial muscles, with any precision. Moreover, it is doubtful whether it would ever be possible to go about describing a language expressed in a new medium in the ideal way. We have to get some idea of what is linguistically relevant before we know what to describe in phonetic terms. In spoken languages, we know now that absolute pitch is not linguistically relevant and that, in many spoken languages, relative pitch is not relevant at the morphological level. This kind of information is what we use when we start analysing a new spoken language. But with signed languages, we do not yet know all that is relevant. For instance, early descriptions of signed languages tended to focus only on what the hands did and ignored the muscle activities of the body, the head, and the face. Now we know that the hands are only part of the story. Jacobowitz and Stokoe found that extension of the wrist, elbow, and shoulder joints is relevant to expressing future time in some ASL verbs, but before they found this out, they probably did not transcribe or even notice the extension of the joints in these verbs.

In many signs the position and orientation of the hand(s) as a result of particular muscle activities are morphologically relevant. From a perceptual point of view, the easiest way of describing that is by claiming that there is "something out there" which determines the muscle activity, no matter the actual production of any individual sign. Loci are an abstraction of the same kind as tense. Tense is the grammatical (inflectional) expression of time. It is a grammatical category that is expressed through tense markers in paradigmatic contrast. Similarly, *locus* can be seen as a category that is expressed through locus markers in paradigmatic contrast. Locus markers cause a spatial change in the production of a sign. The meaning of the category *locus* involves referentiality. As I will show, the meaning and function of the category overlaps with many categories of spoken languages, but its expression is unique to signed languages. By distinguishing *locus* and *locus marker,* we meet Jacobowitz and Stokoe's criticism: the locus as such is not expressed in signing, only the locus marker is; but we need the category of locus to talk about discourse (see in particular II.2 The frame of reference, and III.8.6 Polymorphemic verbs and space).

In Liddell and Johnson's model, loci defined in relation to the signer's centre can be seen as a substitute for a phonetic description of part of the muscle activity that goes into making some sign forms, namely signs that are modified for a locus, i.e. take a locus marker. Liddell and Johnson's description of an agreeing verb having cells filled with locus information in the form of p-morphs is in harmony with the idea of locus markers that I have presented here in relation to Danish Sign Language. This is true so long as we do not think of what is filled into the cells, the p-morphs, as expressed by points in space, but by the way they influence the position and orientation of the hand(s) in signs.

The transcription of locus markers
Except in relation to the time lines and in some cases of polymorphemic verbs, I will use the following directional expressions to symbolise the most commonly used locus markers:
— forward (*f*): a direction perpendicular to the signer's surface plane; if outside the shoulders, either forward-right (*fr*) or forward-left (*fl*). The sign form x+ANSWER+c of Ill. 1 will now be transcribed as fr+ANSWER+c;
— sideward (*s*): a direction close to parallel with the signer's surface plane, either sideward-right (*sr*) or sideward-left (*sl*);
— forward-sideward-right/left (*fsr/l*): a direction at an oblique angle in relation to the signer's surface plane;

— upward/downward (*u/d*): directions upward or downward compared with the form of the sign that is morphologically unmarked for height;
— *c*: the *sender locus*, i.e. the form which a verb takes when it is marked for an argument that has first person reference (this form may also be used in other cases and I will return to it in III.6.3 The many uses of the *c*-form);
— neutral (*neu*): does not indicate the locus of a specific referent (see III.6.3 The many uses of the *c*-form).

Distance expressed in pointing signs as more or less raising and extension of the arm can be transcribed as *far* (e.g. *fr.far*) and *cl* (for *close*, e.g. *sr.cl*).

A locus represents a referent, but can only be seen in the way the locus marker influences the production of individual signs. In analysing discourse, we need to talk about specific loci representing specific referents, irrespective of the signs that manifest the locus. In such cases, I will talk about, for instance, *the locus forward-right*.

6.5 Formal description of some different verb types

Single and double agreement verbs

The verb DECEIVE is made with a flat hand with all fingers extended and spread. First the pad of the index finger touches the nose; then, with a non-first person P referent, the hand moves out in the direction of the locus of the referent of the verb's P argument, the palm facing the direction of the movement (see Ill. 14a). At the beginning of c+ANSWER+fr (Ill. 12a), the radial side of the hand is close to the signer's locus (placement in Liddell and Johnson's model) and the ulnar side faces forward right (facing). There are two loci involved in the description of c+ANSWER+fr. At the beginning and at the end of the sign form DECEIVE+fr, the back of the hand also faces somewhere, but it does not matter where it faces. That is, DECEIVE only shows agreement with one argument, namely the argument of the locus that is relevant to the description of the verb's final hold.

The difference between the two verbs is brought out in the following notation of the sign forms:

(1)   1.p DECEIVE+fr   (Ill. 14a)
           I deceive him$_i$

(2)   PRON+fl DECEIVE+fr   (verb form = verb form in (1))
           he$_j$ deceives him$_i$

(3)   PRON+fr DECEIVE+c   (Ill. 14b)
           he$_i$ deceives me

(4)   PRON+fl DECEIVE+c   (verb form = verb form in (3))
      he_j deceives me

(5)   1.p c+ANSWER+fr   (Ill. 12a)
      I answer him_i

(6)   PRON+fr fr+ANSWER+c   (Ill. 1)
      he_i answers me

(7)   PRON+fl fl+ANSWER+c
      he_j answers me

(8)   PRON+fr fr+ANSWER+fl   (Ill. 12b)
      he_i answers him_j

There is no difference between the form of DECEIVE in (1) with 1.p (the first person pronoun) as its A argument and the verb form in (2) with PRON+fl (a form of the non-first person pronoun) as its A argument. Nor is there a difference between the verb form in (3) with PRON+fr (one form of the non-first person pronoun) as its A argument and the verb form in (4) with PRON+fl (another form of the non-first person pronoun) as its A argument. DECEIVE can only agree with one argument, i.e. its root has only one empty cell and this cell can take a P argument agreement marker, a p-morph that makes the verb show agreement with its P argument.[7] Verbs like DECEIVE are *single agreement verbs*. A single agreement verb can agree with its P or IO argument, never with its A argument. This is shown by a symbol for the P/IO argument's locus after the gloss, DECEIVE+*fr*.

By contrast, fr+ANSWER+c in (6) with PRON+fr as its A argument and an IO argument with first person reference differs from fl+ANSWER+c in (7) with PRON+fl as its A argument and from fr+ANSWER+fl in (8) with an IO argument with non-first person reference. ANSWER can agree with both its A argument and its IO argument; it is a *double agreement verb* and its root has two empty cells: one that can take an A argument agreement marker and one that can take an IO argument agreement marker. Other double agreement verbs can take markers for their A argument and their P argument. A double agreement verb is transcribed with a symbol for its A argument's locus before the gloss for the verb and a symbol for its P or IO argument's locus after the gloss.

Regular and backward verbs
There is a morphophonological difference between verbs such as ANSWER and

---

7 When I talk about an agreement verb having an empty cell in which an agreement marker can be inserted, I use Liddell and Johnson's model as a model of the sign's morphological structure.

verbs such as INVITE, PERCEIVE, and TAKE. The verb form in Ill. 15a means 'he invites me', while the form in Ill. 15b means 'I invite him'. Compared with the forms of ANSWER in Ills 1 and 12a, the movement of the hands in INVITE is reversed. While the hand in ANSWER moves from the A argument's locus in the direction of the IO argument's locus, the hands in INVITE move in the opposite direction, i.e. from the P argument's locus in the direction of the A argument's locus. In Liddell and Johnson's terms, the relations between placement and facing are reversed in INVITE compared with ANSWER. In the first segment of ANSWER, the Placement Features Location points to the First Location Features Bundle with the A argument cell, in the final segment it points to the Second Location Features Bundle with the IO argument cell (see Fig. 3 in I.6.3 Liddell and Johnson's sequential form analysis of signs). In the first segment of INVITE, the Placement Features Location points to the Second Location Features Bundle with the P argument cell, in the final segment it points to the First Location Features Bundle with the A argument cell.

This morphophonological difference is also found in ASL where the two kinds of verbs are called *regular* or *typical* (verbs such as ANSWER in Danish Sign Language) and *backward* or *atypical* (verbs such as INVITE in Danish Sign Language) (Padden 1988b, 133, 176-178; Brentari 1988). In both languages, the group of backward verbs is much smaller than the group of regular verbs. Despite the form difference, I transcribe the two kinds of verbs in the same way: c+ANSWER+fr ('I answer him_i') and c+INVITE+fr ('I invite him_i'). The symbol before the gloss for the verb identifies the A argument's locus, while the symbol after the gloss identifies the P/IO argument's locus.

Reciprocal verbs
A morphological difference is the difference between, on the one hand, verbs such as INVITE and ANSWER and, on the other hand, verbs such as DISCUSS. The base form of DISCUSS is seen in Ill. 16a. Some informants can use a modified form of this verb that shows agreement with two arguments, one of which has first person reference. The form is seen in Ill. 16b ('he and I discuss(ed)'). The unmodified form of verbs such as ANSWER and INVITE resembles the forms that are used with an A argument having first person reference. That is, their base forms take a marker symbolised as *c* in their A argument cell (see III.6.3 The many uses of the *c*-form). But verbs such as DISCUSS have unmodified forms with markers having the same expression as the locus markers *sr* and *sl* in their two cells. Such verbs take semantically plural A arguments and have a reciprocal meaning. Other examples of reciprocal verbs are SWAP and QUARREL.

The differences between single and double agreement verbs, between regular and backward verbs, and between reciprocal and nonreciprocal verbs are only three of the many distinctions that cut across the inventory of verbs in Danish Sign Language. A full treatment of these differences is outside the scope of this work.

6.6 The morphological type of signed languages

Signed languages as inflecting languages
A number of modifications of signs has been identified in different signed languages, but the descriptions of them are heterogeneous, to put it mildly. Examples of modifications are: unrealized-inceptive aspect in ASL (Liddell 1984b), fast and slow reduplication in ASL (Fischer 1973; Supalla & Newport 1978) and in Swedish Sign Language (Bergman 1983; Bergman & Dahl in press), manner in ASL (Fischer & Gough 1980), tense in ASL (Jacobowitz & Stokoe 1988), dual in ASL (Supalla & Newport 1978; Klima & Bellugi 1979; Padden 1988b), apportionative internal distribution in ASL (Klima & Bellugi 1979), and twist in Danish Sign Language (Engberg-Pedersen 1989).

As the examples demonstrate, the names of the modifications reflect sometimes their form and sometimes their meaning; sometimes they are terms known from descriptions of spoken languages and sometimes they are more or less fanciful names. The modifications are called modifications, modulations, derivations, and inflections. Sometimes their domain is specified in both semantic and formal terms as when the unrealized-inceptive aspect is said to occur with verbs that refer to volitional processes and to be expressed by one of three specified sequential structures (Liddell 1984b); sometimes it is only reported that the modifications have been found with a number of lexemes, such as 'two dozen ASL verbs' (Jacobowitz & Stokoe 1988, 336). Some modifications are said to be obligatory in a certain linguistic context, some are said to occur partly as 'a matter of choice and focus' (Klima & Bellugi 1979, 284).

Klima and Bellugi compare ASL to inflecting languages such as Latin and claim that 'ASL exhibits a very rich set of inflectional variations on its lexical units' and that 'most of the distinctions that are inflectionally marked in ASL are expressed either lexically or phrasally in English' (Klima & Bellugi 1979, 273). Among the inflections they find in ASL are *'indexical* inflections' (what I call agreement), a reciprocal inflection, number inflections, inflections for distributional aspect, inflections for temporal aspect, inflections for temporal focus, inflections for manner, and inflections for degree (ibid., 273).

A quite contrary view of the morphological type of signed languages is found in Bergman and Dahl (in press). They find that 'SSL [Swedish Sign Language] is basically an inflection-less language with a very well-developed ideophonic morphology' (ibid., 25). This conclusion is based on their analysis of aspectual modifications in Swedish Sign Language, but they add that 'all signed languages which have been the object of closer study are, to our knowledge, similar to SSL in this regard' (ibid., 25).

The prototypes of an *inflecting* (or *inflective* (Sapir 1921(1970), 129-136)) language are Latin and Greek whose words 'do not lend themselves to segmentation into morphs' (Lyons 1968, 191). Moreover, there is no correspondence between 'such segments of the word that we might recognise and morphemes' (ibid., 191). We may segment the Latin word *dominus* into *domin* and *us*, but it is not possible to separate out the parts that mean 'masculine', 'singular', and 'nominative' in *us*.

It is difficult to segment sign words into morphs. Liddell and Johnson's model of a verb modified for agreement does present one or two cells for locus markers, but we cannot point to the expression of the locus markers as a segment separate from the base form of the signs. Rather, the locus markers change the signs' base form. Most other modifications identified for signed languages till now have the same effect. The second criterion of an inflecting language is the lack of correspondence between segments and morphemes, or the occurrence of portmanteau morphemes such as Latin *-us*. Since it is difficult to segment sign words into morphs, the second criterion, which Lyons characterises as the 'more important' (1968, 191), hardly applies. What we might ask is whether several different "modification meanings" merge in their effect on the base forms of some signs. In order for them to be different "modification meanings", they should be kept distinct in some contexts just as 'singular' is kept distinct from 'nominative' in Latin *dominus* if we compare the form with both *domini* (the singular, genitive form) and *dominorum* (the plural, genitive form). There seem to be no examples of this kind of "merged effect" on base forms of signs, which means that signed languages are not inflecting like Latin.

However, the different viewpoints of Klima and Bellugi, on the one hand, and Bergman and Dahl, on the other, seem to focus more on the character of the modifications of signs, whether the modifications are *inflectional* or rather characteristic of 'well-developed ideophonic morphology', which I take to mean *derivational*.

Inflection or derivation
No clear boundary exists between derivational and inflectional morphology. Both types of morphology can be seen as situated on a continuum between, at one end, the most highly fused means of expression, lexical expression, and, at the other end, the most loosely joined means of expression, syntactic or periphrastic expression (Bybee 1985b, 12 and Chapter 4). Matthews (1974) finds that a sufficient criterion for talking about *inflection* is that 'the choice between [two forms] is determined by a general grammatical rule' (111). Bybee also stresses the grammatical character of inflection: 'An *inflectional* category is one...whose expression is *obligatory* in a particular grammatical context' (1985a, 12 – emphasis in the original). But Matthews points out that for some oppositions which we would normally describe as inflectional, the choice between forms may be free. That is true of number in nouns; the choice of the singular or the plural form of a noun is not determined by a grammatical rule and is not an automatic consequence of a particular grammatical context.

Matthews, therefore, supplements some other criteria for distinguishing inflection and derivation. An opposition may be inflectional if it occurs freely with 'one element after another' (Matthews 1974, 48), i.e. it should be possible to choose it freely with all or most of the words of a particular word class as is the case with number in relation to, for instance, Italian nouns. It is not clear whether Matthews finds the criterion sufficient to call the opposition inflectional. Another criterion that he mentions is that two forms are in inflectional opposition if they are not freely substitutable in particular constructions and, moreover, do not parallel simple stem-forms in the contexts. By this double criterion the positive, comparative, and superlative forms of English adjectives can be said to be in inflectional opposition as only the comparative form can occur in the context *They are ___ than the other*s, and only the superlative form in the context *the ___ of the lot*. Neither form can be replaced by a simple stem-form in the particular context. The last part of the criterion guarantees that forms such as *generating* and *generation* are not classified as being in inflectional opposition even though they are not freely substitutable in some contexts (*generating electricity* vs. *the generation of electricity*): *generation* can be replaced by a simple stem-form such as *cost* (*the cost of electricity*). One characteristic that excludes an opposition from the category of inflection is lack of semantic regularity. The meaning of the combination of stem and affix should be predictable.

In order to determine the regularity or generality of a modification in ASL which they call predispositional aspect, Klima and Bellugi asked deaf signers to fill in an adjectival predicate in the context BOY TEND^(HIS) ALL-HIS-LIFE ___ ('That boy has tended to be ___ all his life'). They found that deaf signers 'characteristically supplied' the modified form of signs denoting 'incidental or temporary states' such as ANGRY, AMBITIOUS, AWKWARD, DIRTY, and SICK, but not of signs such as PRETTY, UGLY, and INTELLIGENT that denote 'inherent characteristics or long-lasting qualities' (Klima & Bellugi 1979, 252). Klima and Bellugi also invented nonsense signs and introduced them with a relevant meaning in the same context, and they found that signers modified nonsense signs in the same way. It proves that the modification is productive, has generality, is intersubjectively relevant, and is not just an emotional expression. But it does not prove that the modification is inflectional. The test context is not grammatical as required by the first criterion set up by Matthews and Bybee. In relation to the difference between the positive and the comparative forms of English adjectives, Matthews talks about the choice of form being 'determined by the nature of the construction itself' (1974, 49). It is not clear what is meant by 'the nature of the construction itself'. Does the construction BOY TEND^(HIS) ALL-HIS-LIFE ___ have a 'nature' which determines the occurrence of the 'modulated' or 'inflected' form to the exclusion of the 'uninflected' form? Or is the occurrence of the 'inflected' form simply a consequence of the lexical meaning of the signs? Both the test context and the group of signs that can take the 'modulation' are semantically very restricted which means that predispositional aspect lacks some of the generality that is typical of inflections. The modification is, however, typical of signed languages where it is possible to find many modifications with a semantically highly restricted distribution.

Many modifications also seem quite idiosyncratic. An example from Danish Sign Language is the modification of some verb signs whose form can be embedded in a vertical linear movement, e.g. READ, FIX, TYPE, KNIT. The meaning always relates to the extension of the action, 'read a text to its end', 'fix something properly', 'knit fast (and thereby much)', 'type something to its end', but the meaning is not predictable. While the first three signs acquire a telic meaning in the modified form, the modified form of KNIT does not mean 'knit something entirely'. Moreover, the modification is expressed differently with different verb forms. Some of the formal differences can be explained as a result of iconicity: in READ, the hand can be seen as representing the written page (the base form is seen in Ill. 17), and in the modified form, the hand is moved upward with a transfer of the movement of the eyes *down* the page in the reading process to a movement of the page *upward*; in TYPE, the hands represent the hands of the person typing (the base form is seen in Ill. 18), and they are moved downward in the modified form as a representation of the movement of the hands down over the page with an increasing amount of text. The modification has an idiosyncratic distribution. When asked, signers say that you *may* modify REPAIR by embedding the form in a vertical linear movement ('repair all of'), but they do not express enthusiasm about the result, and I have never seen it produced spontaneously, not even in contexts where it might be semantically appropriate. This modification is, therefore, clearly more derivational than the predispositional aspect described for ASL by Klima and Bellugi. That does not, of course, exclude the possibility that other modifications are inflectional, but it demonstrates a characteristic type of modification of at least Danish Sign Language.

Within an inflectional paradigm such as tense-marking in spoken languages, the semantic dimension of the paradigm, tense, is relevant to all the members of the paradigm. One form, usually the present tense, is the unmarked form in the sense that it occurs when the semantic dimension of the paradigm is irrelevant (in timeless utterances such as definitions), but the form can also occur in semantic opposition to the other forms of the paradigm ('present' vs. 'past' or 'future'). Many modifications in signed languages occur in paradigms where the base form can only be semantically characterised as *not* showing any particular number, aspect, etc. That is, there is no form which is semantically unmarked, but can also occur in opposition to other forms of the paradigm. Rather most modifications in signed languages resemble the verbal prefix in Tiwi meaning 'at a distance'. When the prefix is absent, the verb cannot mean 'close by', a reason why Bybee does not classify the prefix as inflectional (1985a, 12).

One kind of modification of verbs in Danish Sign Language, namely agreement, does, however, have the nature of the tense paradigm mentioned above: there is a paradigm of agreement forms, one of which, the first person agreement form, may be both semantically unmarked for the opposition and semantically opposed to other forms of the paradigm. Moreover, agreement is seen with a very large number of signs. But agreement is not obligatory in specific grammatical contexts; it is only more frequent in some discourse contexts than in others (see III.6 Semantic agreement and marking for a specific point of view, and III.7 Pragmatic agreement). It means that agreement modification is not inflectional in the strict sense, but is closer to the inflectional prototype than any other modification in Danish Sign Language.

When talking about 'a very well-developed ideophonic morphology', Bergman and Dahl (in press) do not merely go against the idea that the modifications are inflectional; they also claim that the modified forms have a very special syntactic distribution, i.e. that they occur in the sentence or discourse positions that are typical of ideophones. All modified forms in Danish Sign Language are clearly not restricted to these positions. In particular, agreement forms, which Bergman and Dahl do not consider, occur in other positions. The overall impression of Danish Sign Language is that a very large number of signs can be modified in meaningful ways, but very few, if any, of the modifications qualify as inflectional in the strict sense. Some, like agreement, are closer to the inflectional prototype; others are either clearly derivational, such as the modification that is expressed by embedding the sign's base form in a vertical linear movement, or else they are somewhere further from the inflectional prototype than agreement.

Linguistic variation

When we see signing in groups of deaf or groups of deaf and hearing people, there is a lot of apparently idiosyncratic variation with respect to all aspects of language and, therefore, also with respect to modification of signs. Woodward and Markowicz (1980) use a model with implicational scales to describe the variation in uses of particular modifications along what they call the Sign-to-English continuum. The Sign-to-English continuum has varieties of ASL at one end and varieties of Manually Coded English at the other end. An individual's variety on this continuum can be seen from, among other things, his use of modified forms of specific signs. In a variety close to the ASL end of the continuum, we find, for instance, forms of nine different verbs modified for what Woodward and Markowicz call 'agent-beneficiary directionality' (ibid., 67), which is similar to what I am calling agreement. In a variety at the other end of the continuum, only one of the verbs occurs in the modified form. The nine verbs can be ranked in such a way that it is possible to characterise individual varieties along the continuum in terms of implications: if signer A uses the modified form of verb X, she also uses the modified forms of verb Z. That is, varieties closer to the ASL end of the continuum include modified forms of verb X and verb Z, while varieties closer to the other end include modified forms of verb Z without having modified forms of verb X. The varieties along the continuum can then be correlated with social variables such as whether the person is deaf or hearing, whether he has deaf parents or hearing parents, and whether he attended college.

One might think that the lack of generality of some modifications in Danish Sign Language resulted from a mixing of data from different varieties of signing, some of which were closer to manually coded versions of Danish. That is not the case. There is also morphological variation within what must be characterised as Danish Sign Language. The variation in modifications in Danish Sign Language depends on internal factors as well as on external factors such as age and educational background. The modifications have a multidimensional character in the sense that their occurrence depends on the frequency of the lexical unit, the latter's frequency of occurrence in a context or linguistic construction that is typical of the modification, and the sign's semantic and formal perspicuity in relation to the modification in question. An alternative way of describing the variation is, therefore, by means of prototypes: the likelihood that a particular modification will occur increases with certain linguistic contexts or constructions, as well as certain signs. In short, most modifications in Danish Sign Language are more like productive derivation than like prototypical inflection.

II

Discourse and Space

1 Introduction

In this part of the book, I will examine the discourse aspects of what has been called the frame of reference (Lillo-Martin & Klima 1990; see also Supalla 1982, 45ff.) or the discourse frame (Padden 1988b, 30). Lillo-Martin and Klima define the frame of reference as, 'the arrangement of R-loci [referential loci] associated with referents for a signing utterance' (Lillo-Martin & Klima 1990, 193). A particular organisation of the *frame of reference* is not limited to a single sentence. If it were, it could not be used to indicate co-reference. On the other hand, the frame of reference is rarely stable over longer stretches of discourse; rather, it is a dynamic structure that is constantly open to change.

In II.2 The frame of reference, I demonstrate some of the conventions that influence the signer's choice of loci. The existence of these conventions show that the space around the signer is to some extent semantically "loaded" or predetermined: the choice of a locus for a given referent is not arbitrary, but influenced by semantic and pragmatic features and semantic relations that are also relevant to the description of spoken languages. The frame of reference, with its spatially expressed semantic relations, often reflects the real or imagined locative relations between the referents; but frequent discrepancies between the frame of reference and the semantic locative relations show that the main function of the frame of reference is not to reproduce a particular locative setting, but to identify referents quickly and unambiguously. Moreover, the frame of reference is used to express a specific point of view, and changes in the frame of reference may signal different layers of meaning or different sections of the discourse.

The time lines that are presented in II.3 make the concept of the signing space as semantically "loaded" especially clear. Time lines are configurations of loci in the sense that if one locus of a time line is used for a time expression, it invests the other loci of the time line with particular meanings.

Not all referents are represented by loci. In II.4 Loci and referentiality, I show that some of the semantic-pragmatic features that constitute referentiality and influence the morphosyntax of nominals in spoken languages also contribute to determining whether a referent is represented by a locus and whether the locus is manifested in pronouns and determiners. Referents that have high discourse value are more likely to be represented by a locus than referents with low discourse value. An inverse tendency in Danish Sign Language is that one of the referents with high discourse value is not represented by a locus different from the sender locus, but in a sense "takes over" the latter in what I call shifted locus constructions. This is expressed in marking for a specific point of view in agreement verbs (III.6.3 The many uses of the *c*-form), the spatial morphology of polymorphemic verbs (III.8.6 Polymorphemic verbs and space), and in gaze direction and body and head orientation (II.5 Shifted reference, shifted attribution of expressive elements, and shifted locus).

In II.5, I discuss three phenomena, *shifted reference, shifted attribution of expressive elements*, and *shifted locus* and their implications for an understanding of the frame of reference and the functions of loci in Danish Sign Language. The term *shifted reference* covers cases where pronouns are chosen from the point of view of a quoted sender. *Shifted attribution of expressive elements* covers cases in which emotions or attitudes expressed by the signer's face or body posture are to be attributed to some referent other than the sender in the context of utterance. Finally, *shifted locus* is a semantic-pragmatic phenomenon unique to signed languages, namely the use of the sender locus for another referent than the signer or the use of another locus than the locus c for the signer. The other referent may be another human being, an animal, or any object that can be personified.

In II.6 Pointing signs, I take a closer look at signs that resemble pointing gestures; these signs can be said to be the basic means of reference via space. I demonstrate that they have different syntactic functions and that differences in their phonetic weight reflect the pragmatics of the *given – new* distinction. I analyse the pointing signs with the syntactic function of pronouns with the aim of determining their linguistic status compared with personal pronouns in spoken languages.

2 The frame of reference

Signers use space to talk about states, events, and processes that exist or take place in space. It is, therefore, tempting to look for an iconic relationship between the use of space in signed languages and the represented locative relations. But there are other conventions for organising the frame of reference besides the iconic mapping relation. This is especially clear when either the frame of reference or the locative relations change without a corresponding change of the other one, as in some of the examples presented in this section.

Deictic and anaphoric frames of reference
The frame of reference is either deictic or anaphoric.[1] If it is deictic, the signer points in the direction of entities or locations in the context of utterance. Here, the frame of reference is determined by the actual locations of the entities or places to which the signer refers. A deictic frame of reference changes in relation to the signer if she changes her location or orientation in space or if the entities change their location. Anaphoric frames of reference are independent of the context of utterance and do not change depending on the signer's change of location in the context of utterance. In what follows, I will focus on anaphoric frames of reference and the kinds of semantic and formal factors that influence their organisation.

The convention of semantic affinity
One convention for the organisation of the anaphoric frame of reference is that referents with semantic affinity to each other are represented by the same locus unless they need to be distinguished for discourse reasons. This convention is demonstrated in the following example in which a signer talked about her childhood. At one point in the monologue, she said that her parents separated and her mother moved to another town. She used the locus forward-sideward-right for her family and the town in which they had lived before her parents' separation, and the locus forward-sideward-left for the town to which her mother moved and from then on also for her mother. Later her parents decided to live together again, this time in the town where her mother had lived during the separation. The family wanted a bigger flat and managed to find one. The signer introduces the flat as follows:

(1) FORTUNATELY OBTAIN SECOND DET+fl LIVE^FLAT /
    Fortunately, we got another flat.

The flat is represented by the locus forward-left. The choice of this locus is influenced by the physical proximity of the new flat to the town where the signer's

---
1 Sometimes *deictic* is used in the pair of terms *exophoric deictic* and *anaphoric deictic*, sometimes it is used in opposition to *anaphoric* (Lyons 1977, 659). I use the latter set of terms.

mother had lived: the signer uses the same side as for the town, namely left, but a different locus within the same main area.

Then the signer makes a digression. She explains how the family found the flat through the factory where her father worked. The signer earlier used the locus forward-sideward-right for her father and now uses the same locus for the factory. The company owned a building with flats, which is also represented by the locus forward-sideward-right.

```
(2)   1.p.POSS FATHER POSS+fsr WORK+fsr FACTORY+fsr /
      PROFORM+fsr------------- WORK+fsr

      PRON+fsr OWN LIVE^HOUSE DET+fsr---- /
                                    OWN
      My father's work [was] in a factory; they owned a building with
      flats.
```

There is greater semantic affinity between the factory and the signer's father than between the factory and, for example, her mother, and there is no need to distinguish the factory and her father. Thus the factory is represented by the same locus as the signer's father.

Semantic affinity covers a number of different semantic relations. In (2), it is the relation that holds between a person and a place or an institution where he or she works. It may also be the relation between a person and a place or an institution that the person frequents, such as a club. Subsumed under the convention of semantic affinity is the convention of *possession*. Possession is the relation that holds between a possessor and the possessum. In (2), it is the relation between the factory, or the factory owner, and the building with flats.

Different layers of meaning
The signer uses the locus forward-left for the new flat in (1), but in the digression, she changes the frame of reference and uses the locus forward-sideward-right for the building with flats and in (3), for the new flat. Subsequent to (2), the signer explains that the family was offered a flat and went to inspect it:

```
(3)   gaze: +----fsr-------------------------------
            1.p PRON+fsr General-entity-Pm+(from-c+move-
            ----------------------------------
            line+fsr) Look-Pm+(A:c+hold+P:fsr) / gesture /

            ALL-RIGHT / 1.p+pl.+sr c+SEND+fl FIRST MAY /
      We went there to see it. Things were settled, and we moved there on
      May first.
```

The signer uses the locus forward-sideward-right for the flat in the first two verbs of (3) (i.e. General-entity-Pm+(from-c+move-line+*fsr* and Look-Pm+(A:c+hold +P: *fsr*), but changes back to the first locus, the locus forward-left in c+SEND+*fl*, when she explains that the family moved in on May first. At that point, she has finished the digression, i.e. the account of how the family got the flat, and returns to the main track of the story, the chronological account of the events in the family's life.

The changes in the frame of reference divide the passage into three sections: 1. the signer introduces the flat; 2. she explains how the family found the flat; and 3. she says that they moved in on May first. Sections 1 and 3 make use of the same locus for the flat (forward-left), while section 2 makes use of a different locus (forward-sideward-right). The choice of locus for the flat in 2 is consistent with two conventions: the general convention of semantic affinity, which associates the factory with the father's locus, and the convention of possession, which associates the possessum with the possessor's locus, in this case the building with flats with the factory's locus (or the factory owner's locus). The changes in the frame of reference are possible because section 2 is a digression from the main track of the monologue. This status is underlined by a special nonmanual feature at the beginning of the digression (furrowed brow, tense upper lip). Examples (1)-(3) represent a case where the frame of reference changes without any corresponding change in the semantic locative relations. The change of frame of reference is due to the convention of semantic affinity and here contributes to signalling different layers of meaning or different sections of the discourse.

The convention of the canonical location
Also subsumed under the convention of semantic affinity is the convention of the *canonical location*. An item's canonical location, or canonical locus as Bruner calls it (1983, 100), is a place where the item is found typically, but not necessarily currently, or a place with which an item is conventionally associated. A canonical location is a relationship between an item and a place, i.e. between referents. It is not a special kind of locus in signed language, and for that reason I prefer to talk about *the canonical location* to using Bruner's term *the canonical locus*.

A canonical location can be reflected in the organisation of the frame of reference. That is seen in a monologue where a signer used the locus sideward-left for a man who lived in a town west from the place where the signer was. The man's canonical location is the town, and since the town is west of the signer's location, it can be represented by the locus sideward-left following the iconic principle (see below). Thus the man is also represented by the locus sideward-left. The convention of the canonical location can interact with the deictic convention for choosing loci. Signers may point in a direction where a referent is typically, but not currently, found. It is, for example, possible to refer to someone by pointing to his or her desk in an office even when the person is absent. That is, when the organisation of the frame of reference is deictic, the loci may reflect the referents' canonical locations rather than their actual locations.

The convention of comparison
Another convention for organising the anaphoric frame of reference is the convention of *comparison*. This is the convention behind a frame of reference where the signer chooses the locus forward-sideward-left for one referent and the locus forward-sideward-right for another referent when she wants to compare or contrast the two referents.

The iconic convention
If the frame of reference reflects the locative relations between the referents, its organisation is consistent with the *iconic* convention (see also Baker & Cokely 1980, 223ff). The iconic convention states that the spatial relation between the locus of a referent A and the locus of a referent B reflects the location of A in relation to the location of B in the described situation on an appropriate scale and leaving out irrelevant detail. For example, a signer described a situation where her daughter's hearing was tested: she had her daughter on her lap and the speech therapist was behind her. When the signer talked about this situation, she referred to the speech therapist using a locus behind her own left shoulder. The locus of the speech therapist in relation to the sender locus maps the semantic locative relation between the speech therapist and the signer in the situation described.

The iconic convention is seen in the choice of loci for many geographical places. Such loci may be chosen to reflect the geographical direction from the signer's location as seen on a map from the point of view of the person reading the map.[2] For example, the locus sideward-left is used for Bristol in England in several monologues by Danish signers, while the sign NORWAY is almost always accompanied by a determiner that is modified for the locus forward-right-upward. The loci are consistent with the iconic convention in relation to a map.

Summary of conventions
The conventions for organising the anaphoric frame of reference that I have presented are the conventions of iconicity, comparison, and semantic affinity including the conventions of possession and the canonical location. The conventions demonstrate that the choice of loci is not arbitrary, but the conventions are neither exhaustive, nor do they have the character of obligatory rules. A signer may choose a locus for a geographical place that does not reflect the relationship on a map between the place where she is and the place that she is talking about, as when a signer in Copenhagen used the locus forward-right of Barcelona and a theatre festival in Barcelona.

Standard choices of loci
The semantic-pragmatic conventions reflect relations between referents, but there are also more or less standard choices of loci. In a dialogue or in very short discourse, the signer often uses loci somewhere forward-sideward-right or -left for a single ref-

---

2 It appears that a few signers conceive the map as seen from the receiver, i.e. they represent a town to the west of where they are by means of a locus to their right (to the receiver's left).

erent, or, in (a section of) a monologue, the locus forward-right or forward-left for a referent that is the only referent with high discourse value. If there are two referents of equal discourse weight, they are usually represented by the loci forward-sideward-right and forward-sideward-left.

Signers often use the locus forward-sideward-upward-right or -left (ipsilateral side) for institutions such as the taxing authorities or foundations. The upward direction reflects most people's attitude to authorities (physical height reflects authority). The loci forward-sideward-right or -left are clearly distinct from the receiver's locus when the receiver is in front of the signer.

Choice of loci and point of view
There are two main dimensions in the signing space: one dimension from side-to-side, and one dimension diagonally across the signing space from close to the signer's right or left side to either forward-left or forward-right. The side-to-side dimension is used in particular for referents with equal discourse weight (*fsr* and *fsl* in Fig. 4). The diagonal dimension is used when the signer empathises with one of the referents. If, for instance, a mother is talking about her child and a day-care institution or a member of a theatre group is talking about her theatre group and a theatre festival, they each represent the referent with which they empathise the least by the locus forward-right or the locus forward-left (*fr* and *fl* in Fig. 4). The other referent is either not represented by any locus different from the sender locus (see II.5 Shifted reference, shifted attribution of expressive elements, and shifted locus), or it is represented by a locus close to the signer's side. This latter locus is often at the side opposite from the locus chosen for the other referent, i.e. either *sr* corresponding to *fl* or *sl* corresponding to *fr*, but also by the loci close to their ipsilateral side. Again, these are conventions which are reflected in much signing, not strict rules.

The loci in Fig. 4 reflect some of the same semantic-pragmatic relations between referents as the conventions mentioned above, but in Fig. 4, the holder of the point of view is one of the referents to be reckoned with. If the signer uses one of the diagonal dimensions and a locus to one of her sides, she indicates greater semantic affinity between the holder of the point of view (represented by the sender locus) and the referent represented by the locus sideward-right (*sr*) or -left (*sl*) than between the holder of the point of view and the referent represented by the locus forward-right (*fr*) or -left (*fl*).

If there are more than two referents, the locus of a third (or any higher number) referent can be chosen consistently with the convention of semantic affinity or the iconic convention. The locus can be identical with one of the first two loci (see the locus of the factory and the signer's father in (2)). Alternatively, if the signer needs to distinguish referents, a new referent is represented by a distinct locus within the same main area (left or right) as the locus of a semantically related referent (see the locus for the new flat in (1)).

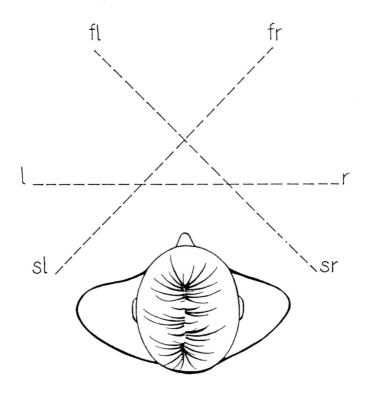

Fig. 4. The side-to-side dimension and the diagonal dimensions

One structuring of the frame of reference can persevere for long parts of a monologue even when the signer talks about situations with different referents. For instance, a signer described a situation where a little girl was going to start kindergarten, and she built up the introduction to the story around the dimension diagonally from herself or the locus sideward-right or -left to the locus forward-right. She used the locus forward-right:
— for the kindergarten in relation to the girl;
— for the kindergarten in relation to the girl's parents;
— for the local authorities in relation to a social worker;
— for the family's car in relation to the girl and her mother; and
— for a kindergarten teacher in relation to the girl and her mother.

As the kindergarten, the local authorities, the family's car, and the kindergarten teacher were all mentioned in different subsections of the introduction, the signer felt no need to distinguish them by means of the frame of reference, but used the same locus for all these different referents, while she clearly indicated which referent (the girl, the girl's parents, the social worker, and the girl and her mother) had the point of view in each section. (For a similar example in ASL, see Padden 1986, 47-48.)

Formal constraints on the frame of reference

There are also some formal constraints on the frame of reference. One formal constraint is that agreement verbs, polymorphemic verbs, and reported speech do not normally make use of loci behind the signer's back. A locus behind the signer's back changes to her side, for instance, when the signer reports speech or signing addressed to a referent previously represented by a locus behind her back. One signer described a situation in which her car had broken down and she had to ask a man living round the corner for help; she first used a locus behind her left shoulder for the man (the iconic convention), but when she quoted her request for help, she used the locus sideward-left:

```
(4)                            _____squint
       NOTIFY+sl (hesitates) DET+sl MAN DET+sl / ...

       I asked uh the man, ...
```

Listing of a number of referents is normally made from left to right by right-dominant signers, and referents may be associated with loci dependent on the listing. A form of nouns which indicates plural number and consists of a reduplication of the noun sign embedded in a linear movement from left to right may influence the choice of locus, as can be seen in the following example. Here the signer changed the locus of a referent because of a noun form indicating plural number. The signer talked about a group of people consisting of five couples and a single man. She first talked about the five couples using the locus forward-right. Then she went on to talking about the single man; she used the locus forward-sideward-left for him (the convention of comparison), but broke off to explain the composition of the group:

```
(5)    _____t      _____t
       SECOND DET+fsl / WHOLE ELEVEN PERSON+pl. / THAT-MEANS

                          _____t
       FIVE COUPLE+pl. / ONE+fsr--------/--------------- /
                            DET+fsr   ALONE PRON+fsr

       The next one - There were eleven people in all, as you know.
       That is, five couples, and the last one, he was single.
```

Both PERSON+pl. and COUPLE+pl. are reduplicated forms embedded in a linear movement of the hand(s) from left to right and these forms entail a change from the locus forward-sideward-left (DET+fsl) to the locus forward-sideward-right (ONE+fsr, DET+fsr, PRON+fsr) for the single man.

The signing space as semantically loaded

In this section, I have shown that the association of loci and referents is not arbitrary, but influenced by semantic-pragmatic conventions and formal constraints on the frame of reference. The choice of locus for a referent is not completely predictable, but the semantic and pragmatic conventions introduce redundancy and show that the signing space is semantically loaded from the moment the signer starts signing. That the choice of loci is neither random nor completely semantically or formally predictable implies that it is meaningful. The locus used for a referent signals semantic-pragmatic relations between referents or the signer's (or holder of the point of view's) attitude to the referent.

Changes in the frame of reference may reflect changes in semantic locative relations or different sections of the discourse, but changes in the frame of reference with different sections of the discourse are not obligatory.

Transcription of locus markers
Because the choice of locus for a particular referent is not random, but invests the referent with meaning, I find it important to indicate the locus markers as approximate directions (*fr, fsr, sr,* etc.) in the transcriptions. This is in contrast to a practice that is developing of using subscript indices in transcriptions of signs modified for loci like the subscripts used to indicate co-referentiality in descriptions of spoken languages, e.g. $_a$PRONOUN or $_b$WANT (see, for example, Padden 1990; Lillo-Martin & Klima 1990). The subscript notation makes the choice of locus appear arbitrary, which it is not in Danish Sign Language.

One or more frames of reference?
In the introduction (II.1), I mentioned that a particular organisation of the frame of reference is not limited to a single sentence; the entire frame of reference is dynamic. It is still not clear whether the proper way of talking about this is in terms of a series of organisations of the frame of reference or in terms of a series of frames of reference. For every single signed utterance, we can describe the frame of reference that is expressed in that utterance. If, however, the utterance occurs in a sequence of utterances and their individual frames of references (or individual organisations of the frame of reference) are consistent, but not identical because not all loci are manifested in all utterances, can we then talk about the same frame of reference (the same organisation of the frame of reference)?

In shifted locus constructions, the signer identifies the sender locus with one of the referents (see further II.5 Shifted reference, shifted attribution of expressive elements, and shifted locus). Earlier in the discourse, the referent may have been represented by a locus different from the sender locus. During the shift, the signer takes on a new perspective, which means that the former locus of the new holder of the point of view "disappears", but the organisation of the frame of reference is consistent with the former organisation combined with the change in point of view. Is this a new frame of reference? Or a new organisation of the frame of reference? Here, at least, the organisation of the loci can be predicted on the basis of the change in point of view. These problems of analysis are related to the problem of describing identical and different reference of anaphoric pronouns in spoken language discourse.

Resolution of anaphoric reference
The problem of resolving anaphoric reference is taken up by Lillo-Martin and Klima (1990) in relation to ASL within the Government and Binding theory of pronominal reference. They analyse what they call R-loci (in my terminology, the expression of loci through modified signs) as the manifestation of referential indices of the kind that appear as subscripts on referential expressions in the linguist's description. Referential indices are a way of showing which expressions have the same or different reference; they are part of the semantic description of all languages, because it is possible to refer in all languages. R-loci, by contrast, are only part of the form description of ASL – and other signed languages (ibid., 196). The problem is now to associate R-loci, R-indices, and referents: how can we know which R-loci are used for which referents in a sequence of clauses in ASL? And how can we know when two R-loci are used for the same referent? Lillo-Martin and Klima suggest a solution that involves 'a discourse representation structure':

> Each indexed noun phrase is assigned a discourse referent, which also has an index. Principles of accessibility in the discourse representation component, along with aspects of the lexical content of the words, determine whether the noun phrase and the discourse referent will be assigned the same index. (ibid., 197)

It is hard to see how this can be a solution to the problem of associating R-loci with R-indices and referents. The 'discourse representation structure' still leaves us with the problem of finding what the 'principles of accessibility' are, no matter the theoretical framework. Moreover, the analysis of R-loci as only expressing referential indices fails to show how the association of referents with specific loci contributes to the meaning of the referring expressions through the semantic-pragmatic conventions described above. Any attempt to solve anaphoric reference in signed discourse must take these conventions into account.

In the following section, I present time lines which are used for time referents in Danish Sign Language. Some of the time lines can influence the organisation of the frame of reference not only for time referents, but also for other referents. Thus they demonstrate particularly clearly how the signing space is loaded semantically.

3 Time lines

3.1 The time lines

Time lines in spoken and signed languages
In an analysis of the expression of spatio-temporal relations in spoken languages, Traugott (1978) distinguishes the expression of tense as a proximal-distal relation without the idea of time line from expressions involving the concept of time line:

> In some languages [±Proximal] may be the only organization of tense, without any concept of time-line … In other languages focus is not exclusively on the term nearest the present; in addition Ego is the (terminal) center of orientation from the past, and the starting point of orientation to the future along the imaginary path of a time-line.
> Orientation to a time-line involves division of <u>then</u> into past and future. (Traugott, p. 375)

In this definition of time line, the notion involves: 1) an orientation from past to future, and 2) Ego as the centre. Only the time line of tense, however, has Ego as its centre. Traugott introduces a different type of time line, i.e. a sequencing line, which may have another reference point than Ego. In order to describe the orientation of time lines, whether they are time lines of tense or of sequencing, Traugott uses the feature [±Prior] which introduces a linearity that is absent in [± Proximal], but makes possible other reference points than Ego.

There are four time lines and a time plane in Danish Sign Language (Fig. 5). I use the term *time line* both of time lines that are expressed in a single dimension and of the calendar plane which is expressed in two dimensions. The time lines are used for expressing sequencing, moments, and periods in time, and they are:

1. the deictic time line (*a* in Fig. 5);
2. the anaphoric time line (*b* in Fig. 5);
3. the sequence line (*c* in Fig. 5);
4. the mixed time line (*d* in Fig. 5); and
5. the calendar plane (not shown in Fig. 5).

The deictic, the anaphoric, and the mixed time lines have a reference point with a spatially fixed locus. Only the deictic and the mixed time lines have Ego as their centre. The reference point of the deictic time line has the utterance time as its default meaning, but its meaning can also be established in the discourse. The meaning of the reference point of the anaphoric time line is always established in the discourse, while the reference point of the mixed time line can be anaphoric or deictic. A time expression that makes use of a locus of a time line with a predetermined locus for a reference point is understood in relation to that reference point. The sequence line and the calendar plane do not have reference points until one is established in discourse; they might, therefore, be said not to be time lines according to the strict definition. I return to this

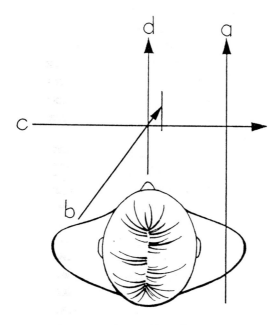

Fig. 5. Time lines

question in II.3.2 A comparison with time lines in spoken languages.

All of the time lines have orientation from earlier to later, but the mixed time line and possibly also the anaphoric time line only have one direction from the reference point. In relation to these time lines, it is only possible to talk about moments or periods that are earlier (the anaphoric time line) or later (the mixed time line) than the reference point.

Time lines have been reported for ASL (in particular Friedman 1975; Cogen 1977; Winston 1989), British Sign Language (Brennan 1983), Danish Sign Language (Engberg-Pedersen, Hansen & Kjær Sørensen 1981), Dutch Sign Language (Schermer & Koolhof 1990), Italian Sign Language (Cameracanna & Corazza 1989), French Sign Language (Vourc'h, Benelhocine & Girod 1989), São Paulo Sign Language (Ferreira Brito 1983), and the signing of a deaf man on a Polynesian island (Kuschel 1974). Most of these studies focus on the use of time lines in lexemes. Ferreira Brito (1983; see also Kakumasu 1968) describes data from a Brazilian Indian signed language, Urubu-Kaapor Sign Language, which is used by a tribe with a high percentage of deaf people. Urubu-Kaapor Sign Language seems not to make use of time lines. Instead Urubu-Kaapor signers indicate 'now' by pointing to the sky. Up to twenty days back in the past can be indicated by the sequence SLEEP ONE/TWO/ etc., and the same sequence followed by the sign DAY indicates a specific number of days into the future. To talk about the remote future, Urubu-Kaapor signers use the signs MOON or SUN or the signs for the seasons.

In signed languages, time lines are expressed spatially in the sense that when a referent is represented by a locus of a time line, the entire line or plane in space is invested with specific referential potential. As soon as the signer uses a time expression with a sign modified for a locus of one of the time lines, that time line is actualised and all its other loci are invested with specific referential potential which may be used in other parts of the discourse. The time lines are always there, ready for the signer to use, and they have different meanings. That means that a time expression whose referent is represented by a locus of a particular time line receives additional meaning from the time line. A particular time line invests a referent with meaning by locating it in time in relation to some reference point, such as 'last Monday' (the deictic time line) in contrast to 'the preceding Monday' (the anaphoric time line or the sequence line). On the other hand, the association of a specific referent with a locus of a time line invests the rest of the loci of the line with meaning ('the time before or after the particular Monday').

Talking about lines and planes simplifies the description of the meaning that a time referent acquires by being represented by a particular locus: the sign FRIDAY modified for a particular locus of a time line in a particular discourse context may acquire the meaning 'Friday before the Sunday when we left for Spain' or 'last Friday' or 'Friday in two weeks', all depending on which time line is used and what locus of the line.

Lines and planes in the signing space
Jacobowitz and Stokoe (1988) strongly criticise the use of the term time line in relation to signed languages. They find that it is 'a mental construct invented in an attempt to describe a language not expressed in sound. The constructs exist only in the minds of those who attempt to explain sign language by metaphor instead of directly' (1988, 333-334; see also *Muscle activity or geometry* in I.6.4 The term *locus*). Further, they state: 'Sign language signs are not propositions of geometry, although many writers on sign languages confuse phonology with geometry' (ibid., 334). They find the notion of time line:

> ...a failed, or an inverse, metaphor. A true metaphor likens something complex or abstract to something simpler, something directly experienced by one or more of our senses. (An inverse metaphor likens something fairly complex to something even more abstract.) There is no gain in describing language behavior with a metaphor that links the abstract system of tense – its semantics, morphology, and phonology – to a feature of another abstract system, that of the classical mathematics of three dimensional space. (ibid., 334)

Instead, they say, 'what are real are the actions performed by ASL signers' (ibid., 334), and 'it is much better to investigate first, and with all the precision possible, the physical structure of the system under study' (ibid., 334-335). Jacobowitz and Stokoe focus on modifications of verbs to express tense and they find that extension and flexion of the muscles are the articulatory basis of the modifications of ASL verbs for past and future tense.

It is beyond discussion that we need a description in physiological terms of the possible articulations of signs and sign modifications, even though what is linguistically important is not necessarily one specific combination of muscle movements.[1] I find, however, that Jacobowitz and Stokoe miss the point when they argue so strongly against the concept of time lines in the analysis of signed languages. First, the concept of time lines is also used in the description of time expressions in spoken languages. Here, the concept of line is used in the semantic description of time expressions to describe orientation in relation to a centre when it is possible to distinguish a before and an after in the meaning of time expressions (see above). Second, the concept of time line in the description of signed languages is useful at the level at which we describe the meaning that results from the association of referents and loci. At this level, time referents can be described as represented by loci expressed by points on lines (one-dimensional) or planes (two-dimensional) in the signing space in the everyday sense of the words. There is no need to invoke 'the propositions of Euclid's first book' as Jacobowitz and Stokoe suggest (1988, 337).

One example of a time line in Danish Sign Language is the deictic time line imagined in space from behind the signer's shoulder to in front and beside her (a in Fig. 5). Just as verbs in verb agreement relate phonetically to many different points in space in relation to one locus (see I.6.4 The term *locus*), the actual points at which signs modified for loci of the deictic time line are made differ in height. The sign MONDAY can be modified for the deictic time line, and if the elbow is flexed and the elbow joint is rotated compared with the base form of the sign, the sign means 'last Monday' (Ill. 19a). If the elbow is extended, the sign means 'next Monday' (Ill. 19b). The hand is held at two different levels in the two signs, but that is irrelevant to their meaning. The point in using the notion of line in relation to some time expressions in signed languages is that it captures the fact that the association of a time referent and a certain locus invests other loci with meaning. Moreover, these other loci can be imagined as relating to lines or a plane in the everyday sense of the words.

Even though signs modified for loci of the deictic time line are made at different levels, the deictic time line can be imagined as a line, because the height differences are phonetic only. The term *plane* characterises a time line as being expressed in such a way that both the vertical and the horizontal dimensions in the signing space are morphologically relevant. Loci of the calendar plane[2] are distinguished with respect to both the horizontal and the vertical dimension.

In contrast to other loci (see I.6.4 The term *locus*), loci of the time lines (except

---

1 Goldsmith (1989) points out that a number of city names in ASL are made with the hand tracing a specific path (like the line of the written symbol 7). This path can be produced by movements of different joints, the wrist, the elbow, the shoulder, or different combinations of these joints: what matters is the path that is traced by the finger tips, not the specific muscles involved in the production.

2 Two dimensions are also used in signing about clock hours. For instance, the semantic equivalent of *from three to seven* may be signed by the signs THREE and SEVEN made at what is most easily described as an imaginary face of a clock.

for loci of the "past section" of the deictic time line) can be imagined as points within the signing space. Therefore, I transcribe locus markers of loci of the time lines differently than other loci (see the examples below).

In this section, I only consider the time lines that are relevant to the representation of referents by loci to the extent that the representation is expressed by *modifications* of signs and through nonmanual means. The time lines are also relevant to the morphological structure of some *lexemes*. For example, the deictic time line is relevant to the lexemes TODAY, TOMORROW, LAST-YEAR, NEXT-YEAR, and the calendar plane is relevant to the lexemes WEEK and MONTH, but I will not go further into that here. Neither will I discuss whether verbs in Danish Sign Language can be modified spatially for tense to express location in time in relation to the utterance time (see Brennan 1983; Jacobowitz & Stokoe 1988; Schermer & Koolhof 1990). If verbs in Danish Sign Language can be modified in that way, the modification is not obligatory and for that reason cannot be described as tense *inflection* (see I.6.6 The morphological type of signed languages). Finally, I will not examine in detail how the representation of time referents by loci is expressed. In the example above, the sign MONDAY is modified for a locus. As with non-time referents other possibilities are to use a determiner or a pronoun modified for the locus.

The deictic time line
The deictic time line can be thought of as a line from behind the signer's dominant-hand shoulder and forward (*a* in Fig. 5). It has a reference point at the sender locus, and its default meaning is the utterance time. The reference point divides the line into three sections: 'before now' (from behind the signer to the reference point), 'now' (the reference point), and 'after now' (from the reference point and outward from the signer). The reference point can be given a nondeictic value in discourse.

The deictic time line can be used both for time referents and for referents which do not by themselves have a temporal meaning. The latter is seen in (1), where a signer was talking about a conference that took place in January, a few months before the utterance time:

```
(1)   RECENTLY GRASS^rod(M)('root')^CONFERENCE /
      JANUARY+deictic-tl-before BEFORE+deictic-tl
      MONTH+deictic-tl-before DET+deictic-tl-before /
      FINE / MANY NEW FACE+pl.  sr+ GO- TO+alt.+c / ALWAYS
                                sl+ GO- TO+alt.+c
                                                         neg
      BEFORE+deictic-tl SAME+redupl. FACE /        /
      DET+deictic-tl-before CONFERENCE / sr+GO-TO+alt.+c
                                         sl+GO-TO+alt.+c
```

```
fra(M)('from') COMMON DEAF GROUND FROM-LOW-TO-HIGH /
FINE /                                            (Ill. 20)
```

Recently there was a grassroots conference - I think it was in January. It was really good. There were many new faces. Previously it had been the same faces again and again. But not this time. At that conference, the people who came ranged from ordinary deaf people to the top. That was good.

The signer uses the deictic time line for the time of the conference (JANUARY+deictic-tl-before BEFORE+deictic-tl MONTH+deictic-tl-before DET+deictic-tl-before, lines 2-3). Later she uses the same locus for the conference (DET+deictic-tl-before, line 5) that took place at the time represented by the locus. The phrase DET+deictic-tl-before CONFERENCE is not by itself a time expression, but like the English expression *the January conference* it can be used to refer to an event in time.

The anaphoric time line

The anaphoric time line can, like the deictic time line, be imagined as a line with a spatially fixed reference point. The line stretches outside the sender's chest from the side of the signer's nondominant hand diagonally to the locus of the reference point (*b* in Fig. 5). The reference point has no default value; its value must always be established in context. I have never seen the anaphoric time line used to talk about events or moments or periods in time after the reference point. Some signers claim that it is possible; others hesitate. Alternatives are to use either the sequence line (see below) or the sign AFTER, which is not related to a time line.

The anaphoric time line is used to fix periods or moments in relation to a moment specified in the discourse. It can also be used for referents that do not by themselves have a temporal meaning, as seen in (2).

```
(2)  AND-THEN / LF NEW ACT^PROGRAMME / PRON+sl WORK MUCH
     BEFORE+anaph.-tl / GROUP+pl.+anaph.-tl-before DISCUSS+
     multiple+anaph.-tl-before / BUT NOW PUT-FORWARD /
     (Ill. 21)
```

The next item [on the agenda] was LF's [the National Association of the Deaf] new objectives. People had worked much on them before [the annual assembly]. Several groups had discussed them prior to [the assembly]. And now they were put forward.

The signer uses a modification of the noun GROUP (reduplication of the sign embedded in a linear movement) that denotes plural number, and a modification for distribution of the verb DISCUSS (reduplication of the sign embedded in a linear movement), so that both sign forms are reduplicated along an imaginary line from the signer's side toward the point imagined as the anaphoric time line's reference point. Thereby she indicates that several groups had discussed the objectives before the annual assembly of the National Association of the Deaf.

Winston (1989) describes an example in ASL of what seems to be a close equivalent to the anaphoric time line and how it influences the organisation of part of a formal presentation. The signer was comparing two historical periods and stepped backward to the left and forward to the right depending on which period he was talking about. I have seen a similar example in a formal presentation in Danish Sign Language in which the signer compared the signing of a single group of children at two different points in time, when they were in grade two and grade four. In this case, there were two reference points, the time of grade two and the time of grade four. The signer represented the referent grade two by the locus forward-sideward-left and the referent grade four by the locus forward-sideward-right. At the same time she implied the progression of time between grade two and grade four by stepping back to the left and forward to the right (the diagonal dimension of the anaphoric time line) depending on which grade she was talking about.

The sequence line

The sequence line can be thought of as a line parallel with the signer's surface plane from her left to her right. For right-handed signers, it has left-to-right orientation in the sense that if A is a locus to the left of another locus B, then A is used for an earlier point in time than B. The sequence line does not have a reference point with a spatially fixed locus. Instead, it is possible to establish reference points by representing time referents by loci of the line and talk about moments or periods before, after or between reference points.

In (3), the signer uses a locus a little outside her right side for Thursday (here transcribed as x) and a locus to the right of the first locus for the following Friday.

```
(3)   WANT TRAVEL^GONE om(M)(prep.)  torsdag(M)('Thursday')
                                     PROFORM+sequence-tl-x-

      DET+sequence-tl-x / DET+sequence-tl-after-x
      ------------------------------------------

      FRIDAY+sequence-tl-after-x BEGIN+after-sequence-tl-x
      --------------------------BEGIN+after-sequence-tl-x

      PRON+sequence-tl-after-x* / torsdag(M)('Thursday')
      PROFORM-sequence-tl-x-----------------------------

      c+GO-TO+neu /
      -----------
```

> *The pronoun is interpreted by native signers as referring to the
> festival which was going to start on Friday.
>
> We wanted to leave on Thursday. On Friday it [the festival] would
> start, so Thursday, we wanted to go there.

The referent Friday is represented by a locus farther right than Thursday. Because of the direction of the sequence line from left to right, FRIDAY+sequence-tl-after-x can only refer to the Friday following the Thursday that is represented by a locus of the sequence line.

Example (4) demonstrates a mixture of manual and nonmanual expression of the sequence line.

```
(4)   COUNTRY^MEETING BEGIN FRIDAY AFTERNOON O'CLOCK FOUR /
      body l---neu-----r----------------------------------
      TIME-PASS / TO SUNDAY O'CLOCK THREE+sequence-tl-right /
      -----------------------------neu
      PRON+sequence-tl-left-to-right /
```

> The national assembly started Friday at four o'clock and lasted
> until Sunday at three.

The signer introduces the beginning point of the period (FRIDAY AFTER-NOON O'CLOCK FOUR) without any manual or nonmanual expression of the sequence line. Then she uses the verb TIME-PASS ('last') while leaning her body to the left. She moves back to the neutral body position and signs SUNDAY O'CLOCK THREE+sequence-tl-right while leaning to the right. The sign THREE+sequence-tl-right is made farther to the right than its base form. Finally, she uses a pronoun, PRON+sequence-tl-left-to-right, of the period. It is made from left to right, modified for the time line.

Loci on the sequence line may also influence the choice of loci for non-time referents. A signer explained that her children's Easter holiday started on Monday while she and her husband had to work until Thursday. The signer modified MONDAY for a locus to the left and THURSDAY for a locus to the right and made the signs TUESDAY and WEDNESDAY in between. She then used the locus sideward-left-downward for her children and the locus sideward-right in the sign TWO+pron.+c+sr ('we (two)') for her husband. That is, she represented both Monday and the children by loci to the left, and both Thursday and the parents by loci to the right. Thereby she underlined the semantic affinity between Monday and the children, on the one hand, and Thursday and the parents, on the other.

The use of the locus sideward-left-downward for the children and the locus sideward-right for the parents under the influence of the sequence line differs from the use of a locus of the deictic time line for the conference in example (1). In the latter case, the locus is a locus of the time line, and the referent has a temporal meaning: the January conference. By contrast, the loci of the children and the parents are not loci of the sequence line. The children's locus is expressed at a lower level than that used for Monday because the children are a relatively small referent. The referents do not have a temporal meaning, but the sequence line and its manifestation in the time expressions (MONDAY+sequence-tl-sl and THURSDAY+sequence-tl-sr) influence the choice of side for loci for the two non-time referents.

The mixed time line
The mixed time line is like a mixture of the three preceding time lines. It can be thought of as a line perpendicular to the signer's body, and it seems to be used for expressing a sequence of moments in time or a period of time seen from a point before its start. In this way, it can supplement the anaphoric time line to the extent that signers do not want to use the anaphoric time line for talking about time after the reference point. The mixed time line replaces the deictic time line in descriptions of a sequence of moments or a period from now into the future. It does not seem possible, however, to reduce the mixed time line to the "future section" of the deictic time line. There is a clear difference between the forms of the sign MONDAY when it is modified for the deictic time line ('next Monday') and when it is modified for the mixed time line. For instance, in one example a signer used the mixed time line to talk about a workshop. She explained that on the first day of the workshop, Sunday, the participants discussed how to organise the week, and she signed the names of the days of the week including MONDAY embedded in a linear outward movement of the hand from the middle of her chest. The example shows that the mixed time line, in contrast to the sequence line, introduces a specific point of view in descriptions of sequences of moments in time: the period of the workshop was seen from its beginning, the day the planning took place.

The mixed time line can also be used for pronominal reference, as when a signer talks about a workshop that takes place over three successive Tuesday evenings and describes what will happen on each evening: she can refer to the evenings by means of pointing signs (functioning as pronouns or determiners) directed at points at different distances from her chest.

The calendar plane
The calendar plane can be thought of as a two-dimensional plane parallel with the surface plane of the signer's body. The plane in two dimensions is like a calendar with vertical columns for the months of the year. The calendar plane is primarily used for a year, but some signers can also use it for a week with the vertical dimension corresponding to hours within the days of the week. Thus, in the equivalent of *The meeting lasted from two to three*, the number sign TWO is modified for a locus up

and the number sign THREE for a lower locus in the same vertical dimension. Others, however, prefer to use a circle corresponding to the surface of a clock.

Every moment or period on the calendar plane is seen in relation to the rest of a calendar period. Its temporal relation to other years or days or to a specific point of view ('May last year', 'the following May') has to be expressed in the discourse context. That is, there are no reference points other than the days, weeks and months of one full year or week.

In (5) the signer uses a determiner that is modified for the calendar plane:

```
(5)  BEGIN JUNE MONTH DET+approximately+calendar-tl-

     ipsilateral-up / fr+SEND-MAIL+c CLEAR /

     In the beginning of June, they wrote that it was OK.
```

The signer uses the locus to her right at forehead level for a specific period, the beginning of June. The use of the horizontal dimension is always context-dependent. As the example shows, the signer does not represent June by a specific vertical column in the left-to-right dimension; ipsilateral articulation of a one-handed sign is neutral. If the calendar plane were an accurate mapping of a calendar, June would be represented by a column to the left of the middle. But in (5), the signer uses a locus expressed outside her right side for June. It is neutral in relation to the left-to-right dimension.

The left-to-right dimension becomes relevant when a signer talks about, for example, the end of March and the beginning of April (Ill. 22). Then she may use a locus downward for the end of March and a locus further right and upward for the beginning of April, making both the vertical and the horizontal dimensions relevant.

In one monologue, a signer used the calendar plane to talk about the school holidays within a year. In February there is a one-week vacation, but different schools close for different weeks. That year, most schools closed the week including February 17th, but the signer's son's school was to close the week before. To explain, the signer placed her left hand with the manual articulator of the sign WEEK in neutral space and left it there all through the following. She asked if the school closed the week with the seventeenth by signing SEVENTEEN DET+l.hand WEEK+l.hand DET+l.hand ("Was it the week with the seventeenth?"), and she answered the question negatively. Then she went on to sign EARLIER ('No, it wasn't that week, it was earlier.'), and, maintaining her left hand with the manual articulator of WEEK in position, she moved her right hand with the articulator of WEEK to her left hand and then in an arc inward toward her body and up above her left hand (Ill. 23). That is, she used the vertical dimension to describe the other referent as 'the week before'.

3.2 A comparison with time lines in spoken languages

Many time expressions in spoken languages make use of the same morphemes as locative expressions. Some see it as a metaphorical extension of locative expressions (Lakoff & Johnson 1980, 42-44; Anderson & Keenan 1985, 296); others analyse it as a result of a common spatial structure underlying both locative expressions and time expressions (Traugott 1978; Jackendoff 1983, 209).

Tense
Traugott defines tense as 'the semantic category that establishes the relationship which holds between the time of the situation or event talked about and the time of utterance' (ibid., 369). The time line of tense is seen in many spoken languages in expressions that make use of the deictic verbs meaning 'come' and 'go' such as French *venir de* about the past (*Je viens de le voir*, literally 'I come from him to see', i.e. 'I have just seen him') and *aller* about the future (*Je vais partir*, literally 'I go to leave', i.e. 'I am going to leave') or English *go* regarding the future. The tense expressions do not necessarily orient the time line in a specific spatial plane, but the horizontal plane is used in what Traugott calls 'idiomatic and metaphorical expressions' such as the English *we look forward to the years ahead* and *we look back on the past*. Expressions with ahead and back employ the plane running perpendicular to the body which separates front from back ([± Front]). Traugott's tense schema is presented in Fig. 6 where T stands for an imaginary time line.

```
      [-Proximal](then) [+Proximal](now) [-Proximal](then)
T------------------------------------------------------T
      [+Prior] (past)              [-Prior] (future)
       Source                       Goal
       come   ──▶                   go   ──▶
      [-Front](behind, back)       [+Front](forward, ahead)
```

(Traugott 1978, 378)

Fig. 6. Tense

Sequencing
Traugott uses the term *sequencing* to mean the 'ordering of events or situations talked about' (ibid., 370). Sequencing is the ordering of events and situations with respect to each other. Expressions such as *first, second*, and *next* indicate succession without the use of a time line, i.e. they are of the type E1 + *other* + *other*. Traugott captures the distinction between E1 and *other* by the feature [±Initial]. By contrast, she claims, sequencing expressions such as *E1 is earlier than E2* and *E2 is later than E1* involve a time line. To describe such expressions, she uses the same feature as for the time line of tense, namely [±Prior]. With the time line of *tense*, the

semantic feature [±Prior] presupposes the feature [-Proximal], i.e. an event is related to the deictic reference point through the feature [±Proximal], which itself presupposes the deictic centre. With the time line of *sequencing*, [±Prior] presupposes the feature [-Initial], which relates one event to another. Traugott's analysis of sequencing is seen in Fig. 7.

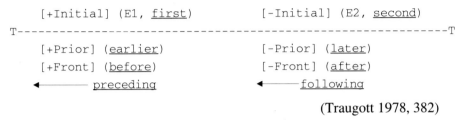

(Traugott 1978, 382)

Fig. 7. Sequencing

By contrast to the pair *earlier* and *later*, the pair *first* and *second* can clearly be described by the feature [±Initial]: the *first* event is [+Initial] and the *second* event is [-Initial]. But the analysis does not make it clear how *earlier* and *later* involve a time line while *first* and *second* do not. Neither pair of expressions, *first – second* and *earlier – later*, has a locative meaning besides their temporal meaning, and as Traugott describes them, neither implies an external reference point, only sequencing in relation to each other. Traugott claims that sequencing expressions only involve a time line if their meaning can be described in terms of the feature [±Prior], and in one place, she says that these features presuppose the feature [-Initial] (ibid., 380). This supposedly provides a parallel to the time line of tense where [±Prior] presupposes [-Proximal] (see Fig. 6). In another place of the same article, Traugott says that '[+Prior] is [+Initial]' and '[-Prior] is [-Initial]' (ibid., 383) as it is also indicated in Fig. 7. That must mean that she describes an *earlier* event as [+Initial], which is clearly not right. Even though event X is *earlier* than event Y, it is not necessarily initial; it may be preceded by event V, which, in its turn, may or may not be the initial event.

Sequencing expressions may involve an external reference point, namely when they are expressions that are also used of locative relations. Then they can be described in relation to a time line with an orientation in a particular plane in space as the expressions *E1 before E2* or the dynamic *E1 precedes E2*. In English [+Prior] correlates with [-Front] on the time line of tense (the past is *behind* us), while [+Prior] correlates with [+Front] on the time line of sequencing (E1 is *before* E2).

The implicit point of view
The difference between the two kinds of time lines, Traugott says, is that the time line of tense has a deictic reference point, while the time line of sequencing has no reference point until one has been specified. That is, Traugott does not describe the

time line of sequencing in relation to an external reference point or point of view. However, when she introduces the feature [±Front] to describe some sequencing expressions, she also introduces an implicit external point of view. She explains the different correlations of [+Prior] with [-Front] on the time line of tense and [+Prior] with [+Front] on the time line of sequencing as follows:

> That E1 selects the positive term front and E2 the negative term back can be explained in terms of the canonical encounter, also known as 'facing'....It was suggested in discussion of tense that [±Front] is assigned on the basis of the basic body-space and perceptual field as we walk along a path. As we walk along this path there may be an encounter (we face the future); in sequencing there necessarily is. The normal, 'canonical,' type is the face-to-face encounter with Speaker as the deictic centre, cf. The type-writer is in front of me (rather than I am in front of the typewriter). From this viewpoint additional type-writers in a row are normally behind the one in front of me. Similarly, there is a canonical encounter with events such that E1 is in front [of] E2, and E2 behind E1. However, there is a difference from assignment of [±Front] to tense in that the assignment of [±Front] to events in sequence, once established in terms of the encounter, remains constant, wherever the speaker is in the sequence of events, because sequence is not deictic in its basic structure.... (ibid., 380)

Sequencing expressions that involve a time line with orientation on a horizontal plane thus imply a reference point: the point of view of an individual in the canonical encounter.

The conclusion in relation to the pairs *first – second* and *earlier – later* must be that either both pairs involve a time line or neither one does. Neither pair involves an external reference point, but both expressions involve a concept of time as progressing. Priority is relevant to both sets of expressions, while initiality is only relevant to *first – second*. In tense expressions that can be described in terms of only [±Proximal], there is a reference point, but no concept of the progression of time.

The fact that [+Prior] sometimes correlates with [+Front] and sometimes with [-Front] has been analysed by Benveniste (1974, 74) as the result of two ways of viewing time (see also Anderson & Keenan 1985, 296; Fillmore 1975; Lakoff & Johnson 1980, 42-44). Either time is seen as moving past the individual. Then [+Prior] correlates with [+Front] as in *E1 precedes E2* (Traugott's sequencing line). Or the individual moves in time. Then [+Prior] correlates with [-Front] as in *the past is behind me* (Traugott's time line of tense).

Traugott criticises this analysis. First, in some languages time expressions do not involve a time line. Second, not all time expressions that can be described in terms of Traugott's two time lines are dynamic; static expressions should not be described in terms of the moving of either the individual or time. Finally, Traugott finds that as the two time lines have different feature combinations and as the sequencing line does not have a deictic reference point, while the tense line does have such a reference point, they cannot be mirror images of each other (ibid., 382). The last argument is weakened, however, to the extent that sequencing terms involve locative expressions from the canonical encounter.

The canonical encounter correlates with what is also called the ego-opposed strategy of assigning front and back to entities without an inherent front-back orientation (Fillmore 1982). It is the ego-opposed strategy which makes a speaker of English say *The ball is in front of the tree*, when the ball is between the speaker and the tree. The tree is assigned a front facing the speaker as in the canonical encounter. Thus the ball is *in front of* the tree. Hausa speakers would describe the same constellation as the equivalent of *The ball is behind the tree* (Hill 1975). Here the speaker, the ball, and the tree are conceived as placed in a line all facing the same way with the speaker at the line's rear. Hausa follows what is called the ego-aligned strategy. The concept of time as moving past – or rather toward – the individual (*the preceding events* are [+Prior] and *the following events* [-Prior]) correlates with the canonical encounter and the ego-opposed strategy except that it is dynamic: the events "approach" or "face" the speaker. Earlier events "confront" us before later events or, in a static description, are closer in the line of events. But as mentioned, the individual can also be seen as moving in time or, in a static description, as located in the middle of a line of events with the past *behind* and the future *ahead of* the individual. The two concepts of time, time moving toward or facing the individual and the individual moving in time or located in the middle of the events, imposes the same basic orientation on time in relation to the individual's front-back orientation: the individual looks in the direction of the future and later events. The basic difference between the time line of sequence and the time line of tense is thus whether all events are seen as "placed" before or "approaching" the individual or whether the individual is seen as "located" in the middle of the events. It is, therefore, misleading to describe the difference between tense (Fig. 6) and sequencing (Fig. 7) in terms of [±Front] as if there were a difference in the conception of the orientation of time. In relation to tense (Fig. 6), [±Front] should be interpreted as the individual's front or back; in relation to sequencing (Fig. 7), [±Front] should be interpreted as an orientation imposed on the events.

Time lines in Danish Sign Language
With respect to time lines in signed languages, Traugott's semantic features [±Proximal] and [±Front] can be given a formal interpretation. The form feature <Proximal> can be used of distance from the signer and the form feature <Front> of orientation in relation to the signer. The feature <Front> has only two values, but proximity to the signer has several values.

In Danish Sign Language, there are three time lines which can be thought of as being more or less perpendicular to the signer, namely the deictic, the mixed, and the anaphoric time lines. While the deictic time line has two directions, the mixed time line and possibly the anaphoric time line are like Traugott's time line of sequencing in that they only have one orientation from the reference point.

The deictic time line can be described in terms of Traugott's tense schema. It has a reference point in the middle and the default value of <+Proximal> is 'now'. The default value of <+Front> is 'future' and of <-Front> 'past'. The deictic time line is most often used in static expressions, as shown by the examples in II.3.1 The time lines. It can, however, also be used in a dynamic expression: a verb with the stem General-entity(B)-Pm (see III.8.5 Categories of stems in polymorphemic verbs) having a movement from outside the signer's ipsilateral side toward her face, relating to an event approaching in time, e.g. a sentence meaning 'Suddenly Christmas came up' (Ill. 24). The mixed time line is like the deictic time line: it has a reference point at the signer and the default value of <+Front> is 'future'. It differs from the deictic time line by not having any <-Front> value.

The anaphoric time line is used to express sequencing in Traugott's sense, i.e. 'ordering of events or situations talked about' (ibid., 372). The reference point of the anaphoric time line is [-Initial]. Traugott showed that, in relation to sequencing, [±Front] is interpreted in the light of the canonical encounter with [+Front] meaning 'earlier' and [-Front] meaning 'later'. But the anaphoric time line does not lend itself to such an interpretation.

Compared with the deictic and the mixed time lines, the reference point of the anaphoric time line is displaced in relation to the signer. Earlier events are expressed as positioned between the reference point and the signer, which means that the signer's position is conceived as earlier in time than the reference point. The anaphoric time line thus has the same basic orientation as the deictic time line and the mixed time line: areas close to the signer represent earlier events, areas further away represent later events. The parallel between the anaphoric time line and the deictic and mixed time lines is in accordance with the conclusion to the preceding subsection: the basic difference between the time line of sequencing and the time line of tense is whether all events are seen as "placed" before or "approaching" the individual or whether the individual is seen as "located" in the middle of the events. The two concepts of time impose the same basic orientation on time in relation to the individual's front-back orientation.

The locus of the reference point of the anaphoric time line represents the event that serves as a temporal reference point; but in contrast to expressions of sequencing in English, the anaphoric time line does not assign any orientation to the event as such. It makes no sense, therefore, to say that the event is "facing" the holder of the point of view (the ego-opposed strategy) (see also *Spatial morphemes* in III.8.6 Polymorphemic verbs and space). An event that is earlier than the reference point of the anaphoric time line is simply conceived as *between* the reference point and the holder of the point of view, not *before* the reference point.

The dimension perpendicular to and through the body is asymmetrical in the sense that a human being's most essential sensory receptors are directed one way which correlates with the side that is relevant to the canonical encounter (Clark 1973). According to Traugott (1978, 387) very few spoken languages make use of expressions for 'side' in time expressions because of the perceptual symmetry of this dimension.

Danish Sign Language employs the symmetrical dimension in both the sequence line and the calendar plane. Here the direction of the time lines can be captured by a form feature <±Left-of> where <+Left-of> means [+Prior]. The correlation of <+Left-of> with 'earlier' and <-Left-of> with 'later' reflects the direction of reading in Western culture which is particularly clear in the calendar plane's mapping of the left-right dimension of calendars.

The feature <±Left-of> relates one locus to two others, a locus of the time line and the sender locus, since *left* must be understood deictically in relation to the signer's centre. Thus, the direction of time lines in Danish Sign Language (i.e. which end is [+Prior]) is determined by the signer's perspective even in relation to the time lines that do not have an explicit reference point at the sender locus.

Traugott concludes that both the absence of time lines in some languages and the fact that time expressions in spoken languages almost exclusively involve the asymmetrical dimensions (front-back, up-down, and not left-right) show that time expressions should not be conceived in terms of a philosophical or physical concept of time as unidirectional, but rather in terms of the perception of space and the canonical encounter. Even though Danish Sign Language does make use of the symmetrical left-right dimension, it also supports Traugott's analysis that time expressions should be understood in terms of the perceiving individual in space

3.3 Conclusion

The five time lines in Danish Sign Language show how the space around the signer is semantically loaded as soon as she starts signing. Loci for time referents and for referents which are given a temporal interpretation are not chosen at random. Each time line has its own meaning and the use of a locus of a time line evokes its meaning and makes reference to earlier or later moments or periods in time fast and precise.

The semantic features that Traugott (1978) uses to describe time lines in spoken languages are also relevant to a description of time lines in Danish Sign Language. Two of the features, [±Proximal] and [±Front], can be interpreted as form features in the description of time lines in Danish Sign Language. It reflects the fact that the basic difference between signed and spoken languages is a difference in means of expression; signed languages use space and movement, spoken languages sound. In spoken languages, expressions with words such as *ahead* or *coming* are only semantically locative; in signed languages, the signs of the corresponding expressions are modified spatially.

In the beginning of II.3.2 A comparison with time lines in spoken languages, I mentioned that some researchers see locative time expressions as a metaphorical extension, while others, and among them Traugott, find that a common spatial[3] struc-

---

3   In this paragraph, I use *space* and *spatial* as semantic terms or as having a cognitive value, and not to talk about a means of expression in signed languages.

ture underlies both locative expressions and time expressions. One argument in favour of talking about a metaphorical extension of spatial expressions in expressions with a temporal meaning is that different languages impose different semantic (locative) structures on time. It only makes sense to talk about metaphorical extension, however, if the locative meaning of the expressions is more basic than their temporal meaning. Different languages also impose different semantic structures on locative relations as seen in the difference between the ego-opposed and the ego-aligned strategy of assigning front-back orientation to items without inherent front-back orientation. Moreover, in the semantic description of dynamic expressions such as the French *venir de* and *aller* and English *precede* and *follow*, we must refer to time as well as location, whether they are used with a primarily temporal or primarily locative meaning. In a semantic description of the locative sense of *venir de*, we have to talk about two moments in time: one where the individual is close to a specific location and a later moment where he is removed from the location and close to the reference point implied by *venir*. Therefore, I find it too early to decide whether we should talk about metaphorical extension or a common spatial structure underlying both locative expressions and time expressions. We need more information on the perception of temporal and locative relations and preferably also on the nonlinguistic cognitive organisation of such relations.

4 Loci and referentiality

Referentiality
In II.2 The frame of reference, and II.3 Time lines, I have demonstrated some conventions for the association of referents and loci. But not all referents are represented by a locus. One key to an understanding of the function of loci is the notion *referentiality*, which has been shown to play a part in spoken languages, as well. Within the group of referential nominals in spoken languages, some are more referential than others and the degree of referentiality is manifested in their morphosyntax. Givón (1984a) demonstrates that some languages distinguish morphologically between expressions with referents which the speaker refers to several times in the discourse, and expressions with referents which the speaker refers to only once. For instance, Bemba distinguishes *a-ka-soma ici-tabo* ('He will read the book/a particular book') and *a-ka-soma ci-tabo* ('He will read some – unspecified – book') (ibid., 123). Thus, Givón finds that reference should be interpreted pragmatically in terms of thematic centrality in the discourse. Hopper and Thompson (1984) show that in spoken languages a prototypical noun is one which denotes 'a visible (tangible etc.) OBJECT' (707), and that this semantic fact is derivative of the prototypical discourse function of nouns, namely that of introducing a participant into the discourse (708). This function correlates with the greatest morphosyntactic marking of the noun. If a noun that denotes a concrete, perceptible object is used for instance with generic reference, its morphological possibilities are more restricted.

The same semantic-pragmatic features that are relevant to distinguishing nominals with high and low referentiality in spoken languages are also relevant to the analysis of what referents are represented by loci in Danish Sign Language. The higher the referentiality of a nominal, the more likely it is that its referent is represented by a locus and that this is manifested in the nominal.

Nominal, referent, and locus
The relationship between nominal, referent, and locus requires a comment here. A nominal can show that its referent is represented by a locus by including one or more signs that are spatially modified for the locus. Such signs are pronouns, determiners, and some nouns. Moreover, a referent's representation by a locus can be expressed in agreement, polymorphemic verbs, and by nonmanual means (gaze direction, body or head orientation, body position). The meaning of a locus is a characteristic of the referent in the same way as natural gender is a feature of the referent in spoken languages. Like natural gender, locus information can be expressed in other places than the nominal; there need not be a nominal manifesting the locus of a particular referent, and the use of the locus for a specific referent usually extends across the clause boundary. Loci are not lexically determined as is grammatical gender in spoken languages.

Concrete anchoring of abstract referents

I will show what semantic-pragmatic features influence whether a referent is represented by a locus, by means of examples from one signer's account of an annual assembly of the Danish National Association of the Deaf. As the monologue is generally about abstract matters, it is particularly suited to demonstrating the semantic-pragmatic features that influence whether a referent is represented by a locus.

The signer introduces her topic thus:

(1)
```
               t
    RECENTLY / FIRST TO THREE+sequence-tl-right
                              t
    maj(M)('May') / PRON+left-to-right / COUNTRY^MEET
    General-entity-Pm+(loc+sl) CLEAR^WOOD^FARM / PRON+sl /
    Recently, from May first to May third, the national convention
    took place at Klarskovgaard.
```

The assembly is represented by the locus sideward-left through the location where it took place, the conference centre CLEAR^WOOD^FARM. The "pointing" sign at the end of the example, PRON+sl, is a resumptive pronoun or pronoun copy used to refer to the conference centre. Since the centre is situated west of the place where the signer is located, it is represented by the locus sideward-left, in keeping with the iconic convention. Later the signer refers to the assembly, or the conference centre at the time of the assembly, by means of the same locus. As an event the assembly is an *abstract* referent, but the signer uses the locus for its concrete *location*, namely the conference centre, as well as for the event. Two minutes and 36 seconds after the last use of the locus sideward-left for the conference centre, the signer explains that new objectives were presented at the assembly and she refers to the time before the assembly by means of the anaphoric time line:

(2)
```
    AND-THEN / LF NEW ACT^PROGRAMME / PRON+sl / WORK MUCH
    BEFORE+anaph.-tl / GROUP+pl.+anaph.-tl-before DISCUSS+
    multiple+anaph.-tl-before / BUT NOW PUT-FORWARD /
                                  neg
    PRON+sl ONE SUGGEST / SIGN ACT / ACTIVE /
    ACTIVE^PROGRAMME /
```

The next item [on the agenda] was LF's [The National Association of the Deaf] new objectives. People had worked much on them before [the annual assembly]. Several groups had discussed them prior to [the assembly]. And now they were put forward. There [at the

```
assembly/conference centre] someone suggested that we didn't use
the sign ACT, but the sign ACTIVE, that is, ACTIVE^PROGRAMME.
```

The long gap between the last use of the locus and its use in this example demonstrates particularly well how loci can be used for keeping track of reference in a particular context. In (2), the signer uses a pronoun modified for the locus of the assembly or the conference centre.

Another example of a concrete anchoring of an abstract referent is seen earlier in the monologue when the signer talks about the old objectives and uses the locus forward-upward for them: she gives them a concrete anchoring to a poster where they had been written. When an abstract referent cannot easily be given such a concrete anchoring, it is much less likely to be represented by a locus even though it may have high thematic value, i.e. the signer refers to it repeatedly. The signer does not represent the new objectives of the National Association by a locus, even though she refers to the objectives several times. If she had compared the old and the new objectives, she might have represented both using loci since another factor which increases the probability that an abstract referent be represented by a locus is *comparison*.

Thematicity and general relevance
Thematicity as a result of repeated mentioning influences whether a concrete referent is represented by a locus. After the introduction in (1), the signer goes on to describe the conference centre. Here, with pronouns and determiners, she makes repeated use of the locus sideward-left. Then she mentions the owner of the conference centre, a savings bank:

```
(3) SAVE^BOX / SDS / OWN PRON+sl /
    The savings bank SDS owns it.
```

The nominals SAVE^BOX and SDS have specific reference and are not just mentioned in passing: example (3) is the answer to a rhetorical question about who the owner is, and in (3), the nominals have much weight because of the nonmanually marked boundaries after each nominal. Still the signer does not associate the referent with a locus because it has low thematic value; she only refers to it this one time.

A concrete referent with low thematicity may be represented by a locus if it has high general relevance to the participants in the conversation. The signer uses spatially modified determiners in a nominal that she uses to refer to the chairman of the National Association of the Deaf. She only refers to him twice and introduces him as follows.

(4)
```
                                    _____
         DET+fr [hesitates] CHAIRMAN COUNTRY^CHAIRMAN ASGER
         _____   t
         Bergmann(M) DET+fr /....

         The uh - chairman, the national chairman Asger Bergmann...
```

The second time the signer refers to the chairman is much later, and here she does not use the same locus as in (4). The second reference to the chairman is seen in (5).

(5) DET COUNTRY^CHAIRMAN AGAIN^ELECT /

   The chairman was re-elected.

The determiner in (5) is made with an index hand with the index finger "pointing" left, but without any movement in the direction. The sign is made in a transition movement between two signs; the signer holds her hand motionless for a brief second.

    The reason that the signer first represents the referent by a locus is not that the referent is human or animate since, later in the monologue, she does not associate the guests who were invited to the assembly's banquet by any locus. It is the combination of concreteness and high general relevance (both the signer and the receiver know the chairman) that makes the signer use determiners in the nominals of (4) and (5). The locus is irrelevant: in (5), the signer uses a determiner without spatial modification for a specific locus, which makes it clear that the locus in (4) does not contribute to keeping track of reference as does the locus of the assembly and the conference centre in (2). Examples (4) and (5) demonstrate a transition from using loci to express specificity, concreteness and relevance to using determiners for this purpose. Moreover, the examples show that high referentiality does not depend on frequency of mentioning only, but can be a result of high general relevance to the participants.

    From the same monologue comes another example of high general relevance resulting in the signer's representing the referent by a locus. The signer refers only once to an institution, the Danish folk high school for the deaf, but uses determiners that are spatially modified for the locus sideward-left following the iconic convention (the institution is situated west of the place where the signer is). The institution can be associated with a specific geographical location, and as an institution it plays an important part in Danish deaf people's culture. Both factors increase the likelihood that it is represented by a locus in spite of its low thematic value.

    In another sequence of the monologue, the signer says that an award was given out at the assembly. She does not use a locus of the award and does not mention the award winner until it turns out that the receiver does not know who got the award.

Then the signer uses a locus for the award winner and for some institutions in a description of the award winner's interaction with the institutions; she explains what the award winner had done to deserve the award. The need to keep apart several referents in a description of their interaction makes the signer use different loci for them.

In summary, concrete, specific referents with high thematic value or high general relevance to the participants in the discourse are more likely to be represented by a locus than either abstract referents or concrete referents with low thematic value or low general relevance to the participants. Another factor in using a locus for a referent is the necessity to keep referents apart in sequences that describe the interaction of several referents. Location referents are as likely to be represented by a locus as are animate or inanimate concrete referents. What matters is the referent's thematic value or general relevance, its concreteness, and the necessity to distinguish referents from other referents.

Animateness
At first sight, it might seem that concreteness plays a greater role than animateness in Danish Sign Language since concrete referents, no matter whether they are animate or not, are more likely to be represented by loci than abstract referents. There is, however, an alternative to representing a referent by a locus away from the signer. An animate referent can in some sense "take over" the sender locus in what I call shifted locus constructions; or the signer can refer implicitly to the referent by her facial expression which then represents the emotions and attitudes of the referent, what I call shifted attribution of expressive elements. (Both concepts were introduced in I.3 The aims of the present analysis, and are further developed in II.5 Shifted reference, shifted attribution of expressive elements, and shifted locus.)

The alternative representation of the referent is seen in another monologue in which a signer explained that once when she was away for a workshop, her house was burgled. When she came back home, she asked her husband Dan what had happened, and he explained that one day when he came home, he felt that something was wrong. He walked in, and suddenly a man ran out from one of the rooms, but Dan managed to catch him, and after some discussion Dan let the burglar go. At the beginning of the monologue, the signer explains that she asked Dan what had happened, and here she uses the locus forward-left for Dan. Then she recounts Dan's explanation, and in this part of the monologue, she does not use the locus forward-left for him. Instead, she refers to him only by his name sign at the beginning of a long sequence where she explains that he came home, found the lock broken, wondered what had happened, walked in, and so forth. As long as the signer talks about what Dan did and thought, she only refers to him implicitly by her facial expression which expresses Dan's emotions (shifted attribution of expressive elements) and by signs modified for her own locus as representing the actor (shifted locus).

The signer goes on to reporting Dan's questioning of the burglar. At first she signs either MAN or DAN (name sign) and in some cases a verb such as ANSWER at the beginning of every remark, but then she switches to another technique available for reported speech in signed languages. She only changes gaze direction and/or changes her facial expression at the beginning of every remark. When she quotes Dan, she looks forward-sideward-right at the beginning of the quotation, then looks at the receiver (here, into the camera). The locus forward-sideward-right represents the original receiver, i.e. the burglar. When she quotes the burglar, she keeps looking at the receiver in the context of utterance, but changes her facial expression, signalling a change in attribution of expressive elements and thereby a new quoted sender. In reporting Dan's questions to the burglar, she also uses a form of the pronoun modified for the locus forward-sideward-right, the burglar's locus, but Dan is not represented by a locus other than the sender locus. At the end of the monologue, the signer comments on Dan's actions, and here she refers to him by means of a pronoun modified for the locus forward-left as in the beginning of the monologue. That is, the signer "reconquers" her own locus when she re-enters the scene as the narrator. Shifted attribution of expressive elements and shifted locus are only possible with animate referents and referents that can be personified, and it explains cases where a referent, in spite of having high thematic value, is not represented by a locus away from the signer.

5 Shifted reference, shifted attribution of expressive elements, and shifted locus

"Role shifting"
An index hand that makes contact with the signer's body at the tip of the index finger (1.p) can be used to refer to the quoted sender in reported speech. Reported speech can, moreover, be accompanied by a number of nonmanual signals that are also seen in special types of signing that are not reported speech.

Nonmanual signals of a similar kind have been reported for a number of signed languages: Swedish Sign Language (Ahlgren 1984b; Nelfelt 1986; Wallin 1987), Italian Sign Language (Pizzuto 1986; Pizzuto, Giuranna & Gambino 1990), and ASL (among others, Friedman 1975, 950; Mandel 1977, 79-80; Thompson 1977, 190; Baker & Cokely 1980, 232; Liddell 1980, 120-21; Bellugi & Klima 1982, 305; Padden 1986; Lentz 1986; Fischer & Janis 1990, 291-292; Lillo-Martin & Klima 1990). The nonmanual signals comprise changes in the position of the signer's body, head, or shoulders, changes in gaze direction, and changes in facial expression.

The changes in nonmanual signals are sometimes called *role shifting*, but it is not always clear how many of the changes are included under this term. Lentz (1986), for instance, talks about '*degrees* of role shifting (i.e., from minimal to maximum), depending on how fully the signer assumes the roles of the characters discussed. Signers, for example, will affect the manner of expression of another person when describing his/her appearance; the role is assumed more fully when telling what a character thought, said, or did' (58 – emphasis in the original). Padden writes: 'In a role-shifting structure, third person pronouns are shifted into first person. Role-shifting is marked by a perceptible shift in body position from neutral position (straight facing) to one side and a change in direction of eye gaze for the duration of "the role"' (48), but she also gives an example of 'role shifting' without a change in body position (ibid., 50).

I would like to show that in relation to Danish Sign Language, we must distinguish three different phenomena functionally, namely,
1. *shifted reference*, i.e. the use of pronouns from a quoted sender's point of view, especially the use of the first person pronoun 1.p to refer to somebody other than the quoting sender;
2. *shifted attribution of expressive elements*, i.e. the use of the signer's face and/or body posture to express the emotions or attitude of somebody other than the sender in the context of utterance;
3. *shifted locus*, i.e. the use of the sender locus for somebody other than the signer or the use of another locus than the locus c for the signer.

These three phenomena may co-occur, but they may also occur individually; and when shifted locus and shifted attribution of expressive elements co-occur, they do not necessarily express a shift to the same referent. That is, the signer may use the sender locus for one referent and at the same time express the emotions or attitude of another referent. Therefore, *role shifting* is not a sufficiently subtle term.

My use of the word *shifted* in *shifted reference, shifted attribution of expressive elements*, and *shifted locus* is calqued on Jakobson's term *shifter* (1971). But I should emphasise that I use the term *shifted* differently than it is sometimes used in descriptions of spoken languages. In descriptions of indirect speech and represented speech in spoken languages, *shifted pronoun* is sometimes used to describe the fact that the pronouns are not identical with the pronouns used in the original utterance (Jespersen 1924, 219). In represented speech such as *She was not interested in his memoirs*, the pronouns *She* and *his* have been shifted compared with the original or "preshifted" utterance *I am not interested in your memoirs* (Jahn 1992, 351). Since shifted locus and shifted attribution of expressive elements are also used in signing that does not have an original, "preshifted", version, I do not use *shifted* in the same sense. By *shifted*, I mean changed in relation to the point of view of the sender of the context of utterance: when the sender uses the first person pronoun 1.p for herself, uses the sender locus for herself, and expresses her current feelings and attitude through her face and body posture, she expresses her point of view as the sender here and now. Whenever she changes the use of one of these factors to express somebody else's point of view, a shift has taken place.

Shifted reference
From descriptions of spoken languages, we know the difference between direct speech and indirect speech. Direct speech is often described as presenting the quoted sender's exact words (Coulmas 1986), which means that nominals, including pronouns, have the form that the quoted sender would have used. Since she would refer to herself by means of *I* in English and the first person pronoun 1.p in Danish Sign Language, these forms are the forms that the quoting sender uses to refer to the quoted sender. I use the term *shifted reference* for the phenomenon that pronouns are chosen from the quoted sender's point of view.

In Danish Sign Language, shifted reference can only occur in reported speech. But there is only partial shifted reference. The first person pronoun 1.p can be used to refer to the quoted sender, but a quoting sender cannot refer to herself by means of another pronoun than 1.p, even when she quotes somebody else's remark about herself. It seems to be impossible to use anaphoric pronouns to refer to any referent present in the context of utterance. Signers do not quote a remark somebody else made about the actual receiver using an anaphoric pronoun, even though the quoted sender used an anaphoric pronoun for the person who is the receiver in the situation where the utterance is quoted. That is, if A signs the equivalent of *He (= C) will be late* to B, and B later reports the utterance to C, B uses the equivalent of *A said that you would be late*, not the equivalent of *A said, 'He will be late.'* In this way, reported speech about present referents is necessarily in the form of indirect speech when the referring nominals are pronouns. As example (4) below will show, signers can use names to refer to present referents in reported speech. It is just pronouns that have to conform to the context of utterance. When signers are asked what they would do if they really wanted to transmit the exact signing of the quoted sender, they say that they might refer to a present referent by means of an anaphoric pronoun, but then they would insert a deictic pronoun with a special nonmanual marking meaning 'that is, (me/you)' after the anaphoric pronoun (Engberg-Pedersen forthcoming).

Also, in languages such as English and Danish, indirect speech seems much more natural than direct speech with anaphoric pronominal reference to the participants in the current context of utterance. That is, it seems more natural to say, *She told me that you would be late* than to say, *She said, 'He will be late'* when *he* is the actual receiver. Gragg (1972) mentions that in Amharic direct speech pronominalization is violated in what he calls first person contexts. The verb *āla* ('say') is combined with main clauses, i.e. direct speech, but in first person contexts, '[p]ure direct discourse, however, would have the awkward effect of making the speaker refer to himself (or, casu quo, the addressee) in the third person' (ibid., 79). In that case only, the quoting sender may use what is indirect speech pronominalization with the verb *āla*.

Shifted attribution of expressive elements
As direct speech is, or pretends to be (Ebert 1986; Tannen 1986), an exact quotation of what somebody said in a certain situation, tense is understood in relation to the time of the quoted speech act, not the time of the quoting speech act. Expressive elements of direct speech are understood as expressive of the quoted sender's mood or attitude. In indirect speech, tense and expressive elements are selected from the point of view of the quoting speech act, i.e. tense is understood in relation to the time of the quoting speech act, and expressive elements are interpreted as expressing the quoting sender's attitude or feelings. In (1) (from Fillmore 1981, 155), *that idiot* expresses the quoting sender's attitude, while *a genius* in predicative function is attributed to the quoted sender. That is why (1) is not contradictory.

(1)   *She thinks that that idiot is a genius.*

By contrast, the direct speech of example (2) is either contradictory, or the manifestation of a sudden realisation, or *That idiot* is quoted from somebody else – it is so to speak used in inverted commas (for a discussion of 'dual voice', i.e. the expression of two points of view in one sentence, see Jahn 1992, 354-358).

(2)   *She said, 'That idiot is a genius.'*

Other expressive elements occurring in relation to indirect speech such as *damn him* in (3) are also attributed to the quoting sender, not the quoted sender (Banfield 1973, 21):

(3)   *Helen reminded me that Jack, damn him, might be late again.*

To the best of my knowledge, there is no established term for the phenomenon that the expressive elements of direct speech should be attributed to the quoted sender. I will talk about *shifted attribution of expressive elements*[1] when the expressive elements do not express the feelings and attitudes of the sender of the context of utterance. It is important to note that even though the expressive elements should be attributed to somebody else, they may be indicative of the sender's interpretation rather than the person's own feelings. What the sender sees as a haughty expression may be something quite different in the other individual's interpretation.

Shifted locus
The third phenomenon that is needed to understand how reported speech and other types of reports from an individual's point of view are expressed in signed languages is *shifted locus*. Shifted locus means that the signer uses another locus than the sender locus *c* for herself or, more often, that she uses the sender locus *c* for a referent other than herself. Shifted locus is expressed in a number of ways: in agreement verbs (III.6.3 The many uses of the *c*-form), in polymorphemic verbs (III.8.6 Polymorphemic verbs and space), and in changes in the signer's gaze direction and body or head orientation in specific contexts, namely when the signer's gaze direction and body or head orientation are imitative of a non-first person's behaviour (see examples below).

Sometimes *body shift* is used to describe changes in the signer's body posture (see, for instance, Meier 1990; Lillo-Martin & Klima 1990), and Lillo-Martin and Klima (ibid., 202) use *shifted framework* of what seems to be a physical reorientation of the loci. I want to emphasise that what I call *shifted locus* is not a matter of expression only, but a semantic phenomenon that can be expressed in several ways that do not always involve a change in the signer's body orientation or position.

The quoted sender and the original receiver
Example (4) includes a case of direct speech from Danish Sign Language.

```
(4)     body:                           back------------------
        head: d---rot.fld---------neu-----nodding-neu----
        brow:                                   frown---------
        gaze: +---fld------+---fld----V---- fru-----V+-----
              MAN c+EXPLAIN+neu / MOTHER /           gesture

        body: ----------------------------------------------
        head: ----------------------------------------------
        brow: ----------------------------------------------
        gaze: ----------------------------------------------
              nok(M)('enough') ANNEGRETHE neu+EXPLAIN+c 1.p
```

[1] I have coined this inelegant phrase on the basis of Banfield's characterisation of free indirect style (represented speech/thought): 'all expressive elements are attributed to a unique subject-of-consciousness' (1973, 30).

```
body:  ---------------------------
head:  ---------------------------
brow:  ---------------------------
gaze:  ---------------------------
       neu+GO-TO+c nok(M)('enough') /
```

The man explained it to her. My mother nodded and said, 'Never mind. It isn't necessary. Annegrethe will explain it to me when she comes. It isn't necessary.'

In this example, there is a contrast between the signer's gaze direction while she signs c+EXPLAIN+neu (line 1) (forward-left-downward) and her gaze direction from the moment she nods after the sign MOTHER (forward-right-upward). Moreover, in the first part of the example, the signer has lowered her chin (head down), and on c+EXPLAIN+neu, her head is rotated slightly to the left. By contrast, in the part starting after MOTHER, she is leaning back. Finally, the signer's facial expression changes right after MOTHER (frown).

The signer of (4) is Annegrethe. In the reported speech, she uses her name sign for herself and the first person pronoun 1.p to refer to her mother, i.e. there is shifted reference. Through the change of body and head position, the change of gaze direction, and the signer's facial expression, this part of the utterance is distinguished from the rest. The signer's facial expression (*frown*) in the sequence from just after MOTHER to the last *nok(M)('enough')* signals the quoted sender's feelings, not the quoting sender's feelings. Another factor in showing that it is reported speech is the sign MOTHER, which introduces the reported speech, specifying the sender. However, especially in reports of several remarks of a conversation between two individuals, the only indication of the change in quoted sender may be the nonmanual signals.

The first part of (4), MAN c+EXPLAIN+neu, is not reported speech. Nevertheless, the nonmanual signals in this part of the example correlate with the nonmanual signals of the second part: the changes in the signer's head orientation, facial expression and gaze direction after MAN parallel the changes after MOTHER (simultaneous with the head nodding). There is a nonmanual contrast (body, head, gaze) between the direction forward-left-downward simultaneous with c+EXPLAIN+neu and the direction forward-right-upward simultaneous with the reported speech. The signer does not quote the man's explanation, but her gaze direction while signing the communication verb c+EXPLAIN+neu shows that she uses the locus forward-left-downward for her mother (i.e. the implied receiver of the explanation). Her gaze direction with the reported speech of the second part of the example indicates that she is using the locus forward-right-upward for the original receiver, the man.

In the original situation, the participants in the conversation, the man and Annegrethe's mother, were probably standing or sitting face-to-face, which means that they would look straight ahead (and maybe a little down and a little up depending on a height difference between them); they would not look slightly to one side, and their bodies or heads would not be rotated. But in quoting their conversation, the signer uses different directions (left and right) to indicate the changes in intended receiver. That is, the different directions do not indicate a particular physical constellation between the participants in the quoted conversation; it is rather a means of indicating the original receiver in signing.

If a signer has earlier used a locus in one particular direction for one of the participants in a conversation, she will maintain the general direction of that locus when she wants to indicate that the referent is the original receiver: she looks in the direction of the referent's locus, and whenever the referent is the quoted sender, she looks in another direction, i.e. in the direction of the locus of the new original receiver. Often signers do not use the exact direction of the original receiver's locus, but just look slightly right or left to indicate an original receiver represented by some locus either right or left.

In the beginning of or all through the reported speech, the signer looks in the direction of the original receiver's locus, not the quoted sender's locus. She thereby indirectly identifies the quoted sender, even if she does not do so by means of a lexical introduction to the reported speech as in (4). Disregarding for the moment cases where the signer herself is either the quoted sender or the original receiver, we have the following possibilities:

1. the signer has already used a locus for both the quoted sender (e.g. the locus forward-sideward-right) and the original receiver (e.g. the locus forward-sideward-left). In that case, she looks in the direction of the original receiver's locus forward-sideward-left (or slightly left);
2. the signer has already used a locus for the quoted sender (e.g. the locus forward-sideward-right), but no locus for the original receiver. In that case, she looks forward-left to indicate the original receiver, i.e. in the opposite direction of the locus of the quoted sender;
3. the signer has already used a locus for the original receiver (e.g. the locus forward-sideward-left), but no locus for the quoted sender. Then she looks in the direction of the original receiver's locus forward-sideward-left (or slightly left);
4. the signer has not earlier used a locus for either of the participants. Then she looks in one direction when she quotes one of the participants and in the other direction when she quotes the other.

In some cases of quoted dialogue, signers look in the direction of a locus to indicate one of the participants in the dialogue as the original receiver, but look straight at the actual receiver when quoting this referent. That is the case in the report of a dialogue between the signer's husband and a burglar described at the end of II.4 Loci and referentiality: when the signer quoted her husband, she looked in the direction of the burglar's locus, and when she quoted the burglar, she looked at the actual receiver (here, into the camera). I am not sure when this strategy is chosen, but it has the effect of identifying the actual receiver with one of the participants in the quoted dialogue, in the actual case the signer's husband in relation to the burglar.

The picture becomes more complex when we look at cases where the signer herself is either the quoted sender or the original receiver. In Danish Sign Language, there are no changes in gaze direction or head or body position or orientation that distinguish somebody other than the signer as quoted sender or original receiver from the signer as quoted sender or original receiver. It is sometimes claimed that "body shift", i.e. a slight change in body or head position or orientation, can identify another agent or quoted sender than the signer (Bellugi & Klima 1982, 305; Lillo-Martin & Klima 1990, 202). This claim seems to be based on the idea that the signer in some sense moves out in the direction of the locus of the quoted sender and thereby lends her own identity to the imagined body in that position. It is, however, only possible to claim that the change in body position identifies a quoted sender different from the signer if there is never a change in body position when the signer quotes herself. But in Danish Sign Language, the signer may change her body or head position or orientation when quoting herself. In one monologue, a signer quotes a conversation between herself and her son when they were sitting in a car; the signer was driving and her son was next to her. Thus she used the locus sideward-right for her son, and when she quoted her own remarks to him, she moved slightly left and rotated her head and body so that she was facing slightly right. Signers usually only change their head or body orientation slightly, if at all, and there is no difference depending on whether they quote themselves or others.

Similarly, a change in gaze direction to indicate an original receiver may indicate either a non-first person or a first-person original receiver. The gaze direction does not signal whether the quoted remark was originally addressed to the quoting sender (i.e. the signer) or to some other person. In a monologue, a signer described a situation where a man approached her and asked her a question:

```
(5) head:                           down---------------
    head:                           rot.fl-neu---------
    brows:                          up-----------------
    gaze:   +----------------------fld----+-----------
            neu+APPROACH+c ASK 1.p / MAY 1.p c+fl+SWAP /

    He came up to me and asked me, 'May I swap with you?'
```

Earlier in the monologue, she had used the locus forward-sideward-right for the man. When she reported his question, she looked forward left for a brief second before returning to eye contact with the actual receiver (see (5)). By means of her gaze direction, she indicated a receiver different from the man and she used lexical identification of the original receiver in the form of the first person pronoun 1.p (ASK 1.p). That is, she used the locus forward-left-downward to represent herself as the original receiver. Thus, changes in gaze direction and body or head position or orientation show the original receiver's locus. Such changes are only sufficient to identify a quoted sender or an original receiver if these have already been associated with loci. Otherwise, both must be identified by lexical means or through inference: if the signer has only introduced two referents and one of them is represented by a locus a, then a gaze direction in the opposite direction indicates the other referent as the original receiver and, by inference, the referent associated with a as the quoted sender. Gaze in the direction of a signals the referent of a as the original receiver and, by inference, the other referent as the quoted sender.

Vertical differences in gaze direction accompanied by changes in body or head posture (such as leaning forward or leaning back, straightening one's back) may be used to indicate a difference in height (for instance, a conversation between an adult and a child) or a difference in level (for instance, one person lying down, the other person standing). The use of a vertical difference in (4) is likely to signal a difference in authority: the signer never saw the man and does not know anything about his height, but he was an expert in relation to her mother.

Signers may also signal the difference between the participants in a conversation simply by changes in facial expression. We can see this from the following example in which there is no change whatsoever in the signer's body and head orientation or gaze direction to signal the changes in receivers. The signer looks sideward left in the direction of the locus of a speech therapist who is the original receiver of the first and the last remark of the example. She also looks to the left during the middle remark, the speech therapist's answer. The changes in quoted sender are indicated by the changes in facial expression from question to neutral expression to incredulous question, and by the use of the pronoun 1.p to introduce the quoted sender of the last speech report:

```
(6) head:   rot.sl---------------------------------
    gaze:   sl------------------------------------
                    ?                  incredulous+?
            gesture   / DEAF  / 1.p PRON+fsrd DEAF /
    mouth: what then    deaf    what              deaf
```

'What then?' (I asked her). (She said,) 'She is deaf.'
'What,' I exclaimed, 'Is she deaf?'

The signer looks sideward-left (the speech therapist's locus) throughout the three speech reports, and her head faces the same direction.

In example (6), there is no need for shifted reference in the reported speech; the only pronoun in the sections of reported speech is PRON+fsrd, which both parties in the conversation can use to refer to the third individual, i.e. the signer's daughter. Moreover, the signer does not use shifted locus, she does not change her gaze direction for the second speech report, and she does not signal in any other way that her locus has shifted. She only indicates the change in quoted sender between the first and the second speech report by means of shifted attribution of expressive elements.

In the first speech report, the questioning expression should be attributed to the person who asks the question, i.e. the signer in another situation; in the second speech report, the matter-of-fact expression should be attributed to the speech therapist; and the final incredulous expression should again be attributed to the signer as quoted sender.

Tannen (1986) finds that in Greek and English oral stories there is a higher percentage of reported speech with no lexicalized introducer of the type 'he said' than in a Greek and an American novel. The way people mark dialogue in oral storytelling when there is no introducer is by changing their voices to take on the characters' voice. That is a clear parallel to the use of shifted attribution of expressive elements to signal changes in quoted sender in Danish Sign Language.

Shifted reference, shifted attribution of expressive elements, and shifted locus as different phenomena
Shifted reference is restricted to reported speech, while shifted attribution of expressive elements and shifted locus can occur in other types of signing. In the first part of (4), the nonmanual signals occurring with c+EXPLAIN+neu are parallel to the nonmanual signals with the reported speech of the second part; but a pronoun with a communication verb such as EXPLAIN in the context of (4) could not have shifted reference. Unless the communication verb occurs within reported speech, the first person pronoun 1.p with such a verb can only be used to refer to the signer; to refer to the man by means of a pronoun, the signer must use PRON+fr. By contrast, a facial expression of emotion or attitude accompanying c+EXPLAIN+neu would usually be interpreted as expressing the explaining person's emotions or attitudes.

Both shifted attribution of expressive elements and shifted locus can be expressed by head and body movements. But the movements differ in the two cases. Shifted locus can be expressed by specific head and body *orientations* in relation to loci, while shifted attribution of expressive elements can be expressed by specific head or body *postures* which are characteristic of the referent such as stooping. The difference becomes particularly clear when the signer's head and body orientation or a polymorphemic verb show that the sender locus is shifted to one referent while the signer's body posture expresses the attitude of another referent. A contrastive example is seen in Ill. 25a and 25b which can both occur in a story where a woman looks arrogantly at a man. In Ill. 25a, the verb is constructed in such a way that the sender locus represents the woman and the signer's face also expresses the woman's arrogance, i.e. there is shifted locus and shifted attribution of expressive elements to the same referent. In Ill. 25b, the sender locus is used for the man in relation to the verb (the orientation of the signer's body and her hand), but the signer's face and body posture still express the woman's attitude. Thus, shifted locus and shifted attribution of expressive elements are two different phenomena (see further III.8.6 Polymorphemic verbs and space).

Point of view

When the signer uses the sender locus locus for another referent than herself, she expresses a particular point of view. Since it is possible for the signer to use the sender locus for another referent not only in reported speech, but also in other types of constructions, it is also possible to express a specific point of view in other constructions than reported speech, as the following examples will demonstrate.

Example (7) demonstrates a context in which we find shifted attribution of expressive elements without shifted reference:

```
(7)    gaze:   +*---+----------V *-------------V +--------V
               KING gesture / TWO+pron. DAMN-IT TWO+pron. /
       mouth:       adh----                tight-lipped--------

       brow:        up--                       up-----
       gaze:   *-------+-------------------*---V-*---V-*-+
               THINK GET-IDEA MAKE CONTEST gesture FINE /
       mouth:  ----- ahh                   ahh

       *: indicates eye gaze behaviour which is imitative of the king's
       eye gaze behaviour.

       The king was at a loss. Damn the two of them! He thought about it
       and got an idea. He would make a contest. That was it. That would
       be fine.
```

Since the facial expression (raised brows and mouth movements) signals the king's feelings and attitudes, the initial reference to the king with the noun KING might introduce reported speech in the same way as MOTHER in example (4) or the first person pronoun 1.p in example (6). But the rest of example (7) is not reported speech. First, no referent is associated with the direction in which the signer looks, i.e. there is no referent that could represent a receiver of the king's utterances. Instead, the signer looks down in an imitation of the king's pondering. Second, it is not possible to use the first person pronoun 1.p to refer to the king with the verbs in (7). The construction mixes predicates which the king might have used in signing to himself or to somebody else (DAMN-IT, MAKE CONTEST, FINE, gesture) and predicates which the signer uses to describe the king's cognitive activity (THINK, GET-IDEA).

In the following example, the signer looks in the direction of a locus while signing an action verb:

```
(8)    gaze: +----------Vfsld-V+----------
             REPAIR+fsld FIX+fsld / FINE /

       He repaired and fixed [the dishwasher] so that it was all fine.
```

The signer has eye contact with the receiver while signing REPAIR+fsld, but looks in the direction of the locus for a dishwasher while signing FIX (Ill. 26). FIX+fsld is accompanied by a mouth pattern (lax, broadened lips, outlet of air) which signals a process. That is, the mouth pattern does not have an expressive, but an aspectual meaning. No facial expression in this utterance signals emotions or attitudes.

Example (8) resembles the first part of example (4) in that the signer looks in the direction of a locus, not at the receiver, while signing the predicate, in (4) c+EXPLAIN+neu and in (8) FIX+fsld. In (7), the signer looks down ponderingly while signing THINK. In all three examples, the gaze direction is imitative of where people would look when they explain something to somebody (at the receiver), repair a dishwasher (at the dishwasher), or think about what to do (at no specific point, but generally not at another person). The parallelism between the three examples demonstrates how signers can take on another person's point of view. In all three cases, the sender locus has shifted in the sense that the sender locus represents someone other than the signer. I describe a referent that is represented by the sender locus, be it the signer or some other referent, as the holder of the point of view.

There is a scale of identification with a referent other than oneself:
1. in reported speech, there may be (partial) shifted reference (the first person pronoun 1.p can be used to refer to the quoted sender), shifted attribution of expressive elements, and shifted locus;
2. with c+EXPLAIN+neu of (4) and in (7), there is shifted attribution of expressive elements and shifted locus, but not shifted reference;
3. with FIX+fld in (8), there is shifted locus, but neither shifted reference nor shifted attribution of expressive elements;
4. with REPAIR+fld in (8), there is neither shifted reference, nor shifted locus, nor shifted attribution of expressive elements, i.e. no identification with the agent referent.

Facial expressions of attitude or character can occur in stative descriptions of a person's permanent or temporary character where the signer keeps eye contact with the receiver. The signer may, for instance, characterise a person who has just walked through a rain shower, by describing his wet hair while looking miserable. I think this phenomenon should not be called shifted attribution of expressive elements as imitative nonmanual signals are more or less obligatory accompaniments of descriptive signs in declarative characterising clauses.

Comparison with spoken languages
Shifted reference and shifted attribution of expressive elements are defining properties of direct speech in spoken languages. In indirect speech, there is no reference shift and expressive elements manifest the quoting sender's feelings and attitudes. Direct and indirect speech are extremes on a continuum with many intermediate types (see articles in Coulmas 1986 and especially DeRoeck in press). A third possibility that has long been recognised and described in the literature is represented

speech or represented thought, or free indirect style (Banfield 1973, 25ff.; Fillmore 1981, 154; Jahn 1992). In this style, there is no reference shift, but 'all expressive elements are attributed to a unique subject-of-consciousness' (Banfield 1973, 30) who is not the representing sender at the utterance time, but someone to whom the representing sender refers by means of a name or a third person pronoun. In the following passage from Virginia Woolf's *Mrs Dalloway* (quoted from Banfield 1973, 10-11), the exclamation should be attributed to Mrs. Dalloway, while the use of the third person pronoun *she* is characteristic of the narrator (as are the verb tenses).

(9) *Mrs Dalloway said she would buy the flowers herself. For Lucy had her work cut out for her. The doors would be taken off their hinges; Rumpelmayer's men were coming. And then, thought Clarissa Dalloway, what a morning – fresh as if issued to children on a beach.*

What characterises free indirect style is shifted attribution of expressive elements without shifted reference. The narrator refers to Mrs. Dalloway as *Mrs Dalloway, she*, and *Clarissa Dalloway*. Moreover, the verbs' tense is not appropriate of the moment when Mrs. Dalloway is thinking about what is going to happen. But *what a morning* must be attributed to Mrs. Dalloway (*thought Clarissa Dalloway*), and the reader understands that the rest of the example, except for the first sentence and *thought Clarissa Dalloway*, is also a representation of Mrs. Dalloway's thoughts.

The same mixture of nominals characteristic of the representing sender and expressive elements attributable to the represented experiencer is seen in example (7) about the king in Danish Sign Language. The noun KING is appropriate of the narrator's point of view, while the facial expression and the gaze direction with the predicates must be attributed to the king, thereby making him the 'subject-of-consciousness'. The signer imitates the king's (imagined) gaze direction which is consistent with the shift in subject-of-consciousness: the sender of the context of utterance momentarily "disappears" in favour of a representation of another person's point of view. That is, to obtain the effect of free indirect style with a subject-of-consciousness, the signing must include both shifted attribution of expressive elements and shifted locus, and both kinds of shift must be to the same referent.

There are, however, some differences between free indirect style or represented speech or thought in spoken languages and examples such as (7) in Danish Sign Language. First, in (7) there is only one nominal referring to the subject-of-consciousness, i.e. KING, and this nominal is outside the scope of the shifted attribution of expressive elements. It is not possible to refer to the subject-of-consciousness by any nominal inside its scope in the way that it is possible to refer to Mrs. Dalloway by *she* in (9). KING in (7) is more like *thought Clarissa Dalloway* in (9): both are part of the narrator's comments.

Second, free indirect style in spoken languages is used to represent speech or thought (see, however, Fillmore 1981, 157), but shifted attribution of expressive elements in Danish Sign Language can be used in "represented action" and with verbs that denote mental states or experiences attributed to the subject-of-consciousness. Some of the predicates in (7) include cognition verbs (THINK, GET-IDEA). Such verbs belong to what Banfield calls 'verbs of consciousness' (including communication verbs and verbs of belief, sensation, and reflection) (ibid., 26). In Banfield's analysis, such verbs can introduce (or follow or occur in the middle of) passages in the free indirect style (*thought Clarissa Dalloway* in (9)), but they are not part of the represented speech or thoughts. In (7), they are used with expressive elements that must be attributed to the subject-of-consciousness. The same is true of the communication verb EXPLAIN in line 1 of example (4). This difference between Danish Sign Language and spoken languages may be only apparent: in oral forms of spoken languages, both intonation and nonverbal behaviour (facial expression) can be used with 'verbs of consciousness' to express the feelings or attitudes of the subject-of-consciousness. Expressive intonation and nonverbal behaviour as in *He squeeeezed the toothpaste from the tube* (pronounced with a long vowel) may be a similar way of expressing a specific point-of-view with an action verb in spoken languages.

The nonmanual expressive signals with action verbs show the relatedness of signed language to mime where the mime uses his body as the represented person would use it. Danish Sign Language resembles mime in its possibility of "representing" actions, but in mime there is nothing like the verb THINK (Ill. 2). A mime has to represent the state of thinking in some other way. Moreover, shift of the sender locus to represent another referent than the signer can be expressed by very small changes in gaze direction and body and head orientation in a signed language. The mime has to make large, time-consuming movements and move around the floor.

Following Dahl (1985, 112), Ahlgren and Bergman (1990, 257) define narrative discourse as 'one where the speaker relates a series of real or fictive events in the order they are supposed to have taken place', and they describe a number of features that are characteristic of narrative discourse in Swedish Sign Language. Example (7) is narrative discourse according to the definition, and it includes some of the features that Ahlgren and Bergman find characteristic of narrative discourse in Swedish Sign Language: it starts with a nominal that introduces a referent (KING), it has a chain of predicates expressing different types of events, intended actions (MAKE CONTEST), and mental states (THINK) (Ahlgren & Bergman: 'any kind of event, from actions expressed with verb-object structure to mental states expressed with false quotations and true quotations' (ibid., 262)), and the signer predominantly avoids eye contact with the receiver. A 'false quotation' is a description in a narrative context of a reaction or an attitude 'in the form of something that looks like an utterance' (ibid., 261), e.g. the gesture and the utterances TWO+pron. DAMN-IT TWO+pron. and FINE of example (7).

Narrative discourse in signing calls for reported speech and a style that can be compared with free indirect style of spoken languages (see also Fischer & Janis 1990, 292). It differs, however, from free indirect style by including "represented action" and "represented mental state or experience" and by excluding nominals referring to the holder of the point of view or the subject-of-consciousness. In all cases, another referent than the signer takes over the sender locus and the signer uses her own body and face to represent the other referent's attitude and emotions.

Reported speech can include all three kinds of shift: shifted reference, shifted attribution of expressive elements, and shifted locus. *Represented thought* and *represented action* can include shifted attribution of expressive elements and shifted locus, but not shifted reference. Further possibilities in Danish Sign Language are:
1. shifted locus with gaze direction and/or head and body orientation imitative of the referent, but without shifted attribution of expressive elements;
2. shifted locus as expressed in marking for a specific point of view in agreement verbs without shifted attribution of expressive elements and with eye contact with the receiver (see III.6.3 The many uses of the *c*-form);
3. shifted locus to one referent and shifted attribution of expressive elements to another referent.

What the appropriate contexts of types 1 and 3 are, is still not clear to me.

6 Pointing signs

6.1 Types of pointing signs

A major functional distinction: referential and predicative use
In the article *Deixis as the source of reference*, Lyons puts forward the thesis that

> the grammatical structure and interpretation of referring expressions (other than proper names) can be accounted for in principle on the basis of a prior understanding of the deictic function of demonstrative pronouns and adverbs in what might be loosely described as concrete or practical situations. (Lyons 1975, 61)

The basis of reference is the situation in which the sender and the receiver can point to the referents in the context of utterance, Lyons says. In order to explain the possibility of nondeictic reference in spoken languages, he starts with a very simple language having a grammar that only includes a deictic particle. The deictic particle is related to a pointing gesture and is neutral with respect to gender, proximity, person, and place; it can occur as both a nominal and a verb. Lyons predicts the development of the system of demonstrative pronouns, adjectives, and adverbs, and the definite article from the deictic particle in a child's acquisition of English (Lyons 1977, 646-657). First, the deictic particle splits into two different forms, the pronominal and the adverbial deictic, reflecting a difference between reference to a person and reference to a place and a functional difference between referential and predicative use. Both forms then develop a proximity distinction: 'this' vs. 'that' in the pronoun, and 'here' vs. 'there' in the adverb. Only the pronoun develops gender distinctions: 'he', 'she', 'it'. The next step is the development of the demonstrative adjectives, whose forms are identical with the demonstrative pronouns, and, finally, the definite article develops from the nonproximal demonstrative adjective (in other languages from a demonstrative which is neutral with respect to proximity (Greenberg 1985, 275-276)). The English definite article is unmarked for the deictic distinction of proximity and its function is to inform 'the addressee that some specific entity is being referred to without however giving him any locative (or qualitative) information about it.' (Lyons 1977, 654). The development is thus:

1. a deictic particle;
2. two forms: a pronominal (person) and an adverbial (place) deictic; and two functions: referential and predicative use;
3. proximity distinctions: pronominal: 'this' – 'that' and adverbial: 'here' – 'there';
4. gender distinctions in the pronoun: 'he' – 'she' – 'it';
5. demonstrative adjectives; and
6. the definite article from the nonproximal demonstrative adjective.

The scenario of the development of the English system is supported by diachronic evidence. In particular, the definite article results from a phonological reduction of 'what is diachronically identifiable with 'that' in certain positions.' (ibid., 654).

The first major distinction is between the pronoun (person) and the adverb (place), which parallels a distinction between referential and predicative use. Since both the pronoun and the adverb can be used to refer, the form distinction parallels a construction where two referring expressions are brought together in a statement about an entity's existence in a location: 'that one (is) there'. Lyons claims that the semantic and the syntactic differentiation of pronouns and adverbs go hand in hand: the semantic difference between reference to an entity and reference to a place correlates a distinction between pronominal and adverbial function as 'deictics with pronominal function (like proper names) cannot be used in predicative expressions' (ibid., 66). That is, a deictic which is part of the VP is interpreted as having an adverbial function.

In what he describes as an 'experiential gestalt', or 'The Pointing-Out Idealized Cognitive Model', Lakoff (1987, 489-491) introduces a three-way distinction between the entity, the location, and a locational predicate or a predicate of motion.[1] The third element, compared with Lyons's model, is the predicate which links the entity and the location and allows the possibility of specifying whether the entity is stationary or moving, the manner in which the entity is either located or moving, and other aspects of the relationship between the entity and the location ('being in/above/etc.', 'moving toward/past/etc.'). But in the description of the Pointing-Out Idealized Cognitive Model as a speech act, Lakoff only talks about the entity and the location: the speaker directs the hearer's attention to the location and focuses his awareness on the entity.

The location thus has a somewhat ambiguous status between being what is predicated of the entity and being an item in its own right. In both descriptions, however, the location is subsidiary to or predicated of the entity. From a grammatical point of view, the main interest is the development of two functionally distinct classes in language: expressions primarily used to refer and expressions primarily used to predicate something of the former or assert the occurrence of a state or event, i.e. a distinction between nominals and predicates or nouns/pronouns and verbs.[2]

Signed discourse abounds with pointing signs, i.e. signs made with the index hand pointing in some direction. The pointing signs clearly have a deictic basis and can be compared with paralinguistic pointing in spoken languages which are ambiguous between reference to entity and reference to location and do not distinguish a

---

[1] There is a fourth element in Lakoff's analysis, namely a final predicate which is expressed as a phrase such as *afraid of his shadow* in *There goes the cop, afraid of his shadow* (1987, 498). This 'semantic element' of the experiential gestalt seems to be very closely linked with the structure of English.

[2] Hopper and Thompson (1984) describe the difference between nouns and verbs as primarily expressing a difference in discourse function: 'the extent to which prototypical nounhood is achieved is a function of the degree to which the form in question serves to introduce a participant into the discourse' and 'To qualify as a prototypical V, a form must ASSERT THE OCCURRENCE OF AN EVENT OF THE DISCOURSE.' (ibid., 708 – emphasis in the original). The prototypical discourse functions correlate with maximal morphological possibilities.

referential and a predicative use. It is, therefore, well worth asking whether Danish Sign Language has developed the major functional distinction between referential and predicative use in the pointing signs.

The pronoun and the determiner
In Danish Sign Language, a major form distinction exists between those pointing signs which function as pronouns and determiners and those which function as stative verbs and particles that link nouns. The division corresponds roughly to Lyons' first acquired distinction, the distinction between the pronoun and the adverb. But the pronoun in Danish Sign Language can refer to places as well as entities, which confirms the ambiguous status of location described above. A pronoun used to refer to a place can be seen in (1); the first sign is made with a lax index finger and a side-to-side movement like unemphatic forms of the pronoun referring to entities.

(1) PRON+u SWEAT-RUN-ON-FACE WARM STUFFY SWEAT-RUN-ON-FACE /

   Up there we were very hot and oppressed by the heat.

That is, there is no form distinction between a pointing sign with reference to a place and a pointing sign with reference to an entity. The pointing sign in (1) can be interpreted as having a topic function in relation to the rest of the construction which means that it has a pronominal, not an adverbial, function.

The unemphatic (singular) pronoun and the unemphatic (singular) determiner[3] are made with a short movement in the direction of a locus or with a short side-to-side movement with the index finger pointing in the direction of the locus. They are made with a lax index finger. Unless the referent or the imagined referent is located above or below the level of the holder of the point of view or the pronoun or determiner is marked for proximity (see below), the index finger is held horizontally (but is lax).

Both the pronoun and the determiner also have "undirected" forms: an index hand with a hold movement (i.e. no movement) or occurring in a transition movement, the direction in which the index finger "points" being irrelevant, i.e. the pronoun or determiner is not modified for a locus. When such forms function as determiners they resemble Lyons' description of the English definite article: the forms are a reduced version of the form of the adjectival pointing signs, and they inform 'the addressee that some specific entity is being referred to without however giving him any locative (or qualitative) information about it' (1977, 654).

Zimmer and Patschke (1990, 207) also distinguish pronouns and determiners in ASL (see also Padden 1988b, 108-111), and they find that the direction of the point in determiners in ASL is 'most often insignificant' and that, '[i]n most cases, the deter-

---
3 Here I only talk about the pronoun and the determiner that are pointing signs. There are other pronouns that can be modified in space.

miners used with different characters [of a story – EEP] point to the same location' (ibid., 207). In some pronouns and determiners of Danish Sign Language, the index finger points in the direction of a locus; in others, it does not. In (2), the pointing sign after the nonmanual boundary resumes the topicalized nominal as a pronoun. The signer uses the locus sideward-right of the referent, but this can only be deduced from her gaze direction at the end of the topicalized constituent. The pronoun after the boundary is not modified for the locus. It occurs in the transition movement from the end position of SISTER to the beginning of the sign INTO and the index hand does not point in any specific direction.

```
(2)                       _____t_____
        gaze:   +----------sr V+-------------------------------
                LITTLE^SISTER / PRON c+INTO[+]+fr CHILD^GARDEN /
        gaze:   --------------V-------V
                FORTUNATELY / PRON+fr /
        Baby sister, fortunately she finally got into the kindergarten.
```

The final pronoun of (2) is used to refer to the kindergarten and is modified for the locus of this referent. It is accompanied by special nonmanual signals (the signer moves her head down, outward, up, and back to neutral), which set off the pronoun from the rest of the clause. Preliminarily, I describe it as a resumptive pronoun.

Since the index finger in the pointing signs functioning as pronouns and determiners can point in many different directions and the difference between the individual forms reflects differences in reference, it might be suggested that there is not one pronoun and one determiner, but many. Lillo-Martin and Klima (1990) argue against an analysis of pointing signs used for anaphoric reference as a list of different forms (lexical items or morphemes) for ASL and suggest the following analysis:

> We propose that it is appropriate to analyze this system as having only one personal pronoun. This pronoun, which we will gloss PRONOUN is marked with an R-index [a referential index, i.e. a notational device that indicates which nouns and pronouns are intended to corefer – EEP] just as are the pronouns and full noun phrases of spoken language....The difference between ASL and English, then, is that in many cases, what are unspoken referential indices in English are overtly manifested in ASL. (Lillo-Martin & Klima 1990, 198)

Lillo-Martin and Klima do not give any evidence for talking about a *personal* pronoun (see II.6.3 Person, place, and shifters). Nor does their analysis suggest a way of coping with undirected determiners and pronouns such as the ones in Danish Sign Language described above, or the undirected determiners in ASL described by Zimmer and Patschke (1990).

The pointing signs which are modified for a locus are demonstrative in that they carry locus information, but they are not emphatic. They may be used both deictically and anaphorically. PRON+(locus-marker) and DET+(locus-marker) vary formally within the same limits. As they have different functions, however, I transcribe them differently. Their different functions can be seen in examples (3)-(5). Examples (3) and (4) have been elicited to demonstrate the difference.

(3)
```
                 t
     DET+fsrd CAT / SLEEP /        (Ill. 27)
     The cat, it's asleep.
```

(4)
```
              t
     PRON+fsrd / CAT /             (Ill. 28)
     That's a cat.
```

In (3), DET+fsr CAT is one topicalized constituent which is used to refer to the cat in question. Example (4) has two constituents, a topicalized nominal which is used to refer to the cat, PRON+fsrd, and a predicate. In (3), the scope of the topicalization marker includes the noun and the point; in (4), the topicalization marker only has the point within its scope. The point in (3) qualifies the noun as a determiner, while the point in (4) functions as a full nominal, i.e. a pronoun. Example (5) is from a monologue and distinguishes noun + determiner and predicate + pronoun:

(5)
```
                                    t                      t
     DET+emphatic+fr Vibely(M) DET+fr / BEFORE+deictic-tl /
                              t             squint
     FIRST 1.p.POSS SON DET+srd / Joakim(M) PRON+srd /
     BE-AT+fr NURSERY ALSO BE-AT+fr /
     Before [now that my daughter is there], my son - his name is
     Joakim - he was at Vibely nursery school.
```

In (5), both the nominal 1.p.POSS SON DET+srd and the clause Joakim(M) PRON+srd consist of a noun (or a possessive pronoun + a noun) followed by a pointing sign. They are distinguished by the nonmanual signals. The scope of the nonmanual signal on the pronoun (squinted eyes) is the pronoun only, while the scope of the special nonmanual signal of topicalization, which here includes squinted eyes, is all of the nominal 1.p.POSS SON DET+srd, including the determiner. The nonmanual signal squinted eyes can be used with referential constituents as a reference check. Since a pronoun can be used to refer as a full nominal, it can be the scope of the nonmanual signal squinted eyes. A determiner cannot be used alone to refer and thus is not an appropriate scope of the signal. In (5), Joakim(M) is used to predicate something of PRON+srd, and PRON+srd is co-referential with 1.p.POSS SON DET+srd. When there is no nonmanual signal to disambiguate the constructions, individual examples can only be distinguished by their external syntactic function as a clause or a nominal and by their meaning.

Specific reference, definiteness, and the determiner
The pronoun and the determiner can only be used in nominals with specific reference. The determiner in Danish Sign Language can occur before and after the noun. The determiner can occur with proper names (see example (5)) as well as in nominals that are used to refer to new referents as in SECOND DET+fl LIVE^FLAT in (6).

```
(6) FORTUNATELY OBTAIN SECOND DET+fl LIVE^FLAT /

    Fortunately, we got another flat.
```

That is, the determiner is neutral with respect to definiteness, but indicates that the nominal has specific reference. Givón (1984b, 399) describes the difference between definite and indefinite referential nominals in terms of the speaker's assumptions about the hearer's ability to identify a unique referent. If the speaker assumes that the hearer can assign unique referential identity to a nominal, he uses a definite nominal; if he believes that the hearer cannot assign unique reference to the nominal, he uses an indefinite nominal. This description of the difference between the use of definite and indefinite nominals throws light on the lack of a form distinction expressing pragmatic definiteness in Danish Sign Language. As Givón points out (ibid., 400), one of the sources of definiteness is immediate deictic availability, and determiners modified for a locus in Danish Sign Language have a deictic basis. Thus, a determiner with a locus marker contributes to identifying a unique referent, whether it has been mentioned before or not.

Lyons mentions that there are two ways in which we can identify an object by referring expressions: 'first, by informing the addressee where it is (i.e. by locating it for him); second, by telling him what it is like' (Lyons 1977, 648). A nominal with a determiner modified for a locus uses both means: the noun (in (6), LIVE^FLAT) tells the receiver what the referent is like. The determiner tells the receiver, not where the referent is, but that the referent is unique, i.e. different from other referents in the universe-of-discourse.

The analysis of a locus-marked determiner as contributing to identifying a unique referent is confirmed by the fact that the forms of the determiner without a locus marker (i.e. forms in which the index finger does not point in the direction of a locus) only occur in nominals with definite reference. Such nominals occur when the sender assumes that the receiver can assign unique reference to the nominal on the basis of factors such as the referent's status in the discourse (the sender has already referred to the referent earlier in the discourse). That is, when the determiner does not have a locus marker, it indicates that the nominal is definite.[4]

The stative locative verb and the particle
The forms of the unemphatic pronoun and the unemphatic determiner are different from the forms of the stative locative verb which is used to assert an entity's location in a place. The pointing signs whose syntactic function is verbal can be analysed as forms of a stative verb and a directional verb related to polymorphemic verbs with the root General-entity-Pm. This root is an alternative to other roots denoting more specific states of being located in a place or moving such as 'stand', 'sit', or '(of a car) be located or move' (see III.8 Polymorphemic verbs). The stative verb forms ('(something) be located somewhere') are made with an index hand with an index finger that is straight, hooked, or bent at the first knuckle (depending on the orientation of the locus direction), and a straight movement in the direction of the tip of the index finger followed by a final hold or a rebound and a hold. The handshape combined with the movement, and in some cases a rebound, give the impression that the finger "touches" the locus or that the locus is a specific point in space. An example of this form, transcribed as BE-AT, is seen in (7).

(7) 1.p BEFORE+deictic-tl CASTBERGGAARD+sr BE-AT+sr /

　　1.p SIGN-LANGUAGE^COURSE BE-AT+sr /

　　Once I was at Castberggaard, for a sign language course.

The equivalent directional verb, GO-TO, is made with a slightly bent finger and an arc movement parallel with the index finger (Ill. 8). The sign BE-AT denotes an entity's location in a place and GO-TO its movement to a place.

　　A pointing sign whose form is very similar to the stative verb BE-AT seems to function as a particle linking two nouns; it is transcribed as LOC:

(8) 　　　　　　　　　　　　　　　　　　　　　　　t
　　SOME+sl DEAF LOC+sl Bristol(M) DET+sl / OFFENDED /

　　Some deaf people in Bristol feel offended.

The topicalized constituent in (8) includes two pointing signs. The form transcribed as LOC+sl is made with a downward movement, a rebound, and a hold, while the form transcribed as DET+sl is made in a transition movement. It is still not clear whether the first part of (8) is clearly distinct from a clause. If it is, the pointing sign between DEAF and Bristol(M) cannot be a finite verb form. Otherwise, it is difficult to maintain a distinction between LOC and BE-AT (see also the ambiguous examples below).

4　In rare cases, the number sign ONE is used as what seems to be an indefinite (singular) determiner rather than as a numeral. In such cases, the nominal including ONE does not include a locus marker.

The proform

Besides the pronoun, the determiner, the stative verb, and maybe the particle, there is one more form of pointing sign that can be distinguished l formally and functionally from the other forms. This form is used as a carrier of information which is otherwise expressed in spatial modifications; the form is usually made with the weak hand:

```
(9)                          t
     DET+fr LEADER DET+fr / AFTER PRON+fr TRAVEL^GONE JUTLAND    /
                                                           PROFORM+sr
     The leader, later she went to Jutland.
```

The sign transcribed as PROFORM+sr consists of an index hand pointing in the direction of the locus sideward-right. It is made with the weak hand with a hold movement simultaneously with the sign JUTLAND. At first, the pointing sign might seem to be a determiner simultaneous with the noun. Then the pointing sign simultaneous with the predicate in (10) could be analysed as a pronoun.

```
(10) 1.p.POSS FAMILY DEAF+redupl.                 /
                     PROFORM+"sideways-movement"
     In my family everyone is deaf.
```

This analysis seems all the more likely since the signer can maintain her hand with the index hand for a pronoun while she signs a predicate:

```
(11)           DEAF /
     PRON+sl-----
     He is deaf.
```

But the proform can occur with predicates where the pronoun is excluded. The proform can, for instance, occur with a sideways movement of the index hand simultaneously with the reduplicated form of DEAF as in (10). But it is not possible to use the reduplicated form of DEAF with a plural form of the pronoun (expressed by a sideways movement of the index hand); example (12) was unanimously rejected by my informants:

```
(12) *PRON+pl. DEAF+redupl. /
```

That is, if the pointing sign in (10) is analysed as a pronoun, we need a constraint on the occurrence of pronouns: the plural form of the pronoun must occur simultaneously with a reduplicated predicative sign. There does not seem to be any plausible explanation of such a constraint.

Another argument against analysing the pointing signs made with the weak hand simultaneously with some other signs as pronouns and determiners is that sometimes they occur in contexts where they can be analysed as neither a pronoun nor a determiner. (Note also that if the pointing sign in (10) is analysed as a pronoun, there are two co-referential nominals in the same clause, 1.p.POSS FAMILY and the pointing sign.) Some verbs can take a modification that consists of a reduplication of the sign embedded in a linear outward movement along the line expressing the mixed time line (see II.3 Time lines). Like DEAF, the verb IN-TROUBLE has a place of articulation on the body and cannot be modified in space, but the modification can be "transferred" to the proform:

```
(13) 1.p  IN-TROUBLE                 /        (Ill. 29)
          PROFORM+multiple+mixed-tl
     I'll run into trouble again and again.
```

In (13), the sideways movement of the index hand is outward from the signer's body. Here, the pointing sign cannot be a determiner since it occurs simultaneously with the predicate, and it cannot be a pronoun since the first person pronoun 1.p occupies the argument position in relation to the stative verb. Instead, I propose to analyse the pointing sign occurring simultaneously with other signs as a form that carries a spatial modification either when the sign which is supposed to be modified cannot be modified for phonological reasons or as an intensification of the spatial modification.[5] In (10) and (13), the proform is modified spatially in ways that the predicate signs cannot be, as they have a place of articulation with body contact. However, there does not seem to be any way of deciding whether a pointing sign which is maintained in the weak hand simultaneously with other signs, as in (11), should be analysed as a token of the proform or as a continuation of the pronoun or the determiner. What they all have in common is that they relate an entity, an event, or a state to an entity or location in the context of utterance or to a cognitive "entity" that is projected into the signing space as a time line or the locus of a referent.

Formal similarities
In their typical functions, the forms of the pronoun and the determiner have less phonetic weight than the forms of LOC and the verbs BE-AT and GO-TO. The pronoun and the determiner are made with either single movement or no movement. They are

---

5 Friedman (1975, 953-955) analyses the use of an 'index' made with the weak hand simultaneously with another sign made with the strong hand in ASL as having an emphatic or contrastive function or serving to 'establish or refer to the location of the NP' (simultaneous with a nominal), to indicate 'the location of the action' (simultaneous with a verb), or to 'incorporate the subject of the verb plus its location' (simultaneous with a verb). She does not mention cases like (12) where the proform is used simultaneously with a verb, but refers neither to the location of an action nor to the subject of the verb.

not made with an initial hold or a rebound and only have a final hold in clause-final position or as the last sign of a topicalized constituent (holds in this position are part of the "intonation" of clause structure). Moreover, the pronoun and the determiner have forms in which the index finger does not point in the direction of a locus.

When they are emphatic, however, forms that function as pronouns can occur with a number of the form features of LOC and BE-AT or their movement is repeated. In (14), the pronoun is made with both hands with index fingers bent at the first knuckle and pointing down, the hands make an upward (reverse) movement and then move down, a handshape and movement that is typical of BE-AT. In (14), the form is used for a contrastive purpose:

```
(14)  PRON+emphatic+fr BAD /
      PRON+emphatic+fr----

      She was the one who was bad.
```

Repetition of the movement, which also adds phonetic weight to the sign, can be seen in forms of the pronoun where the signer wants to give the receiver time to become familiar with the referent (see example (2) in II.6.2 The pronoun, the determiner, and information-packaging).

All pointing signs except for the undirected forms of the pronoun and the determiner can show proximity differences. Forms meaning 'proximal' are made with the index finger pointing downward and the joints of the arm more flexed than the neutral form, and forms meaning 'distal' are made with more extended joints.

Ambiguous cases

Some pointing signs are ambiguous between several interpretations. For instance, the signs for the days of the week can be embedded in an outward linear movement along the line expressing the mixed time line to signify a sequence of days. Here a pointing sign may be used after, for example, the first two weekday signs: MONDAY+mixed-tl-cl. TUESDAY+mixed-tl-forward-from-the-preceding-sign [pointing-sign]+mixed-tl-forward ('Monday, Tuesday, etc.'). In this context, the pointing sign cannot be a determiner of the preceding noun. As it takes over the spatial modification of WEDNESDAY etc., it might be analysed as the proform. It does not, however, occur simultaneously with another sign, but rather at the end of a sequence of "signs" in a modification for distribution[6] and it shares functions with the pronoun by substituting for nouns.

Pointing signs sometimes occur after verbs, where they also seem to take over morphology from another sign. Supalla (1990) analyses certain constructions which

---

6 It is not clear to me how the two first signs of the sequence MONDAY+mixed-tl-cl. TUESDAY+mixed-tl-forward-of-the-preceding-sign [pointing-sign]+mixed-tl-forward should be analysed. The three signs clearly form a rhythmic unit of the same kind as a reduplication of one sign embedded in an outward linear movement, but MONDAY and TUESDAY are two different signs.

have a verb of motion followed by a pointing sign as serial verb constructions, in which the pointing sign functions as a verb that takes over some of the morphology of the first verb. The second sign in such a construction may have other handshapes than the index hand, which strengthens the analysis of these signs as predicative (of the kind which I describe as polymorphemic verbs in III.8). Similar constructions are seen in Danish Sign Language, where a complex polymorphemic verb is often followed by a form with the index hand. Here, a pointing sign takes over morphology from verbs in a sequential construction. In (15), however, a pointing sign occurs after a verb of motion and location with simple morphology:

```
(15)  1.p+pl. THEATRE^PERSON+pl. SIT [pointing-sign]+cu.far
      BALCONY / MUST-NOT [pointing-sign]+cd /
      BALCONY-----------------------------
```
We theatre people sat all the way up in the balcony. We were not allowed to sit down [below, in the stalls].

The sign [pointing-sign]+cu.far in the first clause is accompanied by the mouth pattern of the Danish word *op* ('up'), while the signer does not use any mouth pattern with [pointing-sign]+cd in the last clause. The latter sign follows a modal directly as a verb, but [pointing-sign]+cu.far can be analysed either as a verb in a serial verb construction, as the particle LOC linking a verb and a nominal, or alternatively as a determiner of BALCONY. In (16), there is no noun after the pointing sign in an otherwise similar construction, which makes it possible to analyse it as a verb in a serial construction or as a pronoun referring to a place. The pointing sign is here made with an index finger bent at the first knuckle, a repeated movement, and a final hold, i.e. its form is characteristic of LOC and BE-AT, as well as of the emphatic form of the pronoun and the determiner, and it does have an emphatic meaning:

```
(16)  1.p+pl. WILL-NOT LIVE [pointing-sign]+fr /
```
We won't stay there.

The analysis of such examples must await further analyses of nominal and predicative functions and the notion of clause in Danish Sign Language.

Summary
Lyons (1977) predicted that the first distinction to develop out of the basic deictic particle would be the distinction between a pronoun that can be used to refer to entities and an adverb that can be used to refer to places. This distinction would correlate with a distinction between referential and predicative functions. The pointing signs in Danish Sign Language demonstrate a major form division between a) the pronoun

and the determiner and b) the stative verb and the locative particle. Such a form distinction correlates with a functional distinction between signs that are used to refer and signs that function as predicates, i.e. a distinction between nominals and verbs.[7] In Danish Sign Language, however, there is no form distinction between pronouns that are used to refer to entities and pronouns that are used to refer to places. The pointing signs that can have a predicative function predicate location in a place of an entity; the two semantic aspects of the predicate, being located and the location, are not expressed in separate lexemes (see further III.8.3 Classifiers or verb stems in Danish Sign Language?).

Within the two major groups, the pronoun, which can refer by itself and be the scope of reference check and topicalization marking, is distinguished functionally from the determiner as part of a nominal. There also seems to be a functional distinction between the verb, which forms a clause with a nominal, and the particle, which links one referential nominal to another, apparently without forming a clause. The determiner and the particle then are constituents of nominals, while the pronoun and the verb are major clause constituents. Pointing signs in the form of the proform have the function of carrying information that is otherwise expressed in spatial modification of other signs.

6.2 The pronoun, the determiner, and information-packaging

Compared with the unemphatic, unmarked forms, the emphatic forms of the pronoun and the determiner have more phonetic weight. An emphatic form of the pronoun is seen in example (14) of section II.6.1 Types of pointing signs (repeated here as (1)); it is contrastive.

```
(1)   PRON+emphatic+fr BAD   /
      PRON+emphatic+fr----

      She was the one who was bad.
```

Contrast is one of the semantic-pragmatic features that are relevant in what has been called 'information-packaging' (Prince 1981, 224). Prince defines information-packaging as 'the tailoring of an utterance by a sender to meet the particular assumed needs of the intended receiver. That is, information-packaging in natural language reflects the sender's hypotheses about the receiver's assumptions and beliefs and strategies' (ibid., 224). Other semantic-pragmatic features that are relevant to information-

---

[7] Supalla and Newport (1978) demonstrate that there is often a form difference between related nouns and verbs in ASL. The noun and the verb share handshape, place of articulation, and shape of movement, but differ by systematic changes in directionality, manner, and frequency of movement. The main difference is that nouns are made with 'restrained' movement, while the movement in verb signs is 'continuous' or 'hold'. The difference is, however, almost exclusively seen in the citation form of the signs (ibid., 98) ('Citation form is the form of a sign a native speaker will produce when asked "What is the sign for ___?"' (ibid., 98)).

packaging are assumed familiarity (ibid., 232ff.), predictability, and saliency in the sense of the sender's assumptions about which entity the receiver has in his consciousness at the time of hearing the utterance (ibid., 228).

If a signer assumes that the receiver has little or no familiarity with the referent and she wants to give the receiver time to become acquainted with it, she uses determiners and pronouns with increased phonetic weight. This is demonstrated in the following example where the signer starts by saying that she wants to talk about a nursery school, and then goes on to explaining that it is her second child's nursery school:

```
(2)                                           _____t
      1.p TELL ABOUT NURSERY / THAT-IS 1.p.POSS CHILD NUMBER
                                _____squint
      SECOND+emphatic / PRON+emphatic+l.index / NAME CHARLOTTE /
      SECOND+emphatic---------------------------------------------

      Charlotte(M) DET+emphatic+l.index / DET+fr NURSERY /
      ---------------------------------

      I'll talk about a nursery school. My second child - she is called
      Charlotte [name sign], that is, Charlotte [the Mouth-Hand
      System] - it is her nursery school.
```

The signer uses the sign SECOND (Ill. 30), which is a two-handed sign. She taps the pad of her right index finger against the side of her left index finger four times and then uses the nondominant hand of SECOND in the following pronoun. For the pronoun, she changes the orientation of her dominant hand from palm down to palm facing left (Ill. 31) and taps her right index finger against the side of her left index finger three times. In the determiner (line 3), she makes only two tapping movements.

It is possible to use the fingers of the nondominant hand as loci for referents (called ordinal (tip) loci in ASL by Liddell (1990a, 189-192)). When the signer repeats the tapping movement of her right index finger against her left index finger in SECOND, she "breaks down" the sign SECOND in its parts and uses her left index finger as a locus for her daughter. She makes pronominal reference to her daughter by changing the orientation of her strong hand to the unmarked orientation of the index hand in PRON and continues the tapping movement. The difference between the two signs, SECOND and PRON, is shown by the change in hand orientation and by the nonmanual signals. The nonmanual signal squinted eyes starts when the signer changes her hand orientation. The scope of the nonmanual signal is only PRON+ emphatic+l.index.

What we see here is apparently a very strong emphasis on a particular locus. But when the signer refers to her daughter again, she does not use the locus of her left index finger: after she has explained that her first child went to the same nursery school, she reintroduces Charlotte by using her name only and she does not use the locus of her left index finger again.

(3)   CHARLOTTE START SOME ABOUT FOUR MONTH+pl. /

   c+SEND+fr DET+fr NURSERY /

   Charlotte started when she was about four months old. She was sent to the nursery school.

The apparent emphasis on the locus in the first part of (2) is not an emphasis on the locus, but on the referent. The marked forms of the pronoun in (2) serve to establish an assumedly unfamiliar referent, not a locus, in the receiver's consciousness.

The fact that a referent is not always represented by one and the same locus might lead to the assumption that referents need to be assigned to loci explicitly or that loci must be established (Mandel 1977, 76; Wilbur 1987, 153; Baker & Cokely 1980, 223; Newport & Meier 1985, 916). That is not what we see in Danish Sign Language: the association of referents with loci is not an explicit act or a statement of the kind 'I use this locus for that referent'. That is, the pointing sign that can be analysed as BE-AT does not occur in statements about a referent's association with a locus; it denotes a referent's location in a (referent) place. The verb form manifests the association of the referent with a particular locus, but the association is implied by the verb form; it is not stated explicitly.

The forms of the pronoun and the determiner with least phonetic weight are forms where the index finger does not point anywhere. These forms can occur when the signer assumes that the receiver knows the referent or that the referent is salient by being in the receiver's consciousness at the time of utterance (see example (7) of II.6.1 Types of pointing signs, and example (5) of II.4 Loci and referentiality, and the comments to the example).

In a discussion of the development of anaphoric terms from deictic ones in spoken languages, Greenberg points out a similar correlation between phonetic weight and information packaging:

> ...the use of an accented form in German for the demonstrative, and the same one without stress as an article is one which recurs elsewhere and involves a further iconic factor. Historically, loss of accent and sometimes phonetic reduction in the change from deixis to anaphora, mirrors the loss of prominence which comes with the change from making known to the mere expression of something as already known, a change from new to old information. In Hungarian, stressed az (the father of the two demonstratives) is unstressed as an article and loses final -z if the next word begins with a consonant. (Greenberg 1985, 276)

In Danish Sign Language, morphological variants of the pronoun and the determiner that have more phonetic weight than the unemphatic forms are used for contrast or emphasis and for giving the receiver time to become familiar with the referent. It is not yet clear to me whether the form difference between the undirected forms, the neutral, locus-marked forms, and the emphatic forms with more phonetic weight is so stable that it is possible to talk about a definite article (the undirected forms of the determiner), a determiner, and a demonstrative determiner. With respect to the pronoun, there would be three forms: a light pronoun unmarked for locus, a neutral pronoun marked for locus, and a demonstrative pronoun.

6.3 Person, place, and shifters

Entity and place
There is a basic formal and functional distinction between referential pointing signs and predicative pointing signs, but the referential pointing signs can be used to refer to both entities and locations (II.6.1 Types of pointing signs). The lack of a distinction between entities and locations demonstrates the origin of these signs in the pointing gesture:

> Any theory of deixis must surely take account of the fact (much discussed in philosophical treatments of ostensive definition) that the gesture of pointing itself will never be able to make clear whether it is some entity, some property of an entity, or some location that the addressee's attention is being directed to. (Lyons 1975, 65)

As the referential pointing signs do not distinguish reference to entities and reference to locations, it seems that Danish Sign Language cannot comply with Greenberg's universal 42:

> *Universal 42.* All languages have pronominal categories involving at least three persons and two numbers. (Greenberg 1966, 96)

Personal pronouns are what Jakobson (after Jespersen) calls *shifters* (Jakobson 1971), which means that their reference depends on who uses them. Jakobson uses Peirce's division of signs (in the broader sense of the word) into icons, indices, and symbols to characterise shifters. Shifters have a double status: they are indexical symbols. As a symbol, the form of a shifter is related to its content by convention, i.e. a convention makes *I* in English and *mimi* in Swahili mean 'the sender'. Being indexical, a shifter is in 'existential relation with the object it represents' (ibid., 132). It is the fact that *I* in English occurs with the referent (the sender) that makes it possible for us to know to whom *I* is used to refer on a given occasion.

Pointing gestures have the indexical function of shifters: we understand a pointing gesture's reference by its occurring with (being directed toward) the referent. But the pointing gesture is not a symbol. It has no conventional meaning. A pointing gesture where the index finger is directed toward the receiver does not mean 'the receiver' in the way that the symbol *you* in English means 'the receiver'. The pointing gesture is used to refer by occurring with the referent, directed toward the referent, and a pointing gesture does not specify the type of referent (sender, receiver, spoken-of person, or other).

Greenberg (1985) shows that personal pronouns are often related to demonstratives. He points out that the relations of iconicity and metaphor are asymmetrical relations between an icon or a metaphor and what it stands for: the icon or the metaphor stands for something else, not vice versa. But in the case of personal pronouns being historically derived from demonstratives, the direction of the mapping relation is less clear. The diachronic development is from demonstratives to personal pronouns. Synchronically, or psycholinguistically, however, Greenberg finds that the mapping relation is from person to place.

> Does it make more sense to say that 'here' is where I am or that 'I' am the one who is here? To me, at least, the second locution seems stranger. That is, it seems more "natural" to say that we map the participants in discourse into space than vice versa so that person becomes the model for place as the icon. (Greenberg 1985, 277)

The result is a paradox:

> It does seem...that we must assume that at some point the speakers acted counterintuitively [by deriving the personal pronouns from the demonstratives – EEP] to produce the historical consequences that we found. (ibid., 278)

The paradox can, however, be solved. As shifters, the demonstratives already contain the notion of person; they are understood in relation to the participants in the communication act, and their use depends not only on what they are used to refer to, but also on who uses them. Therefore, it is possible that the historical development of the personal pronouns reflects the perception of space and entities in space in a non-paradoxical way: we use space to keep track of people and other entities, and in that sense, space is primary. But what we focus on in space is humans or entities, and in that sense, they are primary. As mentioned in II.6.1 Types of pointing signs, Lakoff (1987, 491) describes the relation between entity and location as follows: the speech act value of pointing out an entity in a location is to direct the hearer's attention to the location, but the functional condition is to focus the hearer's awareness on the entity.

There is evidence from language acquisition that space is used to keep track of entities and that what we focus on is not space, but the entities found there. Bruner observed a boy who was acquiring English and used *boe* for birds. One evening he tried to recall some birds he had seen during the day, by pointing up while he said *boe*:

> He seemed to be locating in his "present" space an object recalled from memory. His lexeme, *boe*, served as a nominal specifier of his point with a spatial deictic in the absence of an actual object. (Bruner 1983, 76)

It seems that the child spontaneously concentrated on entities, but used places to keep track of them. Bruner also found that a mother pointed to pictures in books and made her child name what he saw. Almost 90% of the mother's names were names for whole objects, and half of the rest was proper names. The child was "trained" to communicate about entities even though the mother used points to locations. Human beings focus on entities, but use space to keep track of them.

Personal pronouns
First and second person pronouns are shifters used to refer to the sender and the receiver of the communication act. The form *I* has a permanent meaning ('the sender'), which is the symbol value of *I*. But when the communication roles change, *I*'s reference also changes: it is used to refer to whoever uses it. That is the index value of *I*. It is the combination of the meaning 'sender' or 'receiver' and changing reference, depending on who uses the words, that constitutes the category of *person* in language.

Pointing signs used for pronominal reference are forms of PRON. To preclude a specific interpretation, in this section I start by using the label PRON+c for the pointing sign in which the tip of the index hand makes contact with the signer's body. That is, I transcribe it as a form of PRON. Before analysing PRON with respect to the category of person, it is important to realise that the pointing signs in Danish Sign Language differ from prelinguistic or paralinguistic pointing gestures. The sign PRON is integrated in Danish Sign Language in a number of ways. PRON occurs in a system with a set of related, but formally and functionally different signs and with rules for their form variants (see II.6.1 Types of pointing signs, and II.6.2 The pronoun, the determiner, and information-packaging). There are morphologically related signs that can be used to refer to two, three, four and an unspecified number of entities. PRON can be modified for reference to many (including or excluding the signer, 'all of us', 'all of them/you'). It can be used both for deictic and for anaphoric reference. The orientation of the index hand in PRON assimilates to the orientation of the manual articulator of other signs in formally predictable ways. Finally, there is a possessive pronoun with a different form, but some of the same possibilities for modification as PRON.

In II.2 The frame of reference, I showed that entities, including humans, are often represented by the same locus as the place with which they have semantic affinity. The examples in II.4 Loci and referentiality, demonstrated that a referent's being animate, inanimate, or locative does not influence the probability of it being represented by a locus. Moreover, in II.6.1 Types of pointing signs, I showed that there is a formal difference between the unemphatic forms of PRON and the verb of location and the locative particle. Yet PRON can be used to refer to a location. All of this seems to indicate that the semantic notion human is not relevant to the pronoun PRON, which is one prerequisite to having personal pronouns.

The issue is more complex, however. The use of the index hand for deictic reference can be described in two ways. First, the pointing signs used for deictic reference can be interpreted in the light of prelinguistic or paralinguistic pointing: if A wants to refer to C, A points to C, and if B wants to refer to C, B points to C. In that sense, the two pointing signs are essentially identical. What determines their form is C's location in relation to A and B, and their reference is understood in this context. The points have no meaning besides their referential function.

Alternatively, because the index hand is used in other signs and may have a phonological value in these, it is possible to analyse pointing signs used for deictic reference in terms of the muscle activity required to produce any individual form of the pointing sign: if A wants to refer to C, A points to C, and if B wants to refer to C, B points to C; but unless A and B are in exactly the same location, the two pointing signs are formally different in terms of muscle activity or form. Conversely, if A and B are facing each other and they use formally identical pointing signs, they refer to different entities. In that sense, pointing signs used for deictic reference resemble shifters such as *here* and *there*: when A and B use the same form, they refer to different places and entities, and in order to refer to the same place or entity, they must use different forms.

The last analysis presupposes that signers perceive every possible form of the pointing sign as a separate symbol because of the differences in muscle activities. That is highly unlikely, since every separate form does not have a distinct meaning. The pointing sign made with the right arm at an angle of 45 degrees from the mid line at the elbow level does not have the same meaning from one use to another in the way that personal pronouns mean either 'the sender' or 'the receiver'.

The first person pronoun
One pointing gesture differs from the rest, namely the pointing sign that makes contact with the signer's body. The sign PRON+c has a stable form (a specific muscle activity) with a stable meaning ('the sender') and its reference depends on who uses it. In order to qualify as a shifter, PRON+c must be an indexical symbol. If it is possible to analyse PRON+c within the same framework as the first analysis presented above, i.e. on a par with prelinguistic or paralinguistic pointing, PRON+c is not a symbol.

Formally, PRON+c differs from other forms of PRON in two ways. First, except for pronouns modified for loci on the tip of the signer's fingers or thumb (see example (2) of II.6.2 The pronoun, the determiner, and information-packaging, and Ill. 31), PRON+c is the only form in which the manual articulator makes contact with something, namely the signer's body as representing the referent. Second, PRON+c is the only version of PRON that is not necessarily made with an index hand. In one monologue, out of 25 points to the signer, only five were made with an index hand. Ten points were made with a very loose index hand with the middle finger, the ring finger and the little finger only slightly bent. Nine points were made with a loose flat hand, and none of the fingers were bent into the hand. Six points were made with the same handshape as the following verb. Other forms of PRON than PRON+c are always made with an index hand.[8]

Semantically, PRON+c deviates from other versions of PRON in two other ways.

---

8 It is possible to make non-first person reference by means of other handshapes than an index hand, e.g. a fist with an extended thumb. The circumstances of the use of this form are not clear to me, but it cannot be analysed as a variant of PRON resulting from assimilation or fast, casual signing as can the variants of PRON+c.

First, it can only be used to refer to humans or entities that can occur as senders in a communication act. Second, it does not necessarily refer to the person whom the index hand is pointing at. In reported speech, PRON+c may be used to refer to the quoted sender, not the quoting sender, even when the index hand is pointing at the quoting sender. Sometimes the quoting sender changes body position, in which case we might say that PRON+c is a different form (the signer is no longer "in the position of the quoting sender"). Such an analysis is, however, refuted by the fact that a change of body position is not a necessary part of reported speech and that it can also occur when the signer quotes her own remark to somebody else (see II.5 Shifted reference, shifted attribution of expressive elements, and shifted locus). No other form of PRON can be directed at one person and refer to somebody else. In that sense, the meaning of PRON+c is conventional and PRON+c is a symbol.

As PRON+c differs from other forms of PRON formally as well as semantically and is an indexical symbol which means 'the sender' and refers to whoever uses it or to a quoted sender, Danish Sign Language does have a first person pronoun. Thus, PRON+c is more appropriately transcribed as 1.p.[9]

The non-first person pronoun
All other forms of PRON than PRON+c always depend on where the referent is located or, with anaphoric reference, on the locus by which the referent is represented. There is no one form of PRON corresponding to a second person pronoun. It is only when A and B are facing each other that A's point to the receiver (B) can be formally identical with (is the same muscle activity) as B's point to the receiver (A). Points to the receiver are usually accompanied by eye contact with the receiver, while points to people not taking part in the communication act may or may not be accompanied by eye contact with the receiver and may or may not be accompanied by eye gaze in the same direction as the pronoun. Gaze direction is not part of the pronoun, however, because eye contact with the receiver is generally found in other contexts, e.g. at the end of a topicalized constituent or at the end of a question, including a question ending with a pronoun which refers to somebody other than the receiver (such as a sentence meaning 'Is he hungry?'). Thus eye contact is a regulator of the communication event rather than part of a second person pronoun (see also Baker 1977; Baker & Padden 1978; Meier 1990). A point to the actual receiver of the context of utterance cannot be used to refer to the original receiver of the quoted speech act. That is, it is not possible to quote a question meaning 'Are you hungry?' and point at the actual receiver, unless the actual receiver is identical with the original receiver. Both semantically and formally, then, PRON used to refer to the receiver differs from the first person pronoun 1.p: it is not a symbol with a fixed form having a particular meaning, but resembles other forms of PRON.

---

9 For reasons which I will come back to in III.6.3 The many uses of the *c*-form, I transcribe agreement forms of verbs which involve the sender locus with +*c*, not +*1.p*.

Disregarding plural forms, the basic distinction in pronouns is then between the pronoun with first person reference and the pronoun with non-first person reference. Within the latter different forms are distinguished with respect to loci.

Meier (1990) presents a somewhat similar analysis of pronouns in ASL. He finds that ASL also has a first person pronoun and a non-first person pronoun, as well as a distinction between singular and plural forms. Besides basing his argumentation on reported speech, Meier mentions the ASL signs WE, OUR, and OURSELVES, whose place of articulation is at best only partially motivated (ibid., 180). There are no such signs in Danish Sign Language.

Alternative analyses of pronouns in signed languages
Within the theory of Government and Binding, Lillo-Martin and Klima (1990) analyse the pronominal pointing signs in ASL as forms of one pronoun. They see locus markers on the pronoun as manifestations of the referential indices, R-indices, that are written as letter subscripts in analyses of nominals. In what they call discourse representation structures, each indexed noun phrase is assigned a discourse referent, which also has an index. Points to the signer that are used to refer to somebody else are handled by means of what they call 'shifting framework': 'shifting the body position, and then signing "me" when you mean "John"' (ibid., 195). A shifting framework introduces a new equation for discourse referents in the discourse representation structure with 'the effect of interpreting an R-index with the discourse referent of another R-index. Which R-index it is interpreted to be depends on the associations made when the shift takes place and on the direction of the shift' (ibid., 202).

The analysis is built on data which include points to the signer that do not refer to the signer, also in contexts that are not reported speech. That is, in Lillo-Martin and Klima's data, what I call shifted reference can occur also in nonquoted signing. Moreover, the data include pronominal reference to the signer by means of a pronoun modified for a locus other than the sender locus (described as 'highly marked' (ibid., 204)). Apparently, the analysis presupposes that there is always 'shifting framework' (i.e. changes in the signer's body position) which can disambiguate the direction of the points. That is clearly not the case in Danish Sign Language. There is, however, generally some contextual clue to the interpretation of an utterance as reported speech. It may be a change in body or head orientation or in gaze direction, it may be a lexical introduction which identifies the quoted sender, or it may be changes in the facial expression. The signals are usually sufficient to disambiguate points to the signer, but then markers of direct discourse in English could also be said to be sufficient to disambiguate occurrences of the pronoun *I* and we could analyse *I* as a variant of one general pronoun. The reason this would be unsatisfactory is, of course, that *I* differs formally from other pronominal forms in English. Lillo-Martin and Klima do not comment on any form differences in points to the signer and points in other directions in ASL.

Lillo-Martin and Klima's analysis also presupposes that signers never change their body position when they quote themselves. Again, that does not hold for Danish Sign Language. In the context of reported speech, changes in body and head orientation or gaze direction primarily indicate the original receiver and only indirectly the quoted sender (see II.5 Shifted reference, shifted attribution of expressive elements, and shifted locus). Signers may also change their head or body orientation when they quote their own remarks; their orientation can be exactly identical in reported speech where the quoted sender is the signer and in reported speech with another quoted sender. In both cases, the signer can move slightly in the opposite direction of the original receiver's locus and rotate her body or head slightly so that she faces the direction of the original receiver's locus, and she may look in that direction as well. What counts is the locus of the original receiver, not what locus the signer has used for the quoted sender earlier in the discourse. Moreover, a signer also may change her body position in nonquoted signing. For instance, one signer talked about the city where his parents live and where he used to live. He used the locus forward-right-up for the city. When he signed NOW LIVE 112
1.p COPENHAGEN HERE ('Now I live here in Copenhagen'), he moved his body back-left to create a maximal contrast between his former and his present place of living. It is not reported speech, and the first person pronoun 1.p is used to refer to the signer even though he has changed his body position.

For Swedish Sign Language, Ahlgren (1984a, 1990) rejects an analysis of pronominal pointing signs as personal pronouns on the following grounds: as in pre- or paralinguistic pointing gestures, the index hand in pointing signs is directed toward the referent, whether the pointing signs are used to refer to the signer or to somebody else. Ahlgren does not, however, consider whether points to the signer can be used in reported speech for other referents than the signer, nor does she comment on possible form differences between pointing signs used to refer to the sender and other pointing signs.

Berenz and Ferreira Brito (1990) find that both ASL and Brazilian Cities Sign Language have first as well as second person pronouns. Their analysis is partly based on the claim that eye gaze is an obligatory part of the second person pronoun; Meier (1990) rejects such an analysis for ASL. Berenz and Ferreira Brito analyse pointing signs used to refer to the sender and the receiver as depending on the front/back axis, and they refer to Fillmore's analysis of the front/back axis in relation to locative expressions in spoken languages as 'determined by certain inherent asymmetries of a reference object' (Fillmore 1982, 37). The front/back axis should, therefore, be understood as anthropocentric. Fillmore further distinguishes two strategies for assigning front and back to entities without inherent front/back orientation: the ego-opposed strategy based on the canonical encounter (the entity is seen as "facing" the speaker), and the ego-aligned strategy where the speaker sees the entity as turning its "back" on the speaker (see also here II.3.2 A comparison with time lines in spoken languages). The choice of strategy is conventional. Even though the sender and the receiver are entities with inherent front/back orientation, Berenz and Ferreira Brito claim that pointing signs referring to the sender and the receiver can be analysed as representing the ego-aligned strategy in that, 'the orientation of the fingertip is *opposite* to the orientation of the referents' bodies' (ibid., 28 – emphasis in the original). They conclude that 'ASL pronouns, based in this anthropocentric axis, are conventional, not transparent' (ibid., 28). That is, the analysis rests on the assumption that the pronouns are based in the anthropocentric, front/back, axis; but this assumption is unfounded, since the index hand of pointing signs points in the direction of the entity referred to no matter its position in relation to the signer.

Acquisition of pronouns
Pointing signs as pronouns have been the focus of research on deaf children's acquisition of signed languages in several studies (Pizzuto & Williams 1979; Petitto 1983, 1985, 1987; Ahlgren 1984b; Ravnholt & Engberg-Pedersen 1986; Hoffmeister summarised in Wilbur 1987, 207-211). Some researchers have focused in particular on the acquisition of pointing signs used to refer to the participants in the communication act, i.e. the potential personal pronouns. Ahlgren found that a Swedish deaf boy had an unproblematic and unbroken transition from using prelinguistic pointing to using pointing signs to refer to himself and the receiver in signing. In contrast, Petitto saw a more complicated development in the language of an American deaf girl. The girl went through a period where she did not use pointing signs to refer to people. Instead, she used the signs MOTHER and FATHER or she used name signs. A few times she referred to herself by means of the sign GIRL. Later the girl used a point outward to refer to herself. Petitto interpreted the form as 'a non-reciprocal, non-deictic, "frozen" lexical sign that stands for her, and her alone. In short, it is her name, rather than a pronoun' (1983, 60 – emphasis in the original). Apparently the girl in Petitto's investigation made a distinction between humans and nonhumans. But it is not clear that she perceived the pronouns in general as shifters.

The children's differential development may be a result of different language input. In interviews, a few Danish mothers of deaf children reported that they had used name signs and nouns to refer to their children and to themselves in communication with their small deaf children. Others always used forms of PRON and the first person pronoun 1.p. All the mothers were native signers (Ravnholt & Engberg-Pedersen 1986).

As the use of the first person pronoun 1.p in reported speech is what makes it an indexical symbol rather than a mere index, we can expect children to encounter problems in acquiring the means for expressing reported speech. That that may indeed be the case is demonstrated by an example from Petitto's study. In a situation where the child, her mother, and Petitto were present, Petitto cut her finger; the child turned to her mother and signed what Petitto transcribes as YOU HURT:

A close examination of the videotape revealed the unusual fact that the child (age 1;11) had taken on my role as if she had been cut rather than me...the child had grossly distorted and painful facial expressions and clutched and pulled at her "bleeding" index finger as if she was in pain. (Petitto 1983, 50 – emphasis in the original)[10]

As mentioned, the child used a pointing sign with the index hand directed outward to refer to herself, and here she seems to use the nonmanual signals of shifted attribution of expressive elements as well as shifted reference (her form meaning 'I') with a sensation verb (see II.5 Shifted reference, shifted attribution of expressive elements, and shifted locus). In Danish Sign Language, and according to Meier (1990) in ASL as well, shifted reference is unacceptable outside reported speech. The example demonstrates the child's problems in acquiring the correct use of pronouns in different contexts with shifted reference and shifted attribution of expressive elements. If she really used the form transcribed as YOU in the sense of 'I', it could not be used in the particular context as it is not reported speech, but a context where shifted attribution of expressive elements is appropriate.

Summary
In summary, the non-first person pronoun PRON in Danish Sign Language differs from prelinguistic or paralinguistic pointing gestures in that it is formally and semantically integrated in a system of signs. It does not distinguish reference to humans from reference to other entities or to places. Especially, there is no distinct form that is used to refer to the receiver of the communication act. The first person pronoun 1.p differs from forms of PRON in that it has variants in free variation (different handshapes), as well as bound form variants (handshape assimilation to the handshapes of verbs). Moreover, the first person pronoun 1.p is the only distinguishable form of pointing signs that is used only to refer to senders of communication acts. It is also the only form that can be used to refer to somebody other than the person toward whom the index finger is directed: in reported speech, the first person pronoun 1.p can be used to refer to the reported sender. This shows that the first person pronoun 1.p is a symbol with a stable meaning, 'the sender.'

---

10   This interpretation seems to indicate that the child used YOU to mean 'I' rather than as a name for herself.

7 Discourse and space: Conclusion

Discourse-dependent and inherent features of referents
The main goal of this part of the book has been to determine the function of loci and the frame of reference in discourse, thereby contributing to an understanding of what loci are. The directions of anaphoric loci are projections of referents. Referents are cognitively relevant products of the discourse, but in talking about entities in the context of utterance, signers can point in the direction of the entities. In talking about absent entities, signers may use the directions of loci as projections of the cognitively "present" referents. That is, loci are based on deixis, but can serve an anaphoric purpose.

The conventions for choosing loci show that, even though loci have a deictic basis, they also reflect discourse-dependent semantic-pragmatic features of the referents. The choice of loci for anaphoric purposes may seem arbitrary when one and the same referent can be represented by different loci in different texts and even within one text. In (1) the referent Castberggaard (an institution) is represented by the locus sideward-left, in (2) (from the same monologue) by the locus forward, and in (3) (from a different monologue) by the locus sideward-right.

(1)   AND-THEN DEAF POSS HIGH^SCHOOL / NOW EXISTENTIAL+sl

        DET+sl CASTBERGGAARD DET+sl / ACCOMPLISH[+] /

        The next item [on the agenda] was a folk high school for the deaf. Now Castberggaard is there. So that has been accomplished.

(2)   ... ALSO DET+f CASTBERGGAARD DET+f / ACCOUNTS ETCETERA /

        [He also helps] Castberggaard with their accounts and so on.

(3)   1.p EARLIER CASTBERGGAARD+sr BE-AT+sr /

        1.p SIGN-LANGUAGE^COURSE BE-AT+sr /

        Once I was at Castberggaard, for a sign language course.

All the same, referents are not associated with loci in a random fashion. In (1), Castberggaard is mentioned in a part of the monologue in which no other referent is represented by a locus. Castberggaard is a significant referent for the signer's line of argumentation and is, therefore, represented by a locus, and she chooses the locus left consistent with the iconic convention for geographical locations as Castberggaard is west of the place where the signer is.

In (2) from another part of the same monologue, Castberggaard is mentioned along with other institutions that receives help from the individual in question. The other referent, the deaf clubs, is represented by the locus forward-left and the man who helps them by the locus sideward-left. The locus forward for Castbergaard underlines the semantic affinity of Castberggaard to the deaf clubs in this particular situation (both receive help from the man), at the same time distinguishing Castberggaard from the clubs.

After (3), the signer goes on to talking about her husband and she uses the locus forward-left for her husband. Castberggaard is only mentioned parenthetically and it has semantic affinity with the signer. The locus right is contrasted with the locus forward-left both with respect to the left-right dimension and with respect to the front-back dimension because it is closer to the signer than the locus forward-left (see Fig. 4 in II.1.2 The frame of reference). By using a locus for Castberggaard here despite the referent's inferior discourse status, the signer underlines the physical distance between herself and her husband and the fact that she was not present at the location that is central to her story.

The semantic-pragmatic value of loci is particularly clear when a new referent is represented by a locus that is already used for a referent. The locus then invests the new referent with a particular meaning. For instance, the sign MEET can be modified for a locus that is already associated with a deaf club. The meaning is then 'a meeting at the deaf club'. Nominals referring to the possessum can include one or more signs modified for the locus of the possessor, and nominals denoting events can include one or more signs modified for a locus of a time line already associated with a time referent and thereby acquire a temporal meaning.

In discussing anaphora in spoken languages, Lyons (1977, 667ff.) contrasts Latin demonstratives used for anaphoric purposes and the English gender-marked pronouns *he* and *she* used for the same purpose. The anaphoric function of the gender-marked pronouns in English is based on a semantic difference reflecting features of the referents, while the foundation of the anaphoric function of the Latin demonstratives is deixis (and gender). In Latin, the distal demonstrative *ille* can be used to refer to the referent of the more remote of two possible antecedents and the proximal demonstrative *hic* to the nearer of the two possible antecedents. Here the locative notions are used of the temporal relation between the anaphoric expression and its antecedent in discourse:

> The basically deictic component in an anaphoric expression directs the attention of the addressee to a certain part of the text or co-text and tells him, as it were, that he will find the referent there. It is not of course the referent itself that is in the text or co-text. The referent is in the universe-of-discourse, which is created by the text and has a temporal structure imposed upon it by the text; and this temporal structure is subject to continuous modification. (Lyons 1977, 670)

Signed discourse has a spatial structure and develops in time. Some of the conventions for choosing loci are independent of the temporal development of the discourse, e.g. the convention of the canonical location and the iconic convention. The iconic convention means that the frame of reference mirrors the situation in point; the frame of reference (or its organisation) may change to the extent that the situation changes (see, however, *Changes in the frame of reference* in III.8.6 Polymorphemic verbs and space). Such changes reflect a temporal development in the situation referred to, not the temporal development of the discourse as such. Other conventions for organising the frame of reference depend on the discourse context. Whether a referent is represented by a locus at all depends on its discourse value, and a number of conventions for choosing loci all state that the association of the referent with a particular locus is influenced by features of the referent which depend on the discourse context. The conventions are the convention of comparison, the convention of possession, and the conventions of the side-to-side and the diagonal dimensions.

Both spatial and temporal factors are reflected in the frame of reference, which is at the same time stable across clause boundaries and dynamic through the discourse. The stability of the frame of reference contributes to the reference-tracking function of the loci and to the possibility of expressing a specific point of view through shifted locus. When signers signal that they use the sender locus for another referent than themselves, by changes in body and head orientation and/or in gaze direction, the receiver's identification of the intended referent is aided by a stable frame of reference. On the other hand, the dynamic nature of the frame of reference makes it possible to signal different layers of discourse meaning and different sections of discourse. The frame of reference and other features of the discourse are interdependent: the frame of reference can only serve the functions which depend on its stability, if other features of the discourse (e.g. the unity of time, place, and action; exposition vs. narration) allow the receiver to recognise its stability in certain sections of the discourse. Conversely, being dynamic, the frame of reference can contribute to signalling different layers of discourse meaning and different sections of the discourse such as changes in time, place, and action, or narration vs. exposition.

Reference-tracking
Foley and Van Valin (1984, Chapter 7) describe four types of reference-tracking mechanisms for spoken languages. They are: 1) pragmatic pivots in combination with voice oppositions; 2) switch reference; 3) assignment of co-reference on the basis of sociolinguistic variables (in particular, honorific speech levels); and 4) gender. Deixis is missing from the list, which is odd since expressions that can be used deictically are relevant to reference-tracking in, for instance, Latin as pointed out by Lyons (1977, 667ff). Loci are based on deixis, but reflect to some extent semantic-pragmatic features other than pure deixis. Therefore, it is well worth examining whether the anaphoric reference-tracking function of loci shares features with anaphoric reference-tracking systems of spoken languages, such as those discussed by Foley and Van Valin. Loci are expressed in nominals and verbs and the only similar category in Foley and Van Valin's list is gender:

> [The 'gender system'] involves the overt morphological coding of a classification of NPs, although it need not be on the basis of sex. These morphological distinctions are carried by anaphoric elements; anaphoric elements of the same class can be interpreted as co-referent, while those of different classes cannot. (Foley & Van Valin 1984, 323)

Gender plays a minor role in English. Still, English has a three-way classification of nouns based on animacy and gender in the third person singular pronouns, and their example from English illustrates the reference-tracking mechanism of gender:

a. John decided to talk to Mary about *her* dog because *it* had been causing problems in the neighbourhood.
b. *She* was very surprised, as *she* had no idea that *it* had been getting into other people's garages and garbage cans.
c. *He* was pleased that *she* did not react defensively to *his* mentioning the situation. (ibid., 323)

In Danish, the same object may be referred to either by the noun *kop* ('cup'), which belongs to one gender class, or by the noun *krus* ('mug'), which belongs to a different gender class. Depending on whether I would refer to the object by *kop* or *krus*, I refer to it by either the pronoun *den* or the pronoun *det*. Danish nouns are inherently marked for one of the two noun classes, a few being marked for both. By contrast, in some languages a nominal and, in English, the third person pronoun can reflect inherent semantic features of the referent or a particular view of the referent (some refer to a particular dog by *it*, others by *he*). A Frenchman may refer to someone as *la nouvelle professeur* in the feminine gender, thereby implying that the new teacher is a woman. That is natural gender (Lyons 1968, 284).

Nouns in Danish Sign Language are not inherently marked as belonging to particular "locus classes". Neither do loci reflect inherent semantic features of the referents as natural gender does. But in particular contexts particular referents are more likely to be associated with some loci than with others. For instance, in a context where the signer has mentioned some guests at a party including herself and her husband, the pronominal form TWO+pron.+c+sl ('the two of us') is immediately understood as referring to the signer and her husband, even when the signer has not previously used the locus sideward-left for her husband. In the context, the signer could not use TWO+pron.+c+fl with the locus forward-left for her husband without an introduction, and, at the same time, no other referent of the context qualifies more for the locus sideward-left, close to the signer. Thus, TWO+pron.+c+sl must refer to the signer and her husband. In the same way, the reference-tracking function of *he* and *she* in Foley and Van Valin's example depends on the meaning of the words and the fact that *John* is used for male referents and *Mary* for female referents.

Summarising, loci can be used for anaphoric purposes like demonstratives in spoken languages. To fulfil their function, spoken language demonstratives depend on the receiver's memory of the temporal structure of the discourse. Similarly, loci depend on the receiver's memory of the spatial and temporal structure of the discourse to fulfil their reference-tracking function. But unlike "pure" demonstratives, loci reflect discourse-dependent semantic-pragmatic features of the referents which may contribute to making it easier for the receiver to remember and sort out the different referents. The closest equivalent to loci as a reference-tracking mechanism in Foley and Van Valin's list is, therefore, gender and in particular natural gender which is a referent-dependent notion. Because they have meaning, loci also contribute to building up the semantic-pragmatic structure of the discourse.

III

Verbs and Space

1 Localism and transitivity

Localism
In the first half of Part III, I focus on the ways primarily verbs in Danish Sign Language are modified to express the relations between the constituents of the clause, and the modifications of verbs and signs from other word classes that express distribution of the state, event or process denoted by the verb, predicate or clause.

In research on spoken languages, linguists have found that the expression of grammatical relations is often related or similar to the expression of locative relations. These findings have given rise to *localist* theories of language (Lyons 1977, 718ff.). Localists point out that the valency roles agent, course, and source, on the one hand, and patient, effect, and goal, on the other, often resemble each other in their use of grammatical cases. An example of the association of goal and recipient is seen in derived verb forms in Swahili where a verb's valency can be changed by an affix *-ia* or *-ea* depending on the previous vowel. The derived form of the verb *-imba* ('sing') is *-imbia* which means 'sing for (someone)', while the derived form *-endea* from *-enda* ('go') means 'go to (a place)' (see Ashton 1944, 218-219). That is, the same affix can change an intransitive verb of verbal activity and an intransitive verb of motion to verb forms which can take either beneficiary or goal arguments.

The parallel between a motion verb and a communication verb in Danish Sign Language is brought out by the following two examples:

(1) CHARLOTTE START SOME ABOUT FOUR MONTH+pl. /
     c+SEND+fr DET+fr NURSERY /   (Ill. 32)
     Charlotte started when she was about four months old. She was sent to the nursery school.

(2) 1.p TELL c+EXPLAIN+sl GRANDMOTHER / PRON+fd DEAF / (Ill. 33)
     I told her grandmother, 'She is deaf.'

The verb c+SEND+fr (Ill. 32) is made with a movement of the hand from outside the right side of the signer's chin forward. The verb c+EXPLAIN+sl (Ill. 33) is made with the tips of the fingers facing left and the bases of the hands facing the signer. Both c+SEND+fr and c+EXPLAIN+sl are followed by a nominal, DET+fr NURSERY and GRANDMOTHER, respectively. In (1), the nominal denotes the goal of the action; in (2), it denotes the recipient. As in Swahili, the relationship between a motion verb and its goal argument is expressed by the same formal means as the relationship between a communication verb and its recipient argument; in Danish Sign Language, the expression is spatial.

Gruber (1976, 33ff.) describes the meaning of clauses like (1) and (2) as both involving motion. He calls the transferred item the Theme: with c+SEND+fr in (1), the Theme is a child; with c+EXPLAIN+sl in (2), it is an utterance. In (1), there is no nominal reference to what Gruber calls the Source of the movement, while in (2), the first person pronoun 1.p represents the Source. In (1), the Goal is DET+fr NURSERY, and in (2), it is GRANDMOTHER. Gee and Kegl (1982; see also Gee & Goodhart 1988, 61; Kegl & Schley 1986; Kegl 1990) find that

> American Sign Language (ASL), a language made in space, expresses the locative base of language, and the way other grammatical and semantic systems are built upon this base, in a particularly perspicuous manner ... the verbal system of ASL represents quite clearly the way in which all languages are ultimately built up from a locative base, thus confirming the locative hypothesis. (Gee & Kegl 1982, 186)

Other researchers likewise claim that the spatial modification of verbs in ASL should be described in terms of the semantic locative cases source and goal (Fischer & Gough 1978; see also Friedman 1975, 956; 1976, 128-29). Still others, however, find form differences between verbs with person agreement and verbs with a locative meaning (see III.3 Earlier verb classifications).

Transitivity
In spoken languages, even though the same form can be used to express both locative and nonlocative relations, subject coding is more typical of agent arguments and object coding more typical of patient arguments. These facts lie behind another type of description of the relations between a verb and its arguments, namely descriptions in terms of transitivity. The notion of transitivity in Hopper and Thompson's definition includes the localist point of view:

> Transitivity is traditionally understood as a global property of an entire clause, such that an activity is 'carried-over' or 'transferred' from an agent to a patient. Transitivity in the traditional view thus necessarily involves at least two participants (...) and an action which is typically EFFECTIVE in some way. (Hopper & Thompson 1980, 251 – emphasis in the original)

That is, transfer is part of transitivity, but transitivity also includes the notion of effect: the action is not only a transfer, it has an effect. Moreover, transitivity includes the notion of agent. A clause that ranks high on the transitivity scale has at least two participants, A and O, where A (for Agent) and O (for Object) are used to 'refer to the two participants in a two-participant clause' (ibid., 252). Hopper and Thompson set up a list of ten parameters as component parts of transitivity. *Volitionality* covers the fact that 'The effect on the patient is typically more apparent when the A is presented as acting purposefully' (ibid., 252). *Agency* is included as a parameter:

> It is obvious that participants high in Agency can effect a transfer of an action in a way that those low in Agency cannot. Thus the normal interpretation of *George startled me* is that of a perceptible event with perceptible consequences; but that of *The picture startled me* could be completely a matter of an internal state. (ibid., 252)

Hopper and Thompson see transitivity as a matter of degree. Each parameter is a scale on which a clause can be ranked.

The difference between a localist description and a description in terms of transitivity is that in the latter, the semantic notions of agent and patient play a more central role than the semantic notions of source and goal. While a localist description points out that nonlocative notions are coded like locative notions, a description in terms of transitivity views the coding of the notions of agent and patient as more central than the coding of locative notions. That is, a description which takes transitivity to be the central notion will take sentences such as *He swam the Channel* or *My guitar broke a string* as marginal or nontypical members, or else as metaphorical extensions of the transitivity construction (Taylor 1989, 210-217). *He swam the Channel* is a transitive construction that correlates with the intransitive construction *He swam across the Channel*; in the transitive construction, 'the path has been incorporated into the verb' (ibid., 211). In *My guitar broke a string*, the subject designates the scope or setting of the event or its location, which means that the subject differs from the prototypical agent subject of transitive constructions.

Many have pointed out that transitive clauses code the events most cognitively salient to the language users (see also Lakoff & Johnson 1980, 69-72; Slobin 1981, 185; DeLancey 1987). Lyons (1977, 490-91) underlines the view that language is a way of coding a particular perception of a situation. The situation where X picks up a knife and stabs Y and Y immediately falls to the ground dead can be described: a) as a single event; b) as a process that is extended in time; or c) as a sequence of two or more situations. If we describe the situation as *X killed Y*, we describe it as a single event. Lyons concludes:

> The fact that there are so many transitive verbs with the same valence as 'kill', not only in English and the Indo-European languages, but possibly in all languages, would suggest that as human beings, we are particularly interested in the results of our purposive actions and in the effects that our actions have upon patients. (ibid., 491)

That is, we are not only interested in the 'transfer' of a knife from one 'location' to another, but in X's intentions and the consequences for Y.

In Danish Sign Language, the verb in a clause meaning 'I gave it to him' (Ill. 34) and the verb in a clause meaning 'I handed it to him on a tray' (Ill. 35) both include movement toward the locus of the referent 'him'. In a localist framework, the difference between the two verbs might be described as the difference between including an element TO in the first verb and including an element TOWARD in the second (see Gee & Kegl 1982). But such an analysis fails to bring out what Lyons points out about *kill*, namely that the verb GIVE in the first clause denotes a single punctual event, while the verb in the second clause denotes a process. Moreover, GIVE denotes a conventional action. GIVE may be used even in cases where no one actually hands over something to somebody, but rather mails it or bequeaths it in a will or the like. GIVE codes these transactions as a type of event that is salient to the language users.

The two verbs in Danish Sign Language also differ formally. The verb in the first sentence is made with a lax flat hand, and the movement of the hand in the direction of the locus of the IO argument is brought about by an extension of the wrist and elbow. The verb in the second clause is made with a tense flat hand which the signer moves toward the locus of the potential recipient by extending the elbow joint to an appropriate degree. Moreover, the signer is likely to shift her gaze either to her hand or in the direction of the recipient's locus in the second clause, but not in the first. The verb in the second clause is a polymorphemic verb (see III.8 Polymorphemic verbs).

Everyday means of communication can be expected to develop the possibility of fulfilling cognitive and social needs to express types of transitive and intransitive events without focusing on their perceptual details. Localist theories underline the locative basis of many meaning relations; but precisely because signs are made in space, it is essential to examine to what extent signs and their modifications signify semantic and pragmatic notions that are not primarily locative.

2 Different types of modifications: An overview

Types of changes in form
In this section, I introduce three types of modifications, leaving the morphology of polymorphemic signs for separate treatment in III.8. In I.6.1 The articulatory means of signed languages, I distinguished five types of form changes:
1. the intensity of the sign's movement is changed (Ill. 7);
2. the sign is reduplicated;
3. the sign undergoes spatial change, i.e. a change in the position or orientation of the hand(s);
4. the sign is embedded in a movement of the hand(s) (Ill. 9b), or an extra movement of the hand(s) is *added* (Ill. 6a); and
5. one-handed signs become two-handed, with both hands moving either alternately or simultaneously.[1]

In relation to the theme of this book, I am particularly interested in types three and four. Type three involves loci, as the orientational or positional change of the base form expresses the sign's modification for one or two loci. Type four does not involve loci, but the extra movement of the hand(s) is extended in space. Form changes of types two and five are often combined with form changes of type four. I leave out of consideration modifications that only affect the intensity of the movement of the sign's base form and modifications that are expressed by reduplication only. Such modifications weaken or intensify the base form's meaning or have a quantificational aspectual meaning (Dik 1989, 187), such as iterative, habitual, or frequentative aspect (for examples from ASL, Swedish Sign Language, and Danish Sign Language of modifications of this kind with an aspectual meaning, see Fischer 1973; Klima & Bellugi 1979, Chapter 11; Fischer & Gough 1978; Anderson 1982; Bergman 1983; Padden & Perlmutter 1987; Engberg-Pedersen 1989; Sandler 1990b; Bergman & Dahl in press). I do include some modifications that are expressed by a combination of reduplication and embedding in a linear movement and have a meaning of distribution over time, i.e. also a form of quantificational aspectual meaning. The reason for including these forms is that they are modified for the time lines (for an example, see Ill. 29) and in this sense make use of space.

As mentioned before, form changes of type four often combine with type two reduplication: the reduplication of the sign is embedded in a linear, circular, semicircular or random movement of the hand(s) as demonstrated by BECKON+ multiple in Ill. 9b. When a sign is reduplicated and embedded in a movement, the movement of the sign's base form may be reduced; the movement is usually retained as a first cycle in the beginning of the linear/circular/semicircular/random movement

---
[1] Some one-handed verb signs have two-handed forms with a distributive meaning, but without a reduplication of the movement of each hand. Whether the "addition" of a hand can be described as reduplication of the sign, I leave for further research. (See also Anderson 1982; Padden & Perlmutter 1987; Bergman & Dahl in press.)

and is then gradually reduced, even to elimination. If the movement of the base form is eliminated, there are of course no further cycles. The gradual reduction (in some cases to zero) of the base form movement has no morphological value. Changes of type four can also consist of a final semicircular, or linear movement, as in c+GIVE+multiple+fr (Ill. 6a). Alternatively, such a movement can be substituted for the movement of the sign's base form.

Modifications for distribution, agreement, and marking for a specific point of view
Changes of type four with an added linear, circular, semicircular, or random movement express different kinds of distribution over entities, locations, or moments or periods in time. I use *distribution* as a superordinate term for these modifications, of which there are many morphologically different kinds. They are not restricted to verbs, but can occur with signs from different sign classes, as well as with clauses. An example with a number sign in predicative function modified for distribution is seen in (1). It comes from a discussion between two deaf persons about shorter working hours:

(1)   THIRTY+multiple /   (Ill. 36)
       Everyone [who works shorter hours works] thirty [hours a week].

The base form of THIRTY is made with a short sideways movement. In (1), the sign is reduplicated and embedded in a horizontal semicircular movement (Ill. 36 shows the initial and the final position of the hand in the modified sign). The modification of THIRTY has an exhaustive meaning.[2]

Another type of spatial modification is the modification of a sign for one or two loci. I describe this kind of modification as *agreement*, except in some cases where a particular group of verbs, agreement verbs, are modified for the sender locus. Very often the sender locus is used for another referent than the signer in agreement verbs: the verb takes a marker for the sender locus in its A cell, i.e. the cell which takes the locus marker for the verb's A argument (see I.6.3 Liddell and Johnson's sequential form analysis of signs). Such verb forms can be analysed as showing *agreement omission* or as being *marked for a specific point of view* (see III.6. The many uses of the *c*-form).

---

2 Padden (1988b, 34-35) distinguishes *exhaustive* and *multiple* inflection in ASL. If an ASL verb is inflected for the exhaustive, the stem is executed at least three times with the end points displaced; the multiple inflection consists of a sweep arc displacement in the horizontal plane. Both forms exist in Danish Sign Language. For instance, THIRTY in (1) can be made with either an unbroken semicircular movement after an initial version of the sign THIRTY, or it can be made with a series of short sideways movements (reduplication of the base form) embedded in the semicircular movement of the hand. But there does not seem to be a semantic difference between the two versions. Whether the modified forms of THIRTY are interpreted as distribution to many or distribution to everyone depends on whether the group is definite or not, but this is not marked in the language. That is, the interpretation of +*multiple* as 'to many' or 'to all' seems to depend on the context only.

Pragmatic organisation of the clause
In order to understand the different kinds of agreement contexts in Danish Sign Language, we must look at a few facts about clause structure in the language. A clause such as (1) is highly ambiguous out of context as is (2):

(2)   PRON+fr THIRTY /

Example (2) may mean 'He/she/it/they are thirty years old/are thirty in number/have thirty cookies/....' The ambiguity can be described as a result of ellipsis, but there are other kinds of ambiguity that cannot be described in this way. The form ANALYSE can occur transitively as in (3):

(3)   1.p ANALYSE SECOND CLASS /
      I analysed grade two.

But it can also occur with a single argument and then the construction is ambiguous:

(4)   SECOND CLASS ANALYSE /
      Grade two analysed [something].
          or Grade two was analysed.

That is, SECOND CLASS in (4) may have the A argument relation or the P argument relation to the verb. The ambiguity may also arise between an A argument relation and a locative argument relation as in (5) and (6), which are, however, disambiguated by the lexical meaning:

(5)   PETER DET+fr / SWIM /
      Peter is swimming.
(6)   SEA DET+fr / SWIM /
      [Somebody] is swimming in the sea.

There need not be any marking, nonmanual or other, of the difference.
   Examples (2) and (4)-(6) point in the direction of a pragmatic analysis of the verb's arguments in Danish Sign Language as we find it in topic-prominent in contrast to subject-prominent languages (Li & Thompson 1976). In Chinese, for instance, *Jeh gua chyj heen tyan* is literally 'This melon eating very sweet' (Chao 1968, 70), with no marker showing that the constituent meaning 'this melon' has the patient relation to the verb. In Chinese, there are also cases of ellipsis that are very similar to example (2) from Danish Sign Language, e.g. a sentence that is literally 'He

is a Japanese woman' when the intended meaning is 'His servant is a Japanese woman', or 'She is an American husband', corresponding to 'She is (a case of being married to) an American husband' (ibid., 71). Constituents with a locative meaning can also occur as topic as in example (6) from Danish Sign Language. A Chinese sentence which is literally 'This place can skate' would in English be *At this place one can skate* (ibid., 73).

A difference between Danish Sign Language and Chinese is that example (3) from Danish Sign Language with two nominals fulfilling the same semantic selection constraints of the verb seems to have only an interpretation with the first person pronoun 1.p as the agent argument, whereas Chinese NVN'-constructions may be ambiguous with respect to the direction of the action. (See also the discussions of word order in ASL in Fischer 1975; Friedman 1976; Liddell 1980, Chapter 3; Wilbur 1987, 141-148.)

Unambiguous constructions: semantic agreement
A small class of verbs, the so-called agreement verbs,[3] is special in that its members have agreement forms which disambiguate the relations between the verb and its arguments. In some contexts, the cell in which a locus marker is inserted into the root of an agreement verb is unambiguously specified as either an A (or source) argument agreement cell or a P/IO argument agreement cell (see I.6.3 Liddell and Johnson's sequential form analysis of signs). I describe the kind of agreement where a form of a verb shows the semantic relations of the arguments to the verb unambiguously as semantic agreement. Agreement verbs that only have a P/IO argument cell are called single agreement verbs; agreement verbs with two cells are called double agreement verbs. Examples of such verbs are the single agreement verb DECEIVE and the double agreement verb ANSWER:

(7)　1.p DECEIVE+fr /　　　　　(Ill. 14a)
　　　I deceived him.
(8)　ANNE fr+ANSWER+c /　　　　(Ill. 1)
　　　Anne answered me.

The base form of an agreement verb is unmarked for loci, but, unlike the verb root, the base form can occur in signed discourse. The base form must be described as having neutral markers in the cells of the root. Most base forms of double agreement verbs are made with a marker for the sender locus in their A cell. The P/IO cell of the

---

3　I have taken over the term *agreement verbs* from research on ASL (see III.3 Earlier verb classifications), but it is important to note that in Danish Sign Language, *agreement verbs* are not the only verbs that can show agreement. They do, however, differ from other verbs in that they can show the special kind of agreement that I call *semantic agreement* (see III.6 Semantic agreement and marking for a specific-point-of-view).

base form of most double and all single agreement verbs takes a neutral locus marker for the direction forward from the signer's body.

A double agreement verb such as ANSWER can be modified for two loci that are both different from the locus *c* (Ill. 12b), but it is not seen often. Rather, double agreement verbs are modified in such ways that the hand(s), loosely speaking, move(s) outward from or inward toward the signer, even when neither argument has first person reference. The reason is that marking for a specific point of view interacts with semantic agreement. A locus marker for the sender locus expresses a specific point of view and supersedes any other locus marker.

Pragmatic agreement
Agreement may also occur with other verbs than agreement verbs and with signs from other sign classes. In such cases, the semantic relation between the agreeing sign and the constituent which refers to the referent of the locus in question is ambiguous; it must be interpreted from syntactic, lexical-semantic, or discourse features. Example (9) involves the same ambiguity as (4); it is not disambiguated through agreement. In such cases, I talk about *pragmatic agreement* in order to underline the pragmatic nature of the relation between the predicate and the argument with which it agrees:

```
(9)                                        t
    SECOND+fsl CLASS+fsl ANALYSE+fsl FINISH+fsl / ... (Ill. 37)
    When grade two had finished analysing...
       or When grade two had been analysed...
```

The base forms of the signs SECOND, CLASS, ANALYSE, and FINISH are made in neutral space a little outside the signer's sternum. The forms in (9), however, are made a little outside the signer's left shoulder. The signer represents the referent grade 2 by a locus because there is a contrast between grade 2 and grade 4.[4] The modification of the signs in (9) serves to emphasise the clause's relation to the referent represented by the locus forward-sideward-left, thereby underlining the contrast. The modification does not disambiguate the relation between the argument and the verb. As the translations demonstrate, the clause is ambiguous.

Agreement in Danish Sign Language is not obligatory in any syntactic context and for that reason the term *agreement* is questionable. I discuss the differences and similarities between locus marking of signs in Danish Sign Language and agreement in spoken languages in III.6.1 Alternative descriptions, and III.6.2 Agreement features, direction, and domain.

---

4 The example is from the presentation that was discussed in relation to the anaphoric time line in II.3.1 The time lines.

Summary

The three types of modifications that I describe in greater detail below are:

1. *Distribution modifications.* The modifications for distribution that I examine are expressed by an added linear, circular, semicircular, or random movement, often combined with reduplication or the addition of the other hand in one-handed signs. Modifications for distribution do not in themselves carry locus information, but they may combine with modification for agreement. Modifications for distribution are found with signs from different sign classes and with clauses. There are several morphologically different types of modifications for distribution.

2. *Agreement.* Agreement markers carry locus information. Agreement can occur with signs from different sign classes. Only some verbs can have agreement markers inserted in cells of the sign that show unambiguously the semantic relation between the verb and its argument. The markers can be inserted in cells of such roots that are labelled as either A or source argument agreement cells or P, IO, or goal argument agreement cells. If a verb can take both a P argument and an IO argument, it agrees with its IO argument. Verbs that have unambiguous cells for agreement markers are called agreement verbs and unambiguous agreement is called semantic agreement. Agreement verbs, as well as many other signs, can show pragmatic agreement. In that case, the agreement marker does not show the semantic relations between the signs. Signs which show pragmatic agreement take one locus marker only.

3. *Marking for a specific point of view.* Marking for a specific point of view is expressed by a locus marker for the sender locus. It interacts with semantic agreement in agreement verbs.

The main focus in treatments of agreement in signed languages has been on agreement verbs with unambiguous argument relations. There is very little published information on what I call pragmatic agreement. In Danish Sign Language, agreement verbs constitute a fairly small group within the group of signs that can show pragmatic agreement.

3 Earlier verb classifications

In her dissertation from 1983 (published 1988), Padden suggests a classification of verbs in ASL based on their morphological use of space. She identifies three classes of verbs, inflecting verbs, spatial verbs, and plain verbs:

> Inflecting verbs, unlike the other two classes, mark for person and number. Spatial verbs mark for location and position, and a sub-class marks for path and manner of movement. In contrast, Plain verbs do not mark for these categories. (Padden 1988b, 25)

Basically the same classification of verbs has been adopted for Italian Sign Language by Pizzuto (1986), for ASL also by Liddell and Johnson (1987; Liddell 1990a), and for Taiwan Sign Language by Smith (1989). Liddell and Johnson and Smith use the term *agreement verb* (or *person-agreement verb*) instead of *inflecting verb,* as some verbs that are classified as not "inflecting" can be modified for aspect, but only agreement verbs can show agreement (see also Padden 1988b, 56). Padden's category "spatial verbs" is renamed *spatial-locative verbs* by Liddell and Johnson (1987), and it includes *classifier predicates* or *spatial-locative predicates*, as well as some verbs without classifiers such as MOVE or PUT in ASL (Padden 1990, 119: subclass 1. See, however, Padden 1981, 241, 243). The basically identical classifications of verbs are seen in Fig. 8.

Padden (1988b)
    inflecting [later, agreement] verbs
    spatial verbs
        classifier predicates = spatial-locative predicates
        locative verbs without classifiers
    plain verbs

Liddell and Johnson (1987), Liddell (1990a)
    agreement verbs
    spatial-locative verbs
        classifier predicates = polysynthetic spatial-locative predicates
        other spatial-locative predicates
    plain verbs

Fig. 8. Two classifications of verbs in ASL

The classifications in Fig. 8 contrast especially with Gee and Kegl (1982), Kegl (1986, 1990), Kegl and Schley (1986), and Gee and Goodhart (1988). They characterise all forms of spatial modification in ASL as agreement, but describe agreement in localist terms. Gee and Goodhart (1988; see also Kegl & Schley 1986, 427) describe the origin of what they call subject and object agreement in ASL as 'locative agreement'. In their analysis, the verb in a sentence with the meaning 'I gave him the telephone number' is said to agree with its subject and object, but the agreement of this verb originates in the kind of locative agreement demonstrated by the verb in a sentence meaning 'I transferred by hand the telephone number from the table to him', where the verb (not *I* as it is written in the article) agrees with 'the initial and final locations of the telephone number' (ibid., 61). That is, Gee and Goodhart describe both kinds of verbs as showing agreement.

Kegl (1990) underlines the formal similarity of different kinds of verbs with respect to spatial modification. The verbs do not differ morphologically, she claims, but it is possible to distinguish, for instance, objects of transitive verbs from applied objects of appearance verbs (e.g. the sign meaning 'horizon' in a sentence meaning 'The sun rose above the horizon'), on the basis of their meaning and their syntactic possibilities: 'The object of a transitive is generally a patient/affected element, but the applied object of an appearance verb is a location. Transitives have a passive (or at least adjectival passive) alternant, appearance verbs do not' (ibid., 164).

Padden (1988b, 1990) and Liddell (1990a) list criteria for distinguishing the three groups of verbs, plain verbs, agreement verbs, and locative (spatial) verbs. They distinguish agreement verbs and locative verbs in terms of meaning. Moreover, Padden (1988b, 25) argues that agreement verbs inflect for person and number, while the markers on locative verbs have a locative meaning. Apparently identical changes of agreement verbs and locative verbs have quite different meanings and should be analysed as different grammatical constructions, she claims. For instance, the exhaustive inflection of agreement verbs is expressed by three or more repetitions of the verb with a change in space of the final segment of each repetition, and means 'any number greater than two'. If a locative verb is made with three repetitions and displacement of the final segment of each repetition, it signifies that the action was made three times. In the ASL sentence meaning *I put candles here, there and there*, the verb PUT is made three times at three different positions. It is a seriated verb construction, not an inflected form (ibid., 49). Liddell (1990a) points out that (locative) classifier predicates may also be modified for number, which makes number inflection invalid as a criterion for distinguishing agreement verbs from locative verbs.

In Danish Sign Language, verbs having a locative meaning can also take the same modifications for distribution (including a modification similar to exhaustive in ASL) as agreement verbs. Moreover, verbs can be modified for number only with a distributive meaning. Number in the verb's arguments does not automatically trigger number modification in the verb. Therefore, I treat number modifications under the general heading *distribution* (see III.5 Modifications for distribution).

Both Padden (1988b) and Liddell (1990a) claim that agreement verbs are marked spatially for subjects and objects, while locative verbs are marked spatially for location. One of Padden's morphosyntactic arguments for the distinction between agreement verbs and locative verbs is that locative verbs do not agree in person with their subjects, as the movement of the hand(s) in a locative verb does not necessarily start at the locus of the subject referent. In the ASL clause meaning 'I walked from there to there', the movement of the locative verb WALK starts and ends at loci away from the signer's body (1988b, 44). The markers on the verb cannot be agreement markers, as the verb is not marked for the locus of the subject, the sender locus; therefore, they must be locative markers.

The example, I find, proves neither that the markers on WALK are not *agreement* markers, *nor* that the markers on agreement verbs are *subject* and *object* agreement markers. Padden discusses subjecthood in ASL in a Relational Grammar framework (1988b, Chapter 5), but she finds 'no clear evidence distinguishing between "initial" and "final" 1s' (ibid., 166). As Padden points out, agreement verbs in ASL agree with arguments having a number of different semantic relations with the verbs which means that the agreement rule cannot be stated in any simple way in semantic terms only. Nonethelesss, in ASL as well as in Danish Sign Language, any individual agreement verb always agrees with arguments having the same semantic relation to the verb. That is, it is possible to state the agreement behaviour of every agreement verb in the lexicon. There is, therefore, no basis for singling out verbs which are marked for a locative argument from verbs which are marked for the agent or the experiencer, except on semantic grounds. Thus WALK can be said to agree with its source and goal argument.

Liddell (1980, 96-99) stresses that in locative constructions, space represents locative relations, while the relations expressed spatially in agreement verbs are more abstract. Liddell and Johnson (1987) and Liddell (1990a) describe a phonological difference between agreement verbs and locative classifier predicates. With agreement verbs, the hand does not necessarily move from one locus to another in Liddell and Johnson's definition of the term *locus* (see I.6.3 Liddell and Johnsons's sequential analysis of signs); it may move only part of the way without starting or ending at a locus. If a classifier predicate is meant to signify that something moved from location *a* to location *b* and the signer uses locus *x* for location *a* and locus *y* for location *b*, the hand must necessarily move all the way from locus *x* to locus *y*. If it stops midway between the two loci, it means that the entity in question stopped midway between location *a* and location *b*. Again, this criterion is problematic in relation to Danish Sign Language, where the absolute length of the hand's movement is irrelevant in most verbs with a locative meaning, just as it is in agreement verbs. What matters is the direction of the movement in both cases.

Liddell (1990a) adds one more criterion for the distinction between agreement verbs and classifier predicates. In ASL, referents can be associated with the tips of the four fingers and the thumb of the hand. Liddell calls these loci 'ordinal (tip) loci' (ibid., 191); he claims that it is possible to direct an agreement verb toward an ordinal locus, but such a locus cannot serve as a locus for a classifier predicate. That is, it is possible to modify, for instance, the agreement verb ASK for an ordinal locus in a clause meaning 'I asked my youngest brother' where the referent is represented by an ordinal locus; but it is not possible to use a locative classifier predicate meaning '(person) stands' in relation to the ordinal locus in a clause meaning 'Somebody stood next to my youngest brother'. Ordinal loci are found also in Danish Sign Language, but it is highly doubtful whether it is possible to modify an agreement verb for such a locus in that language.

Padden (1988b), Liddell and Johnson (1987), and Liddell (1989) all compare two ASL verbs, GIVE and MOVE-FLAT-OBJECT. The verbs are made with the same handshape and their movement may relate to two loci. But while a form of GIVE made between two loci x and y means 'person$_x$ gives to person$_y$', a form of MOVE-FLAT-OBJECT made from x to y means 'move a flat object from location x to location y'. Padden and Liddell and Johnson claim that the spatial modification of GIVE expresses a grammatical relation between the arguments subject and object and the verb, while the spatial modification of MOVE-FLAT-OBJECT expresses a movement between two locations.

In Danish Sign Language, there is a formal difference between a verb meaning 'give' and a verb meaning 'transfer flat object by hand' as we saw in III.1 Localism and transitivity. But the boundary between the two types of verbs, agreement verbs and locative verbs, is less clear-cut than appears in the descriptions of ASL (see also Gee and Goodhart's comparison of the signs meaning 'give' and 'transfer by hand' summarised above). The major difference in Danish Sign Language is between polymorphemic verbs and nonpolymorphemic verbs, with agreement verbs belonging to the latter group. Polymorphemic verbs can include movement morphemes that are not seen in agreement verbs (see III.8.4 Movement morphemes in polymorphemic verbs); they can take other kinds of morphemes expressed spatially (see III.8.6 Polymorphemic verbs and space); and by contrast to agreement verbs, polymorphemic verbs can occur in backgrounded constructions that describe locative configurations (see III.8.6 Polymorphemic verbs and space).

In what follows, I describe different kinds of morphology in Danish Sign Language. I distinguish different types of verbs (Fig. 9) on the basis of a distinction between modifications for distribution, semantic agreement, and pragmatic agreement and the spatial and movement morphology of polymorphemic verbs. The major distinction is between polymorphemic verbs and nonpolymorphemic verbs as prototypes at each end of a continuum. The category of nonpolymorphemic verbs comprises plain verbs, agreement verbs, and other nonpolymorphemic verbs. The two last types can show pragmatic agreement and be modified for distribution, but only agreement verbs can show semantic agreement. Pragmatic agreement has only been treated sparingly in descriptions of other signed languages (Padden 1988b, 27; 1990, 121-123), or has not been distinguished from semantic agreement or the behaviour of locative verbs; it therefore plays no part in earlier verb classifications.

Nonpolymorphemic verbs   Polymorphemic verbs
    agreement verbs (can be modified
        to show semantic and
        pragmatic agreement)
    verbs that can be modified
        to show pragmatic, but not
        semantic agreement
    plain verbs

Fig. 9. Classification of verbs in Danish Sign Language

The main difference between my classification of verbs in Danish Sign Language and the classifications of verbs in ASL presented in Fig. 8 is that I make a major two-way distinction between nonpolymorphemic verbs and polymorphemic verbs. The equivalents of what I call polymorphemic verbs, i.e. classifier predicates, are treated as a subgroup of spatial or locative verbs in the classifications in Fig. 8, i.e. they are grouped with nonpolymorphemic verbs having a locative meaning. My reasons for not following the classifications presented in Fig. 8 is that the distinction between nonpolymorphemic verbs having a locative meaning and transitive verbs is primarily a semantic one. By contrast, the difference between polymorphemic and nonpolymorphemic verbs is both morphological and semantic. But I will show that the two types are extremes on a continuum: when we go from the nonpolymorphemic end toward the polymorphemic end with verbs of motion and location, the verbs become increasingly locative in meaning and start to be potentially polymorphemic. Tokens of these verbs in the middle, however, often have so few morphemes that they look like nonpolymorphemic verbs. It seems to be such verbs that are grouped in Fig. 8 with the polymorphemic ('classifier') verbs, as opposed to the verbs showing person and number agreement. The classifications in Fig. 8 emphasise a more or less absolute distinction between subject and object agreement and morphology that manifests locative relations. Moreover, Fig. 8 does not recognise a group of verbs that can be modified to show pragmatic agreement only, since pragmatic agreement is not part of the analyses behind the classifications.

4 Plain signs

Some signs always have the same place of articulation with the hand(s) touching the head, face, trunk, or contralateral arm. The place of articulation may change in a fluent, casual style without semantic consequences. Examples of signs that cannot be modified spatially are the verbs CONTROL-ONE'S-TEMPER (with the hand touching the chest), TRAVEL (with the hands touching the chest), and VERY-CURIOUS (with the hand touching first the nose and then the contralateral side of the chest). Such verbs were early separated out as a special category in research on ASL (Friedman 1976, 130; Fischer & Gough 1978, 163f.). Padden later named verbs that cannot inflect for person and number *plain verbs* (1988b, 38). She emphasised that this category cannot be distinguished by a form criterion, as many verbs which cannot show agreement do not have a place of articulation on the body, head, face, or arm. With respect to semantic agreement this holds for Danish Sign Language as well. But many signs that have a base form with neutral space as their place of articulation can be modified spatially for distribution or can show pragmatic agreement. Therefore, I reserve the term *plain* for signs that cannot be modified spatially at all. The group includes verbs, as well as signs from other classes. The majority of these signs does have a place of articulation on the body, head, face, or arm. The boundary between signs that can be modified spatially and signs that cannot is not sharp, however. A sign's place of articulation is only one among several characteristics that are typical of signs belonging to either group.

Plain verbs constitute a very large group in Danish Sign Language. They may be transitive (LOVE, HATE, USE) or intransitive (CRY, SLEEP, SWEAR, PEE); denote states (BE-ASHAMED, BE-CALLED, KNOW, BE-BORED), events (FORGET, GO-TO-BED, TRY), or processes (STARE, STUDY, WORK-HARD). Although many of these verbs have an iconic origin (SMELL made at the nose, SMILE made at the mouth), not all can be described as iconic. There is no reason why BE-CALLED should have the chin or TRY the chest as a place of articulation.

In Danish Sign Language, some verbs that have a HMH (hold, movement, hold) structure and have contact with the body or head during the first hold are agreement verbs and can be modified in space. Verbs of this kind are TELL, SEE, THAT'S-UP-TO, and DECEIVE (Ill. 14). They are agreement verbs, even though their place of articulation at the beginning of the sign is an area on the body or head.

Some verbs have an iconic origin in depicting states or actions where the arms and hands form a picture with the signer's body and head. In RUN, the arms and hands represent the movements of the arms and hands which are typical of running; the hands do not touch the head or body, but the movements of the hands form one "picture" with the body. Other verbs of this kind are those that denote the playing of musical instruments. Such verbs tend not to be modified spatially. In (1), however, TYPE (Ill. 18), which also has an iconic origin where the hands depict the action of typing in relation to the body, is modified spatially; it shows pragmatic agreement:

```
(1)    body:                       left------------
       right: TAKE-NOTES           TYPE[+]+sl CLEAN /
       left:  TAKE-NOTES c+GIVE+sl TYPE[+]+sl CLEAN
       They would take notes and give them to someone to type out.
```

The verb TYPE[+]+sl is made with the hands outside the left side of the chest. It is made in relation to the same locus as c+GIVE+sl. This locus represents the referents of the A argument of TYPE[+]+sl and the IO argument of c+GIVE+sl (the person who is meant to type the notes). The iconicity of the hands in relation to the body is broken in TYPE[+]+sl in order to emphasise the co-reference of the two arguments.

The intransitive verb TELEPHONE is made with a hold at the ear (Ill. 38). It cannot be modified spatially to show pragmatic agreement as can other intransitive verbs. Some signers have a transitive verb TELEPHONE-TO that can show agreement, while others use the plain verb TELEPHONE both transitively and intransitively. TELEPHONE-TO can be used by some as a double agreement verb with the hand completely dislocated from the place of articulation at the ear: the hand moves in relation to two loci. In the case of a first person A or P argument, the hand may approach the ear at some point. Another possibility is that the verb is used as a single agreement verb agreeing only with its P argument. Yet another possibility is that it shows a mixed agreement pattern, agreeing with its A argument only when the P argument has first person reference: with a non-first person P argument ('X calls him'), it shows single agreement, i.e. agrees with its P argument, but not its A argument; with a first person P argument ('X calls me'), it shows double agreement. The verb is clearly in a transition phase, in which the more conservative norm is the transitive and intransitive use of the plain verb TELEPHONE and the most advanced stage is the double agreement verb. The transitive form TELEPHONE-TO can also be modified for distribution by some signers: the hand starts at the signer's ear and moves out in a semicircle and the meaning is 'call many/all of them'.

TELEPHONE-TO has one characteristic of prototypical plain verbs: its place of articulation is on the signer's head or body, not in neutral space. It also has some characteristics of many agreement verbs: it is a transitive verb whose P argument is high on the animacy scale and it denotes a transfer (communication) between individuals. It is therefore an obvious case for a verb that fluctuates between plain verbs and agreement verbs.

Even though plain signs cannot be modified spatially, it is possible to express distributional meaning or the sign's relation to a locus as in agreement by other means. In II.6.1 Types of pointing signs, I described how a pointing sign, i.e. the proform, can "take over" the spatial modification that cannot be expressed on the sign. Another possibility is the signer's gaze direction and/or head and body orientation. In a monologue, a signer described her great disappointment in seeing a bed by rotating her body so that she was facing the direction of the locus representing the bed and looking in this direction while signing GREATLY-DISAPPOINTED (Ill. 39). The construction is equivalent to a construction with a predicate showing pragmatic agreement (see III.7.1 Pragmatic agreement, semantic agreement, and point of view marking).

5 Modifications for distribution

Distribution is used here as a superordinate term for a number of different modifications. What they have in common is that they all denote distribution over entities, places, and/or points or periods in time. Not every sign which can take a modification for distribution can take all modifications of this kind. The modifications for distribution that I focus on here include a circular, semicircular, linear, or random horizontal or vertical movement which is not part of the sign's root form. If the sign is one-handed, the modification may consist of a doubling of the sign root by using the second hand and/or sometimes reduplication, with the hands moving alternately. Loosely speaking, random movement means that the hand moves back and forth, left and right between each cycle of the reduplication in an unsystematic pattern. Random distribution is primarily, but not only, seen in modifications for distribution of verbs close to the polymorphemic end of the verb continuum (from nonpolymorphemic to polymorphemic verbs) (see III.3 Earlier verb classifications, III.8 Polymorphemic verbs, and IV Conclusion).

Most modifications for distribution include reduplication of the sign root, but some agreement verbs modify for distribution without reduplication. Then the verb signs are made either with a final circular, semicircular, or linear movement (e.g. GIVE-KEY (Ill. 40)), or such a movement is substituted for the movement of their base form (e.g. TEACH). In those cases where both are possible, it is not yet clear whether there is a difference in meaning between forms with and without reduplication (see note [2] in III.2 Different types of modifications: An overview).

Modifications for distribution can occur with signs from different sign classes in predicative function, with interrogative signs, and with clauses. Modifications for distribution differ from those for agreement, in that modifications for distribution *per se* do not involve loci. A form modified for distribution can show agreement, but the two kinds of modifications can be distinguished.

Number agreement or modification for distribution
Klima and Bellugi (1979) distinguish grammatical number and distributional aspect in ASL. The term *grammatical number* covers examples where 'internal changes in the form of the verb' reflect 'whether certain arguments of the verb (its object, or subject) are singular or plural', whereas '[o]ther internal changes in the form of the verb reflect distinctions in the number of actions referred to as well as distinctions in the nature and extent of the distribution of those actions over arguments (inflections for distributional aspect)' (Klima & Bellugi 1979, 280). Thus Klima and Bellugi distinguish grammatical number as an agreement phenomenon from distributional aspect. Padden (1981, 1988b, 1990) describes several forms of number agreement in ASL: 'Number agreement may be either unmarked, for singular or collective plurals...or marked for dual, trial (three) or more than three.' (Padden 1988b, 31).

In Danish Sign Language, verbs are never modified for number just because their arguments are nonsingular. Signs in predicative use, with an added linear, circular, semicircular, or random movement, with or without reduplication, have a distributive meaning besides denoting number. A few verbs are exceptions, notably INFORM and TEACH. The signs INFORM+multiple and TEACH+multiple seem to be more or less lexicalized with a nondistributive, plural meaning used in particular with implicit or unspecified plural IO arguments. But the form in (1) with the verb GIVE-KEY made with a semicircular movement means that the keys were distributed among the members of the group; each couple in the group got a key for their room in the hotel:

(1)   1.p+pl.+sl GET KEY neu+GIVE-KEY+multiple+c+sl /   (Ill. 40)

       Then we all got keys.

It is possible to use a form of GIVE-KEY without a semicircular movement, even when the verb has a plural IO argument. For instance, this form is used in a clause meaning, 'He gave them the keys' where the action does not have a distributive meaning. That is, a final semicircular movement of the hand in GIVE-KEY does not merely signal plural number of the IO argument; for that reason it is not number agreement.[1]

In her description of the morphology of spoken languages, Bybee draws forth the difference between categories of person and gender, on the one hand, and, on the other, categories of number in relation to the meaning of verbs:

> While person and gender categories seem to have little effect on the meaning of a verb, and are ... rarely lexicalized, number is somewhat different. The number of participants in a situation, whether agents or recipients of an action, can affect the situation profoundly. (Bybee 1985b, 23 – emphasis in the original)

Bybee relates verbal plurality to aspect: both have an effect on the inherent meaning of the verb, and they are often expressed in very similar ways. Kwakiutl, for example, has three plurality forms with reduplication of the verb. One of them indicates plurality of the subject ('many are boiling'), another repeated activity ('it is boiling repeatedly'), and the third form expresses an activity occurring at the same time in different parts of a unit ('is boiling in all of its parts') (Bybee 1985b 103f.; see also Anderson 1982; Bybee 1985a, 34ff.; Bergman & Dahl in press).

---

1   Bergman and Dahl (in press) present an analysis of reduplicated forms in Swedish Sign Language as parallel to ideophones. Moreover, they suggest that the occurrence of reduplicated forms is dependent on phenomena such as topic and focus structure (see also Liddell 1980, 102-104). Bergman and Dahl mention that 'Typically, an ideophone/reduplicated verb expands a sentence with a 'normal' verb as the main predicate' (in press). Note that the IO argument occurs before the verb in (1) and that the unmodified verb GET with a more general meaning than GIVE-KEY precedes GIVE-KEY. In (1), the verb is not reduplicated, but modified for distribution in another way. I find, however, that it is too early to say whether signs modified for distribution in Danish Sign Language resemble ideophones.

Bybee links the difference in meaning between different kinds of number in relation to the verb with a difference between inflectional and either lexical or derivational expression. Derivational and lexical number in verbs is not redundant in the way that inflectional number (agreement) often is (1985b, 104ff.). In Danish Sign Language, modifications for distribution are not redundant; they add specific meaning to the base form.

Examples of modifications for distribution
Signs from classes other than verbs can be modified for distribution, e.g. a number sign in predicative function in (2), a conjunction in (3), and a clause in (4):

(2)   THIRTY+multiple /   (Ill. 36)

   Everyone [who works shorter hours works] thirty [hours a week].

(3)   _____t
   IF+multiple+deictic-loci WANT WITH / MUST PAY FIFTY CROWN /[2]
                                              (Ill. 41)

   If anyone of you wants to participate, he should pay 50 crowns.

(4)   [PRON SUGGEST]+multiple /[3]   (Ill. 42)

   They all made different suggestions.

An alternative to (3) suggested by some informants has the sign YES modified for distribution:

(3') IF YES+multiple+deictic-loci / MUST ...

Modifications for distribution and agreement
The difference between distribution and agreement can be demonstrated by exam-

---

[2] When I discussed example (3) with a group of informants, there was much disagreement. One informant rejected the example downright; she would instead modify the sign WITH. Another felt that the example was acceptable if it was addressed to a group of people who were present in the context of utterance (which it was); it would not be acceptable for nonpresent referents ('If anyone of them wanted to...'). A third informant rejected the modified form IF+multiple +deictic-loci, but suggested instead a modified form of another conditional conjunction, PRETEND^ hvis(M)('if'). The informant who originally produced the example found her own sentence (3) acceptable.

[3] Example (4) is reminiscent of reduplication of sentences used to express distribution, for instance, in Swahili:

   A: *Wauzaje machungwa haya?*
       How do you sell these oranges?

   B: *Moja senti tatu, moja senti tatu*
       one   cent   three
       Three cents each.   (after Ashton 1944, 317)

ples (1) and (5). Distribution modifications denote distribution over a number of entities or distribution over time and often the two kinds of distribution are intertwined, as in (5) where a signer used the verb JUMP ('skip') to say that interpreters often leave out names and numbers in their interpretation:

(5) JUMP+multiple+mixed-tl /   (Ill. 43)
    Then they skip them as they go along.[4]

The sign in (5) was reduplicated and embedded in a linear movement outward from the signer's chest. The modification of JUMP denotes the plural number of the referent (names, numbers), as well as iterative action. The distribution modification is combined with the use of the time line which denotes the process in time as the interpretation takes place.

GIVE-KEY in (1) is a double agreement verb; it has an A argument cell, which in this case takes a neutral marker, and an IO argument cell which takes a marker for the IO argument's locus. The referent of the IO argument is represented by the sender locus and the locus *sl*. The form in (1) contrasts with a form also being modified for distribution, but having a different IO argument agreement marker, e.g. c+GIVE-KEY+multiple+fsr ('give to all of them'). The latter form includes the same modification for distribution, but a different agreement marker. The form in (1) also contrasts with a form without a distributive meaning, neu+GIVE-KEY+c ('give to us'), i.e. a form taking no marker for distribution, but showing the same agreement as the form in (1). The claim that it is an example of 'the same agreement' needs a comment. The form neu+GIVE-KEY+c can be used in a situation where the referents of the IO argument of the verb are represented by two different loci, the locus *c* and some other locus. That is, the IO argument is used to refer to two or more people including the sender and at least one more person represented by another locus, e.g. the locus sideward-left. In that situation, there is agreement conflict: the verb is supposed to agree with one argument having two different values for the feature expressed in agreement. A similar example from French is the sentence *Mon frère et moi, nous sommes heureux* ('My brother and I, we are happy'), when it is said by a woman. In French, the adjective *heureux* ('happy') must agree in gender with the subject *nous* ('we'), which is used to refer to a male and a female. Thus, there is agreement conflict between a masculine and a feminine form of the adjective. The agreement conflict is solved by the use of the masculine form. In the example from Danish Sign Language, the agreement conflict arises from the IO argument having referents represented by two loci, the sender locus and another locus; here the agreement conflict is solved by the use of the sender locus only. The distributive form in (1), neu+GIVE-KEY+multiple+c+sl, allows the verb to take two locus markers in its IO argument cell, but the distribution

---

4 The Danish equivalent of *skip* is *hoppe over*, literally *jump over*. The use of JUMP in (6) may be an example of lexical borrowing from Danish.

modification is not required to solve the agreement conflict. The distribution modification adds meaning: each one was given a key. That is, it is possible to distinguish the distribution marker from the agreement marker in agreement verbs modified for agreement as well as for distribution.[5]

In (6), a modification for distribution is combined with pragmatic agreement.

(6) TALK-WITH-EACH-OTHER+group+p.a.:fsr / (Ill. 44)
    They'll all just talk with each other.

The verb TALK-WITH-EACH-OTHER is a lexically reciprocal verb, which means that in the form modified for *group*, the movement of the hands form a circle. The form in (6) contrasts with two forms: TALK-WITH-EACH-OTHER+p.a.:fsr ('they talked with each other') without modification for distribution (no circular movement); and TALK-WITH-EACH-OTHER+group ('talk in a group') made in neutral space, but modified for distribution.

Verb forms showing agreement always include locus markers, whereas modifications for distribution do not *per se* involve locus markers. In (1), neu+GIVE-KEY+multiple+c+sl has a distribution marker which permits the verb to take two locus markers for its IO argument, *c* and *sl*. The forms in (3) and (6), IF+multiple +deictic-loci and TALK-WITH-EACH-OTHER+group+p.a.:fsr, are modified both for agreement (locus markers) and for distribution. The form in (5), JUMP+multiple +mixed-tl-forward, is modified for distribution and has a marker for a time line. In all these cases, the modification for distribution is combined with another marker expressed spatially. But there are cases where a form modified for distribution apparently does not take any other spatially expressed markers. When a signer uses a form with a semicircular or linear horizontal movement in front of her (as in (2) and (4)), it is only possible to decide whether there is actually any use of loci, if it is possible to refer, for instance, to the persons working thirty hours a week (see (2)) by means of a form of PRON with the same horizontal movement.

The scope of modifications for distribution
Even though the semantic domain of modifications for distribution is the predicate or all of the clause, the modification appears only on one sign of the clause, unless the clause is modified as in (4). In (2), (3), and (4), the semantic scope of the distribution modification is the clause ('He works thirty hours, and so does she, and he, etc.', 'If you want to participate, or you, or you, ...'); but the distribution modification appears

---

[5] It is not clear to me how the form of GIVE-KEY modified for distribution should be analysed in Liddell and Johnson's model (see I.6.3 Liddell and Johnson's sequential form analysis of signs): the base form of GIVE-KEY has a HMH structure with cells for the A argument and IO argument agreement markers in the two H segments. The modification for distribution in example (1) can loosely be described as having an M segment with a semicircular movement inserted before its last H segment.

in three different places: on the predicative sign only (2), on the conjunction only (3), and on the clause (4).

In reduplicative constructions in spoken languages, Moravcsik (1978b) has found a distinction between simple plurality of the participants of an event, as expressed by noun reduplication, and distributive meanings, as expressed by either noun or verb reduplication. Dressler distinguishes nominal and verbal plurality and points out that verbal plurality has a global meaning involving all of the clause (1968, 92-93). This is also what lies behind Bybee's statement: 'The number of participants in a situation, whether agents or recipients of an action, can affect the situation profoundly' (Bybee 1985b, 23). Danish Sign Language makes it particularly clear that modifications for distribution do not only involve the meaning of the verb, but the meaning of the predicate or the clause, as even clauses can be modified for distribution. Moreover, the distributive constructions often have the kind of ambiguity that Dressler mentions as evidence that verbal plurality has a global, clausal, meaning: Seneca *háihsak·hɔh* means 'he is looking for several things = in several places = at various times' (Dressler 1968, 93). The modifications for distribution in Danish Sign Language can also mean distribution over P argument referents, over locative referents, and distribution in time (see example (5)), and the forms are often ambiguous.

The exact place where the modification for distribution is expressed in Danish Sign Language seems not to matter. Haiman (1985b, 182ff.) lists a number of categories in different languages that have this characteristic. Tagalog nouns are marked for the singular and the plural and adjectival predicates agree with their subjects in number:

```
(7)  a.  Ma-Ø-gandaʔ          ang babae
         adj.-sg.-beautiful   the woman
         The woman is beautiful.

     b.  Ma-ga-gandaʔ         ang mga babae
         adj.-pl.-beautiful   the pl. woman
         The women are beautiful.      (= (50a-b), ibid., 185)
```

But the following constructions are also possible as alternative ways of expressing 'The women are beautiful':

```
     c.  Ma-Ø-gandaʔ          ang mga babae
         adj.-sg.-beautiful   the pl. woman

     d.  Ma-ga-gandaʔ         ang babae
         adj.-pl.-beautiful   the woman    (= (50c-d), ibid., 185)
```

That is, number can be marked on the subject, on the predicate, or on both.

Nouns in nonpredicative function

In Danish Sign Language, both noun signs and verb signs as well as signs from other classes may be reduplicated and embedded in movements of various shapes. Embedding of some reduplicated noun signs in a movement denotes plurality without a distributive meaning when the nouns are not used in a predicative function. The most common form is reduplication of the sign embedded in a linear movement. Example (8), however, which is rather unique, shows a modification which seems to have a collective meaning:

(8) TWO+pron.+c+sr TRAVEL^GONE AUSTRIA / TOGETHER SOME+sl DEAF

 FRIEND+"redupl.-circle"+sl / WITH ALL+sl /

 The two of us were going to Austria, together with some deaf
 friends.

The signer of (8) reduplicates the sign FRIEND embedded in a circular movement in the direction of the locus which she uses for the referent. The meaning is not distributive: 'they were all friends among themselves' or 'each one of them was a friend'. The signer simply refers to the group as her friends.

 The signer of (9) reduplicates the sign GROUP embedded in a linear movement along the line of the anaphoric time line:

(9) PRON+sl WORK MUCH BEFORE+anaph.-tl / GROUP+pl.+anaph.-tl-

 before DISCUSS+multiple+anaph.-tl-before / (Ill. 21)

 Several groups had discussed them prior to [the assembly].

When GROUP is made along the line of a time line, it acquires additional meaning ('groups before the assembly').

Distribution and telicity

The form and meaning of some modifications for distribution depend on the form and lexical meaning of the modified signs in ways that are only partially predictable. The verb TYPE (Ill. 18) is a two-handed symmetrical sign. It can be made with a vertical, downward movement of the arms with the meaning 'type up' (see also I.6.6 The morphological type of signed languages). This modification of TYPE has a telic meaning; unlike the unmodified form, it denotes 'a process leading up to a terminal point as well as the terminal point' (Comrie 1976, 47). Another sign that can be made with a vertical, linear movement is READ (Ill. 17). Its base form is made with a flat hand and bidirectional, sideways movements (as if the hand represents a page that is moved back and forth before the eyes). To indicate 'read something to the end', signers move their hand upward, eliminating the sideways movement of the base form. By contrast to the telic form of TYPE, the modification of READ is made with an upward vertical movement because of the sign's iconic origin: in the culture in which Danish Sign Language is used, the reader's eyes move from the top of the page downward. The upward movement of the hand gives the impression of the reader's eyes moving downward, just as the downward movement of the arms in TYPE creates the impression of the paper moving upward. The meaning of the vertical movement is not predictable, but rather depends on the lexical meaning of the verbs. If KNIT is made with an upward vertical movement, it means 'knit fast (and thereby much)'; in this case, the modified form does not have a telic meaning.

In READ and TYPE, distribution and telecity converge: the activity denoted by the verb is seen as applied to the referent as a unit (a page in reading or typing). Chung and Timberlake (1985) describe how expressions specifying locative limits make predicates telic in spoken languages. Compare, for example, *John walked in the city* (atelic) and *John walked from Madison Avenue to 91st Street* (telic) or *The fire burned the log* (atelic) and *The fire burned the log up* (telic). The linear, vertical movement of distribution in Danish Sign Language that gives the verb, or rather the predicate in which the verb occurs, a telic meaning also iconically visualises Chung and Timberlake's description of telicity:

> A process may either have the potential of continuing indefinitely, or it may have associated with it a natural boundary or limit on the degree of change, such that when the limit is reached, the event cannot continue. Traditionally a process without an inherent limit is called atelic, one with a limit is called telic (from Greek *telos* 'limit, end, goal') ... The notion of inherent limit depends both on the semantic content of a verb and on the content of its arguments at the predicate level. (Chung & Timberlake 1985, 217)

The linear, vertical movement in the modified versions of verbs such as READ and TYPE marks the outline of the "imagined" referents (the top and the bottom of the page) and in this way changes the processes of reading or typing into events with 'a natural boundary or limit.'

6 Semantic agreement and marking for a specific point of view

6.1 Alternative descriptions

In example (1) below, the narrator signs a form of NOTIFY with her hand at chin level and the tips of her fingers facing the locus forward-left, a locus that represents the person named Dan. The signer makes the sign EXPLAIN at throat level with the bases of her hands facing the locus and the tips of her fingers facing herself (Ill. 45a-b):

```
(1)                                         ?
    1.p c+NOTIFY+fl DAN / PRON+fl / STEAL HOW   / fl+EXPLAIN+c /
    (Ill. 45b)
    I asked Dan, 'Tell me, how did the burglary take place?' He told
    me.
```

The modification of verbs in space as in example (1) has been described as *agreement* in several signed languages (see the references in section III.3 Earlier verb classifications; also Kegl & Wilbur 1976, 388; Engberg-Pedersen, Hansen & Kjær Sørensen 1981, 144; Bellugi & Klima 1982, 302; Lillo-Martin 1986; Pizzuto 1986). Some researchers describe the spatial modification of verbs in terms of *incorporation*, either 'subject-object incorporation' in British Sign Language (Brennan, Colville & Lawson 1984, 182, 200) or, in ASL, 'incorporating a pronoun (or a case-marking copy of from one to three arguments) into a verb. The pronoun copy is then deleted, leaving behind a trace – the direction in which the sign moves' (Fischer & Gough 1978, 26; see also Edge & Herrmann 1977). Deuchar (1984) describes the direction of movement in verbs such as GIVE and EXPLAIN in British Sign Language as 'a *marker of case* in an egocentric system where, if there is a first person argument (that is, if the signer needs to refer to himself or herself), direction of movement will show the case of the first person, whether 'agent' or 'patient'. If the first person is agent (or source) then there is movement away from the signer, while movement toward the signer indicates a first person patient (or goal)' (86 – emphasis added). Here, Deuchar only mentions clauses in which one of the arguments has first person reference. Apparently, she describes locus differences between non-first person arguments in terms of incorporated pronouns (ibid., 208), but she does not discuss the distinction between case-marking expressed by direction of movement and pronoun incorporation expressed by locus differences.

Descriptions in terms of pronoun incorporation include agreement, as the relation between an incorporated pronoun and its antecedent can be subsumed under agreement (Corbett 1991, 112, 169-170). But in descriptions of the phenomenon as verb agreement, the marker on the verb is not regarded as an incorporated pronoun; it is a marker showing grammatical agreement within the clause. The main difference between the agreement descriptions and the descriptions in terms of incorporated pronouns is then the status of the markers on the verbs: Are they agreement markers or are they pronouns that in their turn agree across clause boundaries? I will first look at the difference between case-marking and agreement.

Agreement and case-marking on verbs
In spoken languages, marking of the semantic case of an argument on the verb is seen, for example, in the Philippine language Tagalog (Schachter 1977). In this language, each nontopic nominal has a prenominal marker indicating its semantic case. The topic nominal is marked by a special topic marker which is neutral with respect to semantic case, but the semantic case of the topic nominal is indicated by a prefix on the verb. If the nominal that Schachter calls 'actor' is topic, the verb has an actor-topic prefix; if the topic-marked nominal is goal, the verb has a goal-topic prefix. In (2), A stands for actor, T for topic, AT for actor-topic, GT for goal-topic, and D for direction:

(2) a. *Magbibigay   ang   babae   ng   bigas   sa   bata*
       AT-will-give T   woman   G   rice   D   child

   The woman will give some rice to a/the child.

   b. *Ibibigay   ng   babae   ang   bigas   sa   bata*
       GT-will-give A   woman   T   rice   D   child

   A/the woman will give the rice to a/the child.
                    (= Schachter's examples (1a-b), ibid., 280-281)

That is, the verbal prefix indicates the semantic case of whichever nominal is the topic. The verbal prefix signals, for example, that the clause has an actor-topic in the case where the actor nominal is marked as the topic, rather than as the actor.

In Danish Sign Language, a double agreement verb such as GIVE has two cells for markers: in one cell it takes a marker for the A argument, in another cell a marker for the IO argument. But by contrast to the Tagalog verbs, the sign verb is marked for a feature of its argument that is independent of the argument's semantic case. This feature is the locus of the argument's referent. Moreover, the features which are inserted into the cells are features that are independent of the clause in which the verb occurs (see, however, the description of marking for a specific point of view in III.6.3 The many uses of the *c*-form). The agreement marker itself carries information about a locus that is independent of the individual clause; which cell the marker occupies in the verb depends on whether the argument is the A or the IO argument.

Agreement is defined as the formal expression of a syntactic relation with respect to some grammatical feature. In the relationship between the verb and its arguments, case is what constitutes the grammatical relation (see also Lehmann 1988, 63-64). We can only talk about a verb agreeing with one or more of its arguments if the marker on the verb includes some grammatical category other than case, namely gender, number, or person.[1] In Danish Sign Language, the other category is locus and person (see III.6.2 Agreement features, direction, and domain).

Agreement markers in spoken languages always involve two aspects: they signal a syntactic relation, e.g. the relation between the subject and the verb, and they carry a meaning different from the syntactic relation. In Swahili, the verb agrees with the subject and some objects in person or noun class.

```
(3)  wa-toto      wa-na-kula    mkate
     CL2-child    CL2-PRES-eat  bread

     The children are eating bread.
```

The marker *wa-* on the verb shows that *watoto* is the subject of the verb and that the subject belongs to class 2 of the Swahili noun classes. In (3), the agreement marker *wa-* occurs before the tense marker *na-*. The same agreement marker can occur after the tense marker. Then it shows that *watoto* is the object and that the object belongs to class 2:[2]

```
(4)  ni-me-wa-pa         wa-toto     mkate
     1.p-PERF-CL2-give   CL2-child   bread

     I have given the children bread.
```

By contrast to (3) and (4) from Swahili, the markers in the Tagalog clauses do not carry a semantic feature of the topic argument that is independent of the argument's relation to the verb. Therefore, it is not an agreement marker. But parallel to the Swahili examples, fl+EXPLAIN+c in (5) signals two things: that DAN is the verb's A argument, and that the A argument is non-first person, with its referent represented by the locus *fl*. As in the Swahili verb, the position of the agreement marker in the verb stem shows the nominal's argument relation to the verb.

1 In Tlahuitoltepec Mixe (Mexico) (Lyon 1967), markers on the verb show whether the clause is actor-oriented or goal-oriented, i.e. the verbs are case-marked. The selection of actor orientation versus goal orientation is predictable from a hierarchy of importance depending on person, definiteness, and animacy. The only difference between the sentences meaning 'I hit the person' and 'The person hit me' is the marker on the verb which indicates that the highest ranking argument is either the actor or the goal. This is a parallel to case-marking in Tagalog. But in Tlahuitoltepec Mixe, the marker on the verb also indicates the 'mood' of the clause ('conjunct' or 'nonconjunct' depending on the introductory particle) as well as the person of the highest ranking argument, i.e. there are different markers for first, second, and third person. The latter kind of information is already found in the clause, which makes it reasonable to say that the verb agrees with the highest ranking argument in person. The reason why we would not say that the verb also agrees with this argument in case rests on the linguistic theory of case as being clause-dependent and constituting the relationship between the verb and its argument. Corbett (1988, 28) does, however, talk about case agreement in West Slavonic languages where adjectival predicates are said to agree with the subject in case.

2 Not all subject and object agreement markers in Swahili are identical.

(5)   DAN fl+EXPLAIN+c /   (Ill. 45b)
      Dan explained it to me.

An agreement verb in signed languages includes two kinds of information: information on characteristics of the arguments that are independent of the argument relation to the verb, and information on which nominal has which argument relation to the verb. The two kinds of information are separated in Liddell and Johnson's notation (see I.6.3 Liddell and Johnson's sequential form analysis of signs). Agreement verbs have cells for the agreement markers, and it is the position of a cell in the verb root that determines which argument relation a given nominal has to the verb. The information that is carried by the marker in the cell, the p-morph, is information on the nominal's independent characteristics, i.e. locus information. This information is independent of where the p-morph is inserted into the verb. It is the p-morph that is the agreement marker.

Before analysing the p-morphs' status as agreement markers, I consider the suggestion that they are incorporated pronouns. Some agreement markers in spoken languages derive diachronically from anaphoric pronouns through incorporation (e.g. Givón 1976; Moravcsik 1978a; Bresnan & Mchombo 1987; Lehmann 1988). There are two possible intermediate stages between free pronouns and agreement markers, clitics and incorporated pronouns.

Clitics or affixes

In Danish Sign Language, the handshape or orientation of pronominal signs whose base form has an index hand can be assimilated to the handshape or orientation of an adjacent sign. With respect to assimilation, the first person pronoun 1.p differs from the non-first person pronoun PRON: the handshape of 1.p may assimilate to the handshape of the verb in pre- or postverbal position, while the hand orientation in PRON assimilates to the orientation of the hand in the verb in postverbal position. Orientation assimilation in PRON is obligatory, while handshape assimilation in the first person pronoun 1.p is optional. The handshape of PRON always approximates an index hand: the index finger is stretched out and the three other fingers are bent in the proximal joint. By contrast, the first person pronoun 1.p is often made with a lax hand with no fingers bent into the hand irrespective of the verb. When the first person pronoun 1.p shows assimilation, it is, however, the handshape that assimilates to the verb's handshape.

Zwicky and Pullum (1983) list six criteria for distinguishing clitics and affixes. One criterion is that clitics can attach to words of many categories, while inflectional affixes are quite specific in their selection of stems. According to this criterion, the assimilated forms of PRON are clitics. The orientation of the hand of PRON can be assimilated to the orientation of the hand of signs from other categories than verbs, for instance, a number sign (6) and an interrogative pronoun (7):

(6)
```
                    [+]
EIGHT DEAF / THIRTY+sl..PRON+sl / EIGHT  DEAF / REST HEARING
PRON+pl.+sl / (orientation assim.)
```
Eight were deaf. That is, there were thirty. Eight were deaf, and the rest were hearing.

(7)
```
                 ?
WHO+r..PRON+sr / (orientation assim.)
```
Who is that?

Another criterion is that clitics have fewer morphophonological idiosyncrasies than affixes. Again PRON with assimilated hand orientation is a clitic, as the forms are completely predictable from the context. Moreover, there are no semantic idiosyncrasies in the use of the assimilated forms of PRON, which is another argument in favour of analysing assimilated forms of PRON as clitics rather than affixes, according to Zwicky and Pullum's argumentation. Finally, whether a form of PRON will show hand orientation assimilation can be predicted from the syntactic context. By this criterion, the assimilated forms of PRON are also clitics.

The next question is then whether the markers on the verbs, i.e. the p-morphs inserted into the verbs' A and P/IO argument cells, can be analysed as incorporated pronouns.

Incorporated pronouns or agreement markers
The relationship between pronouns and agreement markers has been extensively studied within the last decade in both the theory of Government and Binding and in more functional approaches to grammar. The theories are difficult to compare, partly because the term *pronoun* is used sometimes for a particular form and sometimes for a function.

Lehmann (1982, 234ff.) distinguishes form and function in verb-object agreement. On a scale of forms he lists, at one end, full NPs as in (8) from German, where *die Frau* ('the woman') is semantically in agreement with *seiner Haushälterin* ('his (female) housekeeper'); both are also the feminine gender. Along the scale set up by Lehmann we find free pronouns, clitic pronouns, and variable affixes. The opposite end of the scale from full NPs is constituted by invariable affixes such as the transitivity marker in Tok Pisin in (9) which does not have an anaphoric function:

(8) *Der Professor fragte nach seiner Haushälterin. Niemand hatte die Frau gesehen.*

> The professor asked for his housekeeper. Nobody had seen the woman.   (= Lehmann's example (47), ibid., 234)

(9) Man i-mek-im   singsing long Mbabmu
     man Sbj.3-make-TRANS   spell   to   Mbabmu

     Men utter a spell over Mbabmu.
                            (= Lehmann's example (55b), ibid., 235)

Lehmann compares the scale of forms with a functional scale set up according to two criteria: whether the element can function anaphorically, and whether it can co-occur with the NP in the clause where the agreement is. The two criteria are not mutually independent. If an agreeing element cannot co-occur with the NP in the clause, it does function anaphorically; but if it can co-occur with the NP, there are two possibilities: it may also be able to function anaphorically (i.e. without the NP in the same clause), or it may not be able to function anaphorically (i.e. it requires an NP in the same clause). Lehmann defines *anaphoric agreement* as the relation between the NP and a free or clitic pronoun which can function anaphorically and cannot co-occur with the NP. *Syntactic agreement* is defined as the relation between the NP and a clitic pronoun or variable affix which can co-occur with the NP, but also may occur without it. That is, in syntactic agreement, there is a syntactic place for the NP in the agreement construction (ibid., 219). This means that clitic pronouns may show either anaphoric agreement or syntactic agreement. The difference depends on whether or not the clitic pronoun can co-occur with the NP. The difference is demonstrated by examples (10) and (11) from Italian and Spanish (= Lehmann's examples (50) and (51), ibid., 234):

(10) *Giovanni, l'ho visto ieri.*
     John, I saw him yesterday.
(11) *Ayer lo vi a mi amigo.*
     Yesterday I saw my friend.

In both sentences, the NP's, *Giovanni* and *a mi amigo*, can be left out. In (10), the pronoun is obligatory, but could not be present if the NP was part of the clause, i.e. there is anaphoric agreement between the pronoun and the NP in the Italian sentence. In (11), the pronoun is optional and the NP is part of the clause and identified as the object by the case marker *a*; here there is syntactic agreement between the NP and the pronoun. But Lehmann finds that (11) is not typical of syntactic agreement. Following Boas, he describes the relationship between the pronoun and the NP in (11) as 'a sort of appositive relationship' (ibid., 237; see also Bloomfield's description of cross-reference (1935, 193)). Lehmann finds that the crystallisation point of syntactic agreement on the scale is affixes that can function anaphorically as well as co-occur with the NP in the agreement relation. Examples of such affixes are the subject agreement markers in Latin and Swahili where the agreement markers can occur with or without nominals; if the personal pronouns occur in the clause with the agreement markers, they are emphatic. In approaches in terms of 'Pro-Drop', languages where the nominal is required, such as German, represent the unmarked case (see also Dik 1989, 133).

Lehmann leaves out of consideration one possibility which is represented by the Bantu language Chicheŵa: an affix which cannot co-occur with the NP in the agreement relation (Bresnan & Mchombo 1987). In Chicheŵa, one form – the subject marker which has the form of a prefix on the verb – has the qualities of the crystallisation point of syntactic agreement on Lehmann's scale: it may occur with as well as without a subject NP. In Bresnan and Mchombo's terms, it may be used for both anaphoric (when an NP is not present) and grammatical (when an NP is present) agreement. When the subject NP is absent, the marker is given 'a pronominal subject interpretation' (ibid., 745; see also 765). The object marker, which is also a verbal prefix, is used unambiguously for anaphoric agreement. It cannot co-occur with an object NP, but only with an 'object' topic which is not part of the VP. Therefore, Bresnan and Mchombo categorise the object marker as an incorporated pronoun. Within their framework, Lexical Functional Grammar, the functional uniqueness condition 'requires that, regardless of where it may be expressed in the word and phrase structure, information about the same function must be consistent – and, in the case of meaning, unique' (ibid., 745). The uniqueness requirement makes it impossible to analyse an agreeing element as having an anaphoric relation to an NP that has the same argument relation to the verb, i.e. what Lehmann describes as 'a sort of appositive relationship.' As the NP in (11) from Spanish is case-marked and thus an argument of the verb, Bresnan and Mchombo would analyse the pronoun *lo* as showing grammatical agreement, just as the Chicheŵa subject marker when it occurs with a subject NP. The completeness condition of Lexical Functional Grammar 'requires that every argument which is lexically required must be present' (ibid., 745). Therefore, the subject marker is given 'a pronominal subject interpretation' when the subject NP is omitted, and this is also how the pronoun in Spanish would have to be analysed when the NP is not present in the clause.

Lehmann reserves the term *anaphoric agreement* for occurrences of forms (free pronouns and clitic pronouns) which never co-occur with the NP in the agreement relation. What he misses here is the Chicheŵa object marker which has this functional characteristic, but the form of an affix. Bresnan and Mchombo use only one criterion to distinguish grammatical agreement from anaphoric agreement, namely whether the NP in the agreement relation has an argument relation to the verb. Whenever the NP co-occurs with the agreeing element, the agreeing element shows grammatical agreement. Otherwise, it shows anaphoric (pronominal) agreement irrespective of its form. Bresnan and Mchombo use the term *pronoun* to distinguish elements that agree anaphorically from elements that agree grammatically. That is, when they claim that the object marker in Chicheŵa is an 'incorporated pronoun' or that the subject marker is given 'a pronominal subject interpretation', what they mean is not that the agreeing element has the form of a pronoun, but that it shows anaphoric agreement. Their analysis characterises elements as (incorporated) pronouns or affixes on a syntactic basis and disregards a synchronic form analysis of the elements as free pronouns, clitics, or affixes.

Bresnan and Mchombo adhere to the theory that grammatical agreement has evolved from incorporation of pronouns (1987, 741). As a general claim for all cases of grammatical agreement, the theory is clearly false as there are many languages in which agreement markers do not have the same phonological form as any pronoun of the language (Moravcsik 1978a). But the claim can be true for individual languages or for some agreement markers in a language. In Danish Sign Language, pronouns and agreement markers share the features locus and person; neither pronouns nor agreement markers include any generic properties of nominals, which means that there is no semantic reason why agreement markers could not have developed from pronouns.

A verb marked for agreement can occur either when the nominal in the agreement relation has an argument relation to the verb or when it is outside the clause, e.g. when it is topicalized. There is a form difference between cliticized pronouns and agreement markers. In (12), neu+EXPLAIN+c is followed by a pronoun, the first person pronoun 1.p, whose handshape is assimilated to the handshape of the verb. In (13), there is no nominal. In (12), the cliticized pronoun consists of all the features of the first person pronoun 1.p except for the handshape features which have been substituted by the handshape features of EXPLAIN (Ill. 46). In (13), there is no form cliticized to fl+EXPLAIN+c (Ill. 45b).

(12)   <u>nodding</u>
    MOTHER /   gesture nok(M)('enough') ANNEGRETHE
    neu+EXPLAIN+c..1.p neu+GO-TO+c nok(M)('enough') / (Ill. 46)

    My mother nodded and said, 'Never mind. It's not necessary. Annegrethe will explain it to me when she comes. It's not necessary.'

(13)   <u>   ?</u>
    1.p c+NOTIFY+fl DAN / PRON+fl / STEAL HOW / fl+EXPLAIN+c /
    (Ill. 45b)

    I asked Dan, 'Tell me, how did the burglary take place?' He told me.

In Bresnan and Mchombo's terms, the agreeing element is alternately an incorporated pronoun showing anaphoric agreement and an affix showing grammatical agreement; in Lehmann's terms, the agreement marker in Danish Sign Language shows syntactic agreement with a sort of appositive relationship between the agreement marker and the nominal when the latter is present in the clause. That is, functionally, the agreement marker is parallel to the clitic pronoun in Spanish in example

(11); formally, however, the agreement marker is not a clitic pronoun, but an affix like the subject prefix in Chicheŵa. Like Latin and Swahili agreement markers, the agreement markers in Danish Sign Language thus have the characteristics of what Lehmann analyses as the crystallisation point of syntactic agreement. But in one respect the constructions in Danish Sign Language differ from Latin and Swahili: apparently, there is free variation between constructions with a nominal in the clause as in (12), and constructions without the nominal as in (13). Informants report that there is no difference between using a pronoun in examples such as (12) and (13) and leaving out the pronoun. The pronoun in (12) is not stressed or focal.

Lillo-Martin (1986; see also Kegl 1986) finds that, morphologically, verb agreement in ASL is an inflectional process rather than a process of cliticization. Syntactically, a verb showing agreement may occur by itself or co-occur with an NP.[3] She analyses these facts in terms of null arguments: verbs which show agreement in ASL behave 'as if an overt pronoun were present, in that structure [sic] which otherwise would need an overt pronoun are grammatical, and structures in which island violations would have occurred are "saved"' (ibid., 420). Specifically, verbs which show agreement may occur with null arguments in constructions where verbs without agreement demand a pronoun (or another nominal). The nonagreement verb DON'T-KNOW in ASL must take an object pronoun in (14), while the ASL agreement verb GIVE in (15) can occur without a pronoun ("br' stands for a brow raise which is sometimes used as a clause marker' (ibid., 442)):

```
(14)           t            br
      aTHAT aMAN, bJOHN SAY cMARY DON'T-KNOW aINDEX.
      That man_i, John said Mary doesn't know him_i.
                  (= Lillo-Martin's example (11a), ibid., 424)
(15)           t            br
      aTHAT aMAN, bJOHN SAY cMARY FINISH cGIVEa BOOK.
      That man_i, John said Mary already gave a book to (-him_i).
                  (= Lillo-Martin's example (10), ibid., 424)
```

In Danish Sign Language, we see the same difference between an agreement verb such as INVITE in example (16) and a nonagreement verb such as KNOW in (17).

```
(16)     t                     affirm
      PALLE / BRITTA SAY SUSSI c+INVITE+fr /
      As for Palle, Britta says that Sussi has already invited him.
```

---

3 Liddell (personal communication) finds that an object pronoun cannot occur after a verb agreeing with the object in ASL. Smith (1989, 109) has found a similar constraint in Taiwan Sign Language. In Danish Sign Language, such constructions are quite common in native signers' natural discourse (see example (12)).

(17) ```
         t
      KRESTEN / SUSSI SAY ANNE KNOW PRON+fr /
```
As for Kresten, Sussi says that Anne knows him.

But an anaphoric pronoun is not obligatory with a nonagreement verb as shown by the following examples:

(18)  ```
                          t                    affirm
      THAT-IS DET+fs1 BOOK / BRITTA SAY SUSSI READ   /
```
As for that book, Britta says that Sussi has already read it.

(19) ```
      ___t___   _____t_____
      MARINA / WHEN neu+GO-TO+c / SUSSI SAY BRITTA KNOW-WELL /
```
As for Marina, when she will come, Sussi says that Britta knows.

(Examples (16)-(19) were elicited to demonstrate the pronoun use in question.)

It seems that the possibility of leaving out the nominal depends on a number of features which all contribute to identifying the argument of the verb. If the verb shows agreement, the argument is sufficiently identified as in (16), but a verb's semantic co-occurrence constraints combined with the context may also be sufficient to identify the argument: in (17), all the nominals may semantically be P arguments of the verb KNOW, and my informants feel that a pronoun is required, while in (18), only the first nominal satisfies the semantic requirements of the verb READ and the sentence is acceptable without a pronoun.[4] The verb KNOW-WELL (example (19)) must take a propositional P argument. That is, the syntactic requirements of KNOW-WELL identify the topicalized clause as the argument. My informants felt that a form of PRON at the end of the construction would be a resumptive pronoun co-referential with BRITTA.

The conclusion is that there does not seem to be a *syntactic* requirement of a "pronominal" element (a pronoun or an agreement marker) in Danish Sign Language. Moreover, the description of the agreement markers as incorporated pronouns would obscure the form difference between pronouns and affixes. Therefore, I prefer as an

---

4  Informants were not comfortable about judging the grammaticality of constructions like (16)-(19) and differed in their judgments of the following example:

(Context: two adults looking at a group of children eating. The day before, there had not been enough food)

```
          1.p HOPE TODAY (PRON+pl.+deictic-loci) SATISFIED /
```
I hope they will get enough today.

Some signers felt that the example was acceptable without PRON+deictic-loci, and one signer that the pronoun was obligatory. There is reason to believe that the more context dependent a feature is (the less syntactically determined), the harder it is to judge the grammaticality of the construction.
```

analysis the one suggested by Lehmann for spoken languages: agreement markers in Danish Sign Language are affixes, or p-morphs, which can function anaphorically, but also co-occur with the nominal in the agreement relation. When they co-occur with the nominal, there is an appositive relation (cross-reference) between the agreement marker and the nominal.

6.2 Agreement features, direction, and domain

Definitions of agreement

In III.6.1 Alternative descriptions, I showed that the p-morphs with locus information inserted into cells specified for particular arguments cannot be described as case markers on the verbs, and that the p-morphs are not clitic pronouns, but fulfil some of the syntactic criteria for being regarded as agreement markers set up by Lehmann. Before the p-morphs can properly be said to be agreement markers, there are many questions that have to be discussed, particularly in relation to the controller of the agreement, i.e. the direction and domain of the agreement and the origin of the agreement feature. Lehmann (1982) defines agreement as follows:[1]

> Constituent B agrees with constituent A (in category C) if and only if the following holds true:
> 1. There is a grammatical or semantic syntagmatic relation between A and B.
> 2. A grammatical category C with a form paradigm of subcategories exists.
> 3. A belongs to a subcategory c of C, and A's belonging to c is independent of the presence or nature of B.
> 4. C is expressed on B and forms a constituent with it. (Lehmann 1982, 203)

Corbett (1988, 24) points out that whether directionality is taken into consideration (which constituent is the controller and which the target) depends on the grammatical theory. Ferguson and Barlow (1988, 1) do not include direction in their definition. They point out that an advantage of nondirectional accounts of agreement is that they can easily handle cases in which the controllers are not fully specified with respect to agreement features as, for instance, when the predicative adjective in French is gender-marked even though the first person pronoun is not (ibid., 13):

(1) a. *Je suis heureux (masc.)*
       I am happy (said by a male)
    b. *Je suis heureuse (fem.)*
       I am happy (said by a female)

---

1 Moravcsik (1978a, 333) defines agreement very similarly to Lehmann except that she apparently switches the relationship between agreeing and agreed with constituent ('a grammatical constituent A will be said to agree with a grammatical constituent B in properties C' (1978a, 333)). The example of verb – subject agreement in English following her definition shows, however, that the phrase *agree with* in the beginning of the definition is a mistake: B in the definition agrees with A, not vice versa.

Ferguson and Barlow emphasise the grammatical relation between the constituents when they define agreement as the phenomenon that in some languages 'a grammatical element X matches a grammatical element Y in property Z within some grammatical configuration' (ibid., 1). Here the requirement is that the agreeing constituents occur in a 'grammatical configuration', while Lehmann also includes cases where there is a 'semantic syntagmatic relation between A and B' (see the quotation above). But Ferguson and Barlow also mention the possibility of including 'intersentential pronominal anaphora' in agreement (ibid., 5).

The agreement features
The potential agreement features in Danish Sign Language are *locus* and *person*. Within the non-first person category, locus is not an inherent feature of nouns like gender or a feature of the nominal like number. The nominal arguments of the verb may include a locus marker, but there are many clauses in which the arguments of the verb are not present as nominals or the nominals are not overtly marked for locus. Moreover, a verb may be modified spatially for the loci of referents present in the context of utterance. This is reminiscent of the French example (1) where the gender difference does not inhere in the first person pronoun, but derives from the referent of the subject nominal. The category of locus differs from natural gender, however, in that it is not an inherent, but a temporary feature of the referent, as the same referent can be represented by different loci.

An alternative to talking about loci as an agreement feature is to regard the agreement feature as person with two subcategories, first and non-first person. This brings us relatively closer to well-known territory from analyses of spoken languages. Even though the category of person in Danish Sign Language only includes two subcategories (lacking the second person category), person agreement between the verb and its arguments is found in languages such as Latin, German, and Swahili. Moreover, in Latin and Swahili the controller may be absent as the pronoun is only present when it is emphatic. The differences between loci within the subcategory of the non-first person category in Danish Sign Language could then be explained as explicit indices of co-referentiality of the kind which is needed to account for co-referentiality in spoken languages (see Lillo-Martin & Klima 1990, discussed here in II.6.1 Types of pointing signs, and II.6.3 Person, place, and shifters).

That is partly the analysis adopted for ASL agreement verbs by Padden (1990). She claims that verb agreement categories in natural languages, person, number, and gender, 'are made up of a very small number of elements, specifically no more than three, sometimes only two' (ibid., 127), and she refers to an article from 1989 by Corbett who argues that what is sometimes claimed to be fifteen gender classes of Serbo-Croatian can be reanalysed as consisting of three controller genders: masculine, feminine, and neuter, with subgenders. Subgenders are predictable morphological variations within the same gender class, in the case of Serbo-Croatian distinguished by animacy.

To obtain a category with as few elements as she claims is common in spoken languages, Padden analyses agreement in ASL as person (and number) agreement. It is not clear how she views locus distinctions in agreement verbs, but she finishes her article thus:

> Finally, there remains one set of elements that exploit the spatial dimension and appear to do so in a way unmatched in oral languages: the indexical segments. The challenge to those constructing a grammar of ASL will be to account for these segments in a principled way. (ibid., 131)

Padden does not analyse locus as an agreement category, apparently because it would be an agreement category with more than three elements, and she leaves it to future study to determine the linguistic status of locus distinctions.

In a reworked version of the 1989 article, Corbett (1991, chapter 6) describes several techniques to reduce a large number of agreement classes to fewer genders. He does, however, give an example of a language where the reduction leads to five genders (ibid., 172) and another language where ten agreement classes are reduced to six genders (ibid., 174). But the problem is not so much whether there are two, three, or maybe six elements in the agreement category. It is rather whether there is an infinite number as seems to be the case with locus distinctions in signed languages. An infinite number of different linguistic forms presents both a descriptive problem, in that we would have to deal with an infinite inventory, and a psycholinguistic problem. In processing the language, the language user would have to deal with an infinite number of elements (see the discussion of these problems in relation to ASL pronouns in Lillo-Martin & Klima 1990, 198).

What Padden states is a fact: signed languages exploit space in a way unmatched by spoken languages, but they do not use space in loci in the non-first person category for creating symbols. That is, there is no demand put on the signer that she store an infinite number of symbols in her memory. The value of a locus must always be deduced from its context, and in any given context only a limited number of loci are used without indication of the value of the different loci through lexical means. The demands on the signed language user's memory are not part of the language system, but of its use.

Two agreement categories: person and locus
In II.6.3 Person, place, and shifters, I showed that Danish Sign Language distinguishes first person from non-first person pronouns. But even though there is a person category of pronouns, it is possible that there is no person distinction in verb agreement. We can apply the same criteria here as for the pronouns.

First, we should examine whether there is a form difference (besides the difference in direction) between the locus marker used with first person arguments and the locus markers used with non-first person arguments, as there are form differences between the first person pronoun 1.p and the non-first person pronoun PRON. In some verbs, the locus marker for the sender locus in the verbs' P/IO cell results in forms with body contact; such forms are highly marked in relation to the (present) referents of non-first person arguments. Body contact is lexically idiosyncratic; COMFORT+c is made with contact with the signer's cheeks, while fr+TEACH+c is made without contact, and fr+ANSWER+c is made with or without contact with the signer's chest, apparently with no semantic difference. That is, formally, the marker for the sender locus differs from other locus markers in that the form changes on agreement verbs resulting from other locus markers are predictable, while the locus marker c causes lexically idiosyncratic form changes. The first person pronoun 1.p triggers verb forms with a locus marker for the sender locus no matter whether 1.p is used to refer to the sender of the context of utterance or to a quoted sender. But the locus marker c may be used in agreement verbs for referents that do not have the role of sender of a communication act. In marking for a specific point of view (see III.6.3 The many uses of the c-form), the sender locus can be used for other referents than the signer herself or a quoted sender. That is, the locus marker c is not restricted to expressing first person, but its other function, marking for a specific point of view, derives from its ability to express the first person category (see III.6.4 First person, point of view, and agentivity).

What I suggest is a description in terms of two agreement categories, *person* and *locus*, with person having two subcategories and the number of loci in the locus category depending on any given context. The category of locus is only distinguished within the non-first person subcategory of the person category. That is, there is a hierarchical relation between the agreement categories:

> person
> > first person
> > non-first person; locus differences within the non-first person category

A parallel to the hierarchy of categories in Danish Sign Language would be the distinction in some spoken languages between genders or between obviative and nonobviative within the third person subcategory of the person category only (Moravcsik 1978a, 357):

> person
> > first person
> > second person
> > third person; gender differences within the third person category

We are, however, still left with the problem that the clause often does not include a controller of the agreement in terms of a nominal that is inherently or explicitly marked for the agreement feature.

The function of agreement: 'Apprehension of a linguistic object'

Lehmann (1982, 228ff.) discusses directional accounts of agreement, i.e. accounts that seek to determine which constituent is the controller and which the target of the agreement, and he states that the agreement categories (number, gender, etc.) are all of nominal or pronominal nature and the agreement direction is always 'from an NP to either a governing or modifying expression' (ibid., 228). Lehmann gives a functional explanation of why the agreement direction is always from an NP and never to an NP. He rejects the possibility of finding anything shared by agreeing elements in NP internal and NP external agreement in terms of syntax. Instead, he uses the semantic notion of argument by which he understands a nominal concept or a referent:

> The relation between an argument and an NP is one of designation: an NP designates an argument. Other constituents may be in some construction with an NP, and make reference to the argument. To signal the reference to an argument is to open an argument slot. (ibid., 232)

An agreeing expression is an expression with an argument slot (e.g. a determiner or an attributive adjective in internal agreement or a verb in external agreement). If the argument is designated by an NP, the expression in question may agree with the NP. Agreement appears in argument slots because agreement markers show the categories of the NP triggering the agreement and can therefore represent the NP. Agreement can now be understood as having the function of keeping 'a linguistic object' constant:

> ...part of the **apprehension of a linguistic object** is to keep it **constant**. This presupposes that the same object (i.e. nominal concept or referent, something that can serve as an argument in the above sense) can make its appearance at various places in the sentence or text. The fact that each time the same object is involved is expressed in formal languages by means of differential referential indices. In natural languages it is expressed by means of agreement in grammatical categories, i.e. by categorizing, mentioning the categories of, the apprehended object. (ibid., 233 – emphasis in the original)

Lehmann further points out that it is not the case that there is one place in a sentence (a noun or an NP) where the linguistic object is apprehended, nor that the agreement markers are only reappearances of the same already fully apprehended object. We can see that from the fact that the grammatical category need not be expressed on the noun or NP:

> What is more, the NP may not even belong to a cetagory [sic] which the agreement marker shows. This means that the categorisation is in part only achieved through agreement, through the recurrence of the object. (ibid., 233)

In Danish Sign Language, a locus is often only expressed in verb agreement.

In the passage quoted, Lehmann explicitly links the function of differential referential indices in formal languages with agreement in natural languages. What serves to keep the linguistic object constant is the mentioning of certain semantic features of the linguistic object in various places of the sentence or text. The semantic features appear as grammatical categories in agreement markers, and here Lehmann distinguishes grammatical categories depending on whether they contribute to the apprehension of the linguistic object or not. In order to apprehend the linguistic object, we must refer to it as an individual, and this can only be done if we at the same time subsume it under a class (see also Givón 1976, 171-172). That is, apprehension depends on the converse principles of generalisation and individualisation, which constitute nominal classes (including noun classes and genders) and the category of number, Lehmann claims. By contrast, the agreement categories of person and definiteness are determined by operations of deixis and determination which are outside the dimension of apprehension of the linguistic object (ibid., 258). That is, according to Lehmann, deixis does not contribute to keeping the linguistic object constant. Lehmann does not expand on this point, but the reason why he excludes deixis as a means of keeping the linguistic object constant is probably that deictic expressions in *spoken* languages are shifters, i.e. indexical symbols, whose reference shifts with the sender.

One function of loci is to keep the linguistic object constant: loci serve to keep track of reference (see II.7 Discourse and space: Conclusion), even though they are based on deixis. The reason why this is possible is that except for the first person pronoun 1.p and the marker for the sender locus, locus markers are not indexical symbols, i.e. they are not shifters (see II.6.3 Person, place, and shifter). Loci within the non-first person category are more constant than the deictic category of person[2] of spoken languages as they do not change with the sender. The choice of locus depends on semantic and contextually-bound features of the referent, and not on nouns being inherently marked for the category of locus or on loci being predictable on the basis of semantic features of the noun. Thus, loci contribute to keeping the linguistic object constant and thereby to its apprehension especially through deictic individualisation, but also to some extent through generalisation, namely to the extent that loci have meaning in themselves.

Would we then in spoken languages accept as an agreement category a category which depends on transient features of the referent conditioned by the context of utterance or the discourse context? Person is indeed a transient feature of the referent and in languages such as Latin and Swahili and in the following examples from Spanish (from Moravcsik 1978a, 351), we do talk about person agreement even when there is no personal pronoun to control the agreement:

(2) a. *nadie lo vimos*
 nobody him saw-we

 None of us saw him.

---

2 In so far as third person pronouns contrast with first and second person pronouns in spoken languages, they may be described as shifters: even though some will refer to A by means of *he*, A will refer to himself by means of *I*. There is, however, general agreement that third person pronouns do not have the same deictic status as the first and second person pronouns. This is true also of the forms of PRON in Danish Sign Language as compared with the first person pronoun 1.p.

b. *toda   la   familia   fuimos*
   whole the   family   went-we

   My whole family, including me, went.

That is, the category of locus resembles the category of person by being transient and not an inherent feature of either nouns or referents. By not being shifters, however, locus markers are more like gender and especially natural gender and can, like gender or differential referential indices, contribute to keeping the linguistic object constant.

Agreement in Danish Sign Language
If we take another look at Lehmann's definition of agreement (quoted above), we see that we now have two interrelated categories C, person and locus, with a form paradigm, although this may not be a closed paradigm, as it is as yet unclear whether there is an infinite number of loci. Moreover, 'c' in Lehmann's agreement definition, which in Danish Sign Language is a subcategory of person/locus, is expressed on B, the verb, and forms a constituent with it. It is always possible to make A explicit, either by a pronoun or by another nominal, and to make the agreement feature explicit on the nominal, either in a pronoun or in a determiner. Moreover, it is always possible to specify the semantic syntagmatic relation between B, the verb, and the nominal: the nominal is either the A or source argument or the P, IO, or goal argument of the verb. But as in other cases in which the source of the agreement feature is not fully specified with respect to agreement features (Ferguson & Barlow 1988, 13), it is an advantage to give a nondirectional account of agreement in Danish Sign Language. This means that it would be more appropriate to say that the verb is in agreement with its arguments. I will, however, continue to use the more traditional phrase that the verb agrees with its arguments.

The peculiarities of the agreement categories, in particular locus, are what makes agreement in Danish Sign Language nonprototypical with respect to agreement features, direction, and domain. But except for the fact that the agreement category as such is unknown in spoken languages, I find that the agreement type does not deviate from what is also called (nonprototypical) agreement with sources of the agreement feature(s) not fully specified in spoken languages. Therefore, agreement is the appropriate term for the spatial modification of verbs that indicates the A/source and/or P/IO/goal argument by loci.

Agreement in Danish Sign Language differs from prototypical agreement in another respect. While agreement usually occurs in all constructions fulfilling the syntactic and semantic requirements, agreement in Danish Sign Language is limited to a lexically determined subclass of the verbs. By far not all clauses have verb-argument agreement. Only clauses with an agreement verb can show this kind of agreement. Moreover, the arguments must have specific reference. Even within these lexical and semantic restrictions, there are contextual, individual, and generational differences (see below).

Agreement with semantic arguments

I mentioned in III.3 Earlier verb classifications, that some researchers (notably Padden 1988b; Liddell 1990a) analyse verb agreement in ASL as agreement with the syntactic arguments subject and object. In her analysis of ASL within the framework of Relational Grammar, Padden shows that many syntactic rules can be given a more general formulation if the category of subject is used to characterise one of the arguments of the verb rather than some semantic role. One example of such a rule is that nominals that precede modals must be subjects, Padden claims. The rule cannot be stated in terms of semantic roles since (3) with the patient preceding the modal is acceptable and (4), also with the patient preceding the modal, is unacceptable:

(3) HOUSE CAN BLOW-UP.   (= (56), Padden 1988b, 148)
    The house could blow up.
(4) *BOOK CAN WOMAN $_i$GIVE$_j$ MAN.   (= (60), ibid., 149)

But Padden does not find any evidence for a distinction between "initial" and "final" 1s (i.e. "deep" and "surface" subjects) in ASL (ibid., 166).

In Danish Sign Language, agreement verbs are always marked for the same semantic arguments. The agreement pattern of some verbs makes it necessary to distinguish source and A arguments (see III.6.3 The many uses of the c-form); but any individual verb is unambiguously marked for either its A or its source argument or either its P, its IO, or its goal argument. A verb that is marked for its source argument cannot be marked for its A argument. And a verb that takes an IO or a goal argument is marked for this argument and not for its P argument. There is no form difference between marking for a P, an IO, or a goal argument, and the marking of one excludes the marking of the others within the same verb. The distinction between a goal and a P argument with a verb taking only one argument besides its A argument is purely semantic, and so is the distinction between a goal and an IO argument with verbs taking two arguments besides its A argument. Therefore, we might reduce all three to one category: object. Such a category would, however, obscure the fact that the semantic category is unambiguously marked, given the lexical semantics of the verb. As in ASL, the agreement rules for verbs that show agreement in Danish Sign Language can be stated without reference to different levels of syntactic representation.

As mentioned, agreement verbs that take both a P and an IO or goal argument (verbs like GIVE and SEND) agree with the IO argument. That is, agreement verbs in Danish Sign Language require what Faltz (1978; see also Givón 1976, 160-166), in talking about spoken languages, terms 'the DO type of indirect object marking': the indirect object takes the grammatical coding of the direct object of the verb. Moravcsik (1988, 103-104) points out that there is here a mismatch between language-internal and cross-language distribution of agreement, as no language has indirect object agreement without also having direct object agreement. That is, indirect object agreement presupposes direct object agreement cross-linguistically. In some spoken languages, however, ditransitive verbs agree with their indirect object only, just as agreement verbs in Danish Sign Language agree with the IO argument and not the P argument. Croft (1988, 167-168) suggests a solution to the "mismatch": agreement indexes the important or salient arguments, and since indirect object nominals usually refer to humans with high salience, case roles such as recipient or experiencer enter into the agreement relation before case roles such as patient.

Danish Sign Language differs, however, from most spoken languages in that it treats arguments referring to locations as P/IO arguments; locative nominals are treated like human nominals with respect to verb agreement:

(5)   CHARLOTTE START SOME ABOUT FOUR MONTH+pl. /

    c+SEND+fr DET+fr NURSERY /

    Charlotte started when she was about four months old. She was
    sent to the nursery school.

Some agreement verbs, e.g. SEND, SEND-MAIL, may agree with a human or a locative IO argument. The fact that in Danish Sign Language both P arguments and IO arguments are coded like goal arguments points to the locative origin of agreement in this language.

Types of agreement verbs
Double agreement verbs agree with their A or source argument and their P, IO, or goal argument; *single agreement verbs* agree with their P or IO argument, i.e. all agreement verbs are transitive (see also I.6.5 Formal description of some different verb types). Examples of double agreement verbs are EXPLAIN, SEND, SEND-MAIL, GIVE, SCOLD, TEACH, CRITICISE, TELEPHONE-TO, PERCEIVE, TEASE, NOTIFY, ANSWER, GIVE-KEY, HELP, VISIT, INVITE, APPLY-FOR, EMPLOY, DISCUSS, and SWAP. Examples of single agreement verbs are INFORM, BECKON, DECEIVE, COMFORT, SHOOT-AT ('tease'), TELL, and SEE.

It is not possible to find one semantic or formal criterion that determines whether a verb is a single agreement verb, a double agreement verb, or a verb that can only show pragmatic agreement. Some single agreement verbs have a form with contact on the head or body in their first segment, e.g. DECEIVE (Ill. 14a), INFORM, TELL; but that is not the case with BECKON (Ill. 9a) or COMFORT. In general, verbs with a vertical movement cannot show semantic agreement. However, one verb, HELP, has a single vertical movement and is a double agreement verb (the orientation of the hands and the movement change slightly so that the movement is from the direction of the A argument's locus toward the direction of the IO argument's locus and the palms face in the direction of the IO argument's locus). This is probably because the verb may take an animate IO argument and denotes some kind of transfer. The sign SHOOT-AT ('tease') is also made with a vertical movement, but here the handshape (two index hands) can be seen as iconically representing guns directed at the patient referent.

There is no absolute boundary between double and single agreement verbs. Some people use a *mixed agreement pattern* with verbs which others treat as double agreement verbs (see also III.4 Plain signs). The mixed agreement type is verbs which can agree with two arguments only when their P/IO argument has first person reference; otherwise they agree with only their P/IO argument, i.e. they behave like single agreement verbs. Another type of defective paradigm is single agreement verbs which cannot take the first person agreement marker, e.g. SHOOT-AT. If the P argument of such verbs has first person reference, they do not show agreement.

A generational difference

The defective paradigms can be understood in terms of a diachronic development. People above fifty or sixty tend to construct all agreement verbs as single agreement verbs agreeing with their P/IO argument, except when the P/IO argument has first person reference;[3] then agreement is left out as in (6):

```
(6)                                    squint
    BLIND^INSTITUTE OFTEN / BLIND        c+TEASE+neu 1.p+pl.+sr. /
                                   PROFORM+pl.

    (Ill. 47)

    This institute for the blind, the blind there often teased us.
```

Many younger people would construct TEASE as a double agreement verb, in this case with the P argument cell filled with the first person agreement marker (neu+TEASE+c).[4] The agreement pattern of many elderly people is unusual, because P/IO argument agreement presupposes A argument agreement in the world's lan-

---

3   There is some variation with respect to individual verbs. For instance, elderly people may use first person P/IO agreement forms of the agreement verbs NOTIFY, INFORM, and DECEIVE (Ill. 14b), even though they would not use a form of TEASE with first person P argument agreement.

4   It is reasonable to expect that the informational load of sign order is higher when the verb does not show agreement (see the discussion of this issue in ASL in Wilbur 1987, 141ff.), even though verb agreement does not always coincide with flexible word order in the world's languages. In a study of techniques for expressing semantic roles and locative relations in Swiss French Sign Language and Italian Sign Language (Boyes Braem et al. 1990), it was found that in clauses with reversible subject and object, Swiss informants relied on spatial morphology as well as sign order while the Italian informants tended to mention the agent first and rely on sign order only, as in example (6) from a Danish deaf man of about 60. I have, however, not studied sign order in Danish Sign Language.

guages. Keenan (1976, 316; see also Lehmann 1988, 64) mentions a few languages in which the verb may agree with its object, but cannot agree with its subject; otherwise spoken languages only have object agreement if they also have subject agreement. I will return to an explanation of the agreement pattern with only P/IO argument agreement in III.6.3 The many uses of the *c*-form.

The following three stages can be seen as stages in the development from the "earlier" agreement pattern to the "younger" agreement pattern, but there is no clear linear transition. Younger people also often use the "earlier" pattern:

1. The verb agrees with its P/IO argument except when this argument has first person reference; then there is no agreement. This is the agreement pattern of the older generation and the defective agreement pattern of single agreement verbs of a younger generation.
2. The verbs develop the possibility of agreeing with a first person P/IO argument:
   a. The verb can show P/IO argument agreement also with a first person argument, i.e. the full agreement pattern of a single agreement verb;
   b. The verb can show P/IO argument agreement also with a first person argument simultaneously with A argument agreement with a non-first person argument. There is no A argument agreement when the verb agrees with a non-first person P/IO argument. This is the mixed agreement pattern, i.e. the defective paradigm of double agreement verbs.
3. The verb shows A argument agreement and P/IO argument agreement with all kinds of arguments with specific reference, including two non-first person arguments. This is the full paradigm of double agreement verbs.

When asked, signers are often in doubt how they would use a given verb. Can SHOOT-AT ('tease') agree with a first person P/IO argument? If it can, can it then agree with a non-first person A argument at the same time? That is, does it have the full potential of a single agreement verb or even of a double agreement verb, or is it defective? Does TEACH have the full paradigm of a double agreement verb, or does it have a mixed agreement pattern, i.e. can it agree with two non-first person arguments? My informants hesitate about the answers to questions testing these issues and do not always agree with each other or even with themselves over time. The agreement pattern depends on the verb, the signer, and probably also the receiver, the text type, and other features of the situation. The full double agreement pattern does occur, but very seldom (see also III.6.3 The many uses of the *c*-form).

The categories single and double agreement verbs have been found in a number of signed languages, notably Italian Sign Language (Pizzuto 1986), Taiwan Sign Language (Smith 1989, 81-112), and ASL (Padden 1988b, 26-28; note, however, that WANT, which is described as an inflecting verb that can agree with one argument in Padden 1988b (27-28), is described as a plain verb which may take a pronoun clitic in Padden 1990).

The tendency to avoid A argument agreement
Danish Sign Language verbs tend to avoid A argument agreement or to make all verbs appear as if the verb had a first person A argument, i.e. there is a tendency to direct or orientate the hand(s) in verbs outward from the signer's body irrespective of agreement. This tendency is seen in the following facts:
1. Single agreement verbs agree with their P/IO argument only, and the defective verbs do not even agree with a first person P/IO argument which means that the hand(s) is/are not directed or oriented inward.
2. The mixed agreement pattern means that only when the verb has a P/IO argument with first person reference, is the A argument cell of the verb filled with a locus marker other than the locus marker c, i.e. the marker for the sender locus. Only then is the verb sign made with an inward direction or orientation.
3. The older generation tends to use what appears to be a defective paradigm of single agreement verbs, seen from the point of view of the younger generation's language. They leave out agreement with a first person P/IO argument. This means that in all verbs which do show agreement the hand(s) is/are directed or oriented outward from the signer's body.

In Italian Sign Language, subject agreement is optional in certain contexts, e.g. in 'simple declarative, one-argument sentences' (Pizzuto 1986, 25-26). In ASL, the subject agreement marker may also be omitted (Padden 1988b, 136-139 and 167). What happens in cases of so-called agreement omission is that the verb is made in relation to the sender locus. In the following sections, I discuss the tendency to avoid A argument agreement in relation to agreement omission and marking for a specific point of view.

6.3 The many uses of the c-form

The base form
In Liddell and Johnson's notation, the root of an agreement verb is an incomplete s-morph with empty cells for one or two agreement markers (see I.6.3 Liddell and Johnson's sequential form analysis of signs), whereas a base form is a "pronounceable" sign. In order to convert a root into a base form, one or two p-morphs must be inserted into the empty cell(s) of the verb's root. It means that a base form of an agreement verb necessarily has at least two morphemes: the root and a marker in the empty cell (see Johnson & Liddell 1984, 179-180). There are also spoken languages in which the root of verbs cannot occur by itself. In Swahili, for instance, the base form of a verb has the prefix *ku-* which is one of the noun class markers, and Danish infinitives have a suffix *-e* which is added to the verb's root.

In Danish Sign Language, the base forms of most double agreement verbs have a marker for the sender locus c in their A cells and a marker for the forward direction in their P/IO cells. The base forms of single agreement verbs have a marker for the forward direction in their P/IO cell. The term *c-form* serves as a cover term for all markers which specify the sender locus, no matter their morphological value. I use the symbol *neu* (for *neutral*) for a marker which has a different effect on the verb form than the *c-form* and does not indicate the locus of a specific referent, but turns the root into a base form. Its influence on the verb's form depends both on the type of verb and the kind of cell (either an A or a P/IO cell) into which it is inserted.

A few verbs which can take two agreement markers distinguish the base form and the form with first person A argument agreement, namely reciprocal verbs that take two A arguments such as DISCUSS, SWAP, and QUARREL. The base form of DISCUSS is shown in Ill. 16a and the agreement form c+fsl+DISCUSS in Ill. 16b.

Agreement with a non-first person argument means that the verb has, in either its A cell or its P/IO cell, a p-morph that specifies a locus different from *c* and different from *neu*. But in discourse that involves a number of different loci, very few clauses contain signs modified for more than one locus different from *c*. That is, even when signers talk about the interaction of two referents associated with two loci different from *c* at some point in the discourse, they rarely use both loci within a single clause.

Two examples
As the following example is fairly long, I first give the translation. The letters in parentheses refer to the loci:

(1) Afterwards Ole Plum's commemorative award was given out [A:*c* and IO:*neu*]. You don't know who it was given [A:*c* and IO:*neu*] to? [Question to the receiver, who has asked.] To Henning Ravn Larsen, from Kolding *[sl]* [the name of a town]. He *[sl]* is a - uh, chartered accountant, so he *[sl]* is indeed. He *[sl]* does - uh, a lot for deaf people. He often helps [A:*c* and IO:*fl*] them with their accounts. The deaf clubs *[fl]* ask [P: *sl*] him and he *[sl]* comes over and over again [A:*sl* and goal:*c*]. Castberggaard *[f]*, too, their accounts and so on. That's why they gave [A:*c* and IO:*sl*] him the award. I [1.p] think it was 9000 crowns. They gave [A:*c* and IO:*sl*] it to him.

```
AFTER Ole(M) PLUM(name) REMEMBER^legat(M) ('award')^Outline
two-dimensional-entity-Pm+(extension-rectangle) / c+DONATE+neu
                              neg,?
KNOW-NOT WHO TO c+DONATE+neu / TO Henning(M) Ravn(M) / Larsen(M) /
FROM COLD^Kolding(M) DET+sl / SELF STATE auto(M) [beginning of
'authorised'] [hesitates] ACCOUNTANT / PRON+sl SELF PRON+sl /
DO BIG [hesitates] WORK FOR DEAF DET+fsl / OFTEN c+HELP+fl
                                       gaze:sl V+
ACCOUNTS+pl. / DEAF^CLUB DET+pl.+fl / KNOW-NOT-HOW / BECKON+sl
```

```
            PRON+sl sl+GO-TO+redupl.+c / ALSO DET+f CASTBERGGAARD DET+f /
            ACCOUNTS ETCETERA / c+GIVE+sl MONEY legat(M)^Outline-two-
            dimensional-entity-Pm+(extension-rectangle) / THINK 1.p NINE
            THOUSAND CROWN / c+GIVE+sl gesture /
```
(Except for the end of the sign KNOW-NOT-HOW, when she looks in the direction of *sl*, the signer has either eye contact with the receiver or, when she hesitates, looks away, but not in the direction of a locus.)

In the extract, the signer uses *sl* for the town where the receiver of the award lives, *sl* for the receiver himself, *fl* for the deaf clubs, *f* for the institution Castberggaard, and she refers to herself by means of the first person pronoun 1.p. The agreement verbs are:
— c+DONATE+neu with unspecific A and IO arguments;
— c+GIVE+sl with an unspecific A argument and a specific IO argument whose referent is represented by *sl*;
— BECKON+sl with a specific A argument whose referent is represented by *fl* and a specific P argument whose referent is represented by *sl*;
— c+HELP+fl with a specific A argument whose referent is represented by *sl* and a specific IO argument whose referent is represented by *fl*;
— sl+GO-TO+redupl.+c with a specific A argument whose referent is represented by *sl*, and a specific goal argument whose referent is represented by *fl*.

That is, the *c*-form is used in the verbs for an unspecific A argument, for an A argument whose referent is represented by the locus sideward-left, and for a goal argument whose referent is represented by the locus forward-left. The use of the *c*-form in the verbs divides the passage into the following thematic parts:
1. From the beginning to 'to Henning Ravn Larsen, from Kolding *[sl]*', with the *c*-form used for the unspecific agent who gives away the award (c+DONATE+neu);
2. 'He *[sl]* is a – uh, chartered accountant, so he *[sl]* is indeed. He *[sl]* does – uh, a lot for deaf people. He often helps [A:*c* and IO:*fl*] them with their accounts', with the *c*-form used for the award winner, i.e. the agent of c+HELP+fl;
3. 'The deaf clubs *[fl]* ask *[sl]* him and he *[sl]* comes again and again [A:*sl* and IO:*c*]', with the *c*-form used for the deaf clubs (sl+GO-TO+redupl.+c);
4. 'Castberggaard *[f]*, too, their accounts and other things', with no agreement verb;
5. 'That is why they gave [A:*c* and IO:*sl*] him the award', with the *c*-form used for the unspecific agent who gave away the award (c+GIVE+sl);
6. 'I [1.p] think it was 9000 crowns', with 1.p used for the signer;
7. 'They gave [A:*c* and IO:*sl*] it to him', with the *c*-form used for the unspecific agent (c+GIVE+sl).

No single clause of example (1) has a verb with two loci different from *c* or a pronoun or determiner with a locus different from *c* plus a verb with another locus different from *c*. Very few clauses in Danish Sign Language contain two nominals that are modified for two loci that are both different from *c*. In example (2), there are two such nominals, but the first nominal is topicalized, i.e. it is outside the clause, and even examples like (2) are rare:

```
(2)                                     gaze:r-+------------------
                             t       affirm
    Jette(M)(name) DET+fsl / UNDERSTAND DET+pl.+fsr YOUNG /

    r-----+----------------------------------------------------
    affirm
    WANT   c+HELP+fsr / PROGRAMME CHANGE / c+HELP+fsr / WANT YOUNG

    ---------
    SATISFIED /
```

Jette understands the young people. She really wants to support them, change the activities and support them. She wants the young people to be content.

In the first clause, the determiner DET+fsl is modified for the locus forward-sideward-left, while the determiner DET+pl.+fsr is modified for the locus forward-sideward-right. The sign UNDERSTAND cannot be modified in space, while HELP as a double agreement verb takes the *c*-form in its A argument cell and the locus marker for the young people's locus in its IO argument cell. Earlier in the same monologue, the referent Jette was represented by the locus forward-sideward-right, but just before (2), the signer uses this locus for the referent the young people. She reintroduces the referent Jette by using the topicalized nominal Jette(M) DET+fsl with the determiner modified for the locus forward-sideward-left. Nevertheless, the double agreement verb HELP has the *c*-form in its A cell.

The point-of-view marker
The signers of (1) and (2) take on the point of view of different referents during the discourse by representing them by means of the sender locus in the verbs. They express a specific point of view by using the verb forms that would be appropriate if the argument had first person reference. This is particularly clear in (1), in the changes in point of view between the award winner (c+HELP+fl) (part 2) and the deaf clubs (sl+GO-TO+redupl.+c, where the goal is represented by the sender locus) (part 3). In c+HELP+fl, *c* is used for the award winner and *fl* for the deaf clubs; in sl+GO-TO+redupl.+c, *c* is used for the deaf clubs and *sl* for the award winner. In clauses with a non-first person argument, the *c*-form is a point-of-view marker.

In II.5 Shifted reference, shifted attribution of expressive elements, and shifted locus, I described *shifted locus* as the use of the sender locus for another referent than the signer or the use of another locus than *c* for the signer. The *c*-form used as a point-of-view marker is one type of shifted locus as the occurrence of the point-of-view marker means that the sender locus is used for another referent than the signer in an agreement verb.

The *c*-form may, however, also be used for an unspecific referent, which makes it impossible to talk about a transfer of the point of view to the referent. In example (1), there are two verbs, c+DONATE+neu and c+GIVE+sl, that are used with the *c*-form in their A arguments cells, but the A arguments are left unspecified. That is, in some cases it seems possible to analyse the use of the *c*-form as a result of changes in point-of-view; but the *c*-form is also used in cases where the referent is unspecific.

Body and head movements
Sometimes when the *c*-form is used in a verb whose argument does not refer to the sender, the signer changes her head or body orientation slightly; she may also change her gaze direction. In the first half of (3), the signer moves her body slightly to the left and rotates it a little so that her front faces forward right; in the second part, her body is moved slightly to the right and rotated so that it faces forward left and she looks in the same direction.

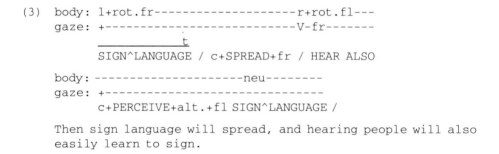

```
(3)   body: l+rot.fr-------------------r+rot.fl---
      gaze: +--------------------------V-fr-------
                              t
             SIGN^LANGUAGE / c+SPREAD+fr / HEAR ALSO
      body: --------------------neu--------
      gaze: +-------------------------------
             c+PERCEIVE+alt.+fl SIGN^LANGUAGE /
```

Then sign language will spread, and hearing people will also easily learn to sign.

The signer uses the locus forward-right for the hearing people (c+SPREAD+*fr*) and the locus forward-left for the entity perceived, i.e. sign language or sign language users (c+PERCEIVE+alt.+*fl*). The body rotation (and gaze direction) depends on the locus of the recipients of the spreading and the entity or persons perceived. The same forms of SPREAD and PERCEIVE, with body rotation and change in gaze direction, could have been used if the signer herself was active in spreading or perceiving sign language. As (3) describes an interaction between two parties, the second party is represented by a locus to one side when the signer describes the first party's actions (spreading sign language), and the first party is represented by a locus to the opposite side in the description of the second party's actions (perceiving their language). (See also the description of gaze directions in reported speech in II.5 Shifted reference, shifted attribution of expressive elements, and shifted locus.)

Kegl (1986, 289; also Kegl 1990; Bellugi & Klima 1982, 305) analyses 'a subtle shift of the body into a specific position in the signing space' in ASL as a clitic indicating role prominence. The role prominence clitic indicates the person from whose perspective the action of the verb is viewed (Kegl 1985, 136). This analysis of the function of the role prominence clitic in ASL resembles my analysis of the *c*-form as a point-of-view marker in some contexts in Danish Sign Language. There is a form difference, however. In ASL, the signer's body moves in the direction of the referent's locus; in Danish Sign Language, a non-first person referent "takes over" the sender locus. There are cases such as (3) from Danish Sign Language where the signer moves her body in some direction, but such changes in body position cannot be analysed as indicating role prominence because they depend on the locus of the referent whose argument is not prominent: in example (3), the recipients of signed language in the first clause, and the entity perceived in the second clause. Moreover, there are many examples of verbs taking the *c*-form with a non-first person argument and without accompanying body or head movements; in examples (1) and (2), there is no change of body orientation or posture which can be interpreted as a means of indicating the loci of the A arguments' referents. In (3), the body movements serve to underline the contrast between the two parties, but the use of the *c*-form is independent of the body movements.

Locative relations and egocentricity
Up to this point, I have shown that the modifications of agreement verbs in space can be seen as influenced by two principles. The first principle is agreement, where a verb is marked for the loci of its arguments' referents. The second principle is marking for a specific point of view where the *c*-form is used as a point-of-view marker. The first principle has its origin in locative relations; agreement reflects transactions between the holders' of locations or actions in locations. The second principle is shifted locus, which has its origin in egocentricity and the ability of human beings to take on the point of view of somebody else. We conceptualise space as organised around the centre of our body, but we can imagine what space looks like from another individual's centre. The holder of the sender's position is the centre of the universe of discourse and from there she views its actions and events.

In III.6.2 Agreement features, direction, and domain, I pointed out that verbs tend to occur in forms where their movement is outward from the signer's body irrespective of agreement, and that this tendency is particularly manifest in many elderly people's language. This variety has only P/IO argument agreement, but with the remarkable exclusion of first person P/IO argument agreement in most agreement verbs. In elderly people's language, what develops into the A argument agreement cell in double agreement verbs is so thoroughly bound to having a place of articulation near the signer's body that a P/IO argument with first person reference cannot change the orientation or direction of the sign's movement. In the younger variety, double agreement verbs can agree with two non-first person arguments, but usually take the *c*-form in their A argument agreement cell. In the varieties with only P/IO argument agreement, it is not possible to talk about a point-of-view marker in the A argument cell; since there is no alternative to the point-of-view marker, there is no A cell. But in the varieties where there is an alternative, the verbs do have an A argument agreement cell, and this cell can take either an agreement marker or the point-of-view marker.

Agreement omission
An alternative to talking about marking for a specific point of view would be to consider the *c*-form a marker of agreement omission or the neutral marker of the base form. By talking about the *c*-form, I imply that the form of the verb is identical with a form where the verb agrees with a first person argument. I have not been able to identify a difference between the form of HELP used in (2) with a non-first person A argument and a form of HELP used with a first person A argument. However, with respect to the p-morph inserted in the A argument cell, neither is there any difference between the form in (2) and the verb's base form. Therefore, it might be argued that the form in (2), c+HELP+fsl, has a neutral marker in its A argument cell, a marker that is used in cases of agreement omission and in base forms of the verbs, e.g. "neu"+HELP+fsl.

Agreement omission in agreement verbs occurs when the arguments have unspecific reference, when the referent of an A argument is not represented by a locus, and in cases of agreement conflict. In (4), the referent of the A argument, Annegrethe, is not represented by a locus:

```
(4)            nodding
    MOTHER /        gesture nok(M)('enough') ANNEGRETHE
    neu+EXPLAIN+c 1.p neu+GO-TO+c nok(M)('enough') / (Ill. 46)
    My mother nodded and said, 'Never mind. It's not necessary. Anne-
    grethe will explain it to me when she comes. It's not necessary.'
```

The form of EXPLAIN in (4), with A argument agreement omission (Ill. 46), differs from the verb's base form which has the *c*-form in its A argument cell, i.e. c+EXPLAIN+neu (Ill. 45a). That is, the form in (4) has a neutral marker in the A argument cell, and the marker differs from the *c*-form. If the *c*-form in c+HELP+fsl in (2) is analysed as showing agreement omission, we have to claim that the marker inserted in the verb's A argument cell in cases of agreement omission depends on whether the verb shows first person P/IO argument agreement. If it does, the marker in its A argument cell is *neu*; otherwise, it is *c*. Such an analysis fails to bring out the semantic and formal similarity between the first person agreement marker and the so-called marker of agreement omission.

Agreement conflict may arise with the verb INVITE. The sign agrees with its A argument whose referent is usually, but not always, identical with the goal of the invitation. In (5), the group that issues the invitation (the deaf people, DEAF DET+pl.+fsl) and the goal of the invitation (the deaf club in Bristol, DEAF^CLUB / BRISTOL DET+fl) are represented by different loci. That creates an agreement conflict in relation to INVITE. The signer hesitated and chose a single agreement verb, BECKON, which should agree with the first person pronoun 1.p, but there is some doubt whether the verb can agree with a first person P argument. The result is agreement omission.

```
(5)   DEAF DET+pl.+fsl / [hesitates] BECKON+neu 1.p c+GO-TO+fl
      DEAF^CLUB / BRISTOL DET+fl /
      The deaf people [at the workshop] invited me to the deaf club in
      Bristol.
```

Examples (4) and (5) demonstrate that agreement omission does occur. Agreement omission may also occur in certain discourse contexts such as introductory statements, but I am still uncertain about exactly when agreement is used or left out. As it appears from III.6.2 Agreement features, direction, and domain, agreement is an area with much individual variation (see also III.7 Pragmatic agreement). However, not all occurrences of the *c*-form can be described as agreement omission. In the following examples, the *c*-form occurs in verb forms that differ from the base forms of the verbs. In (6), the *c*-form is used in the P cell of the single agreement verb COMFORT, even though its P argument does not have first person reference:

```
(6)   Context: At a summer camp for deaf children, the teachers read the
      messages from the parents. One parent had written that her son
      needed to be comforted if he had bad dreams. A signer used the verb
      COMFORT:
         ... / COMFORT+c /                              (Ill. 48a)
      [If Peter has bad dreams,] he should be comforted.
```

The form COMFORT+c in (6) (Ill. 48a) contrasts with the base form of the verb (Ill. 48b). In COMFORT+c, the palms of both hands touch the signer's cheeks; in the base form the palms face away from the signer. COMFORT+c in (6) also contrasts with COMFORT+fsr in (7), which was elicited for the sake of illustrating a contrast to (6):

```
(7)   BOY FALL+fsr / MOTHER COMFORT+fsrd /             (Ill. 48c)
      The boy fell; his mother comforted him.
```

By contrast to the form in (6), COMFORT+fsr in (7) (Ill. 48c) shows P argument agreement.

In (6), where the *c*-form is used in COMFORT+c for a non-first person P argument, the A argument is not specified. In (8), the double agreement verb TEACH occurs with the *c*-form in its IO cell even though the IO argument does not have first person reference. In this case, too, the A argument is not specified.

```
(8)                             affirm
     PARTICIPANT DET+pl.+fsr neu+TEACH[+]+c B^PROFORM /
            affirm
     neu+TEACH[+]+c /                           (Ill. 49a)
     The participants have already learnt the B-proform.¹
```

The base form of TEACH and the form used in example (8) can be seen in Ills. 49a and 49b.

The verbs in (6) and (8) do not agree with their P/IO arguments; neither do they occur in their base forms. The behaviour of the verbs can only be described as the use of the *c*-form as a point-of-view marker. In the P/IO cell of a verb, the point-of-view marker differs from the non-first person agreement marker and from the marker of the base form, and it is identical with the first person agreement marker. In the A cell of a double agreement verb, it differs from the non-first person agreement markers and is identical with the first person agreement marker and the neutral marker of the base form. Clauses like (6) and (8), where the point-of-view marker is used in a P/IO cell and the A argument is not specified, are passive-like in that the P/IO argument is assigned the point of view of the clause.

But my informants disagree about the acceptability of examples such as (6) and (8), which are both from actual discourse. The argument for the analysis of the *c*-form as a point-of-view marker in some constructions rests in particular on the avoidance of sentences with more than one locus different from *c* and on the use of the *c*-form in P/IO argument cells with non-first person arguments. As the latter kind of construction is rare, it may seem hazardous to base any argumentation on it. I will show later, however, that the use of the sender locus for what can be described as nonagent arguments is widespread with polymorphemic verbs (III.8.6 Polymorphemic verbs and space), and that such constructions are probably one of the sources of constructions such as (6) and (8).

Overview

The relationship among base forms, forms showing agreement, forms marking for a

---

[1] The term *proform* is the term used in Danish for what has in some signed languages been called *classifier*, and which I describe as stems of polymorphemic verbs in III.8 Polymorphemic verbs. The B-proform is the stem used in verbs of motion and location for cars, trucks, and similar vehicles.

specific point of view, and cases of agreement omission appear in Fig. 10. The use of the *c*-form in P/IO cells as a point-of-view marker is only possible when the P/IO argument is animate or, more particularly, when its referent is of a kind with which human beings can identify. If the point-of-view marker is used with a non-first person P/IO argument, it seems that the A argument must be left unspecified and, in the case of a double agreement verb, the A argument cell is filled with the neutral marker.

Double agreement verbs:

A cell: base form: *c*
first person agreement: *c*
non-first person agreement: locus marker that differs from *c*
agreement omission:
neu, if the P/IO cell is filled with *c* ((4): neu+EXPLAIN+c);
otherwise *c* ((1): c+DONATE+neu)
? point-of-view marker (= base form)

P/IO cell: base form: *neu*
first person agreement: *c*
non-first person agreement: locus marker that differs from *c*
agreement omission:
neu ((1): c+DONATE+neu; the A cell is filled with *c*)
point-of-view marker:
c, only if the A argument is left unspecified, only some verbs, and only some signers ((8): neu+TEACH+c)

Single agreement verbs:

P/IO cell: base form: *neu*
first person agreement: *c*
non-first person agreement: locus marker that differs from *c*
agreement omission: *neu* ((5): BECKON+neu)
point-of-view marker:
c, only if the A argument is left unspecified, only some verbs, and only some signers ((6): COMFORT+c)

Fig. 10. Base forms, agreement forms, forms marked for a specific point of view, and forms with agreement omission

It is not possible to reduce forms with the point-of-view marker to base forms, as the forms differ in the P/IO cells of some agreement verbs. Neither is it possible to reduce agreement omission to base forms, since the forms differ in double agreement verbs where the P/IO cell is occupied by the first person agreement marker or the point-of-view marker. Finally, it is not possible to reduce marking for a specific point of view to agreement omission, because the forms differ in the P/IO cells of agreement verbs such as COMFORT and TEACH.

On the other hand, the following forms are alike in that they take the *c*-form in the relevant cell:
— double agreement verbs with a point-of-view marker in their A cell;
— base forms with respect to the A cell (except for reciprocal verbs such as DISCUSS);
— forms with first person A argument agreement;[2] and
— double agreement verbs with agreement omission in the A cell (unless the P/IO cell is occupied by the point-of-view marker, in which case the A cell takes the neutral marker).

The c-form in the younger variety of the language
There is a hierarchy of the use of the *c*-form in the younger variety:
1. If the verb has a first person P/IO argument, the *c*-form may be inserted into the P/IO cell of the verb. It is then a first person agreement marker.
2. If the *c*-form is not used as stated in 1, it may be inserted into the A cell of the verb, and must be inserted there if the A argument has first person reference. In the former case, its status is ambiguous; it may be analysed as a marker of agreement omission or as a point-of-view marker. In the latter case, it is ambiguous between showing first person agreement, being a point-of-view marker, and showing agreement omission.
3. If the *c*-form is not used as stated in 1 or 2, it may be inserted into the P/IO cell of what appears to be a small number of verbs, provided that the A argument is not specified and the P/IO argument is animate. Then the *c*-form is a point-of-view marker.

On the one hand, there are uses of the *c*-form which are clearly neutral, i.e. base forms used when the verb's A argument is not specified. On the other hand, the *c*-form can be used as a point-of-view marker in the P/IO cells of some verbs whose P/IO arguments do not have first person reference. In between, there are many cases of association of A arguments with the *c*-form: verbs that show the mixed agreement pattern, single agreement verbs which can only agree with their P/IO argument, many cases of double agreement verbs (as in examples (1) and (2)), and verbs with an A argument with specific reference, but whose referent is not represented by a locus. The ambiguity is built into the system of the spatial modification of the agreement verbs because the point-of-view marker is identical with the first person agreement marker, which is identical with the marker in the A cell of the base form of most verbs.

---

2 While pronouns can be omitted under circumstances that are not yet clear, the first person pronoun 1.p is almost always used when a verb has a first person A argument.

As mentioned above, it is not possible to distinguish among double agreement verbs marked for point of view in the A cell, base forms with respect to this cell, forms with first person A argument agreement, and double agreement verbs with agreement omission in the A cell (unless the P/IO argument cell is occupied by the point-of-view marker). The reason is that marking for a specific point of view and first person agreement coincide with the last principle, which influences the spatial modification of agreement verbs, namely agentivity.

Agentivity
At the end of III.6.2 Agreement features, direction, and domain, I listed the following points as evidence of the tendency to avoid A argument agreement in Danish Sign Language:
1. Single agreement verbs can only show P/IO argument agreement and not A argument agreement. These verbs have P/IO cells and no A cells. Where the latter might have been in the verbs' stems, there is in most cases a phonological specification of a place of articulation on the signer's body or head. Defective single agreement verbs cannot even agree with a first person P/IO argument, which means that, phonologically, the orientation of the hand(s) and the direction of the movement are fixed in relation to the signer's body.
2. The mixed agreement pattern means that the verb only shows A argument agreement when its P/IO argument has first person reference. When the P/IO argument has non-first person reference and there is a specific A argument whose referent is represented by a locus different from c, the verb nevertheless takes the c-form in its A cell.
3. The tendency in the older generation's language to use what, as seen from the point of view of the younger generations' language, seems like the defective paradigm of single agreement verbs means that all agreement verb forms are directed or oriented outward from the signer's body.

These facts cannot be explained in terms of marking for a specific point of view. For instance, in the defective paradigm of single agreement verbs the verb cannot even agree with a first person P/IO argument which otherwise represents the most obvious holder of the point of view. The three items point in the same direction: either the verbs have a place of articulation on or near the signer's body or head as part of their phonological composition or they take a marker specifying the locus expressed near the signer's body in their A cell. In this description, I "mix" the linguistic levels. I compare *place of articulation* (phonological level) with a marker in the verb's *A cell* (morphological level). To be a pronounceable sign a verb must have a place of articulation; but some verbs have a phonological specification of their place of articulation in their roots, while others have empty cells which can be filled with a morphological marker. That is, the agreement markers, the neutral marker, and the point-of-view marker occur in the structure of verb roots in places where other verbs have a phonological specification of a place of articulation which may be identical with the expression of the point-of-view marker and the first person agreement marker. That might be accidental if it were not for the iconicity of many signs.

The concept that can create coherence behind the three points above is agentivity in a slightly extended interpretation. Agentivity is a matter of the degree of control which the referent of an argument has over the situation described by the verb (Comrie 1981, 53). This means that the agent ranks highest on a continuum of control, while the patient ranks lowest. Experiencers are like patients with respect to control (ibid., 55); but in Danish Sign Language animate A arguments, whether agents or experiencers, are opposed to animate (and locative) P/IO arguments. The sender locus encodes agentivity (including agents and experiencers) in iconically motivated signs to the extent of excluding P/IO argument agreement with a first person argument in elderly people's language and creating defective paradigms of both single and double agreement verbs in younger people's language.

The defective paradigm of a single agreement verb such as SHOOT-AT ('tease') means that the verb can only agree with a non-first person P/IO argument; the sender locus is reserved for the agent. In the verb form SHOOT-AT, the hands resemble guns directed at the unfortunate target. The defective paradigm of double agreement verbs, the mixed agreement pattern, means that the verb cannot agree with a non-first person A argument unless its P/IO argument has first person reference, i.e. unless the sender locus is used for a nonagent argument. An example of such a verb is EXPLAIN (Ill. 45a), which depicts an opening motion of the hands as if to lay something open for the recipient. Verbs having a mixed agreement pattern are more likely to agree with a non-first person A argument (i.e. show the full agreement pattern of a double agreement verb) when the referent of this argument is present in the context of utterance, i.e. when the agentivity is more or less represented in another "body" present.

In order to explain handshape variants in signs in ASL that cannot be explained as phonetic variants (because they go against a feature analysis of handshapes based on perception), Boyes Braem (1981) proposes a lexical description of signs that involves a level of symbolic representation. At this level, 'the underlying semantic concept is matched up with a visual symbolic representation or kind of visual metaphor' (ibid, 43; see also Brennan 1990a, 1990b). For instance, the underlying concept behind BUILD in ASL is the concept of constructing an edifice or building, and the visual metaphor is one of flat objects being piled on top of each other. Through the morphophonemic and the phonemic levels, the underlying visual metaphor is "transferred" to a surface form at the phonetic level (BUILD is made with either two flat hands or two hands with the index and middle fingers extended and held together). A lexical model along these lines, combined with Liddell and Johnson's segmental model (I.6.3), would be needed to describe how the change in agreement patterns and the defective agreement paradigms in Danish Sign Language are related to the notion of agentivity.

The agreement pattern of a verb such as MOVE-PERSON can also be understood when the verb is analysed as encoding agentivity lexically. The verb MOVE-PERSON means 'employ' or 'transfer (a person) from one place or institution to another'. It is a double agreement verb, but by contrast to the verbs of the examples above, it agrees with its source/patient and its goal arguments. It can only take the c-form in one of its cells if its argument has first person reference, i.e. in, for instance, clauses meaning 'I employed him', 'I was employed there' or 'I was transferred to (somewhere)'. In a sentence meaning 'She was employed there' or 'He employed her', the verb must take a locus marker for the source/patient and goal arguments of the verb or a neutral marker clearly different from *c*. This pattern can be explained in the light of the verb's form and meaning: the verb's meaning is related to a polymorphemic verb ('handle (a cylindrical entity)') and the handshape by which it is expressed is identical with the handshape of the polymorphemic verb's stem, which is of the handle type (Ill. 50) (see further III.8.5 Categories of stems in polymorphemic verbs). Handle stems encode agentivity in the signer's hand and in unmarked cases in her body. The form MOVE-PERSON depicts the handling of an entity from its present position to another position. Thus it agrees with its source/patient argument and its goal argument. The unmarked form of the verb cannot have the *c*-form in one of its cells because the sender locus represents the agent referent, not the source/patient referent or the goal referent.

A contrast to this verb is the verb GO-TO (Ill. 8), which is also formally and semantically related to a polymorphemic verb ('(of a general entity) move or be located') with a stem of the whole entity type. Although GO-TO also has the meaning of transfer from one place to another, it can be used with the *c*-form in its cells even when its arguments do not have first person reference, for example with the *c*-form in the A cell in c+GO-TO+fr ('He went there') and in the goal cell in fsr+GO-TO+c ('He came')). Here the sender locus is not blocked by "an implicit agent" in the lexeme as in the case of MOVE-PERSON because GO-TO, like polymorphemic verbs with whole entity stems, denotes an entity's own movement, not an entity's being moved by someone, i.e. agentivity is not encoded in the signer's body in this case. (See also Kegl 1985, 120-121.)

Another contrast to MOVE-PERSON is GIVE which is also related to a polymorphemic verb with a stem of the handle type ('handle (flat entity)'). Even though this verb also denotes a transfer from one place to another and encodes an agent in the signer's hand, it can take the *c*-form in its A argument cell when the argument does not have first person reference. The reason is that the verb has the conventional meaning 'give' and the prototypical situation of 'giving' is one where the agent is in possession of the entity given, i.e. the entity given is at the location of the agent.

In conclusion, the sender locus expresses three semantic-pragmatic functions: agentivity, first person reference, and point of view. The sender locus is associated with agentivity in the verbs; at the same time, it is used for arguments with first person reference. In relation to nominals with first person reference, the sender locus loses its association with agentivity when a verb develops the possibility of taking a first person agreement marker in its P/IO cell (see the development of agreement verbs outlined at the end of III.6.2 Agreement features, direction, and domain). The deictic value of the *c*-form established when the *c*-form occurs as a first person agreement marker makes possible the further development of the *c*-form into a marker for point of view. The diachronic development is from agentivity over deixis (first person agreement) to point of view; marking for a specific point of view is introduced via first person agreement.

The spatial modifications of agreement verbs in Danish Sign Language are the result of the interaction of three different principles:

1. The first principle is agreement: verbs agree with both their A arguments and their P/IO arguments in that p-morphs specifying the loci of these arguments' referents are inserted into the appropriate cells. The origin of this principle is locative relations. Agreement unrestricted by the two other principles is not very frequent in Danish Sign Language.
2. The second principle is agentivity: the sender locus stands for agentivity in the verbs' lexical structure and the verbs agree with their P/IO arguments. The origin of this principle is the iconic motivation of verbs depicting the actor of the event or process described by the verb.
3. The third principle is point of view: the sender locus expresses a specific point of view which means that the *c*-form is used as a point-of-view marker. The origin of this principle lies in the deictic value of the sender locus, in egocentricity combined with the ability of human beings to see the world from another individual's centre.

The second principle, agentivity, is stronger in the "earlier" pattern of verb agreement, while the first (locative) principle and the third principle, the sender locus as expressing a specific point of view, are stronger in the "younger" pattern that I described in III.6.2 Agreement features, direction, and domain.

6.4 First person, point of view, and agentivity

First person reference, point of view, and agentivity are well-known notions from analyses of spoken languages, and it has been shown that they are often interrelated in ways that are very similar to what we see in Danish Sign Language. The interrelation of agentivity and point of view is of course particularly clear in the definition of the prototypical subject as the intersection of agent and topic (Comrie 1981, 114).

The point-of-view marker in Danish Sign Language is expressed in the same way as the first person agreement marker, and first person is basically a deictic category. In spoken languages, deictic expressions are also used to express point of view. The sentence *Several years ago he lived near the beach* (from Fillmore 1982), with the basically deictic word *ago*, has the utterance time as its temporal reference point. *Several years earlier he had lived near the beach*, with the basically nondeictic *earlier*, has a textually-established temporal reference point. If we say *Several years ago he had lived near the beach*, mixing basically deictic (*ago*) and nondeictic (*had lived*) elements, the temporal reference point is still the nondeictic one that was established in the discourse context. The use of ago, however, with a nondeictic reference point has the effect of expressing 'the inner experience of a central character' (Fillmore 1982, 38), or a point of view. In *Several years ago he had lived near the beach*, the word *ago* is interpreted in relation to the textually relevant point in time, but the form *ago* retains its 'now'-value: we look at the past event as if it were related to the time of the communication act, and that creates the point-of-view effect.

An equivalent locative example with the basically deictic verb *come* is the sentence *The men came into her room*, where the point of view is with the woman inside the room. By using the verb *come*, the speaker places herself inside the room and sees the situation from the woman's perspective (Fillmore 1972, 377). This example mixes the basically deictic verb (*came*) of *The men came into my room* with the basically nondeictic verb *enter* (cf. the third person pronoun) of *The men entered her room*. The effect is one of transfer of the point of view: the sender is present as the narrator by saying *her*, but identifies with the woman by using *came*, which retains its 'here'-value.

In Danish Sign Language, the verb agreement system makes use of a deictic element, namely the sender locus, for nondeictic reference; at the same time, the signer can be present as the narrator in the way she refers to non-first person referents by means of nominals, including pronouns. The system of spatial modification of verbs introduces a deictic element, the sender locus, in nondeictic signing and thereby makes it possible to express point of view. When the signer uses her own locus for either the A argument's or the P/IO argument's referent, she places the point of view with that referent.

The use of basically deictic words with words which are not basically deictic creates an effect similar to the one created by the techniques of represented speech or represented thought (free indirect style). In II.5 Shifted reference, shifted attribution of expressive elements, and shifted locus, I demonstrated how shifted attribution of expressive elements and shifted locus could be used to represent thoughts and actions: the signer uses her own body and face to obtain the effect. In marking for a specific point of view on agreement verbs, a non-first person referent takes over the sender locus, but marking for a specific point of view in agreement verbs may take place without shifted attribution of expressive elements. That is, there is a scale of identification with the referent in point. Complete identification is seen in reported speech with shifted reference (the first person pronoun 1.p used for the quoted sender), shifted attribution of expressive elements, and first person agreement in verbs. Less complete identification consists of shifted attribution of expressive elements and shifted locus without shifted reference. Still less identification with the referent is found in constructions with marking for a specific point of view in verbs without shifted reference and without shifted attribution of expressive elements.

In two dialects of Nahuatl (Mexico), Zitlala (Una Canger – personal communication) and Ameyaltepec (Amith 1988), many verbs have affixes that can signify direction toward (intraverse action) or direction away from (extraverse action) a specific deictic reference point. For instance, the verb in a construction meaning 'I sent word there with someone' has the affix of extraverse action in Ameyaltepec, while the verb in a sentence meaning 'I sent it back here with someone' has the affix of intraverse action. The use of the intraverse and extraverse prefixes in Nahuatl is not fully understood. It seems that the most usual reference point is the sender location, but that

> ... in certain situations a speaker is free to choose a deictic reference point, and this freedom is reflected in the fact that in these situations either an intraverse or extraverse directional is correct, with corresponding changes in meaning of the verbal compound. Thus, within the context of the speech act the speaker may at times manipulate the pivot of the deixis in accordance with a particular conversational or narrative strategy and exercise some control over the orientation and identification of the addressee or audience. (Amith 1988, 396)

The transfer of 'the pivot of the deixis' to a nondeictic reference point resembles the use of the point-of-view marker of non-first person referents in Danish Sign Language as the point-of-view marker is identical with the basically deictic first person agreement marker. The transfer is exemplified (with Una Canger's help) by the following excerpts in Aztec (Classical Nahuatl) from Book 12: The Conquest of Mexico, Second Chapter, of *Florentine Codex: General History of the Things of New Spain* (Anderson & Dibble 1975, 5ff.). A Spanish ship approaches the east coast of Mexico and the ruler sends a delegation from the inland to the coast to meet the Spaniards. The conversation between the delegation and the Spaniards is described from the delegation's point of view by the use of the affixes for intraverse and extraverse action:

```
(1)   Ø-qujn-oal-notz-que in españoles
      3.pl.S-3.pl.O-INTRA-call-pl.S

      [To make the transcriptions easier to read, the marking of tense
      is not specified.]

      The Spaniards called out to them (the delegation)
```

In (1), the affix of the intraverse action is used of an action going from the Spaniards to the delegation, i.e. the point of view is with the delegation. In (2), the action goes from the delegation to the Spaniards and, accordingly, the affix of the extraverse action is used:

```
(2)   Ø-qujm-Ø-on-jlhuj-que...
      3.pl.S-3.sg.O-3.pl.O-EXTRA-say-pl.S

      They (the delegation) said (it) to them (the Spaniards): ...
```

The affixes of the intraverse and extraverse actions are sufficient to identify the participants in the conversation. This is particularly clear in (3) about the exchange of gifts:

(3)　*in jzqujtlamãtli in in Ø-qujm-Ø-õ-maca-que,*
　　　　　　　3.pl.S-3.pl.O-3.sg.O-EXTRA-give-pl.S

　　Ø-qujn-Ø-oal-cuepcaiotili-que
　　3.pl.S-3.pl.O-3.sg.O-INTRA-give in return-pl.S

　　Ø-qujn-Ø-oal-maca-que
　　3.pl.S-3.pl.O.-3.sg.O-INTRA-give-pl.S

　　cozcatl, xoxoctic, coztic...

　　All this they (the delegation) gave them (the Spaniards). They (the Spaniards) gave them (the delegation) (it) in return. They offered them green and yellow necklaces....

The first transfer of gifts is from the delegation to the Spaniards and the extraverse prefix is used. The next two verbs are about the transfer of gifts from the Spaniards to the delegation. Here the intraverse prefix is used. Only the intraverse and extraverse prefixes indicate who is the agent and who the recipient in the transactions. In Danish Sign Language, the agreement markers and the point-of-view marker are also sufficient to identify the participants in such an interaction.

After the exchange of gifts, the Spaniards return to Castille and the delegation to the Mexican ruler. About the delegation's return the text uses a verb with the affix of intraverse action:

(4)　*oal-mo-cuep-que*
　　INTRA-reflex-return-pl.S

　　They returned to here.

From this place on in the text, the point of view is with the ruler. That is, the point of view can be manipulated in the course of the text by the use of the affixes of intraverse and extraverse action, which are basically deictic, signalling the sender position. In the same way, the sender's locus as a point-of-view marker was used to signal changes in point of view in example (1) about the award winner in III.6.3 The many uses of the *c*-form.

In Danish Sign Language, there is only one marker, not two like the intraverse and extraverse prefixes of Nahuatl; but in Danish Sign Language the marker can occupy two positions in some agreement verbs (the A argument position and the P/IO argument position) and in polymorphemic verbs. This produces the effect of direction outward from the signer (the point-of-view marker in the A cell) or inward toward the signer (the point-of-view marker in the P/IO cell). But in many cases of reported dialogue, signers would use reported speech with a complete change of point of view between the two parties in the dialogue with each new turn. In Nahuatl, the dialogue can be reported from one point of view, irrespective of the changes in sender. The difference between the two parties in Danish Sign Language would then be shown by a difference in direction, right or left, in both cases outward from the signer.

Another example of the linking of first person reference and point-of-view marking comes from Japanese. In this language, there are two different verbs meaning 'give'. One is used when the action is looked at from the point of view of the A argument's referent, the other when the action is looked at from the point of view of the IO argument's referent. With these verbs, first person outranks third person in the sense that it is not possible to use the verb with the IO argument point of view when the A argument has first person reference (Kuno & Kaburaki 1977).

In Danish Sign Language, when the P/IO argument has first person reference, it is not possible to use the point-of-view marker for a non-first person A argument, simply because a verb cannot take two tokens of the c-form. The c-form as the first person agreement marker outranks the c-form as the point-of-view marker. This restriction correlates with the obligatoriness in some languages, for instance Southern Tiwa (Allen & Frantz 1978, 12) and the Wakashan languages (Mallinson & Blake 1981, 73), of passive constructions when the P argument has first person reference (a sentence meaning, for instance, 'I was seen by the man'). Here the point of view is obligatorily with the first person referent. (See also Comrie 1981, 185.)

A similar constraint on the interaction of marking for a specific point of view and person reference comes from languages with so-called direct and inverse verb forms. In Tlahuitoltepec Mixe (Lyon 1967), markers on the verb show whether the clause is actor oriented or goal oriented. The selection of marker depends on a hierarchy: first person, second person, third person definite, third person indefinite, animal, and thing. The difference between the sentences meaning 'I hit the person' and 'The person hit me' is that the verb of the former clause has the marker of actor orientation (the highest ranking argument, here the first person argument, is the verb's A argument); the verb of the latter clause has the marker of goal orientation (here the highest ranking argument is the verb's P argument). (See also Comrie 1981, 122, on direct and inverse verb forms in Algonquian languages.)

In Danish Sign Language, whether the first person argument is the A or the P argument, the point of view is with that argument. In the Danish Sign Language equivalent of the first clause above, the verb would have the c-form in its A cell and the verb of the last clause would have the c-form in its P cell. In younger people's language, first person outranks non-first person in that a first person argument prevents any other argument from being marked by the c-form in the verb.

Comrie (1981, chapter 9), among others, points out that many linguistic distinctions correlate with, or are determined by, what he calls the animacy hierarchy. The animacy hierarchy 'cannot be reduced to any single parameter, including animacy itself in its literal sense, but rather reflects a natural human interaction among several parameters' (ibid., 192). Among the other parameters mentioned in the chapter are the person scale and salience. As I have shown, these parameters also play a part in Danish Sign Language. With respect to the person scale, first person ranks higher than non-first person reference in relation to the c-form. The distinction between human/animate and inanimate in the literal sense of animacy is seen in the restriction on the point-of-view marker: it can only be used for arguments which have referents with which a human being can identify. Salience plays a part in the representation of referents by loci: only salient referents are represented by loci and verbs only agree with arguments whose referents are represented by loci.

Danish Sign Language illuminates in particular the relation between marking for first person and marking for a specific point of view. Agentivity plays a role in the spatial modification of some agreement verbs which can only be understood if the sender locus is seen as encoding agentivity.

7 Pragmatic agreement

7.1 Pragmatic agreement, semantic agreement, and point-of-view marking

The nature of the relationship between the controller and the agreeing constituent
Semantic agreement, which is the agreement of particular verbs with their A argument and/or P/IO argument, reflects the semantic relations between the participants in dynamic situations in relation to each other and in relation to the process or event in which they take part. This pattern is complicated by the encoding of agentivity in the sender locus, which restricts the spatial modification of the verbs, and by the emergence of marking for a specific point of view, which introduces a particular perspective on the relationships (see III.6.3 The many uses of the *c*-form).

Pragmatic agreement shows that there is a relation of some kind between static and dynamic situations and the entities and locations which are part of them, but the semantic nature of the relation is not clear from the form of the agreeing constituent. That is, the nature of the relation is as much or as little ambiguous as the construction may be, irrespective of agreement. As pointed out in III.2 Different types of modifications: An overview, the main constituents of many clauses in Danish Sign Language seem to be best described in pragmatic terms. The term *pragmatic agreement* is meant to emphasise the difference between this other kind of agreement and semantic agreement, which shows the semantic relationship between the verb and its arguments. The relationship between the agreeing constituents and the controller in pragmatic agreement may be a locative relationship between a state and an entity in a location, but loci for referents are selected on criteria other than to reflect locative relations (especially various kinds of semantic affinity (see II.2 The frame of reference)). Thus, pragmatic agreement may occur when there are relations between a constituent and the controller other than locative ones.

Example (1) shows two clauses with an ambiguous relation between the nominal and the predicate; the verbs in both clauses – in the first clause, also the auxiliary – are modified for the locus of the nominal's referent:

(1)
```
                                              t
SECOND+fsl CLASS+fsl ANALYSE+fsl FINISH+fsl /
FOURTH+fsr ANALYSE+fsr /  (Ill. 37)
When grade two had finished analysing, grade four analysed.
or When grade two had been analysed, grade four was analysed.
```

If none of the signs in (1) were modified for loci, it would still be ambiguous. That is, pragmatic agreement neither disambiguates the clause nor causes the ambiguity.

While a double agreement verb can take two locus markers when it shows semantic agreement, a verb showing pragmatic agreement takes only one locus marker and its form is the same no matter the semantic relation of the controller to the verb. Pragmatic agreement also differs from semantic agreement in that signs other than verbs can show pragmatic agreement. In (1), both ANALYSE and the auxiliary FINISH are marked for the locus of SECOND+fsl CLASS+fsl. In (2), the sign GOOD with an adverbial function is spatially modified. Example (2) is from a description of a teaching situation where two groups had been asked to discuss the same problem:

```
(2)  PRON+fsl GOOD+fsl EXPLAIN+p.a.:fsl         /    PRON+fsr
                                          GOOD+fsl------------

     SO-SO+fsr /
     ---------

     One group was good at exposing their ideas, whereas the other one
     wasn't really so good.
```

Pragmatic agreement and semantic agreement are mutually exclusive. Agreement verbs may show each kind of agreement, but not at the same time. The verb PAY is either a single agreement verb or a double agreement verb that shows the mixed agreement pattern (see I.6.5 Formal description of some different verb types, and III.6.2 Agreement features, direction, and domain); in (3), it agrees with its IO argument.

```
(3)  CAN Car-Pm+(c+move-arc+fr) SCHOOL+fr / c+PAY+fr TEACHER+fr

     TEN TEN-CROWN c+GIVE+fr /  (Ill. 51)

     He could drive round the school and pay the teacher ten crowns.
```

In (4) with pragmatic agreement, PAY agrees with one argument only, its A argument:

```
(4)  DET+fr LEADER DET+fr / gesture / PRON+fr PAY+p.a.:fr WHOLE+fr /

     (Ill. 52)

     The leader said, oh calm down, and he would pay it all.
```

The form of PAY in Ill. 51 has two locus markers: the locus marker *fr* in its IO argument cell and the point-of-view marker in its A argument cell. The form of PAY in Ill. 52 has only one locus marker, the locus marker *fr*, whose position in the verb was not foreseen in Liddell and Johnson's model (see I.6.3 Liddell and Johnson's sequential form analysis of signs). Loosely speaking, what matters in the form showing semantic agreement (Ill. 51) is where the base of the weak hand faces and the direction in which the strong hand moves. What matters in the form showing pragmatic agreement (Ill. 52) is where both hands are; their orientation is not important.

Another example of a verb with two clearly distinct forms is EXPLAIN, which is a double agreement verb. The form of EXPLAIN showing pragmatic agreement in example (2) can be seen in Ill. 53, its base form is in Ill. 45a, and a semantic agreement form in Ill. 45b. When EXPLAIN shows semantic agreement, the bases of the two hands face the direction of the locus of its A argument and the fingertips face the direction of its IO argument's locus. When the verb shows pragmatic agreement, as in (2), the orientation of the hands is irrelevant. What matters is the direction in which the signer has moved her hands compared with the neutral position outside the midline of her body. In Liddell and Johnson's model, the verb root has empty cells for the A and IO argument agreement markers, and the p-morphs that are inserted here specify the sign's placement and facing, i.e. the direction of the bases of the hands and the direction of the fingertips. When EXPLAIN is modified for pragmatic agreement, only one locus is involved. The hands are positioned somewhere in the locus direction, but their orientation is irrelevant.

The reciprocal subgroup of agreement verbs, i.e. verbs such as DISCUSS, QUARREL, and SWAP, can also show both semantic and pragmatic agreement. These verbs are two-handed, symmetrical signs whose base forms differ from the forms showing first person A argument agreement; they can show semantic agreement with a first person argument and a non-first person argument. Then they take two locus markers. They can also show pragmatic agreement with only one locus marker. Ills 16a, 16b, and 54 show the base form, a form showing semantic agreement, and a form showing pragmatic agreement of the verb DISCUSS.

Whether an agreement verb shows semantic or pragmatic agreement depends on the construction of the entire clause and the number of specified arguments. In (4), there is only one argument that fulfils the semantic criteria for being either the A argument or IO argument of PAY+p.a.:fr, namely PRON+fr. In the context in which the example was used, there was no doubt that PRON+fr had the A argument relation to PAY+p.a:fr, but it might also have the IO argument relation, in which case the clause would mean 'He should be paid it all'. In either case, the other argument, the IO argument or the A argument respectively, is left unspecified.

Only verbs can show semantic agreement; but signs in the predicate other than the verb can show pragmatic agreement. In example (4), WHOLE+fr is modified for the locus forward-right even though as a pronoun it does not refer to the referent represented by this locus. The background of (4) is a situation where the signer explains that a Spanish festival leader insisted that the Danish theatre group pay for their hotel and meals, contrary to an earlier agreement according to the Danish group of which the signer was part. WHOLE+fr is used to refer to the expenses that the Danish group had had and which the signer has just described in a sentence meaning, 'We would have to pay for the hotel and the food and everything'. That is, WHOLE+fr is used to refer to the Danish group's expenses and the group is represented by the sender locus; but in (4), all of the signs are locus marked for the festival leader's locus forward-right.

In summary, semantic and pragmatic agreement are expressed by the same markers, but the contexts in which they occur differ. Moreover, agreement verbs which show semantic agreement take agreement markers in cells that are unambiguously determined for semantically specified arguments, while the cell into which the agreement marker is inserted in a pragmatic agreement context is semantically ambiguous. In the latter case, the semantic relation between the constituent showing agreement and the controller must be deduced from the context or from the lexical semantics of the signs. With double agreement verbs, a formal difference exists between pragmatic agreement and semantic agreement.

The discourse function of pragmatic agreement
Pragmatic agreement is not obligatory in a particular grammatical context, but is used for specific discourse purposes, especially to underline a contrast as in examples (1), (2), and (4). For persuasive purposes or as a sort of imperative, signs can take a locus marker for the receiver's locus. For example, RECOMMEND can take a locus marker for the receiver in a summing up of a recommendation ('I recommend that to you') or WAIT can take a locus marker for the receiver in an imperative ('You must wait!'). Moreover, pragmatic agreement is often used in descriptions of what somebody witnessed or what took place somewhere away from the holder of the point of view. It may emphasise mental distance as in descriptions of actions, states, or opinions that the signer or the holder of the point of view does not share or approve of, e.g. the following example where a signer quotes a man's reason for not wanting to go to a party:

(5)   REASON HEAR ALL+fsr / TALK-WITH-EACH-OTHER+group+p.a.:fsr /[1]

(Ill. 44)

Because they are all hearing. They'll all just talk with each other.

Pragmatic agreement is also typical of a formal register. In formal presentations addressed to a larger group or in teaching, signers often move their body in the direction of a locus or even take a step in a particular direction (see the example discussed in relation to the anaphoric time line in II.3.1 The time lines, and, for similar examples from a formal register of ASL, Zimmer 1989).

Pragmatic agreement is a matter of choice. It is used to underline the relationship between the content of a predicate and the referent of the locus in question, often, but not always, as distinct from or in opposition to some other referent. Without specifying the type of semantic relation, the agreement markers in pragmatic agreement emphasises the relation between the agreeing items and the controller by representing the controller on the agreeing items (see Lehmann's explanation of agreement in

1   The notation +*group* indicates a modification for distribution that can be used with reciprocal verbs. It is expressed by a circular movement and means that the action took place in a group.

III.6.2 Agreement features, direction, and domain). They show which argument is topic or theme in relation to the agreeing items. In examples (1), (2) and (4), either the A argument or the P/IO argument, depending on the meaning, is not specified; they are not of interest.

It is not clear to me whether there are sign forms that can be described as showing pragmatic agreement with a first person argument. The problem is that the base form of signs that can show pragmatic agreement are made near the signer's body and that is also how pragmatic agreement with a first person argument would have to be expressed. That is, it seems impossible to distinguish the base form of the sign from a form that shows pragmatic agreement with a first person argument. There are, however, contexts where a signer underlines a contrast between herself and another referent by moving her body in the opposite direction of the locus that represents the other referent. An example of that was mentioned in II.6.3 Person, place, and shifters: a signer underlined the contrast between the city in which he used to live (represented by the locus forward-right-upward) and the city in which he now lives, by moving his body slightly backward left while signing NOW LIVE 1.p COPENHAGEN HERE ('Now I live here in Copenhagen').

The function of pragmatic agreement can also be illuminated by comparing it with marking for a specific point of view. In examples (1), (2), (4), and (5), pragmatic agreement is expressed by locus markers different from the c-form, i.e. by sign forms where the hands have been moved away from the proximity of the signer. By contrast, marking for a specific point of view is expressed by the c-form (see III.6.3 The many uses of the c-form), which means that part of the verb form is made close to the signer's body. While marking for a specific point of view is based on the signer's identification with the referent of the A or P/IO argument, pragmatic agreement underlines a distance. The difference between point-of-view marking and pragmatic agreement appears when a predicate agrees with an A argument as in one of the meanings of examples (1), (2), and (4) and in example (5). Here, the verb forms are made at a distance from the signer and what is brought into focus is the predicate's relevance to one particular argument. The point-of-view marker in the A argument cell of agreement verbs results in verb forms made near the signer. While the point-of-view marker can express a certain point of view in relation to the process or event described by the verb, pragmatic agreement brings the relation between the predicate and the topic into focus, especially when the signer wishes to emphasise a contrast, a mental distance, or the relevance of a predicate to a particular argument.

The use of the point-of-view marker for non-first person referents in agreement verbs can be said to express an internal point of view of a situation, while pragmatic agreement often emphasises an external point of view (contrast, mental or physical distance). The same is true of a double agreement verb showing semantic agreement with two non-first person arguments; in such verb forms, the movement or the orientation of the hands is related to two loci that are both different from the sender locus.

Here the point of view is external in relation to both referents. As mentioned in III.6.3 The many uses of the *c*-form, such forms are rare in Danish Sign Language, because marking for a specific point of view almost always "interferes" with semantic agreement. The forms with semantic agreement with two non-first person arguments can, however, be found, namely in the same contexts where we find pragmatic agreement. That is, when signers want to underline both arguments, in persuasive utterances where the referents are present in the context of utterance (e.g. an utterance meaning 'Do send it to her!'), and when there is a third implicit referent, a holder of the point of view who feels a physical or mental distance to the transaction between the other two parties ('I had nothing to do with it. He sent it to her.').

In other words, "pure" semantic agreement with two non-first person arguments without the "interference" of marking for a specific point of view is functionally similar to pragmatic agreement: the sign form is made away from the signer, and it represents an external point of view or a physical or mental distance to the event.

By contrast to the above examples of pragmatic agreement with an argument that may be the verb's A argument, in some cases of pragmatic agreement, the ambiguity is eliminated by the signer's use of shifted locus. In example (6), the semantic relation between the actions denoted by the verb FIX+fsld and the referent of the locus *fsld* is clearly that of action to patient, because, by her use of shifted locus (the gaze direction, see Ill. 26), the signer represents the agent by her own locus:

(6)   t
    EARLIER / DET+fsld DISHWASHER+fsld BROKEN+fsld / PRON+fsld / 1.p
    gesture / NECESSARY BECKON+fr DISHWASHER^MAN /
    Index-Pm+(fr+move-line+c) / REPAIR+fsld FIX+fsld / FINE /
    (Ill. 26)
    Before that, the dishwasher had broken down. What should I do? I had to call the dishwasher man. He came and he repaired and fixed it so that it was all fine.

In another context, REPAIR and FIX might be modified for the locus of their A argument. By using shifted locus with FIX+fsld, the signer assigns an internal point of view (the dishwasher man as the agent) to the situation and thereby eliminates the ambiguity of the form FIX+fsld. The A argument referent is represented by the sender locus. Thus the construction with FIX+fsld and shifted locus looks like a construction with a double agreement verb showing semantic agreement and taking the point-of-view marker in its A argument cell. This again shows that semantic and pragmatic agreement are two related phenomena; the difference between them is a result of the types of constructions in which they occur.

Focal information and topic
Dik (1989, 277) defines focal information as 'that information which is relatively the most important or salient in the given communicative setting, and considered by S [the sender – EEP] to be most essential for A [the addressee – EEP] to integrate into his pragmatic information'. Topicality 'characterises those entities "about" which information is provided or requested in the discourse' (ibid., 266). That is, whereas focal information is generally new to the receiver, topics are presupposed. In pragmatic agreement, the controller, whether present in the clause or not, is given, while the predicate is focal. That is, in a predicate showing pragmatic agreement, there is overlap in time of topical (the agreement marker representing a given referent) and focal (the predicate) elements.

Topicality and focality may overlap in contrastive contexts of the kind that Dik characterises as Parallel Focus (Dik 1989, 282; see also Chafe 1976, 33-38):

```
(7)  John and Bill came to see me. JOHN was NICE, but BILL was rather
     BORing.

     (= (34), Dik 1989, 278)
```

In the second clause of (7), *JOHN* and *BILL* are topics and focused. This is exactly a discourse context that might trigger pragmatic agreement in Danish Sign Language (see example (2)). Sometimes the contrast is less explicit, as when pragmatic agreement is used to indicate that the holder of the point of view does not share or approve of an action, state, or opinion (see example (5)). But also in that case, there is a second locus, namely the sender locus, which represents the holder of the point of view.

Another context where topicality and focality may overlap is question words. Question words signal a gap in the sender's information, and as such they are focal elements. Dik claims that 'if a language has special strategies for the expression of Focus constituents, these strategies will typically be also used for question words' (1989, 280). A question may relate to the identity or character of an entity whose existence is already taken for granted: here again focality and topicality overlap. In Danish Sign Language, question signs may show agreement when the existence of the questioned referent is presupposed. The question signs WHO and WHAT can take a deictic locus marker for a present entity in sentences meaning 'Who/What is that?' (Ill. 55). That is a parallel to the question word showing gender agreement in French in *Laquelle veux-tu*? ('Which one do you want?', a choice between two oranges). The question word *laquelle* ('which one') agrees in gender with the implicit feminine noun *orange*. In describing the damage to her home where water flooded the kitchen, a signer quoted her husband, HOW+multiple+sld ('How did it happen (that there is water here)?'), with HOW modified for the same locus as was used for the water. A question sign can only show agreement when it pertains to a specific referent. It cannot do so in a sentence meaning 'Who is coming for dinner?', when the sender does not request information about the identity of a specific entity and there is no overlap of focality and topicality in the question sign.

In a discussion of the scope of focus, Dik et al. (1981, 52-53) point out that its scope may be the predication as a whole. Then the focus concerns the illocutionary point of the predication. That is, if the predication is an assertion, the focus will fall on the truth value of the assertion; and if the predication is an invitation or a piece of advice, the focus will concern the force with which the speech act is presented to the receiver as in the English clause:

(8) *DO come over for dinner!* (= Dik et al.'s example (32), ibid., 53)

That is a parallel to the use of pragmatic agreement where a verb such as RECOMMEND or WAIT is modified for the receiver's locus in an advice or an order. The focus is on the relationship of the predicate to the receiver.

7.2 Other treatments of phenomena like pragmatic agreement

Taiwan Sign Language (Smith)
There is very little mentioning of phenomena like pragmatic agreement in the literature on other signed languages. Smith (1989, 101-102) notes that Taiwan Sign Language has a small number of verbs which appear to be able to agree with either their subject or their object, 'depending on the demands of the discourse situation'. The examples Smith gives include HAVE and HAVE-NOT in contrastive contexts. Except for pointing out that the verbs can agree with either their subject or their object and that '[t]he determination as to whether the agreement is with the subject or the object depends on syntactic and contextual clues' (ibid., 102), Smith does not treat these cases of agreement as different from what I call semantic agreement.

ASL (Padden)
Padden (1990) describes some forms of spatially modified verbs in ASL as forms with pronoun clitics. An example is (1) (Padden's example (1), ibid., 121).

(1) WOMAN $_a$WANT; MAN $_b$WANT.

The woman$_i$ is wanting and the man$_j$ is wanting, too.
The woman wants it$_i$ and the man wants it$_j$.

As the translations indicate, the subscripts *a* and *b* may represent either the A arguments' or the P arguments' loci. Padden argues that WANT in (1) does not show agreement; instead, she claims, the markers on the verbs are pronoun clitics as the verbs can also occur with what she calls overt pronouns. In that case, the base form of the verb is used as in (2) (Padden's example (3), ibid., 122); S stands for 'strong hand', W for 'weak hand'):

(2) S: WOMAN WANT; MAN WANT
     W: $_a$PRO $_b$PRO

   (WOMAN and MAN in ASL are made with contact with the face and cannot be modified in space.)

   The woman$_i$ is wanting and the man$_j$ is wanting, too.
   The woman wants it$_i$ and the man wants it$_j$.

Moreover, the same alternation between an overt form of PRO and a spatial modification of the sign is seen with nouns and adjectives (Padden's examples (6) and (5), ibid., 122):

(3) I SEE $_a$DOG $_b$DOG $_c$DOG
     I saw a dog here, there and there, too.
(4) S: I SEE DOG DOG DOG
     W: $_a$PRO $_b$PRO $_c$PRO
     I saw a dog here, there and there, too.

In III.6.2 Agreement features, direction, and domain, I discussed the analysis of spatial modification in signed languages as pronoun clitics; Padden's analysis suffers from the same problem as was mentioned there. If the markers on the verbs are derived from pronoun clitics, example (1) could only be ambiguous if the so-called pronoun clitics could enter into the kind of relationship between arguments and markers that Lehmann characterises as 'a sort of appositive relationship' (Lehmann 1982, 237). This kind of relationship is seen in spoken languages when a free pronoun or a clitic pronoun can occur with or without the nominal just like the subject agreement markers in, for instance, Latin. In the first interpretation of (1), the so-called pronoun clitics occur with the nominals that they cross-reference, i.e. MAN and WOMAN; in the second interpretation, they occur without a nominal used to refer to the patient. As the agreement markers and the pronouns or pronoun clitics behave alike syntactically, it is not possible to distinguish the clitic pronouns from the agreement markers on any other criterion than form. But there is no form difference between the so-called clitic pronouns in (1) and the agreement markers in other contexts.

Moreover, it does not make sense to describe spatially modified nouns such as $_a$DOG or DOG accompanied by what Padden transcribes as $_a$PRO as having a pronoun clitic. A pronoun cannot be part of a nominal with a head noun such as DOG.

Instead, the form that Padden describes as PRO may be an ASL equivalent to the pro-form which I have identified in Danish Sign Language (see II.6.1 Types of pointing signs) and which is distinct from the pronoun: it occurs simultaneously with another sign and carries spatial information relevant to the sign. Padden mentions that PRO can occur simultaneously with verbs that have a place of articulation on the face or the body and cannot themselves be spatially modified, and it can occur simultaneously with agreement verbs that show agreement obligatorily. ASL agreement verbs show semantically unambiguous agreement. Just as with ANALYSE in (1) from Danish Sign Language in III.7.1 Pragmatic agreement, semantic agreement, and point-of-view marking, the modified form of ASL WANT in (1) differs from agreement verbs by being ambiguous. What Padden describes here may thus be similar to what I call pragmatic agreement in Danish Sign Language.

ASL (Kegl)
Kegl adheres to Padden's analysis of plain verbs. She writes:

> The analysis here adopts Padden's analysis of plain verbs. In my thesis...the class of plain verbs was instead analyzed as having spatial agreement with objects. They appeared to have spatial agreement because the cliticization of a pronominal enclitic results in assimilation of orientation of the verb with respect to the indexed location of the object NP. I was misanalyzing this phonetic effect as evidence of spatial agreement. (Kegl 1986, 302)

and

> The cliticization of a pronominal enclitic results in an assimilation on the part of LIKE to orientation toward the index point of the goal argument. Such assimilation makes a plain verb such as LIKE appear to have spatial agreement with the goal. (ibid., 303)

The sign LIKE in ASL has initial body contact, and when it is followed by a pronoun modified for a particular locus, the place of articulation of the final segment of LIKE tends to be assimilated to the place of articulation of the pronoun.

Assimilation
Pragmatic agreement may result in a sequence of signs being made with the hands moved away from the neutral space in one particular direction. Thus, pragmatic agreement might be a purely phonetic feature, i.e. a result of assimilation between the places of articulation of adjacent signs, as suggested for some verbs by Kegl. Informants often describe the phenomenon as 'When your hands are out there, it feels strange to move them in and make the sign near your body', a description that might be taken as evidence of assimilation. Of course a description in terms of assimilation presupposes that at least one sign in the sequence is modified spatially for reasons other than assimilation. Otherwise there would be nothing to trigger the assimilation. A candidate for the sign (or signs) that is modified for other reasons could be nominals that refer to the referent of the locus in question. In (1) of III.7.1 Pragmatic agreement, semantic agreement, and point-of-view marking, there is the nominal

SECOND+fsl CLASS+fsl; in (2), there is a pronoun, PRON+fsr, in the second clause. There is, however, not always such a nominal to trigger the assimilation. In (5) of III.7.1, there is a clause boundary between the pronoun ALL+fsr and the verb TALK-WITH-EACH-OTHER+group+p.a.: fsr. Conversely, a modified nominal is sometimes followed by a predicate with signs in base forms; in (5) below, the forms MARRY and ALSO both of which can be modified in space are made near the signer's body even though the pronoun TWO+pron.+fr is made with the hand moved out in the direction of the locus forward-right:

```
(5)            ____t____    ____t____
    SECOND      / DEAF       / TWO+pon.+fr MARRY ALSO /
        DET+fu---PROFORM+fr--------------MARRY ALSO
    The next ones, they were deaf, they were also a couple.
```

That is, assimilation of place of articulation is not a general phenomenon in Danish Sign Language, and we have to explain the difference between the predicates in examples (1), (2), and (4) of III.7.1 Pragmatic agreement, semantic agreement, and point-of-view marking, and the predicate in (5) here. Moreover, the parallel between the modified form of WANT and WANT accompanied by a modified form of PRO in Padden's examples from ASL cannot be subsumed under an assimilation analysis.

7.3 Equivalents to pragmatic agreement in spoken languages

Are there then any equivalents to pragmatic agreement in spoken languages? To answer this question, we must distinguish the form from the function of pragmatic agreement. In one sense, the form is of course unique to signed languages, since spoken languages do not have loci. But are there languages where agreement is marked on all words of a predicate? There are examples of clauses where a particular agreement marker occurs on all words as in the following sentence from Swahili (Ashton 1944, 346):

```
(1) Wa-toto     wa-li-o-kimbia    wa-me-rudi        w-ote
    Cl2-child   Cl2-past-rel.-run Cl2-perf.-return  Cl2-all
    The children who ran away have all returned.
```

But it is accidental that there is no word in this sentence without the Class 2 agreement marker. In Swahili, there is nominal internal agreement; the verb agrees with its subject and sometimes its object, and a "floating" determiner like *wote* ('all') agrees with the head noun. A temporal adverb, for instance, would be unmarked for agreement. Nichols (1985, 281), however, describes an example from Avar, in which all constituents except for the ergative argument, but including an adverb, agree with the nominative argument, *ʕičal-gi* ('apples'), in number:

(2) Re-ʂ   ʂa-r   dede-r-e   ʕičal-gi   r-ošun r-o'a
     she-Erg here-Pl Fa-Dat-Pl apples(Pl)-Ptc Pl-buy Pl-Aux

     She bought apples here for her father.

Another question is whether we find agreement between the same types of constituents as in Danish Sign Language. I have already (end of III.7.1 Pragmatic agreement, semantic agreement, and point-of-view marking) shown an example of the question word *laquelle* ('which one') in French agreeing in gender with the implicit noun. In the Muskogean language Chickasaw, numerals and nominals may take agreement markers as predicates (Munro & Gordon 1982, 85 and 92, examples (12a) and (40)):

(3) KII-hanna'li
     1p.I-six

     [KII is the 1st person plural marker of the set I ('active' argument) agreement markers]

     There are six of us.

(4) ã-hattak-at   in-tochchi'na
     1s.III-man-SU 1s.III-three

     [ã- is the first person singular marker of the set III ('dative' argument) agreement markers]

     Literally: My husbands are three [to me], i.e. I have three husbands.

The Chickasaw examples (3) and (4) resemble constructions where numerals show pragmatic agreement in Danish Sign Language:

(5) FIVE+sl /
     There are five of them.

(6) FIVE+fsr EXISTENTIAL+fsr PRON+fsr /
     He has five.

In (3) and (4) from Chickasaw, the semantic relations between the predicates and the controllers of the agreement ('active' in (3) and 'dative' in (4)) are expressed by agreement markers from different sets (I or III). In Danish Sign Language, only agreement verbs have unambiguous cells. In pragmatic agreement the relation between the controller and the modified signs is ambiguous and can only be deduced from the context or from lexical semantics.

The function of pragmatic agreement is to bring into focus the relation between a predicate or a clause and its topic. A functional parallel to this in spoken languages is cases where the verb only agrees with a particular syntactic argument if it is salient, as in Swahili where verbs agree only with salient objects (Ashton 1944, 45; see also Croft 1988, 167-169). There are also spoken languages in which the verb agrees with whichever argument is more salient. In Tangut, verb agreement is optional and can only be with a first or second person nominal (Comrie 1981, 184). When a transitive construction has only one first or second person argument, the verb agrees with this argument regardless of its grammatical relation to the verb. In Danish Sign Language, a predicate can also take a locus marker for the referent of a salient argument irrespective of the semantic relationship between the predicate and the argument.

8 Polymorphemic verbs

8.1 Introduction

An example

Some of the characteristics of polymorphemic verbs of motion and location in Danish Sign Language can be demonstrated by the following example from a monologue in which a signer described the sporting activities that she took part in during a stay in the United States. She found the rules of basketball, which she did not know before, very strict and she exemplified their strictness: if you see someone from the opponent team approaching your goal with the ball, you are not allowed to come from behind and cut his way short so that he bumps into you. You must overtake him and stop so that he bumps into you when you are not in motion.

Because of the complexity of the example, I start by giving the translation, then follows the transcription, and finally, I explain the example in ordinary prose:

(1) At the goal, when I'm in the defence and I see someone moving forward and I pursue him and overtake him and he bumps into me, then I'm out. I must run around and in front of him and stop so that he bumps into me. Then it's his fault, not mine. I stand innocently, and he bumps into me and falls. If we're both running and bump into each other, that's against the rules. I have to be ahead. I have to be ahead and stop and he bumps into me. Then it's his fault.

```
A
body:                                              move forward-
face:                    frightened------------------------
gaze:   +-up+----down+------------------------------------
right:  AT GOAL /       DEFEND              1-Pm+(near-r.
left:            1.p          1.p  1-Pm+(hold+c)+(move-line--+
mouth:                         a----------- a-----------

B
body:   ---------------------
face:   ---------------------
gaze:   ------------------+-hands------------------------
right:  shoulder+move-line+forward)+(hold)----------------
left:   forward)-------------------+(move-arc+forward-of-r.
mouth:  ------------------------- tongue out-----------

C
gaze:   ------+----------------------V+--------V+-----down
right:  ------+(move-line+into-1.hand) / 1.p    / MUST /
left:   hand)+(hold)----------------          OUT
mouth:  ----- bu
```

```
D
gaze:   ------------------------------------+-----------
right:  1.p 1-Pm+(hold+near-r.shoulder)
left:       1-Pm+(hold+c)--------------+(move-arc+ahead-of-
mouth:                                  run---------------

E
gaze:   -------V+-----down-----+--------------------
right:  -------------+(move+into-l.hand)+(orientation-
left:   r.hand)+(loc)+(hold)------------------------
mouth:  --------stay   tongue out-------------------

F
face:                                            neg
gaze:   ------------V+---------------------------------V
right:  change:fall) / ERROR PRON+where-r.hand-was / 1.p /
left:   ----------------------------------------
mouth:  -------------------

G
body:   rot. r.-----------------------------------------
gaze:   down srd---------------------------------------
right:  1.p V-Pm+(loc+c) gesture Index-Pm+(right+move-line+
left:                    gesture
mouth:      stand------- tongue out----------------------

H
body:   --------------------neu
gaze:   ---------------------+-------------------#+----
right:  into-signer's-body)+ (orientation:fall) / IF 1.p
left:
mouth:  ---------------------------------------

I
gaze:   -------------------------------------------------V
right:  SIMULTANEOUSLY 1-Pm+(right+move-line+into-l.hand+
left:                  1-Pm+(left+move-line+into-r.hand) /

J
gaze:   +--------V+-------down-------------------------
right:  (hold)---- BEFORE /
left:   MUST-NOT /           1.p 1-Pm+(c+move-arc+loc+for-
mouth:                            stop--------------------

K
gaze:   -----V---r.hand-----------------+----------------V
right:          THEN 1-Pm+(r.shoulder+move-line+into-l.hand) /
left:   ward)+(hold)------------------------------------
mouth:  -----
```

```
L
gaze:   +------------V
right:
left:   ERROR PRON+sr  /
```

(Mouth movements are only indicated with predicates of motion and location.)

In lines A-C of the example, the signer uses the stem 1-Pm on both hands. This stem can be used for the motion and location of a human being, and here the signer uses two such stems to describe the activities of the two individuals involved, herself and her opponent. She begins by placing her left hand close to her body. The instant she starts moving this articulator outward, she also moves her right hand outward, starting a little outside her right shoulder (the initial position of the signer's hands is seen in Ill. 56). That is, her right hand is a little farther out from her body than her left hand. The outward movement of her hands gives the impression that her left hand "pursues" her right hand and "overtakes" it. She then makes her right hand bump into her left hand.

In lines D-F, the signer explains how the defence should be carried out. Here she starts by bringing both hands into position, and immediately afterwards she moves her left hand outward in an arc to a position farther away from her body than her right hand. Then she moves her left hand downward with a short movement to an abrupt stop, a movement that means that something is located somewhere or that a motion is brought to a stop (for instance, in a verb meaning 'arrive (somewhere)'). This movement, which is transcribed as *loc*, contrasts with *hold*, which has no movement other than what it takes to bring the hand into position (a transition movement). In lines E-F, the signer moves her right hand forward so that it bumps into her left hand.

The signer explains the correct defence again in lines G-H by means of two other polymorphemic verbs. The first is a sign with the stem V-Pm which is used for two-legged beings in certain predicates of motion and location, and the second is a sign with the stem Index-Pm, which can be used for human beings. She starts by rotating her body so that she faces right while at the same time she places her right hand with the stem V-Pm close to her body (Ill. 57). Then she makes a gesture of innocence and, finally, she moves her right lower arm and hand, with the index finger pointing upward and the palm facing the direction of the movement, from far out right in toward her body, bumps it into her chest, and moves it outward again while rotating her elbow so that her lower arm and hand end up in a horizontal position ('bumps into me and falls'). In lines H-J, the signer explains once more that she is not allowed to bump into her opponent while running and, in lines J-L, repeats that she must stop before her opponent bumps into her.

What is striking here is the rich variation in the signer's explanations combined with the recurrence of the same units in the different explanations. The signer explains the same thing in several different ways and uses the same units again and again in new combinations. The 1-handshape is used with a number of different movements. In line A, the signer places her left hand with the 1-handshape close to her body without any other movement than what it takes to bring the hand into this position (*hold+c*). Then she moves her hand forward in a straight line (*move-line+forward*). The instant she starts this movement, she also starts moving forward her right hand with the same handshape (*near-r.shoulder+move-line+forward*). But she stops the movement of her right hand (*hold*) when she starts the arc-shaped movement that brings her left hand into a position farther out from her body than her right hand (*move-arc+forward-of-r.hand*) ("the overtaking part" of the defence). When her left hand is in line with her right hand in relation to her body, the signer stops the movement of her left hand (*hold*) and immediately starts the movement of her right hand forward so that it bumps into her left hand (*move-line+into-l.hand*). Thus, the movements of the signer's two hands are coordinated in such a way that the activities of one hand can be used to segment the activities of the other.

The arc-shaped movement recurs in lines D-E, but here both hands are brought into position at the same time. Also there is no forward movement of the signer's right hand in this case. The signer brings her right hand into position and keeps it there (*hold+near-r.shoulder*) without moving it forward. Compared to lines A-C, the movement of her left hand in lines D and E is reduced to the arc-shaped movement. The arc-shaped movement of her left hand is coordinated with a hold in her right hand. But by contrast to the first case (line C), the signer brings her hand to a stop with a clearly marked downward movement (transcribed as *loc* on the left hand of line E).

As the movements of the hands are finely coordinated, so are the activities of the other articulators coordinated with the movements of the hands. In lines A-B, the signer uses a mouth pattern indicating fear (transcribed *a*). This mouth pattern starts when the signer first places her left hand (*1-Pm+(hold+c)* (line A)) close to her body and is renewed when she starts moving both her hands forward (line A). At the same instant, she starts moving her body forward and both her body movement and the mouth pattern as well as the frightened facial expression stop when she stops the forward movement of her hands.[1] There she switches from eye contact with the receiver and looks down at her hands.

In lines E and F, the activities of the signer's eyes and her hands are coordinated. Just before the downward movement of her left hand (*loc*), the signer blinks (line E), one of the most common signals of a constituent boundary. The downward movement is accompanied by the mouth pattern of the Danish word *blive* ('stay').

Example (1) demonstrates that motion can be described more or less elaborately. We have already seen how the forward movement of the signer's hands used in lines A and B does not recur in lines D and E, even though the actions described in both cases include a forward motion of the two opponents. In lines A-C and in lines I-J, the

---

1 Affective facial expressions tend to have a peak early in their scope and fade out towards the end which sometimes makes it difficult to say exactly when they finish. In this case, however, the frightened expression clearly stops when the signer looks down at her hands.

signer describes the same event, namely the prohibited way of shortcutting an opponent's path. Lines D-F and lines J-L both describe the correct behaviour. But the descriptions of the prohibited behaviour in line J and the correct behaviour in lines J-L are both reduced compared with the descriptions of the prohibited behaviour in lines A-C and the correct behaviour in lines D-F, respectively. In lines I-J, the signer simply moves her hands from both sides toward the middle until they bump into each other. The number of movement units are compared in Fig. 11. The first description of the prohibited behaviour includes seven movement units, the second only three. The first description of the correct behaviour also includes seven movement segments, while the second description includes three, of which one, *move-arc+loc*, merges two units, *move-arc* and *loc*. Instead of moving her hand first in an arc-shaped movement and then down to an abrupt stop, the signer moves her hand upward and simultaneously in an arc-shaped movement down to an abrupt stop.

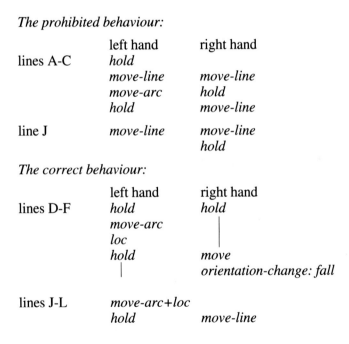

Fig. 11. Number of movement units in some polymorphemic verbs of example (1)

Besides the reduction in the number of units and segments, there are other differences between the descriptions of the "same" action. In lines A-C, the forward movement of the hands is accompanied by a mouth pattern that is part of the facial expression of fear (transcribed as *a*). In lines D-E, the forward movement of the hands is accompanied by the mouth pattern of the Danish verb *løbe* ('run'), while the downward movement of the signer's left hand, which is an addition compared with lines A-

C, is accompanied by the mouth pattern of the Danish verb *blive* ('stay') (line E). In line J, we again find a Danish mouth pattern, in this case the Danish word *stop* ('stop'). That is, the signer increases her use of mouth patterns of Danish verbs as she reduces the number of movement units.

One more difference between the examples is the signer's gaze direction. Especially in lines A-C, the first example in the series, the signer looks at her hands, first when she moves both her hands forward, later when she moves her left hand in an arc ahead of her right hand. For a brief moment, she looks at the receiver at the end of the forward movement unit (line B). She re-establishes eye contact with the receiver when she bumps her right hand into her left hand (line C). These changes between looking at her hands and having eye contact with the receiver are repeated in lines D-F and J-L, but in line I, the signer maintains eye contact with the receiver all through the predicate. Line I is where we find the least complex predicate with one movement unit in each hand and symmetrical movements of the hands.

In lines G-H, the signer describes part of the same event as in lines D-F and J-L (the correct behaviour), but here she uses two other stems, V-Pm and Index-Pm. In lines A-B, the signer moves her body forward while moving her hands forward. The body movement, so to speak, reinforces the information expressed by the hands. That is also the case with the signer's body orientation in line G: she places the manual articulator with the V-handshape of the stem V-Pm close to her body and rotates her body so that she faces slightly right (Ill. 57). But when she signs Index-Pm+(right+move-line+into-signer's-body)+(orientation-change:fall), the information conveyed by her body does not reinforce, but supplements the information conveyed by her hand: she describes how the person from the opponent team bumps into her, by moving her right hand and lower arm into her own body.

Example (1) demonstrates that the articulators are finely coordinated in this type of construction and the activities of the different articulators can be segmented. A segment may consist of a merger of two units that occur as separate segments in other places. The example raises a number of questions:

— What are the handshape units that can be used in constructions of the kind demonstrated in example (1), and what are the differences between these handshape units?
— What is the status of the signer's body in relation to the handshape units?
— What is the relation between two sequences of units articulated simultaneously by the two hands?
— What is the inventory of movement units?
— Which movement units can co-occur simultaneously in two hands and sequentially in one hand?
— What do reductions in sequences of units describing motion and location consist of, when do they occur, and what is their function?
— What is the function of the signer's gaze?

— What is the function of the signer's mouth patterns?
— How do the complexes of units exemplified in (1) relate to other signs, to modifications for distribution and agreement, and to the frame of reference?
— And what is the linguistic status of this kind of complexes of units compared with spoken languages?

Predicates or clauses

The constructions in example (1) in all cases come after a pronoun identifying one of the participants in the action, namely the first person pronoun 1.p. In one case, lines H-I, a time adverbial is inserted between the pronoun and the complex of units. Seemingly, the constructions are exact parallells to clause structures such as 1.p DEFEND (line A), 1.p OUT (line C), ERROR PRON+where-r.hand-was (line F), ERROR PRON+sr (line L), except that the order of the pronoun and the predicate is reversed in two of these clauses. But complex constructions such as those seen in (1) also resemble constructions with reported speech in which the signer identifies the sender by means of a name, a noun, or a pronoun and then proceeds with the reported speech (part of example (4) in II.5 Shifted reference, shifted attribution of expressive elements, and shifted locus, is repeated here as (2) for convenience):

```
(2)  body:     back----------------------------------
     head:        neu-----nodding-neu----------------
     brow:                   frown--------------------
     gaze: fld----V----fru-----V+---------------------
              MOTHER /           gesture nok(M)('enough')

     body:  ----------------------------------------
     head:  ----------------------------------------
     brow:  ----------------------------------------
     gaze:  ----------------------------------------
              ANNEGRETHE neu+EXPLAIN+c 1.p neu+GO-TO+c

     body:  ----------------
     head:  ----------------
     brow:  ----------------
     gaze:  ----------------
              nok(M)('enough') /
```

My mother nodded and said, 'Never mind. It's not necessary. Annegrethe will explain it to me when she comes. It's not necessary.'

Like the signer of (2), the signer of (1) shifts the attribution of expressive elements (face: frightened, mouth: a—, tongue out in lines A-C). In (1), the signer is talking about herself (or herself as a general person); she would have used the same constructions in talking about somebody else, in which case the locus would have been shifted (body: rot.r, gaze: down srd in lines G-H; the use of *c* in the predicates). One difference from the construction with reported speech in (2) is, however, that the constructions in (1) do not include any referential nominals.

Another conspicuous characteristic of the constructions in (1) is that in no case is there a constituent after the complex construction. Although the signer starts by identifying one of the participants by means of the first person pronoun 1.p, she does not and cannot insert a sign identifying the other participant in the interaction after the complex construction, as she might do after a double agreement verb. Thus, the complex constructions in (1) resemble both full clauses as reported speech and single verbs having a predicative function. They have a predicative meaning describing the motion and location of entities.

I will show that a continuum exists with, at one end, polymorphemic constructions that can occur in the same environment as reported speech, but are "reports" of states, events, and processes of motion and location; at the other end, we find internally unanalysable lexemes some of which can be modified for agreement and distribution. Constructions like the one in line I are somewhere on the continuum between full-blown polymorphemic constructions and lexical verbs. The construction in lines I-J has the fewest number of movement units, it has continuous eye contact, a time adverbial is inserted between the pronoun and the complex unit, and it occurs in a conditional clause.

As the polymorphemic constructions have a verbal character, I refer to them as *polymorphemic verbs*. In signed language research, such constructions are usually described as *classifier verbs*.

Classifiers
In her article on arbitrariness and iconicity in historical change in American Sign Language, Frishberg introduced the term *classifier* in the description of ASL:

> ASL uses certain hand-shapes in particular orientations for certain semantic features of noun arguments. Thus the verb MEET has no 'neutral' form; the citation form actually means 'one person meets one person', or perhaps more specifically 'one self-moving object with a dominant vertical dimension meets one self-moving object with a dominant vertical dimension'. If trees started walking, they would MEET one another in the same way. Many of these classifiers are productive and analysable, although not strictly transparent. (Frishberg 1975, 715)

Classifier is here used for a unit of a verb of motion expressed by a particular handshape. Frishberg does not compare what she calls classifiers with classifiers in spoken languages. In later studies, however, such units in verbs of motion and location have been compared with the classificatory verb stems of Athapaskan languages, especially Navaho, and the term *classifier* has been used in studies of a number of signed languages.[2]

---

2 ASL, Thai Sign Language, Italian Sign Language, Swedish Sign Language, British Sign Language, Taiwan Sign Language, New Zealand Sign Language, and Danish Sign Language

The importance of these so-called classifiers in signed languages has also been demonstrated in some studies of deaf children's acquisition of ASL (Newport & Supalla 1980; Newport 1982; Supalla 1982; Ellenberger & Steyaert 1978; Kantor 1980) and in a study of children's acquisition of Danish Sign Language (Toft & Hansen 1988). Moreover, their role in the creation of new signs has been described for ASL (Bellugi & Newkirk 1981), British Sign Language (Brennan 1990a, 1990b), and Danish Sign Language (Engberg-Pedersen & Pedersen 1985a). There is therefore no doubt that we are here dealing with an important feature of the structure of signed languages. It has even been claimed that all signs in ASL include classifiers (Kegl 1986, 438; see also McDonald 1982, 1983). In earlier studies (Engberg-Pedersen 1985; Engberg-Pedersen & Pedersen 1985a), I have argued against an analysis of the polymorphemic verbs of motion and location as including classifiers.

In what follows, I will focus on the aspects of the polymorphemic verbs of motion and location that show how they differ from other verbs with respect to the use of space. I will show that they are polymorphemic verbs built around a stem expressed by the handshape of the sign. Polymorphemic verbs can take two or more consecutive or simultaneous morphemes denoting path and motion or location, and the handshapes by which some of the stems are expressed can change in morphologically relevant ways. Both of these features are excluded with verbs that have been described up to now, including verbs that can show agreement. That changes in the handshape of some polymorphemic verbs are morphologically relevant (for a morphological analysis of such handshapes in ASL, see Supalla 1986) means that the stem of these verbs includes more than one morpheme. But as such changes of handshape are not relevant to the use of space, I will only mention examples of the changes in passing. First, in III.8.2 Predicate classifiers and classificatory verbs in spoken languages, I will describe the use of the term classifier in relation to predicates in spoken languages, and after that discuss the use of this term in relation to Danish Sign Language in III.8.3 Classifiers or verb stems in Danish Sign Language?

8.2 Predicate classifiers and classificatory verbs in spoken languages

Predicate classifiers or co-occurrence constraints
Allan (1977) defines classifiers in spoken languages on two criteria:

> (a) they occur as morphemes in surface structures under specifiable conditions; (b) they have meaning, in the sense that a classifier denotes some salient perceived or imputed characteristic of the entity to which an associated noun refers (or may refer).
> (Allan 1977, 285)

(Kegl & Wilbur 1976; Supalla 1978, 1982, 1986; Baker & Cokely 1980, 287-329; Liddell 1980, 93-101; Engberg-Pedersen 1981; Gee & Kegl 1982; McIntire 1982; McDonald 1982, 1983; Padden 1988b, 200-241; Brennan, Colville & Lawson 1984, 185; Suwanarat et al. 1986, 17-72; Kegl 1985, 1986, 1990; Wilbur, Bernstein & Kantor 1985; Wilbur 1987, 85-100; Smith 1989; Collins-Ahlgren 1990; Corazza 1990; Lucas & Valli 1990; Schick 1990; Wallin 1990).

The definition is problematic because it does not specify what is meant by *morpheme*. Allan sets up a contrast between verbs in Athapaskan languages such as Navaho, on the one hand, and verbs in languages such as English and Tarascan, on the other hand. In talking about numeral classifiers in Tarascan, he underlines that classifiers should be kept distinct from stems which are subject to semantic co-occurrence constraints. The Tarascan verbs *ekuá-*, 'pile up long things', and *takú-*, 'pile up flat things', denote different events, they have different semantic co-occurrence constraints, and are not classifiers.

> ... the shape characteristics of referents which are identified by numeral classifiers are, not unexpectedly, relevant in some noun-verb collocations in Tarascan – whereas English, e.g., has no identical constraints. But the co-occurrence of the Tarascan verbs with particular classes of nouns is not marked by any set of formatives in the verbal group which can be seen to classify those nouns in a way comparable to the Athapaskan classificatory stems. Instead, noun-verb collocation in Tarascan is conditioned by covert co-occurrence constraints of the kind familiar in English. (ibid., 289)

As an example of verbs with similar co-occurrence constraints in English, Allan mentions *drink* and *eat* where *drink* classifies the stuff consumed as liquid, while *eat* classifies the stuff consumed as solid. Allan concludes:

> The relevant difference between the Athapaskan languages and the English verbal group is the inclusion of a classificatory stem in Athapaskan ... as a surface marker of noun classification which has no counterpart in English, nor indeed in Tarascan. Therefore neither English nor Tarascan is a predicate classifier language. More generally, if a language has noun classes entailed by co-occurrence constraints between nouns and their modifiers or predicates, this does not make it a classifier language; if it did, every language would be a classifier language, and the label would become meaningless. (ibid., 289-90)

Allan does not see, however, that this conclusion undermines his own analysis of the Athapaskan languages as predicate classifier languages. His analysis of Tarascan and English verbs presupposes that classifiers are formatives that do not include the predicative meaning of the verb complex, but only classificatory meaning such as shape. In Navaho, the classificatory meaning and the predicative meaning are merged in one form and the Athapaskan linguists do not describe the stems as classifiers, but as classificatory verb stems.

Classificatory verbs in Koyukon

As an example of a language with classificatory verb stems, I will use Koyukon, an Athapaskan language belonging to the Northern Group (Thompson, Axelrod & Jones 1983). Verbs in Koyukon consist of a stem, a number of prefixes, and some suffixes. The suffixes are irrelevant to my point and I will leave them out of consideration. The stem can historically be analysed as a root and a suffix indicating aspect, e.g. momentaneous, continuative, perambulative aspects. For each aspect, there are four different stems, a so-called *stem set* with one stem for each of the four modes, imperfective, perfective, future, and optative mode. The modes also determine one of the prefixes of the verbs. If a verb has seven different aspectual forms, it has seven stem sets of four stems (imp., perf., fut., and opt.), i.e. altogether 28 stems.

Prefixes in Koyukon may express meanings such as 'out into the open', 'arrive carrying or bringing (an object of a particular kind)', or 'in a line or row'. The prefixes occur in so-called derivational strings, some of which must combine with a particular aspectual stem and specific mode prefixes. Other derivational strings are non-aspectual, i.e. they can combine with any stem of the verb. The *derivational strings* always change the meaning of the verbs in the same way, regardless of verb. The derivational strings are relevant to the categorisation of verbs in Koyukon.

Koyukon linguists also talk about *verb themes*. A theme is an abstract form of the verb with an indication of the obligatory prefixes with that particular verb. The Koyukon themes are divided into categories according to three criteria: their mean-ing, the kinds of aspects of their stems, and the derivational strings that they can occur with. Examples of such verb categories are positional verbs, extension verbs, classificatory stative verbs, motion verbs, and classificatory motion verbs. Classificatory stative verbs and positional verbs have only one aspectual form, the neuter aspect, while motion verbs and classificatory motion verbs have seven aspectual forms.

With classificatory stative stems, the choice of stem depends on characteristics of the subject referent; with classificatory motion verbs, it depends on characteristics of the object referent. The classificatory verb stems relate to the nonclassificatory stems in the following way:

	classificatory verbs:	*nonclassificatory verbs:*
stative verbs:	classificatory stative verbs	positional verbs
motion verbs:	classificatory motion verbs	motion verbs

The classificatory verbs can be used for entities that can be characterised as, for instance, 'compact object' or 'flat, rigid, or stick-like object'. But it is not always easy to see in what way the classificatory verbs are more semantically classificatory than the positional verbs and the nonclassificatory motion verbs. A verb meaning 'burning object be located' or a verb meaning 'plural object be located', both of which are classificatory stative verbs, can hardly be said to be more semantically classificatory than a (nonclassificatory) positional verb meaning 'stand' which can be used only with animates.

The classificatory verb stems are classificatory in the sense that they group nouns in the same classes across the stative – motion distinction (Hoijer 1945, 17). There are eleven classificatory stative verb themes that correlate semantically with eleven classificatory motion verb themes. Corresponding to a classificatory stative verb theme meaning 'compact object be located', there is a classificatory motion verb theme meaning '(agent) move compact object'. The stems of the classificatory motion verbs and the stems of the classificatory stative verbs are historically related: the classificatory motion verb stems in the momentaneous aspect perfective mode are identical with the neuter imperfective stems of the classificatory stative verbs. That is, a motion described as momentaneous and perfective leads to a state. The morphological relatedness is not, however, criterial for the categorisation of the verbs as classificatory.

The difference between the classificatory verbs and the nonclassificatory verbs is: 1) that the same noun classes are distinguished in the classificatory stative verbs as in the classificatory motion verbs; there is no such correlation between the positional verbs and the nonclassificatory motion verbs; and 2) that there is a form difference between the classificatory stative and the classificatory motion verbs; if there was not such a difference, the verbs would constitute one series of stems which could be used in verbs both with a stative meaning and to denote motion. Disregarding the morphological and semantic relation between the classificatory stative verbs and the classificatory motion verbs, the positional verbs and the classificatory stative verbs have the same morphological composition and resemble each other semantically in that both kinds denote the location of some entity, either animate or inanimate. In the case of animates (the positional verbs), Koyukon lexically distinguishes more different ways of being located than in the case of inanimates (the classificatory stative verbs), as probably all languages do (see III.8.3 Classifiers or verb stems in Danish Sign Language?). Leaving out details about the affixes of the verbs, Fig. 12 demonstrates the interaction of stems and derivational strings in verbs with the classificatory stems for 'compact object'.[1]

Classificatory stative stems:
The stem set: *'onh* (impf.)   *'o'* (perf.)   *'o'* (fut.)   *'o'* (opt.)
1. derivation: '(classified object) be there, be in position of rest'
     saahal la-'onh   'a sugar-cube is there' (134)
2. derivation: '(classified object) be completely submerged'
     taal-'onh   'the fishtrap is set', lit. 'a compact object is there under water' (143)
3. derivation: 'wear (classified object)'
     ts'ah nidaanla-'onh   'you are wearing a hat' (143)

---

[1] The classification of entities depends on the interaction of the stem with gender markers; therefore, the classification may sometimes seem somewhat unusual as when a hat is classified as a compact object.

The meaning of a verb is the result of, among other things, the combination of aspect and mode (the four modes being imperfective, perfective, future, and optative). As can be seen from Fig. 12, the classificatory stative stem imperfective mode is identical with the motion stem in the momentaneous aspect perfective mode: the state is a result of the momentaneous perfective motion. That is why verbs with the stative stems in the perfective mode are translated by English verbs in the present tense.

4. derivation: '(classified object) be in a line or row'
   kkanh ditaałt'-onh   'there is a line of beaver lodges' (144)

Classificatory motion stems:
Momentaneous aspect
   stem set: *'oyh* (impf.)   *'onh* (perf.)   *ol* (fut.)   *'ol/'o'* (opt.)
1. derivation: 'arrive carrying (classified object), bring (classified object)'
   ts'ah nis-'onh   'I arrived carrying a hat, I brought a hat' (148)
2. derivation: 'carry, bring (classified object) into the house'
   ts'ah hadonis-'onh   'I brought the hat into the house' (154)

Classificatory verbs of involuntary motion:
Momentaneous aspect
   stem set: *leeyh* (impf.)   *ninh* (perf.)   *liyhtl* (fut.)   *leeyh* (opt.)
1. derivation: '(classified object) arrives'
   daal-ninh   'it (package) arrived' (209)
2. derivation: '(classified object) goes down'
   ts'ah nodol-ninh   'the hat fell, dropped' (210)
3. derivation: causative derivation
   saasee anditaatl-ninh   'he threw the clock away' (211)

(The numbers in parentheses refer to pages in Thompson, Axelrod & Jones 1983.)

Fig. 12.
Examples of verbs with the classificatory stems for 'compact object' in Koyukon

Barron (1982, 134) sets up three criteria for classificatory verbs. The first two are generalised versions of the two criteria mentioned above for distinguishing classificatory and nonclassificatory verbs in Koyukon. These two criteria together demand that the classificatory verbs constitute a relatively closed subsystem within the verbs of the language. Barron's third criterion is that the classification of the nouns should depend only on the verb forms. This is to exclude agreement phenomena. But it does not matter whether the classification is made through affixes, composition, or stem variation. In Koyukon, the classification is made through stem variation.

The Koyukon stems are called *classificatory verb stems*, and not *classifiers*.[2] They constitute a subclass within the category of verbs, a subclass with systematic

---
[2] Koyukon and other Athapaskan languages have verbal prefixes which are called classifiers, but they do not have a classificatory function. Landar (1967, 265) describes the Navaho classifiers as 'prefixes of voice' changing, for example, an active verb to a passive verb or a transitive verb to an intransitive verb. The forms which are called classifiers by Athapaskan linguists are not the forms Allan (1977) talks about in his analysis of Navaho as a predicate classifier language. Allan leaves out of consideration the forms called classifiers by Athapaskan linguists, as they cannot really be said to classify nouns or referents. Instead, Allan focuses on the *classificatory stems*; it is these forms that he interprets as classifiers.

relations between groups of verbs. Classificatory verbs have two semantic components, a classificatory element that ascribes an argument of the verb to a certain noun class and a predicative element which predicates something of the classified object (Barron 1982, 141). The classificatory verbs in Koyukon differ from the nonclassificatory in that they are semantically and morphologically, in some cases only semantically,[3] related across the stative–motion distinction. Otherwise, like the nonclassificatory stems, the classificatory stems can historically be analysed as consisting of a root and an aspect marker, they have one or more aspects like the nonclassificatory stems, and like them they can take derivational strings. That is, the classificatory verbs do not have a different morphological composition and they cannot even be said to differ radically semantically from the nonclassificatory stems.

Talmy's analysis of conflation patterns
Tarascan (nonclassificatory) verbs (see the beginning of this section) as well as the Koyukon verb stems are restricted to occur with a more limited number of nouns than most English verbs. This means that the number of events that any single Tarascan verb or Koyukon stem can be used to denote is more limited than the number of events that, for instance, the English verb *move* can be used for; *move* can be used with many more objects, both concrete and abstract, and to denote both an object moving freely and an agent's moving of an object.

Talmy (1985) gives a general definition of a *motion event* as 'a situation containing movement or the maintenance of a stationary location' (ibid., 60). The basic motion event consists of four components: 'the Figure is a moving or *conceptually movable* object whose path or site is at issue'; 'the Ground is a reference-frame, or a reference-point stationary within a reference-frame, with respect to which the Figure's path or site is characterised'; the Path is 'the course followed or site occupied by the Figure object with respect to the Ground object'; and the Motion 'refers to the presence *per se* in the event of motion or location' (ibid., 61 – emphasis in the original). The two types of Motion are represented by the symbols *move* and be_L, respectively. In addition to these internal components, a motion event can have a Manner and a Cause.

Talmy further shows that different languages lexicalise different combinations of Motion and other components of the motion event, or, in his words, different languages have different *conflation* patterns (ibid., 74-75). English expressions of Motion typically conflate Motion and Manner or Cause as in *stand, lie, lean* (be_L + Manner), *slide, swing, twist* (move + Manner), and *blow, push, hammer* (move + Cause). By contrast, Spanish expressions of motion typically conflate Motion and Path as in *entrar* ('move-in'), *salir* ('move-out'), *subir* ('move-up'), *bajar* ('move-down'), *cruzar* ('move-across'), while expressions of motion events in Atsugewi (Hokan) conflate Motion and Figure as seen in the following examples:

---
3   There are other classificatory and nonclassificatory groups of verbs in Koyukon than the ones I have focused on here.

-lup- 'for a small shiny spherical object (e.g. a round candy, an eyeball, a hailstone) to move/be-located'
-caq- 'for a slimy lumpish object (e.g. a toad, a cow dropping) to move/be-located'
-qput- 'for loose dry dirt to move/be-located' (after Talmy 1985, 73)

The conflation type of Atsugewi verbs is identical to the conflation type of the stative and motion verbs of Koyukon and some verb stems of Danish Sign Language, as I will show. Talmy's analysis demonstrates how the meanings of these verb stems have a predicative element, Motion (*move* and be_L), and a classificatory element, Figure.

Judging from Allan's English translations (see the beginning of this section), the Tarascan verbs *ekuá-* ('pile up long things') and *takú-* ('pile up flat things') can be analysed as conflating Motion, Figure, Cause, and what Talmy calls *distribution of an actor*, which 'refers to the arrangement of multiple patients' (ibid., 133). That is, the Tarascan verb roots conflate more components than the Koyukon verb stems, but there is no morphological distinction between verbs in Tarascan and verbs in Koyukon which might warrant Allan's characterisation of the Athapaskan languages as predicate *classifier* languages and Tarascan as not belonging to this type. Both have verb stems with a classificatory element (or semantic co-occurrence constraints) and an element of predicative meaning. Because the verb roots in Tarascan conflate more components of the motion event, they have more specific meanings than the verb stems in Koyukon. But the Koyukon verbs have more specific meanings than the English verb *move* because *move* conflates even fewer components than the Koyukon verb stems.

Classifiers and agreement

In writing about classifiers in general, Edmondson (1990a; see also Bos 1990, 234) finds that the analysis of classifiers as primarily having a classificatory or categorisational function is wrong. The so-called classifiers are much more arbitrary and syntactic 'than linguists have previously been prepared to admit' (ibid., 189). He suggests instead that the notion underlying "classifiers" is agreement (see also Supalla 1982, 24ff.).

Lehmann (1982) points out that the relationship between a noun and a classifier does not fulfil one of the criteria of agreement, namely that the assignment of the agreement-triggering term to the agreement category be independent of the agreeing term. One of the characteristics of classifiers is that, by contrast to noun classes, they are not completely predictable from the choice of noun. A classifier can classify a noun, and in this way, the assignment of the noun to the "agreement" category is not independent of the "agreeing" term, the classifier. Thus classifiers and classificatory verbs cannot be analysed as forms showing agreement. Instead, Lehmann suggests that we understand the relationship between classifiers and nouns in terms of semantic compatibility or concord. He defines concord as a relationship that obtains between two constituents when their meanings are compatible and the same conditions are fulfilled as for agreement except that one constituent's belonging to a certain subcategory of the grammatical category is not independent of the presence or nature of the other constituent, as it is required for agreement.[4]

Classifiers and noun classes

Dixon (1986) distinguishes the grammatical category of *noun classes* involving a grouping of all nouns of a language into a smallish number of classes, on the one hand, and, on the other hand, the lexico-syntactic phenomenon of *noun classification* through noun classifier as free forms in syntactic construction with a head noun. A classifier occurs in the same noun phrase as the noun it qualifies, and classifiers provide information about 'physical design (size, shape, animacy, etc.), function or use (edible, habitable, etc.), cognitive categories in a given culture...and also about social role and interaction.' (ibid., 108). In Dixon's view, a classifier cannot be an affix on a verb. But Dixon sees some parallells between classifiers and the classificatory verb stems of the Athapaskan languages. He finds that as the Athapaskan classificatory verb stems involve 'a verbal element and also a classificatory element, referring to the type of object that is being discussed' (ibid., 107), the classificatory verbs do not fall clearly into either the scheme of noun classes or the scheme of noun classification (classifiers):

> The Athapaskan-type system satisfies some of the criteria set out for noun classes – there is a small, closed system of stem-types, and there is an indication of the class of a noun on a constituent other than the noun itself i.e. in the verb. However, only some nouns are classified (those with concrete reference), and then only on some semantic types of verb, characteristics that are more reminiscent of classifiers. (ibid., 107)

Classifiers and incorporation of a classifying noun

Another classificatory system that Dixon describes as 'unusual' is incorporation of a classifying noun into the verb as described by Mithun (1986). Dixon does not describe this 'unusual' system as a classifier system. He finds 'that it is quite possible that the kind of classificatory incorporation described by Mithun could develop into a system of classificatory verb stems, as in Athapaskan and other languages; and that this may parallel one avenue for the development of noun classes, from noun classifiers...' (Dixon 1986, 107). That is, noun classes may develop from noun classifiers just as classificatory verb stems may develop from noun incorporation, but classificatory verb stems are not classifiers.

Mithun does talk about classifiers in her analysis of noun incorporation. She defines noun incorporation as 'a lexical process whereby a noun stem and verb stem

---

4 It is not clear whether Lehmann wants to include in his definition of concord all kinds of semantic co-occurrence constraints irrespective of the morphological form of the entities which contribute to the constraints.

are compounded to form a derived verb stem' (1986, 380). An incorporated noun does not refer, but narrows the scope of the host verb, i.e. it makes the meaning of the compound more specific. Mithun describes several types – or stages – of noun incorporation. In one type, the process of noun incorporation is highly productive. Even though the incorporated noun is not referential (it is not marked for distinctions such as definiteness, specificity, or number), incorporation is used as a means of backgrounding known information: a verb with an incorporated noun is used when a referent has already been mentioned and a pronoun alone would not be sufficient to reidentify the referent. The presence of the incorporated noun narrows the scope of the verb.

Mithun refers to the incorporated nouns as classifiers. They are identifiable as separate morphemes in the verb complex. At some point, the noun incorporation process may lose its productivity, so that the set of incorporated "classifiers" becomes closed, and the morpheme boundaries may become blurred. What started out as a productive process of noun incorporation may end up as semantic co-occurrence constraints between verbs and separate nominals (ibid., 393).[5]

Conclusion
This is clearly an area with much terminological confusion. The definitions and terms fit the language or language group for which they were first made better than other languages. Some linguists, like Dixon, use the term *classifier* only for free forms in noun phrases. Others, like Mithun, use the term also for nouns incorporated into the verb complexes. And still others, like Allan, use the term for classificatory verb stems, i.e. lexemes with a predicative meaning as well as a classificatory meaning. Apart from Allan, however, everyone seems to agree that a *classifier* is a morpheme separate from either the noun or the verb root. In order to determine the status of the units of the polymorphemic verbs of motion and location expressed by different handshapes in Danish Sign Language, it is, therefore, necessary to analyse the morphological composition of the entire verb complex. Are there verb roots or stems separate from the handshape units, such that the latter could be analysed as purely classificatory elements integrated into the verb complexes, i.e. as classifiers in Mithun's sense?

8.3 Classifiers or verb stems in Danish Sign Language?

The handshape unit and the movement unit
The term *classifier* is widely used in signed language research, probably because of the pervasiveness of the elements that it is used to describe. A strong need for terminology exists, but there is no agreement on how the entities for which the term is used and the verb complexes in which they occur should be analysed. Supalla (1978)

---

[5] There is no reason to believe that the classificatory verb stems of Koyukon or any other Athapaskan language have developed from noun incorporation (Michael Fortescue - personal communication).

and McDonald (1982, 169-188; 1983) both compare the handshape unit of the ASL verbs in question to the classificatory verb stems of the Athapaskan language Navaho. Supalla, basing his discussion on Allan's analysis of Navaho verbs (1977, see also here III.8.2 Predicate classifiers and classificatory verbs in spoken languages), draws the conclusion that the handshape unit is a classifier (an affix) and the movement units of the verb complexes are roots (Supalla 1982, 11). In contrast, McDonald describes the handshape units as 'the core or the stem of the ASL verb' which 'is used to signal the motion or location of a given type of object.' (1983, 35). In her thesis (1982), McDonald uses the term *classifier* for the handshape units of ASL verbs of motion and location, even though she finds that the handshape units play a central role in the predicate. The reason is that she also accepts Allan's analysis of "predicate classifier languages", i.e. languages like Navaho with classificatory verb stems, as having classifiers (ibid., 171-172).

Supalla (1978, 1982) presents no arguments in favour of analysing the units expressed by movement as roots and the units expressed by handshapes as affixes. The reason for his analysis seems to be primarily semantic: the movement units denote the motion or location meaning of verbs of motion and location. Moreover, Supalla implies that the movement units can be held constant, while the handshape units can be substituted one for the other, depending only on the class to which the noun of the nominal (or the nominal's referent) belongs.

Some researchers (Kegl & Wilbur 1976; Klima & Bellugi 1979, 13) suggest that the handshape units have a pronominal function. Such an analysis is tempting when we consider examples such as the following from Danish Sign Language. The signer described how her husband pursued and caught a burglar:

```
(1) right:   1-Pm+(near-r.shoulder+move-line+near-l.hand+
    left:    1-Pm+(hold+forward-left)-------------------

    right:   slow-and-tense) / GRASS FIELD+fl / Handle-hand-
    left:    ---------------------------------------------

    right:   Pm+(c+move-line+l.hand+closing) / FORTUNATELY /
    left:    ---------------------------------------------

    (Ill. 58)

    Making an effort he gained on him, and on a grass field, he finally
    caught him, fortunately.
```

The signer almost grasps her left thumb with her right hand (Ill. 58), which suggests an analysis of the thumb as a form used like a pronoun to refer to the burglar.

McDonald finds that analyses of the handshape units as pronouns and Supalla's analysis of handshape units as (classifier) affixes entail two assumptions: first, that 'there exists other "linguistic" material which can be characterised structurally as a "verb" (the movement in Supalla's analysis) or which unambiguously communicates a single "verbal" meaning across these "pronominal" forms'; and second, that 'the "pronouns" "add" information to the verb and do not somehow govern or control its meaning' (1982, 161ff.). But the classificatory morphemes (i.e. the morphemes expressed by the handshape units) control the resultant meaning of the verb complexes, McDonald claims. She compares two ASL verb forms that describe the handling and the existence in a location of an entity. One means 'move x-type of object in a certain way to a certain location' and the other means 'x-type of object existed in a certain way in a certain location'. The two verbs have different handshape units, but the same movement, 'a slightly arcing forward movement with an abrupt held end' (ibid., 163). Examples are verbs meaning '(I) put (a book) on (the table)' and '(a bird) perched up on (a branch)', each expressed by different handshapes, but the same movement. If the movement unit constituted the verb root, the two verb forms should denote the same type of motion, but they do not; the former expresses caused motion, the latter an entity's own motion. The "verbal" meaning not only depends on the movement units, but on the interaction of the classificatory morpheme (expressed by the handshape) and the morphemes expressed by the movement. Or put differently, the choice of handshape unit contributes to the predicative meaning of the verb complex, not just the classificatory meaning.

Similarly, the same movement in Danish Sign Language, a linear movement, can express either an entity's own motion (with Car-Pm or Index-Pm), distribution (with Flat-entity-Pm), extension (with Flat-surface-Pm), or motion caused by an agent (with Handle-two-dimensional-entity-Pm), all depending on the handshape unit. With some handshape units (e.g. V-Pm, see Ill. 66), the linear movement can mean either motion or distribution, but the orientation of the hand in relation to the direction of the movement then varies. That is, in Danish Sign Language as well, the "verbal" meaning of the complex depends on the interaction of the movement unit and the handshape unit.

McDonald also argues against Supalla's analysis of the movement units as roots by pointing out that movement in verbs of motion and location may express other things than motion. This is also true of Danish Sign language: the movement unit *loc* means 'be located' and a specific up-and-down movement of the hand with some stems means 'energetically, resolutely' (see further III.8.4 Movement morphemes in polymorphemic verbs).

McDonald's conclusion is that the assumptions behind the analysis of the handshape units as pronouns and peripheral to the verb are invalid: the same movement may express different meanings depending on the handshape units. The movement does not unambiguously communicate a single "verbal" meaning across the alleged pronouns, and the handshape units do control the meaning of the verb. In example (1) about the catching of the burglar, the articulator of the polymorphemic verb serves as what I call a referent projection in the same way that the directions of loci do; but referent projections are not pronouns (see further III.8.6 Polymorphemic verbs and space).

Three stems used for the motion and location of human beings
The contribution of handshape units of polymorphemic verbs to the predicative meaning of the verb complex can be demonstrated for Danish Sign Language by a closer analysis of three handshape units in polymorphemic verbs that can all be used for the motion or location of a human being, namely 1-Pm, V-Pm, and Index-Pm.[1] The three handshape units are not the only ones that can be used for human beings in polymorphemic verbs; neither are they restricted to predicates about human beings. In that use, however, they can combine with the largest selection of movement units.

Craig (1986, 5-6) mentions that 'linguistic classifications mark humanness and animacy first, then shape, then use and consistency', and she refers to Supalla's article on ASL in the same volume (1986) for an example of a language that conforms to this hierarchy of classes. Polymorphemic verbs of Danish Sign Language also distinguish between animate and inanimate, but the sheer number of handshape units that can be used in polymorphemic verbs of human beings is evidence that the handshape units have more than classificatory meaning. If they only had that, there would not be many different forms that could all be used for the same type of referent, unless, of course, they were in free variation, and they are not. In Koyukon, the verbs used for animates are nonclassificatory; many of the nonclassificatory motion verb stems and the (nonclassificatory) positional verb stems denote specific motion events that animates take part in, such as stems meaning 'to be sitting', 'to be standing', 'to be lying down', 'to walk, go by foot', 'to swim', and 'to paddle a canoe, go by boat'. All of these stems can occur in polysynthetic verbs in Koyukon. In the same way, the different handshape units that can be used for human beings in Danish Sign Language reflect different aspects of the motion events, or different perspectives on those events, rather than different classes of referents involved. The number of different forms (including verbs that are not polymorphemic such as SWIM, SIT, LIE, RUN, LEAVE, and TRAVEL) that can be used for human beings reflects the social need within this semantic area of central importance to language users to be able to talk in a concise and detailed way about the different kinds of motion events that human beings are involved in. It may, therefore, be begging the question to draw on forms that can be used for human beings in order to show that these forms do include a predicative meaning besides their "classificatory" meaning; but forms like 1-Pm, V-Pm, and Index-Pm which can be used for human beings are among the most frequently used forms in polymorphemic verbs and among the forms which can combine with the most movement units. In that sense, they are central to an understanding of these verbs.

Some of the handshape units in polymorphemic verbs can be analysed as including more than one morpheme (Boyes Braem 1981; McDonald 1982; Supalla 1982,

---

[1] Because the meanings of these three stems are very complex, I transcribe them with symbols indicating their form rather than their meaning. The stem transcribed Index-Pm resembles in form the ASL form often described as 'general person'-classifier (e.g. Wilbur 1987, 90). It seems, however, to differ from the ASL form semantically and with respect to the movement units with which it can combine. The stem symbolised 1-Pm is formally identical with the handshape of the number sign ONE in Danish Sign Language (a fist with the thumb extended).

1986). An example is the V-handshape in Danish Sign Language (see below). For this reason, I do not talk about *morphemes* expressed by handshape units; I will anticipate my conclusion, however, and refer to the handshape units of polymorphemic verbs as *verb stems*.

The stem 1-Pm
The stem 1-Pm (Ill. 59) is used in verbs that denote a human being in opposition to or in the company of one or more other human beings. That is, 1-Pm is used in verbs that mean 'accompany', 'compete with', 'separate', 'move away from', 'lag behind', 'catch up with', 'overtake'. It can be used in verbs to describe both the motion of two individuals away from the holder of the point of view and the motion of the holder of the point of view and somebody else, in both cases with a movement outward from the signer's body (see Ill. 56, which shows the beginning of the construction that describes how the signer pursues and overtakes someone in basketball).

The same handshape is used to express verbs of location when one is contrasted with a higher number, for instance, in instructions to children to stand in line, one by one, as contrasted with two by two. I am not certain whether this use of the handshape should be seen as expressing the same stem as in the verbs of motion mentioned in the preceding paragraph; the handshape of the sign TWO can also be used to express stative verbs, but is less widely used in verbs denoting motion.

The handshape by which 1-Pm is expressed can change its orientation in semantically significant ways only in constructions involving both hands and meaning 'two bump into each other and fall'. 1-Pm cannot be used in verbs to describe:
— the manner of a stative verb, whether the human being is sitting, standing, or lying (instead: V-Pm);
— (someone) walking backward (instead: the stem Legs-Pm (Ill. 60), in some contexts (see below): V-Pm);
— (someone) approaching the holder of the point of view (instead: Index-Pm);
— (someone) passing the holder of the point of view, unless it is someone passing the holder of the point of view in a contest (use instead: Index-Pm or V-Pm);
— (someone) going somewhere by himself or changing location (instead: Index-Pm or V-Pm);
— (someone) entering or leaving a container-like object, such as a house or a car (instead: V-Pm or General-entity-Pm; the latter is expressed by an index hand).

The stem V-Pm
The meaning of V-Pm (Ill. 61) can be divided into two main areas: 1) motion or location of human beings with special reference to their legs or feet; and 2) motion by foot in a certain direction, to a goal, or within an area. With the first sense, the fingers are usually wiggled; forms with the second sense usually have no finger-wiggling and the index and middle fingers are more relaxed, in a half-bent position. The semantic

differences and the differences in expression between what is here described as two meanings of the same stem may be so substantial that the forms should be described as belonging to two different stems.

With respect to the first main sense, V-Pm is used when the signer wants to contrast manners of stative verbs ('sit', 'lie', or 'stand') or contrast walking to, for instance, bicycling or driving a car. The handshape unit of V-Pm can change its orientation (verbs meaning, for instance, 'lie', 'lie on one's side', 'stand', and 'stand on one's head') and the handshape unit can be analysed into meaningful parts as can be seen in the contrast between a verb meaning 'sit' (the index and middle fingers are bent at the joints) and a verb meaning 'stand' (the two fingers are extended). To describe more specific manners with respect to the position or motion of the legs, the stem Legs-Pm (Ill. 60) is often preferred. The backside of the hand of V-Pm denotes the front of a human being, which can be seen in the contrast between verbs meaning 'lie on one's back' (backside up) and 'lie on one's stomach' (palm up).

The second semantic area of V-Pm is seen in verbs denoting motion by foot in a certain direction, to a goal, or within an area. Verbs of this kind do not underline the walking aspect as a contrast to other ways of moving, and here V-Pm overlaps and, to some extent, contrasts with Index-Pm (see below). V-Pm is often used in verbs denoting a change of location ('I went into the kitchen, then into the living room'). In this use, V-Pm can be used in verbs to describe somebody walking away from the holder of the point of view or the holder of the point of view going somewhere. Some signers claim that it cannot be used for somebody approaching the holder of the point of view, unless it takes a manner morpheme like a morpheme meaning 'limp'; in that case, the verb has a meaning that is subsumed under the first semantic area. V-Pm can be used in verbs that mean 'withdraw' rather than *walk* backward', for instance, in a sentence meaning 'I went into the room, but realised that it was the wrong room and backed out'. Here Index-Pm is impossible.

V-Pm cannot be used in verbs to describe:
— (someone) lagging behind a group or another individual (instead: 1-Pm);
— (someone) walking backward when walking is emphasised (instead: Legs-Pm);
— (someone) being separated from a group or another individual (instead: 1-Pm), unless it is underlined that it is by *walking* away, in which case the form with finger-wiggling is acceptable.

Moreover, V-Pm is not generally used in verbs about somebody approaching the holder of the point of view (use instead: Index-Pm).

The stem Index-Pm
The third stem, Index-Pm (Ill. 62), covers a semantic area that can be divided into three subsections. First, Index-Pm is used in verbs that denote an individual's approaching or passing the holder of the point of view. If it is preceded by a verb about the individual's approaching the holder of the point of view and if the

individual stays within the holder of the point of view's visual field when he moves away, especially if he stays within the same room, then it can also be used of an individual's going away from the holder of the point of view. If the individual passes out of the visual field of the holder of the point of view or the receiver (as in a sentence meaning 'I'm leaving'), the nonpolymorphemic verb LEAVE (Ill. 63) is used instead.

Second, Index-Pm can be used in verbs of motion with a goal or along a route, unless the route is very complicated like a maze. With this meaning, Index-Pm overlaps with the second meaning of V-Pm. Here, Index-Pm can be used in verbs of both the motion of the holder of the point of view and the motion of another individual. Examples are: run in a stadium, swim the length of a pool, make a detour, go ask someone a favour, go check something. By contrast to V-Pm, Index-Pm is not used in verbs whose function is mainly to describe a change of location, especially not if the verb is followed by a nominal such as KITCHEN or WINDOW ('He went into the kitchen/over to the window').[2] In one context, where we might expect 1-Pm, Index-Pm is used, namely in a verb meaning 'push one's way through (a mass of people)'.

Finally, Index-Pm is used in verbs to denote two people meeting each other, and to denote their leaving each other, but only if the same stem is used about their meeting each other in the first place.

Signers are very reluctant to use Index-Pm in a stative verb with *loc* as a foregrounded verb ('(somebody) was standing somewhere').

Index-Pm cannot be used in verbs to describe:
— the manner of a stative verb ('sit', 'lie', 'stand') (instead: V-Pm);
— (someone) jumping (instead: V-Pm);
— (someone) walking by contrast to other ways of moving like bicycling or driving a car (instead: V-Pm);
— (someone) lagging behind a group or another individual (instead: 1-Pm);
— (someone) walking backward (instead: Legs-Pm).

The three stems compared
The three stems overlap semantically. Especially, Index-Pm and V-Pm overlap in the area of an individual moving in a certain direction or to a goal, and in many cases, both forms are acceptable. In other areas, they clearly contrast in a way that cannot be attributed to any classificatory element of their meaning. Some examples can illuminate the differences between the three forms. If a person describes a situation in which she is buying shoes and she asks the salesperson to get her another pair, she will describe the salesperson's moving away from her by using a verb with V-Pm (moving away from the holder of the point of view out of her visual field, but not

---

2 In III.8.1 Introduction, I mentioned that the complex predicates in the basketball example could not be followed by a nominal. If a form with V-Pm is followed by a nominal such as KITCHEN or KITCHEN DET+(locus-marker), the form is closer to the nonpolymorphemic end of the verb continuum (see further III.8.6 Polymorphemic verbs and space).

leaving altogether, which would be described by LEAVE). The salesperson's return can be described by a verb with Index-Pm (someone approaching the holder of the point of view).

If a group of scouts are walking in the woods and one is lagging behind and suddenly realises that he cannot see the others, his catching up with them will be described by a verb with 1-Pm. Here the point of view is with the person lagging behind. But if a hunter approaches the group of scouts, his approaching the group will be described by a verb with Index-Pm (someone approaching the holder of the point of view).

A football player dribbling toward the opponents' goal is described by a verb with 1-Pm (one seen in competition with others), but seen from the goalkeeper's point of view the same player is described by a verb with Index-Pm (someone approaching the holder of the point of view).

A signer described an African hotel surrounded by walls; the residents were warned not to go outside the walls because of the wild animals. Instead, they could walk around inside the walls. Here, the signer used a verb with V-Pm and a repeated circular movement. If she had used Index-Pm with a similar movement, it would mean that the tourists had to walk the length of a circular route repeatedly. Such a verb with Index-Pm is typically used of a runner in a stadium.

The handshape units denote different motion events in interaction with units expressed by movement.[3] In many cases, substitution of the handshape units is not possible in identical contexts because the different stems highlight different aspects of the motion events described. In short, the choice of handshape unit does not depend only on the choice of noun in the verb's argument or on nontemporary[4] features of the referent, but on the kind of motion event the verb is used to describe. The handshape units are not predicate classifiers, but have some similarity to

---

3 Supalla (1990, 136) reaches a similar conclusion: 'The selection of a classifier for a given noun, from the inventory of permissible classifiers for this noun, is determined by which aspect of the event of motion the discourse will focus on....' and note 1: 'This description of the selectional constraints in the classifier-movement combinations may sound at some points as though I mean to imply that classifiers select movement morphemes, and at other points as though I mean to imply that movement morphemes select classifiers. Speaking more technically, however, no directionality is intended in this description: more neutrally, classifier-movement combinations are jointly restricted.' In this article, the idea of substitutability of handshapes depending only on the referents has disappeared. Supalla defines different types of *verbs* on the basis of different types of classifiers, or, as I would say, different types of stems.

4 Some languages have classifiers that classify nouns on the basis of a temporary state of the referent. Toba (Guaykuruan) has a classifier, *ñi*, used of nonextended (three-dimensional) items. This classifier can be used with the noun meaning 'girl' of a seated girl, *ha-ñi-nogotole* (Denny 1986, 304) and, therefore, might be taken as a classifier having a verbal meaning. But the classifier classifies the noun (or the referent) by shape ('nonextended') and it is only by contrast to the neutral way of classifying the noun meaning 'girl' by means of another classifier, 'vertical', that the meaning 'seated' appears. Moreover, the phrase *ha-ñi-nogotole* is a nominal; there is no predicate in the construction, by contrast to constructions with the classificatory verb stems.

Koyukon verb stems. The stems of Koyukon polysynthetic verbs denote not only an entity of a particular kind, but also a potential state or process of which the entity is a part, i.e. they conflate Motion and Figure in Talmy's sense (1985, see here III.8.2 Predicate classifiers and classificatory verb stems). The same is true of handshape units in polymorphemic verbs of Danish Sign Language.

Classificatory stems?
The question is now whether the stems of polymorphemic verbs in Danish Sign Language are classificatory. The handshape units of the stems of polymorphemic verbs reflect features of the referents that also play a part in the semantics of classifiers and classificatory verbs of spoken languages, in particular shape (see McDonald 1982; Supalla 1986). This, at least, is evidence that the semantics of signed languages reflect the same general perceptual categories as other languages. The reason for distinguishing classificatory from nonclassificatory verb stems in Koyukon is that the classificatory verbs group nouns into the same classes across the stative – motion boundary and that there is a form difference between stative and motion verb themes (see III.8.2 Predicate classifiers and classificatory verb stems).

In Danish Sign Language, the major division is not between stative stems and motion stems, but between stems in verbs describing the state or motion of an entity (or a mass regarded as an entity or a group of entities regarded as a whole) without an external agent or a visible cause, on the one hand, and, on the other, stems in verbs that describe an agent's handling something or moving while holding something. I call the first category *whole entity stems* (Index-Pm, V-Pm, and 1-Pm all belong to this category) and the latter category *handle stems* (see further III.8.5 Categories of stems in polymorphemic verbs). The choice of a whole entity stem depends on the type of entity being located or moving, while the choice of a handle stem depends on the type of agent (most, but not all, of the handle stems require a human agent) and the type of entity handled.

A few stems have the same form and are semantically related across the whole entity – handle boundary. One example is the form in Ill. 50 which can be used both in sentences meaning 'The glass is on the table' and 'The glass fell off the table' (the whole entity stem Cylindrical-entity-Pm) and in a sentence meaning 'I put the glass on the table' (the handle stem Handle-cylindrical-entity-Pm). But while the whole entity stem Cylindrical-entity-Pm can be used for glasses as well as mugs, the handle stem Handle-cylindrical-entity-Pm is not usually used for mugs. Instead, the handle stem Handle-handle-Pm is preferred.

It is, moreover, not always easy to decide whether stems of the same form also have related meanings. The form in Ill. 64 occurs in the noun GROUP, in the nonpolymorphemic verb FORM-GROUP ('form a group'), and in polymorphemic verbs meaning '(of a group) move somewhere' (a whole entity stem), '(of a pillar) fall' (a whole entity stem), and 'hold something massive' (a handle stem). It is possible to see the iconic origin behind these meanings, but it is likely that once a form is used in lexical signs (GROUP, FORM-GROUP), the polymorphemic verbs that denote the same kind of entities ('(of a group) move somewhere') are no longer seen as related to other verbs with the same handshape unit ('(of a pillar) fall', 'hold something massive'), which would make them separate stems: Group-Pm, Pillar-Pm, Medium-sized-cylindrical-entity-Pm, and Handle-medium-sized-cylindrical-entity-Pm with lexical meanings that makes it difficult to predict the choice of stem only on the basis of physical characteristics of the entities talked about.

In conclusion, it is not the case that the noun classes that result from the classification imposed by whole entity stems and by handle stems respectively are identical or similar. For that reason, it is less obvious to talk about classificatory verbs in Danish Sign Language.

Mutual dependency of handshape units and movement units
There is an important morphological difference between the handshape units in polymorphemic verbs of Danish Sign Language and the verb stems in Koyukon. Verb stems in Koyukon can occur with derivational strings having general meanings such as causative ('keep, have O in position'), and quite specific meanings such as 'in the fork of a tree'. But a verb stem in Koyukon does not require such a derivational string. A stative verb stem in a particular aspect can occur with only a subject prefix. In Danish Sign Language, the handshape unit of a polymorphemic verb requires at least one morpheme expressed by movement. The handshape units select particular movement morphemes and the movement morphemes select particular handshape units.

The reason why I talk about the handshape units as the stems of the verbs is that the most frequently used polymorphemic verbs have handshape units that have the most lexically idiosyncratic meanings (examples are Index-Pm, V-Pm, and 1-Pm). The frequently used handshape units have to be listed in the lexicon with a description of their meaning, the kinds of movement morphemes they can take, and the kinds of spatial arrangements that they can occur in. Moreover, the frequently used handshape units are much more numerous than the frequently used movement morphemes. The most frequently used movement morphemes denoting motion or location are not very numerous (see III.8.4 Movement morphemes in polymorphemic verbs).

It is not yet clear how the movement morphemes should be classified morphologically, as stems, derivational affixes, or inflectional affixes. As the movement morphemes that denote motion and location are both in paradigmatic contrast and can occur syntagmatically within the same predicate (see the basketball example, (1), in III.8.1), it is unsatisfactory to classify them as inflectional affixes. Classifying them as stems or derivational affixes entails that the polymorphemic verbs are either compounds whose stems cannot occur independently from another stem or that their stem cannot occur independently from a derivational affix, which would mean that it is not possible to make the distinction between stem and derivational affix on the basis of distribution.

Polysynthetic or polymorphemic
First, I used the term *polysynthetic* for the polymorphemic subgroup of verbs in Danish Sign Language because of their similarity to polysynthetic verbs in Koyukon.[5] In language typology, however, the term polysynthetic is used for languages having other characteristics than the verbs in Danish Sign Language. Among these are specific scope relations between the components, the possibility of changing the word class of a word several times during the derivation, and incorporation of noun stems into the verb.

Sapir describes a synthetic language as a language where 'the concepts cluster more thickly [than in analytic languages – EEP], the words are more richly chambered, but there is a tendency, on the whole, to keep the range of concrete significance in the single word down to a moderate compass' (1921/1970, 128). A polysynthetic language is then a language which is 'more than ordinarily synthetic. The elaboration of the word is extreme. Concepts which we should never dream of treating in a subordinate fashion are symbolised by derivational affixes or "symbolic" changes in the radical element, while the more abstract notions, including the syntactic relations, may also be conveyed by the word' (ibid., 128). This is indeed not a very precise definition for which reason the term is discarded by Bloomfield (1935, 208). Nevertheless, the term is used especially about a number of North American languages. Fortescue (forthcoming) lists nine traits that 'tend to cluster in languages displaying polysynthetic morphology (none of them criterial on their own)' and talks about 'various types of complex morphological systems related by a kind of family resemblance.' It is too early to say how many of the criteria are met by Danish Sign Language, but there are striking similarities between the polymorphemic verbs of this language and the polysynthetic morphological subtype that Fortescue describes as having 'a wide range of 'field' affixes in the verbal complex (indicating, for instance, precise location of an action or the instrument with which it is carried out)'; the subtype is exemplified by Atsugewi, a language having the same conflation pattern (Talmy 1985, 73) as the verbs of motion and location in Danish Sign Language (see III.8.2 Predicate classifiers and classificatory verb stems in spoken languages).

My main point here, however, is to distinguish two major groups of verbs in Danish Sign Language, and the primary difference between them is that verbs belonging to one group have base forms with from one to three morphemes, while the others are characterised by a stem that can combine with a large number of morphemes denoting motion and location, orientation, direction, relative position, manner, aspect, and distribution. I will therefore use the term *polymorphemic* of the lat-

---

5 The term *polysynthetic* is also used in an unpublished paper by Liddell and Johnson (1987; see also here Fig. 8 in III.3 Earlier verb classifications) for a subgroup of what they call spatial-locative predicates in ASL.

ter group and avoid the term *polysynthetic* with its implication of a specific typological class.

Summary
The handshape units of polymorphemic verbs of motion and location in Danish Sign Language contribute to the predicative meaning of the verbs. The closest parallel to these verb stems in spoken languages is the verb stems of polysynthetic verbs of Athapaskan languages. The latter are not classifiers, but classificatory or nonclassificatory verb stems. The handshape units in polymorphemic verbs in Danish Sign Language differ from the verbs in Athapaskan languages in that they must combine with at least one morpheme denoting motion or the state of being located and at least one morpheme denoting relative location.

8.4 Movement morphemes in polymorphemic verbs

Morphemes expressed by movement or spatially
In III.8.1 Introduction, I showed that the movements of the hands in the polymorphemic verbs of the basketball example, example (1), could be segmented into units by the activities of the other articulators and that the units recurred with the same meaning in several verbs. In this section, I develop the analysis of the units as morphemes, but I also show examples of the problems of analysing into discrete units something so iconic as the movement of many verb forms denoting motion or an entity's outline. At the present stage of research, it is not possible to set up a definitive list of morphemes expressed by movement in polymorphemic verbs of a signed language, and it may turn out that this is not even desirable. There is an area where productive morphology overlaps with artistic expression; this is an extremely interesting research area, but we may never be able to make a precise boundary between the two.

In the analysis of the modifications of the sign vocabulary with base forms (see III.5-7), the crucial factor in modifications expressed spatially is the direction or orientation of the manual articulator(s) in relation to loci, while the movement of these signs is lexically fixed (see I.6.3 Liddell and Johnson's sequential form analysis of signs). We can use this fact to distinguish two types of morphemes in polymorphemic verbs that do not have a base form with any lexically determined movement. Morphemes that are expressed by the direction of the movement from the signer (e.g. whether the movement is outward or inward, to the left or the right, from face level to chest level or the other way), as well as the orientation or position of the hand(s), can be said to be expressed primarily spatially. Morphemes that are expressed by the shape of the path traced by the moving hand(s) (e.g. whether the hand(s) trace(s) a line or an arc) and the quality of the movement (e.g. the tension of the muscles, reduplication) are expressed primarily by movement. That is, by *movement morpheme*, I mean a morpheme expressed in one of these ways, not necessarily a morpheme denoting motion. Two polymorphemic verb forms may contrast only in the shape of the movements, such as a linear movement vs. an arc movement in sentences meaning 'He walked up to it' and 'She walked round something up to it' (with the stem V-Pm). I will describe this as a difference in movement, not a spatial difference. By contrast, if two verb forms differ only with respect to the direction of the movement, the difference between the two forms is spatial. Both may have, for instance, a linear movement, but the movement of one verb form starts at the signer's body at chest level and goes outward ('He went over there'), while the movement of the other verb form starts outside the signer's face and goes down to chest level ('She went down one floor').

Modifications for distribution that involve reduplication of a movement as well as displacement of the hand(s) in space are expressed both spatially and by movement. They often denote distribution or some locative configuration. As I am primarily interested in examining how polymorphemic verbs differ from nonpolymorphemic verbs in their use of loci, I list distribution morphemes under morphemes primarily expressed by movement in this section.

In what follows, I leave out of consideration morphologically relevant hand-internal movement such as the change of the handshape of V-Pm from bent to stretched fingers meaning 'get up (from a sitting position)'.

Movement morphemes or movement analogues
The iconicity of many movements in signing invites the question: how should the movements of polymorphemic verbs be analysed, as separate morphemes or as unanalysable wholes?

For ASL, DeMatteo (1977) claims that movement in what I call polymorphemic verbs is best analysed as analogous to the motion that it describes. In analysing what he calls the sign MEET in ASL and the form changes it may undergo, DeMatteo claims that there is 'an unlimited number of variations in the single sign MEET' (ibid., 114). The sign is expressed by two index hands with the fingers pointing upward, moved toward each other, or moved in relation to each other in 'an unlimited number' of ways. To capture the rich variation, DeMatteo suggests a model that includes, among other things, 'a set of analogue rules that map certain continuous or iconic aspects of the scene onto continuous or iconic sign phenomena' (ibid., 131). DeMatteo regards it as a problem that a traditional analysis would have to claim either that 'with each change in the movement parameter of MEET we have another distinct sign' (ibid., 114), i.e. an unlimited number of lexemes, or that 'the rule specifying the proper movement value of MEET can contain an unlimited number of markings' (ibid., 114), i.e. an unlimited number of inflections or derivations.

If we analyse the constructions, not as variants of one lexeme MEET, but as polymorphemic verbs with the same stem combined with different (sets of) movement morphemes, the problem of an indefinite number of lexemes does not arise. Such an analysis, however, still leaves us with the problem of whether there is an analogous relationship between the movements of the verbs in signed language and the motion events or some visual representation of them (DeMatteo 1977, 130). That is, can the hands in these constructions be moved in relation to each other in an unlimited number of ways having distinct meanings and corresponding to the unlimited number of ways in which two persons can actually approach or move in relation to each other?

Supalla and Newport, in their joint and separate work (Supalla 1978; 1982; Newport & Supalla 1980; Newport 1982), find that even though the movements of verbs of motion and location in ASL are iconic, they can and should be described in terms of a system of discrete units rather than as analogues. They describe the movements as expressing one or a combination of more than one of seven 'movement roots'. But Newport (see also Supalla 1978, 36) also acknowledge the occurrence of movements that cannot be analysed into discrete units:

> On very rare occasions signers may attempt to outline the precise path of a moving object or the precise shape of an object. However, this continuous type of movement differs in a number of ways from the discrete movement forms already described. First, it is produced very slowly, with the eyes oriented towards the hands rather than towards the listener's face. Second, its use is restricted to the special purpose of specifying precise outlines; it is considered unacceptable for ordinary conversation. (Newport 1982, 486)

The basketball example from Danish Sign Language shows that signers may look at their hands even in cases where the verbs they are using can be described as having discrete morphemes expressed by movement. Furthermore, there are cases which are best described as a standardised analogue to a visual representation of a particular motion where the signer does not look at her hands. Still, I also find a difference between the kind of outlining that Newport describes and instances of polymorphemic verbs in Danish Sign Language.

One problem for a model which describes the movements of polymorphemic verbs as visual analogues is that the movement units of polymorphemic verbs do not always denote motion. Some stems (e.g. Index-Pm) can take a movement unit consisting of a repeated up-and-down movement, which may combine with a movement unit denoting path and motion (e.g. a linear movement). The combination is not a visual analogue of 'move in a certain direction along a certain path while jumping'. The up-and-down movement means 'energetically, resolutely'. In talking about an assembly in a deaf club, a signer said that a man got up to criticise the chairman's report, using a verb with Index-Pm and a movement unit denoting path and motion combined with the up-and-down movement: the man did not jump all the way to the podium, but walked there resolutely, determinedly. An up-and-down movement may mean 'jump', but then it cannot combine with the stem Index-Pm. Another example of a movement unit that does not denote motion is *loc*, which is expressed by a short movement and an abrupt stop. Occurring as the only movement unit of a polymorphemic verb, *loc* means 'be located somewhere', it does not mean 'move a short way and stop'.

Another problem for an analysis of the movement units of polymorphemic verbs as visual analogues is cases where signers themselves break up complex forms into their component units. That was seen in the basketball example, where the signer changed between a sequential use of *move-arc* and *loc* and a simultaneous use of the same two units. In another example, a signer described a bus ride in Africa on a bumpy, winding road. She used the stem Car-Pm (for cars, trucks, busses, etc.) starting with a combination of the motion unit *move-zigzag*, which denotes a path of a specific shape, and the manner unit *random* (see below). The combination described motion along the winding road. To indicate that the road was bumpy, she then used a combination of the manner expressing unit *random* and the motion expressing unit *move-back-and-forth* (here expressed by an up-and-down movement of the hand at the same position in space). After the part with the combination of *move-back-and-forth* and *random*, the signer signed BAD ROAD Curved-surface-Pm+(extension-hemispherical+distribution-line) ('It was a bad road having many bumps') and went on to another demonstration of the ride by means of a polymorphemic verb with Car-Pm, again with "the winding parts" before the "bumpy parts". But at the end of this part, for a brief second, she combined the two kinds of information in one unit including the *move-zigzag* (winding path) and *move-back-and-forth*+ *random* (bumping up and down). The sequence has the following parts:
— Car-Pm with *move-zigzag* and *random* ('run in irregular winds');
— Car-Pm with *move-back-and-forth* and *random* ('run on a bumpy road');
— BAD ROAD Curved-surface-Pm+(extension-hemispherical+distribution-line) ('It was a bad road having many bumps');
— Car-Pm with *move-zigzag* and *random* ('run in winds');
— Car-Pm with *move-back-and-forth* and *random* ('run on a bumpy road'); and
— a very brief version of Car-Pm with *move-zigzag* simultaneously with *move-back-and-forth* and *random* ('run in winds on a bumpy road').

In the basketball example, the signer also first used a sequence of units, and then later combined them:
— 1-Pm with a sequence of *hold, move-arc, loc, hold* and
— 1-Pm with a combination of *move-arc* and *loc*, followed by *hold*.

That is, we see the same pattern in both examples: what is sequential at first is combined in a later simultaneous complex. There is, however, an important difference between the two examples. In the basketball example, the units *move-arc* and *loc* denote two events that are sequential in time: the person runs forward and then stops. That is, the first version with a sequential use of *move-arc* and *loc* is more "analogous" to the real-world event than the simultaneous version, *move-arc+loc*. By contrast, in the bus example, the real-world events are simultaneous: the bus runs on a bumpy and winding road. In the latter case, the version with the combination of the movement units in one complex is the more "analogous" version. In both examples, the signers start with the sequential version and end with the simultaneous complexes. This is evidence that segmentation dominates over analogy in at least some instances of polymorphemic verbs: sequentiality precedes simultaneity, regardless of the iconicity or analogy of these examples.

In summary, the evidence in favour of analysing some movement units of polymorphemic verbs as morphemes is that:
— even though the segmentation is not always straightforward (see examples below), a sequence of movements can be divided into units on the basis of the activities of the other articulators;
— the units that we find in this way recur with the same meanings in other sequential and simultaneous combinations;
— signers break up more complex simultaneous "bundles" into sequences of units or sequences of less complex "bundles" irrespective of the iconicity; and
— it is generally possible to specify the distribution of the units, both in relation to other movement units and in relation to stems.

In what follows, I will present a preliminary and far from exhaustive analysis of the different types of movement morphemes that can occur in polymorphemic verbs. The types are:
1) morphemes denoting location
2) morphemes denoting motion
3) morphemes denoting manner
4) morphemes denoting distribution
5) morphemes denoting extension
6) morphemes denoting aspect

I focus especially on the problems of sequential segmentation, segmentation of simultaneous "bundles", and the classification of the different types of morphemes in the above-mentioned categories. I will mention which stem types the different kinds of movement morphemes can combine with, but that is further developed in III.8.5 Categories of stems in polymorphemic verbs.

Location

loc: is expressed by a short movement followed by an abrupt stop. The morpheme seems to be identical with the *contact* morpheme in ASL described by Supalla (1978, 1982), McDonald (1982), and Liddell and Johnson (1987). It can occur with whole entity stems as follows:
— by itself ('X is located somewhere'),
— reduplicated with a distribution morpheme ('Xs are located in a certain pattern'), or
— in a serial construction with a definite number of *loc* ('an X is located here, another one here, etc.').

With most whole entity stems and with handle stems, *loc* can furthermore occur after *move-line* or another path expressing motion morpheme (see below) to denote someone's arrival at a location (whole entity stems), or someone's putting an entity in a location (handle stems). Also, it can occur simultaneously with some path motion morphemes merged with this morpheme. In the basketball example, for instance, *loc* merges with *move-arc*: the semicircular movement expressing *move-arc* and the downward movement followed by an abrupt stop are combined in one semicircular upward and then downward movement, followed by a stop.

hold: can occur at the beginning or end of a path movement. It can also occur by itself in a backgrounded verb (see III.8.6 Polymorphemic verbs and space); in that syntactic context, the semantic contrast between location and motion is neutralised. Finally, *hold* can occur with limb stems, handle stems, and Look-Pm in combination with shifted attribution of expressive elements to describe the posture of an animate being.

orientation-change: Some whole entity stems can be used in verbs that describe either a change of orientation or a state of "abnormal" orientation. The handshapes by which the stems are expressed have an unmarked orientation that denotes the canonical orientation of the entity in question: a car with the wheels downward, an upright bicycle, a person standing on his feet, etc. To describe an entity in a state of noncanonical orientation, the signer starts by holding her hand with the unmarked orientation (e.g. the articulator of Car-Pm, the flat hand, has an unmarked orientation with the palm down); she then changes the orientation with a rotating movement of the lower arm and wrist (to a flat hand with the palm up). There may be a difference in the rotating movement depending on whether the verb denotes a state ('(the car) was lying upside down') or a process ('(the car) turned upside down'). It is not clear, however, exactly what the difference is or whether the difference is the same for all stems that occur with *orientation-change*. Thus *orientation-change* is a preliminary term for a number of different morphemes that denote change of orientation (i.e. motion) or different states of noncanonical orientations (i.e. location).

Motion

The orientation and the direction of the movements of the following morphemes depend on spatially expressed morphemes. For instance, the morpheme *jump-path* can combine with morphemes expressed by particular orientations of the hand(s) to describe jumping in the vertical dimension or in the horizontal dimension, toward or away from the signer, and combinations of these dimensions.

move: expressed by a very short movement. It can occur before *loc* and, in this combination, it denotes that the state of being located somewhere is preceded by motion. It can also combine with reduplication to denote continuous motion.

move-line: belongs to the path-denoting motion morphemes. It is expressed by a linear movement; if the starting and ending points are at different vertical levels and at different distances from the signer, the movement may be slightly arcing. It means 'move to or from somewhere regardless of the exact path' or 'move straight'. Depending on spatial morphology it can be expressed by only horizontal, by only vertical, or by both horizontal and vertical displacement of the hand.

move-arc: another path-denoting morpheme. The shape of the arc may be a quarter of a circle or a semicircle which gives rise to a segmentation problem: should the semicircle be segmented into two "quarter-circles"? The m*ove-arc* morpheme denotes motion around something, motion around to something (i.e. making a detour) or an arc-shaped motion. The length of the arc and its exact shape are determined by the starting and ending points of the movement. As this is a matter of spatial relations, however, there is no linguistic reason to segment a semicircular movement into smaller movements.

The arc movement may have different sizes expressing different sizes of motion ('make a big detour to avoid someone' (big arc), 'pass someone in a line' (small arc)). There seem to be no more than three sizes, neutral, small, and big. The size differences can be described as follows: 1) as expressing locative relations (spatial morphology); 2) as two manner morphemes (*small* and *big*) that can be combined with some motion morphemes; or 3) as three different move-arc morphemes. Movements expressing other morphemes can have different sizes (e.g. the movements of *move-zigzag* and *jump*); the changes in size of these movements do not imply a change in distance to something as the difference between big and small arc movements may do. As other movements show size differences without implying locative relations, I will preliminarily analyse all size differences as differences in manner, i.e. as expressions of *small* and *big*.

move-circles: is expressed by repeated circular movements of the hand and means 'move around somewhere'. Repeated circular movements are also used in some manner denoting morphemes (see below).

move-(specific-shape): covers a series of movements that denote path motions of specific shapes such as a circle, an oval, or a zigzag path. When *move-line* or *move-arc* are used to denote paths of specific shapes, they belong to this type, but as they (like *move-circles*) can also denote motions of less specific shapes, they are singled out here.

Repeated circular movements can be 1) an instance of *move-circles*, which means 'move around somewhere' (a "loose" (not tense) movement); 2) an instance of aspectual reduplication of the *move*-(specific shape) type of morpheme *move-circle* ('move in circles again and again/for a long time and intensely') (a fairly tense movement an unspecific number of times; a "tense" facial expression); or 3) a series of the same morpheme meaning 'move in a circle a specific number of times' (a specific number of movements).

A movement of a specific shape may be the result of a combination of several movement morphemes of other shapes, such as when a signer explained circuit training in a stadium by means of a verb with Index-Pm and an oval-shaped movement. The movement was clearly divided into a sequence of *move-line* + *move-arc* + *move-line* + *move-arc*, because the individual segments were combined with different manner morphemes denoting speed ('You run fast on the straight stretches and slowly in the curves').

move-random-path: can be expressed in a number of different ways. What is typical of the expression of this morpheme is that the hand follows a course that is not recognisable as one of the other path movements and its exact path is irrelevant. The movement, however, is in one general direction. The morpheme *move-random-path* is used for motion somewhere in a non-straight way. It can be used, for instance, with 1-Pm for a football player dribbling the length of the field.

jump-path: is expressed by an arc movement, but its meaning is different from the morpheme *move-arc*. It can be used with some whole entity stems and denotes jumping with displacement, not necessarily the motion around something or the avoidance of something. The morpheme *move-arc* can combine with Index-Pm; *jump-path* cannot.

move-back-and-forth: is expressed by up-and-down movements or sideways movements where the hand returns to its initial position. By contrast to the morphemes of the group of *move*-(specific-shape), it does not denote a path motion as the hand returns to its initial position. It can combine with, for instance, *move-line* or, as in the example of the bus driving on a bumpy road (see above), with *random* manner.

analogue-(type): some verbs include movements that are best described as analogues of specific motions. V-Pm can, for instance, be used to describe an acrobat jumping on a trampoline turning and twisting his body: the signer's hand moves up, twists in loops, and moves down again. The number of loops and their size can change as a sort of embellishment. It is a standardised way of describing loops which can also be seen with the stems Aeroplane-Pm and Fly-Pm.

Other examples of *analogue*-(type) are more productive and are restricted to special styles of signing of a more poetic kind. One such example was made by a signer who is especially skillful at this kind of signing: he described a leopard's stalking and running by means of movements of his shoulders, arms, and fists representing the leopard's body, legs, and paws (a limb stem). He also made a representation of an elephant, but corrected himself for flicking his wrists: that would be more appropriate of a leopard or a lion, while an elephant's foot does not move in relation to its leg, he claimed. The point here is as close an imitation of the motion contour and rhythm of the real-world event as possible. But even this stylised use abides by rules of signing that make it different from mime (see III.8.6 Polymorphemic verbs and space).

The stem Legs-Pm (Ill. 60) occurs in a number of more or less standardised movement patterns denoting such motions as limping, walking like a woman on high heels, and walking like a fat person. Supalla (1990) describes such movement patterns as expressing *manner of locomotion*. As analogues they combine the notions of motion and manner. It is not always clear whether a certain movement unit should be analysed as a particular motion morpheme, as a motion morpheme combined with a certain manner morpheme, or as an analogue kind of morpheme. An example is the description of the acrobat's loops. When such units are highly standardised and have a very restricted distribution, it may be preferable to list them as unanalysable wholes with specific meanings. This is to some extent a parallel to what is seen in Koyukon which has about 270 combinations of morphemes, the so-called derivational strings, which can be added to different categories of verb themes (see III.8.2 Predicate classifiers and classificatory verbs in spoken languages, and Fortescue 1990). Like the movement units of Danish Sign Language the derivational strings can have very specific meanings such as 'in the fork of a tree' or 'ashore'.

Manner
As mentioned, it is often difficult to decide whether a specific movement unit should be analysed as denoting a particular motion or a more general motion with a particular manner. In the case of *move-random-path*, we can compare the unit with other instances of random motion in which a path motion denoting movement is modified to denote a less regular path. Examples are *move-zigzag* and *move-back-and-forth*. When the manner denoting morpheme *random* is added to these path morphemes, the result is irregular sizes of the zigzag or back-and-forth movements as seen, for instance, in the example with the bus driving on a bumpy (*move-back-and-forth+random*), winding (*move-zigzag+random*) road. Here the "regular" paths are recognisable semantically as well as in the expression of the combinations. The meaning of *move-line* is not part of the meaning of *move-random-path*, nor does the expression of *move-random-path* include a linear movement. The morpheme *move-line* means 'move somewhere regardless of the exact path' or 'move straight', and neither meaning is included in *move-random-path*, which does not denote that the entity moved to a specific point.

Some manner constructions seem to have developed from a morpheme denoting motion. Handle stems that take human agents can be used with a repeated circular movement and a facial expression of perplexity to indicate the holder of the point of view's doubts concerning the entity handled. I transcribe this morpheme as *at-a-loss*. When a signer described a situation in which her children's school was closed and she and her husband had to go to work, she used the stem Handle-large-cylindrical-entity-Pm and moved her hands round while protruding her tongue and looking around in despair ('What should we do with the children?') (Ill. 65). It is not difficult to see the motion origin of this construction (moving something around in search for a place to put it), but it is not reasonable to analyse it as actually denoting motion. The movement pattern with the particular facial expression can occur with other handle stems with the same meaning and is productive as a manner morpheme.

Some verbs meaning 'isolated' include the whole entity stems V-Pm and 1-Pm, repeated circular movements, and a pointed, slightly protruding tongue. Again it is possible to see the motion origin of the construction, but the meaning of these forms is so specific and the distribution of the circular movement and the protruding tongue so restricted (probably to only the stems V-Pm and 1-Pm) that the signs are best listed as unanalysable lexemes. Some of the manner morphemes found in Danish Sign Language are:

random: expressed by a change of a regularly shaped movement denoting motion along a path to an irregular movement with the same general shape.

big and *small*: expressed by an increase or decrease in the contour of a movement. They are very often accompanied by manner morphemes expressed by changes in the intensity of the movement.

resolutely: expressed by an up-and-down movement; it can occur with some whole entity stems and some handle stems that can be used of animates and it denotes a determined attitude on the part of the moving being.

at-a-loss: the morpheme described above; it only occurs with handle stems, is expressed by circular movements and an affective facial expression, and denotes the agent's uncertainty about what to do with the entity handled.

speed: a cover term for several different ways of expressing speed: through the intensity and speed of the movement of the hand, through initial holds (high speed), and through more specific movement patterns like a rotating movement of the lower arm simultaneous with *move*-(specific-shape) used with Car-Pm of a car moving fast.

Manner of motion can also be expressed by certain mouth patterns, but they have not been studied yet. Apart from *speed* morphemes, which can also be used with the nonpolymorphemic verb LEAVE (Ill. 63), manner morphemes can only be used in polymorphemic verbs.

Distribution

The distribution morphemes denote the location and configuration of an unspecified number of entities or the motion of an entity to an unspecified number of locations in a particular configuration. Distribution morphemes presuppose one of the following types of morphemes: *loc*, path motion morphemes, especially *move-line*, and extension morphemes (see below). The effect of the distribution morphemes is that the movements of *loc* and *move-line* and the extension morphemes are reduplicated and embedded in another movement with displacement of the hand(s). The number of movement morphemes that polymorphemic verbs can take when they also take a distribution morpheme is much more restricted than when they do not take a distribution morpheme. The movements by which the morphemes *loc* and *move-line* are expressed resemble the (phonological) movements that are found in nonpolymorphemic verbs that can be modified for distribution. Thus a polymorphemic verb with *loc* or *move-line* and a distribution morpheme resembles a nonpolymorphemic verb modified for distribution. Similarly, the plural modification of nouns resembles the modifications for distribution of polymorphemic verbs with extension morphemes (see below).

distribution-(specific-shape): the most frequent shapes are *line, arc,* and *circle.* When a distribution morpheme is combined with *loc*, the movement expressing *loc* can be deleted with some stems; it is not yet clear which ones, but the movement of *loc* is retained when there is potential ambiguity. For instance, in the case of a flat hand used for paintings distributed on a wall, the movement of *loc* cannot be deleted as the result would be interpreted as a surface (a flat hand moved linearly). In some cases, the movement of *loc* is seen in the beginning of the distribution movement and is then deleted. *Distribution-*(specific-shape) can be embedded in other distribution patterns. The movement of *loc+distribution-line* can, for example, be reduplicated in a sentence meaning 'There were rows of (books) on the (wall)': the signer moves her hand from the contralateral to the ipsilateral side, brings it back to the contralateral side at a lower level and repeats the sideways movement, etc. Each sideways movement is made at successively lower levels and the number of movements is not important.

Distribution morphemes are often expressed by movements of both hands or by keeping the weak hand with the handshape in question at the starting point of the strong hand, while the strong hand makes the movement. *Distribution-arc* is expressed by a movement of both hands starting at the middle of the semicircle and moving to both sides, for instance, in a sentence meaning 'They were sitting in a half circle' (with V-Pm).

distribution-random: with this morpheme the movement of *loc* is always retained. The morpheme *distribution-random* is expressed by one or two hands producing instances of *loc* or *move-line* in a random pattern.

Some stems can occur with different movement morphemes expressed by the same phonological movement: *move-line* and *loc+distribution-line* are both expressed by a straight line when the movement expressing *loc* is deleted in *loc+distribution-line.* The stem V-Pm can occur with both (Ill. 66). The two forms are distinguished by the orientation of the hand: in the distributive form the hand moves with the palm in the movement's direction ('many/they were in a line'), while the form expressing motion is made with the back of the hand facing the direction of the movement and the fingers wiggle or the fingers are slightly bent ('go somewhere' or 'walk straight').

Extension

A number of handshape units can be used in signs in which the moving hand(s) trace(s) the outline or extension of an entity or a mass of something. Many of these signs are standard nouns such as MOUNTAIN or HOUSE. But sometimes such a sign is used in the same kind of construction as a polymorphemic verb with *loc*, i.e. a stative verb. For instance, a signer described a birthday party where eight people in a line entered the room carrying a long string with presents attached to it:

```
(1) right:  EIGHT PERSON+pl. ... / Handle-handle-Pm+
    right:  over-r.shoulder+resolutely)* / STRING+over-r.shoulder-
    left:                                  STRING+over-r.shoulder-
    mouth:                                 string
    right:  perpendicular-to-body-surface# / General-entity(B)-Pm+
    left:   perpendicular-to-body-surface------------------------
    right:(loc+distribution-line+over-r.shoulder-perpendicular-to-
    left: ------------------------------------------------------
    right:  body-surface)° / VARIOUS+over-r.shoulder / ...
    left:   --------------
    *Ill. 67a    #Ill. 67b    °Ill. 67c
    Eight people...walked in holding a string with various things, ...
```

The sign STRING is the standard noun sign meaning 'string', but its manual articulator is identical with the articulator of the extension stem Tiny-entity-surface-Pm, and in (1), it is used simultaneously with a stative polymorphemic verb having the stem General-entity(B)-Pm and the location morpheme *loc* (Ill. 67c). The two signs, the modified noun and the polymorphemic verb, are both used to describe the state of something. Thus, they have the same function as the predicate Curved-surface-Pm+(extension-hemispherical+distribution-line) in BAD ROAD Curved-surface-Pm+(extension-hemispherical+distribution-line) ('It was a bad road having many bumps'). The latter predicate includes an extension stem that can be used for entities and masses and a movement unit that imitates the outline of the visual representation of the entities ("bumps"). The movement unit can be analysed as a combination of the extension morpheme *extension-hemispherical* and the distribution morpheme *distribution-line*. In III.8.6 Polymorphemic verbs and space, I return to what I call *backgrounded constructions* which may include the manual articulator of nouns such as STRING, that can be analysed as being derived from a sign with an extension stem and a movement morpheme denoting extension.

Stative verbs with an extension morpheme cannot include morphemes denoting location or motion. Instead, their movement specifies the outline or extension of the prototype of the entity or mass in question. I do not analyse the movements into smaller units, but as parallel to the *analogue*-type of motion morphemes.

Signs with extension movements are sometimes called size-and-shape-specifiers (Klima & Bellugi 1979, 237-240; Baker & Cokely 1980, 308ff.; Supalla 1986, 185ff; see also McDonald 1982, 135, 160; Wilbur, Bernstein & Kantor 1985, 3-4).

Aspect
I mention aspect in this section because aspectual modifications are expressed through changes in movement. Since I left out aspectual modifications that are expressed only by change in the intensity of the movement or reduplication in relation to nonpolymorphemic verbs (see III.2 Different types of modifications: An overview, and III.5 Modifications for distribution), I also leave out of consideration such modifications in relation to polymorphemic verbs.

Polymorphemic and nonpolymorphemic verbs
The major difference between polymorphemic verbs and nonpolymorphemic verbs is the capability of the former of including one or more movement morphemes denoting location, motion, and manner. When they only have one such morpheme and this morpheme is *move-line*, a polymorphemic verb such as V-Pm+(c+move-line+forward) is very similar to an agreement verb such as c+SEND-MAIL+f. Polymorphemic verbs, however, differ from agreement verbs in that 1) they can substitute different morphemes denoting motion or location for each other; 2) they can combine such morphemes sequentially; and 3) they can take manner expressing morphemes.

Other analyses of movement
The movement units of what I call polymorphemic verbs have been treated in a number of articles on ASL. In Fig. 13, I summarise the different classifications.

> Supalla (1982)
>> stative roots (hold, tracing movements), denote existence
>> contact roots (contact, stamping), denote location
>> active roots (path movements), denote motion
>> + manner affixes
>
> Schick (1990)
>> IMIT ('prototypical idealisation or distillation of real-world activity')
>> MOV ('can indicate the path of a referent or the extent of the referent')
>> DOT ('the spatial position of a stationary element')
>
> Liddell and Johnson (1987)
>> process roots (movement of entities, changes in the state of entities)
>> stative-descriptive roots (states, physical attributes of the object)
>> the contact root (= Supalla's contact root)
>
>> Fig. 13. Classifications of movement morphemes in ASL

Supalla (1982, 11ff.) analyses movement in verbs of motion and location as movement roots of three types: stative roots denote existence, contact roots denote location, and active roots denote motion. His categorisation of the movements in ASL is based on form features: whether there is displacement of the hand(s); the parameter whose value is changed by the movement (place of articulation, orientation, or handshape); and whether the movement is a tracing, stamping, or path movement. For the difference between a tracing and a stamping movement, Supalla refers to the definitions by Mandel (1977) who, however, talks about a sketching, rather than a tracing movement: in a tracing/sketching movement, 'the articulator is used as an implement that leaves a trace as it moves'; in a stamping movement, 'the implement moves forward and then returns, like a rubber stamp, leaving its trace at the place where it stopped rather than along its course' (Mandel 1977, 67).

Supalla supplements the movement roots with a set of manner affixes. Again, these are defined on the basis of form. For example, the *linear* root combined with the affixes *repeated, mini,* and *contradirectional* means 'move straight with small jumps' or 'hop' (1982, 21). In contrast, the same root combined with the affixes *repeated, mini,* and *bidirectional* means 'move straight randomly' (ibid., 21). In another work, Supalla (1978) analyses a movement denoting random motion as a combination of sideways linear movement with forward linear movement. The difference between analysing a random motion in one general direction as either *linear + repeated + mini + bidirectional* or as a combination of a sideways linear and a forward linear movement reveals the danger of an analysis in which the question asked is: how can more complex movements be analysed as combinations of simpler movements? That is, an analysis in which the categorisation of the movement morphemes is formal rather than linguistic. Physically, a movement in one general direction with small detours to either side may be analysed as a combination of a sideways linear and a forward linear movement, but the meaning 'move randomly in one general direction' cannot be analysed as resulting from the combination of each of the meanings of a sideward linear and a forward linear movement, whatever the morphemes may be.

As mentioned earlier, Supalla correlates broad form categories with the semantic categories existence, location, and motion. In his analysis a *hold*, i.e. no movement, is categorised with *tracing* movements and like them is said to denote existence. In Danish Sign Language, *hold* may have a locative meaning, and in certain contexts it presupposes existence, but it cannot be used in an utterance to make a statement about existence. A statement about existence would include the nonpolymorphemic verb EXIST.[1] Supalla gives no examples of tracing (or stamping) movements, but refers to Mandel (1977) who mentions a number of iconic ASL lexemes in which the hands depict the denotatum by a tracing/sketching movement, e.g. HOUSE where two flat hands sketch the outline of a prototypical house in the Western world, and

---

[1] Liddell and Johnson (1987, 13) describe the hold root as being 'generally used as a base hand to show the interaction between two entities', a function very similar to its use in Danish Sign Language (see III.8.6 Polymorphemic verbs and space) and far from the expression of existence.

SCOTLAND where the fingertip sketches a plaid on the arm.[2] These examples are lexical nouns and, to the extent that they are analysed as having a composite morphological structure, the tracing movement is the movement of extension morphemes, and the signs do not denote existence.

In Danish Sign Language, extension verbs are as little used to make statements about existence as are verbs with *hold*; they are stative verbs describing the physical character or configuration of something. Verbs with extension morphemes cannot occur in backgrounded constructions, but in these constructions their stems can occur with the *hold* morpheme instead of an extension morpheme. Moreover, *hold* can occur with whole entity stems and handle stems, which extension morphemes cannot. That is, *hold* differs from extension morphemes semantically and with respect to syntactic and morphological distribution.

Supalla describes *contact* movement as 'an extremely brief movement (as if to contact something) before the hand stops at a specified place' (Supalla 1982, 14). *Contact* thus has the same form as the Danish Sign Language morpheme *loc*. Supalla categorises *contact* with the stamping movements and say that they have a locative meaning. A nonlexical example of a stamping movement from Mandel (1977, 68) is "a field of flowers', which includes repeated stamping with the *bent-5-hand* (thumb and all fingers spread, bent at the middle knuckles but straight at the base), held palm down, stamping five points at a time all over an imaginary horizontal plane'. The example may be analysed as a verb of location: 'flowers are located here and there'. The same handshape can be combined with the same movement and the result has the same meaning in Danish Sign Language. But in that language, exactly the same handshape with the same movement can also be used to say that there were, for instance, stones or lumps of mud distributed over an area. It contrasts with a sign with the same handshape and a single "stamping" movement indicating that there was a group of flowers or a single stone (or similar mass-like entity) somewhere. The sign can thus be analysed as a verb of location with a stem meaning 'mass-like entity be located/move' and the movement morphemes *loc* (Supalla's *contact*) and *distribution-random*. That is, there is no need to introduce a movement "root" *stamping* different from *contact* – or *loc*. Moreover, the distinction between "stative roots" expressing existence and "contact roots" expressing location is not relevant to Danish Sign Language.

Schick (1990) proposes an analysis with three categories of movement morphemes in ASL. One of them is IMIT, which she describes as 'a prototypical idealisation or distillation of real-world activity but not an imitation or complete analogue image of it' (ibid., 18), i.e. a parallel to the *analogue*-(type) motion morphemes in Danish Sign Language. Schick's other two categories are MOV and DOT: 'A MOV

---

2 Mandel mentions that he does not know of any example where the flat hand leaves an area in a stamping movement (1977, 67). A lexeme of this kind is COLLAGE in Danish Sign Language, where the two flat hands "slap" an imaginary surface in different places alternatingly while moving from face level to chest level.

root indicates simple movement of a hand through space and can indicate the path of the referent or the extent of the referent' (ibid., 17-18); 'The DOT root proposed here is a locative representing the spatial position of a stationary element' (ibid., 19). DOT covers Supalla's *contact* and *hold*, which Schick does not distinguish, as she finds that Supalla's *contact* merely emphasises the location by adding focus to it. In Danish Sign Language, *hold* is rarely used to predicate location in a place of an entity. The syntactic and morphological distribution of the two morphemes differ too; for example, *hold*, and not *loc*, can occur in constructions with limb stems, handle stems, and Look-Pm to describe the posture of an animate being, while *loc*, and not *hold*, can combine with various distribution morphemes.

Schick's MOV category merges path motion morphemes and extension morphemes. Again there is enough morphological and semantic difference between them to keep them separate in Danish Sign Language: they cannot combine with the same stems; motion morphemes can combine with manner morphemes and extension morphemes cannot; motion morphemes can combine with *loc* and each other and extension morphemes cannot; and motion morphemes denote processes, while extension morphemes denote states.

Liddell and Johnson (1987; see also Schick 1990; Supalla 1990) study the combinations of handshape units and movement units and distinguish three types of movement roots in ASL on a semantic basis. The first type is *process* roots where the movement of the hand corresponds to motion of entities or changes in their state. Liddell and Johnson include a unit expressed by lack of movement and denoting lack of motion, as well as units expressed by changes in handshape in the category of process roots. The second type is *stative-descriptive* roots. These roots occur in signs that describe a state, and the movement of the hand corresponds to physical attributes of the entity being described. Included in this type are signs that describe the shape of a surface as well as signs that describe the distribution of entities such as 'cars in a row'. That is, the classification groups together movement units denoting the extension and shape of an entity (e.g. a volcano) with movement units denoting the distribution of single entities (e.g. cars in a row).

Liddell and Johnson's last movement root type contains only one root, *contact*, which is identical with Supalla's *contact* root. It is used in a *stative* predicate 'which establishes the location and orientation of the entity being represented by the handshape' (ibid., 18). To the extent that a hold does not denote a state, the distinguishing factor between the first two types, process roots and stative-descriptive roots, is whether the movement (or lack of movement) denotes an action or a process involving a single entity (process roots) or whether it denotes a state of an entity described by its surface or a state constituted by the distribution of a number of entities (stative-descriptive roots).

The stative-descriptive roots correspond to the distribution morphemes and the extension morphemes of Danish Sign Language. As shown above, these two kinds of morphemes can occur in the same syntactic environment and both types denote stative descriptions. Keeping them apart means, however, that the distribution morphemes used with nonpolymorphemic verbs (see III.5 Modifications for distribution) can be analysed as a subsection of the distribution morphemes occurring in polymorphemic verbs. Moreover, in Danish Sign Language a form meaning '(books) are located in a row' can have either a smooth linear movement or a "broken" movement with small movements of the hand perpendicular to the sideways movement. I analyse both as consisting of *loc* and *distribution-line*, the former with deletion of the movement of *loc*. This is semantically and formally[3] warranted. But such an analysis is not possible if distribution morphemes and extension morphemes are not kept apart, as suggested by Liddell and Johnson's analysis.

Finally, an analysis which does not separate distribution morphemes and extension morphemes obscures the morphological parallel of distribution morphemes when they are combined with the motion morpheme *move-line* (for instance, with V-Pm: 'enter many different (stores)'), the location morpheme *loc* (for instance, with V-Pm: '(many people) sit in a row'), and with the extension morpheme *extension-line* (for instance, with Tiny-entity-surface-Pm: '(many strings) are extended in a row parallel to each other'). In all three cases, the combination can be analysed as a verb with a particular movement unit plus the distribution morpheme *distribution-line*. In the first verb, *distribution-line* is combined with *move-line*, in the second verb with *loc*, and in the third verb with *extension-line*. In all three cases, the combination results in a reduplication of the movements of *move-line, loc,* and *extension-line* with a linear displacement of the hand(s).

The distribution of information over signs
Since several motion and location morphemes can occur sequentially with one and the same stem, it is worth asking whether they constitute one verb or a succession of verbs with the same stem. Another construction type that raises a similar problem is the use of the two hands to articulate the same or different verb stems simultaneously (see *Backgrounded and foregrounded constructions* and *The form of simultaneous verbs* in III.8.6 Polymorphemic verbs and space). That is, the problem of one or several verbs arises both in relation to sequences of movement units and in relation to simultaneous constructions. I have no solution to the problem, but some contributions toward a basis for considering it.

One kind of evidence comes from examples like the basketball example in III.8.1 Introduction, and the bus example mentioned earlier in this section, in which several movement morphemes occur first sequentially and later simultaneously. In the

---

3 The plural modification of some nouns is expressed by reduplication of the sign form embedded in a movement of the hand. In the plural modification of the noun PERSON, which has a downward movement, the downward movement of the hand is usually eliminated after one or two cycles and the hand is simply moved sideways without the movement of the base form of PERSON.

basketball example, *move-arc* and *loc* are first made sequentially, then merged. The simultaneous production of the two might be seen as merely a phonetic effect of fast signing. First, however, the position of the simultaneous productions in the discourse (the second time the signer talks about the same thing) is identical in the basketball and the bus example. Second, the simultaneous production of a *move-* (specific-path) morpheme and *loc* is seen with many stems of both the handle and the whole entity kind, and it is lexicalized in the verb GO-TO (Ill. 8, 'go to', 'arrive'), which is related to a verb with the stem General-entity-Pm. In the bus example, what is astonishing is that the two motion morphemes are at all separated in time since they describe one single motion event. From a semantic point of view, this speaks in favour of analysing the sequences as belonging to one verb.

Supalla (1990) presents examples from ASL in which the description of one motion event is distributed over two verbs with different handshape units in what he calls serial verb constructions. As the constructions use two different handshape units, in my analysis of the handshape unit as constituting the stem of the verb, these have to be described either as separate verbs or as compounds. One of Supalla's examples from ASL is a description of a person limping in a circle; a verb form (resembling a verb in Danish Sign Language with the stem Legs-Pm (Ill. 60)) with a "limping" movement is followed by the tracing of a circle by a "pointing" index hand. Here the manner of motion (limping) is separated from the path of motion (circling). Fischer and Janis (1990) place Supalla's observations in a larger context in their study of what they call "verb sandwiches" in ASL. Verb sandwiches are constructions 'in which the same verb root (or two verbs with highly similar roots) [occur] twice in the same sentence, separated only by the object and/or sentential adjuncts' (ibid., 281). The "filling" between the two layers of verbs may be left out, and the second instance of the verb must be different from the first instance in some respect:

> SUBJECT VERB+SOME-INFLECTION (OBJECT) (ADJUNCTS)
> VERB+DIFFERENT-INFLECTIONS... (ibid., 287)

Fischer and Janis analyse the construction as a mechanism called for by a limit on how "heavy" a verb can be. Supalla's examples of serial verbs and the basketball and bus ride examples from Danish Sign Language resemble the ASL verb sandwiches in that there seems to be a limit on how much information can be "loaded" onto one unit. Fischer and Janis point to one more relevant factor here:

> If we examine these constructions closely, they are at least sometimes marked by a shift in eyegaze after the object or adjunct, signalling the assumption of the subject role by the signer. (Fischer & Janis 1990, 291)

What Fischer and Janis describe here is what I call shifted locus with gaze direction imitative of the referent of a verb's argument (see II.5 Shifted reference, shifted attribution of expressive elements, and shifted locus). The point is further developed in Ahlgren and Bergman (1990; see also Bergman & Dahl in press), who distinguish narrative from non-narrative text or discourse in Swedish Sign Language. Ahlgren and Bergman define narrative discourse as 'one where the speaker relates a series of real or fictive events in the order they are supposed to have taken place' (1990, 257). They identify a lexical difference between verbs of narrative and verbs of non-narrative text and find that narrative verbs 'seem to have a higher degree of iconicity, cannot be negated, nor be accompanied by Swedish mouth patterns, can be combined with various facial expressions expressing the mental state of the referent (rather than that of the signer)' (ibid., 261).

The difference between the sequential and the simultaneous use of *move-arc* and *loc* in the basketball example (III.8.1) can be seen in this light. When the signer uses *move-arc* and *loc* sequentially, her facial expression shows fear, she uses an "un-Danish" mouth pattern, and she looks down at her hands. With the simultaneous use of *move-arc* and *loc*, the signer's face is neutral, she uses the mouth pattern of the Danish word *stop*, and she has eye contact with the receiver. Also, in the bus example, there is a difference in facial expression between the sequential use of the movement units and the simultaneous unit. The latter is very short and the signer is clearly on her way to explaining where the bus was going. The sequential use of the units is much more elaborate and the facial expression is one of hard-won patience with an unpleasant bus ride (i.e. shifted attribution of expressive elements). But the bus example does not fulfil Ahlgren and Bergman's definition of narrative text: the two sequential units describe a single motion event, i.e. the sequential construction is less iconic than the simultaneous construction. It may be that also in narrative text there is a limit to how "heavy" a unit can be, even at the cost of reducing temporal iconicity. Compared with the short simultaneous versions at the end of the examples, the sequential units carry extra semantic load, namely the information that this is narration in the form of shifted attribution of expressive elements and shifted locus. In neither example is there a lexical difference between the narrative and the non-narrative text, as claimed by Ahlgren and Bergman. But the last constructions in both examples are closer to the nonpolymorphemic end of the continuum between nonpolymorphemic verbs and polymorphemic verbs than the first constructions.

Another functional explanation of the sequentialisation may be the pragmatic one that only when the two pieces of information (that the road was winding and that it was bumpy; that, in basketball, you must overtake your opponent and then stop) are separated, do they both constitute asserted information.

The analysis of whether constructions with polymorphemic verbs (or predicates) constitute one or more verbs depends on further analyses regarding which movement morphemes can co-occur simultaneously or sequentially in different types of text and in different syntactic positions.[4] But it must also await a deeper understand-

---

4 That the problem of determining how many verbs a predicate consists of is not only

ing of a characteristic of signed languages which has turned up several times in this analysis of the use of space in Danish Sign Language and which also appears from Supalla's analysis of serial verb constructions and Fischer and Janis's analysis of verb sandwiches in ASL, namely, the fact that certain kinds of information can show up in several different places in the clause: the proform can carry spatial information which in other clauses occurs with a verb or a sequence of signs; modifications for distribution can occur on predicative signs, on conjunctions, and with all of the clause; and in verb sandwiches and serial verb constructions, the information is distributed over two separate verbs.

8.5 Categories of stems in polymorphemic verbs

Types of stems
The stems in polymorphemic verbs can be categorised on the basis of their meaning and the types of movement morphemes that they can combine with, but there are lexical idiosyncrasies. To some extent, the differences between the stem types coincide with their iconic origins. The stems can be divided into four main categories: *whole entity stems, handle stems, limb stems,* and *extension stems.* The following lists of stems of each category are not exhaustive, and the kinds of entities mentioned after each stem are only representative examples.

Whole entity stems
Many whole entity stems can occur in stative verbs as well as process verbs, where the Theme in Gruber's sense (1976, 33ff; see also here III.1 Localism and transitivity) is identical with the actor. Many of these stems can combine with all kinds of movement morphemes except extension morphemes and the manner morpheme *at-a-loss*; but some are restricted in the kinds of movement morphemes which they can take, either idiosyncratically or because the combination of stem and movement morpheme would denote an uncommon phenomenon (see the end of this section). Whole entity stems are used to predicate something about entities, a mass of entities regarded as a whole, or a specific number of entities regarded as a whole. In all cases, the iconic idea behind these stems is that the handshape represents the whole entity.

Besides Index-Pm, 1-Pm, V-Pm (see III.8.3 Classifiers or verb stems in Danish Sign Language?), this category contains such stems as:
— Car-Pm (Ill. 68, the unmarked orientation is with the palm down; for cars, trucks);
— Bicycle-Pm (the flat hand, the unmarked orientation is with the little finger side down; for bicycles, motorcycles);
— Tree-Pm (the lower arm and the hand with all fingers and the thumb extended

---

encountered in signed language research can be seen from the following example from (spoken) Danish (/ indicates intonational units): *Jeg /sov og hostede/ og /hostede og sov/ og /sov og sov og hostede/ i femten timer i træk.* ('I /slept and coughed/ and /coughed and slept/ and /slept and slept and coughed/ for fifteen hours on end.')

and spread, the fingertips pointing upward; for stationary trees with canonical orientation);
— Lumplike-entity-Pm (all the fingers lax, extended, slightly spread, and bent at the joints; for lumps of mud, groups of flowers);
— Mass-Pm (Ill. 69; for masses of people or cattle);
— Flat-entity-Pm (the flat hand, the unmarked orientation has the palm down or away from the signer; the palm turned upward or toward the signer are orientations used to imply that the "content" side (the "text" side of a piece of paper, the picture side of a painting) is visible; for pieces of paper, leaves, books, paintings, plates);
— Animal-Pm (Ill. 70, the unmarked orientation is with the palm down; for animals with four legs);
— Bird-Pm (the fist with the index and middle fingers extended, unspread, and bent at the joints, the unmarked orientation is with the palm down; for small birds);
— Insect-Pm (all fingers stretched out and spread, the pad of the middle finger contacting the pad of the thumb; for flying insects);
— Queue-Pm (all the fingers extended and spread, the fingertips pointing upward; for people in a queue or line);
— Short-thin-entity-Pm (the index hand; for pencils, cutlery);
— Ground-Pm (the lower arm and the flat hand, the palm down; for the ground, rising or lowering water);
— Long-thin-entity-Pm (the index hand and the lower arm; for trees perceived as moving by a moving animate being, trees with noncanonical orientations, wavering columns);
— Group-Pm (Ill. 64; for groups of people);
— Cylindrical-entity-Pm (Ill. 50; the unmarked orientation is with the little finger side down; for glasses, mugs);
— Boat-Pm (the two hands with the fingers extended and slightly curved, held in the shape of the hull of a boat; for boats);
— Liquid-Pm (one or both hands with the fingers extended and slightly spread, the palms down; for liquids; not with *loc*);
— General-entity-Pm (the index hand, lax finger; for everything that can be located or move); and
— General-entity(B)-Pm (the flat hand; for all kinds of inanimates).

The whole entity stem General-entity-Pm can be used in stative or process verbs for anything that can be located or move (for a similar analysis of the index hand in certain verbs in ASL, see McDonald 1982, 56, 123; Supalla 1990). It combines with the movement morpheme *loc* when it is used in a foregrounded verb of location. In verbs of motion, the index hand traces a path, either held perpendicular to the path or with the tip of the finger "leading the movement and the rest of the hand following". Signers explain the difference between the two orientations as a difference in point of view: when the tip of the finger "leads the way", the point of view follows the route; when the hand is held perpendicular to the path, the motion is seen from a distance. There are, however, many examples of changes of the hand's orientation in the middle of the movement.

One very special whole entity stem is expressed by the signer's head and body (see further the subsection *The sender locus vs. the signer's head and body* in III.8.6 Polymorphemic verbs and space).

With some of the stems in the list above I have indicated the unmarked orientation of the hand by which they are expressed. The whole entity stem Car-Pm, which can be used in verbs describing the location or motion of cars and trucks, is expressed by a handshape (a flat hand) whose unmarked orientation is with the palm down. A verb meaning '(the car) was lying upside down' is not expressed simply by the verb Car-Pm+(loc+palm-up+to-the-right), i.e. by moving the flat hand with the palm up down to an abrupt stop somewhere in space. The verb includes an orientation-changing morpheme: the hand starts with the palm down and rotates to the orientation palm up, i.e. a verb that describes the state of a car turned upside down literally means '(the car) was lying upside down as a result of turning over'. A pole or a log does not have a canonical orientation and the articulator of Long-thin-entity-Pm can be used directly with the appropriate (iconic) orientation. There is a common iconic origin behind the whole entity stems Car-Pm, Bicycle-Pm, and Flat-entity-Pm: cars, bicycles, plates, books, paintings, and the like are all entities that can be perceived as saliently two-dimensional. Nevertheless, the fact that different orientation-changing morphemes are required with these stems demonstrates that they have become more lexically specialised.

Handle stems
The next two categories of verb stems, handle stems and limb stems, have an iconic similarity in that the manual articulators used to express the stems imitate human hands handling something, human or animal limbs, or other kinds of instruments. That is, by contrast to the manual articulators of whole entity stems, the manual articulators of the handle and limb stems do not represent all of the entity in the motion event, but in many cases only part of the entity or more than one entity (the handler and the entity handled).

Handle stems are used in verbs that denote:
— an animate agent using primarily hand(s) or forelimbs to handle an entity;
— an animate actor bringing something somewhere by moving there while holding the entity; and
— an animate agent handling an instrument other than the hand.

Handle stems occur primarily in process verbs and can combine with movement morphemes of motion and with *hold* in backgrounded constructions (see III.8.6 Polymorphemic verbs and space). They can combine with *move-line* followed by or merged with *loc* to describe an actor's going somewhere while holding something or an agent's putting something somewhere. A signer used, for instance, Handle-three-dimensional-entity-Pm (Ill. 71) in a verb to state that she went over to a neighbour bringing a number of kitchen utensils. When handle stems combine with *move-line* merged with *loc*, they can also take distribution morphemes ('put an unspecific number of entities in a particular configuration'). Handle stems do occasionally occur in stative verbs with *hold* in foregrounded constructions. In the following example from a signer's description of her daughter's hearing test, a handle stem also occurs with *loc* in a stative verb about an entity being held somewhere:

```
(1) right:   1.p MARIE GIRL / Handle-large-cylindrical-
    left:                    Handle-large-cylindrical-

    right:   entity-Pm +(hold+outside-1.chest) PRON+cd /
    left:    entity-Pm +(hold+outside-1.chest)----------

    right:   Handle-large-cylindrical-entity-Pm+(loc+
    left:    Handle-large-cylindrical-entity-Pm+(loc+

    right:   outside-1.chest) / PRON+behind-1.shoulder
    left:    outside-1.chest)+(hold)------------------

    right:   CLAP-HANDS+above-1.shoulder TINKLE-BELL+above-
    left:    CLAP-HANDS+above-1.shoulder TINKLE-BELL+above-

    right:   1.shoulder / FINISH / 1.p Handle-large-
    left:    1.shoulder                 Handle-large-

    right:   cylindrical-entity-Pm+(outside-chest+move-line+
    left:    cylindrical-entity-Pm+(outside-chest+move-line+

    right:   loc +down -to-the -right) /
    left:    loc +down -to-the -right)
```

I had Marie on my lap; she was there on my lap; and there behind my shoulder the audiologist clapped her hands and tinkled bells. When it was finished, I put Marie down on the floor.

The signer uses the handle stem Handle-large-cylindrical-entity-Pm (the stem is seen in another verb in Ill. 65) both with *hold* only and with *loc* only in the verbs about her holding her daughter on her lap, and she uses the stem with *move-line+loc* in the verb about putting her daughter on the floor.

A handle stem may represent an agent referent while the sender locus or the signer's head and body is used for another referent. A signer can, for instance, describe how a child puts a potato on a snowman's face for a nose by moving her hand with the articulator of Handle-lumplike-entity-Pm toward her own nose, i.e. her hand represents the child's hand with the potato, while her face represent's the snowman's face.

Look-Pm (in verbs which mean 'watch', 'turn one's gaze at', 'look over', etc.) is a handle stem: it is used primarily in process verbs and cannot be used with *loc* only as whole entity stems can. In constructions with Look-Pm, the implied referent relations can be quite complex. In the verb form with Look-Pm in Ill. 25b, meaning '(She) looked at him arrogantly', the sender locus represents the patient argument's referent, while the locus forward-right represents the agent argument's referent. At the same time, the signer's face may imitate an arrogant expression, which expresses the attitude of the agent. That is, the sender locus represents the patient referent as expressed by the signer's gaze direction and the orientation of the manual articulator of Look-Pm, while at the same time the expressive elements on the signer's face are shifted to the agent referent represented by the locus forward-right.

Other examples of handle stems that can be used in constructions where the signer's body or the sender locus is used for one referent while the handle stems represents a different referent are: Handle-scissors-Pm, Handle-gun-Pm, and Mouth-Pm (e.g. in a description of how a lion kills a zebra by biting its throat, demonstrated on the signer's own throat). But Handle-scissors-Pm and Handle-gun-Pm deviate from other handle stems in that they cannot be used in verbs to describe an agent's putting something somewhere or an actor's moving somewhere while hold-ing something. It is, for instance, not possible to use Handle-scissors-Pm in a verb to say that somebody put the scissors somewhere or went somewhere with a pair of scissors. Iconically the manual articulator of the two stems represents a whole entity (a pair of scissors and a gun), but semantically they imply an agent handling the entity.

Handle stems can also be used in backgrounded constructions with *hold*, for instance, for someone sitting in the driver seat of a car while seeing someone approaching (Ill. 72). Then the construction involves shifted attribution of expressive elements. In backgrounded constructions with handle stems, the referent of the expressive elements and the referent represented by the handle stem must be identical.

The perceived iconicity of the handle stems is that of the manual articulator imitating a hand or forelimb holding an entity or doing something, or the manual articulator imitating some other instrument.

Examples of the category are:
— Handle-handle-Pm (the fist with the thumb covering the fingers; for handling a Thermos, a mug, a ski stick, a suitcase);
— Handle-two-dimensional-entity-Pm (Ill. 73; for handling a piece of paper, but also three-dimensional entities which can be manipulated by hand);
— Handle-three-dimensional-entity-Pm (Ill. 71; for handling an entity of some volume or a mass of entities of unspecified size);
— Handle-cylindrical-entity-Pm (Ill. 50; for handling a glass);
— Handle-lumplike-entity-Pm (all fingers and the thumb extended, slightly spread, and bent at the joints; for handling a potato, a lump of mud);
— Handle-telephone-receiver-Pm (the fist with extended and spread thumb and little finger);
— Look-Pm (see above);

— Mouth-Pm (all fingers and the thumb extended, slightly spread, and bent at the joints, the thumb opposed; for animates biting);
— Handle-gun-Pm (the fist with the index finger and thumb extended and spread); and
— Handle-scissors-Pm (the fist with the index and middle fingers extended and spread; for cutting with scissors).

Handle stems can double (use both hands) to denote the handling of two entities (handle two Thermoses), the handling of a larger entity or a larger mass (Handle-three-dimensional-entity-Pm), or the handling of one entity with both hands (handle one piece of paper with both hands).

Limb stems

Limb stems are used in verbs to denote the motion or state of animates indicated by the motion or state of their limbs; limb stems are generally used with shifted attribution of expressive elements. They can occur in process verbs and in foregrounded (stative) verbs with *hold* and shifted attribution of expressive elements. Among the motion morphemes, they combine in particular with the *analogue*-kind, but Legs-Pm and Feet-Pm can also combine with the path expressing motion morpheme *move-line*. They are expressed by the use of both hands and the handshapes of the limb stems are as close an imitation of an animate being's limbs as is possible, using the human arms and hands.

The most common limb stems are the stems for human beings:
— Legs-Pm (Ill. 60; the unmarked orientation is with the fingertips pointing downward; for women walking on high heels, human beings limping, human beings sitting cross-legged);
— Feet-Pm (two flat hands, held like feet with the orientation appropriate for the motion in question; for human beings walking in a carefree way, running); and
— Arms-Pm (the arms and hands held or moved in a way analogous to a standardised version of the state or motion described; for human beings walking determinedly in a certain direction, for human beings waiting (Ill. 74)).

Paws-Pm is an example of a limb stem that can be used in verbs denoting the motion or state of an animal, e.g. a lion, a leopard, or a cat. It is expressed by both hands with the fingers tense, extended, slightly spread, and bent at the joints.

As mentioned above, handle stems and limb stems overlap as categories; in some cases, it is difficult to decide which category the stem of a given verb belongs to. The limb stem Paws-Pm may be used in the same way as Feet-Pm where both hands and the signer's body and head represent one entity (an animal with paws), but also in the same way as handle stems where the hand imitates an animal paw. The main differences between handle stems and limb stems are that handle stems can be used to represent a different actor than the signer's body or the sender locus and they can be used to describe an actor moving somewhere holding something and an agent putting an entity somewhere; limb stems cannot be used to represent a different referent from the referent represented by the signer's body or the sender locus. Neither can they be used for an actor moving somewhere holding something or an agent putting an entity somewhere.

In III.8.3 Classifiers or verb stems in Danish Sign Language? I showed that in the area of the motion and location of human beings there are more options (more different stems) and greater standardisation (of the meaning of the individual stems and the movement morphemes with which they can combine) than in other semantic areas. That is also true of both handle stems and limb stems. Handle stems can be used in verbs denoting a human actor moving somewhere while holding something, but not other animate beings' motion. The limb stems Legs-Pm, Feet-Pm, and Arms-Pm can combine with more different types of movement morphemes than other limb stems and can combine with a greater number of standardised motion morphemes of the *analogue*-kind. Moreover, Legs-Pm and Feet-Pm can combine with the path expressing motion morpheme *move-line* to denote movement in a certain direction or to a goal (e.g. Legs-Pm in a clause meaning 'He limped to the door').[1]

Extension stems
Extension stems are only used with extension morphemes, which do not denote motion, but iconically depict the outline of an entity or a mass. Extension stems are used in verbs that denote the state of an entity or a mass. Verbs with extension stems are stative. Extension stems are often called size-and-shape-specifiers (SASSes) in research on ASL (see the references in relation to extension morphemes in III.8.4 Movement morphemes in polymorphemic verbs).

Examples of extension stems are:
— Flat-surface-Pm (the flat hand; for valleys, buildings, mountains);
— Curved-surface-Pm (the fingers extended, unspread, and slightly bent; for small entities with curved surfaces (bumps, holes) and large entities with curved, smooth surfaces);
— Curved-large-surface-Pm (the fingers and the thumb extended, slightly spread, and slightly bent; for large entities with curved surfaces (a large amount of goods in a supermarket trolley, a big stomach));
— Thin-entity-surface-Pm (the fist with extended index finger and thumb, the index finger is bent at the first knuckle and the thumb is held parallel to the index finger; for thin boards, stick-like entities);
— Tiny-entity-surface-Pm (the fingers extended and spread, the pad of the index finger contacting the pad of the thumb; for very slim entities (a straw or string)); and
— Two-dimensional-outline-Pm (the index hand traces an outline; a sheet of paper).

---

[1] Supalla (1990) describes a category of verbs in ASL, locomotion verbs, which resembles verbs with limb stems in Danish Sign Language. The locomotion verbs in ASL cannot, however, denote path motion as verbs with Legs-Pm and Feet-Pm in Danish Sign Language can.

Contact between articulators
Liddell and Johnson (1987) describe a category of surface morphemes in ASL whose distinguishing characteristic is that the handshapes by which they are expressed can have other articulators, expressing whole entity stems, placed on them. Corazza (1990) finds that Italian Sign Language has many morphemes of this kind. In Danish Sign Language, physical contact between manual articulators is acceptable with Ground-Pm and stems with articulators imitating specific shapes of entities that usually serve as "grounds" (for instance, a springboard) used in backgrounded constructions for the base of takeoff for motion (as in a clause meaning 'He dived from the springboard'). Otherwise, physical contact between articulators expressing two different stems seems to be confined to special styles of signing in Danish Sign Language, namely very creative, poetic signing, signing to children, and very distinct signing to hearing people who are "children" linguistically. Some signers explicitly express distaste for this kind of contact between the hands except when it is seen with the articulators of unusual stems or stem combinations in creative signing. In the basketball example, example (1) in III.8.1, there is physical contact between the articulators of two tokens of 1-Pm and between the signer's right hand and lower arm in Index-Pm and her body. Physical contact between the articulators of two identical stems, especially of the kind where they only touch each other briefly, is more acceptable and is seen in nonpolymorphemic signs related to polymorphemic verbs. Brief physical contact between the hand and the body or the head also seems acceptable, but I have seen signers express the meaning 'Somebody bumped into me' using a verb with Index-Pm where the hand stops a little before actually touching the body and then moves out again.

Stems of polymorphemic verbs and gesturing
In a study of the gestures of a person retelling a comic book story in English, McNeill and Levy (1982) describe two types of iconic gestures: gestures which they find reflect the agent's point of view, and gestures which reflect the patient's point of view. An example of the former is 'the arm extended upward and forward, the hand forming a grip, then the arm moving downward and toward the self; this appeared with the narrative statement, 'and then he bends it way back' (in which 'it' refers to a tree)' (ibid., 282). An example of a gesture reflecting the patient's point of view is 'the right hand extended laterally to the left and rotating around the axis of the arm in a series of circles; this appeared with the statement, 'he finished powering the dynamo', and the gesture represents the movement of the armature of the dynamo' (ibid. 282). The two types resemble verbs with handle stems and verbs with whole entity stems respectively, except that the "whole entity stem" about the dynamo co-occurs with an English transitive verb. The informant in McNeill and Levy's study also used "whole entity stems" with intransitive verbs of an actor's motion: 'the hand with fingers extended moves upward and away from the self in a single thrust as J said 'she dashes out of the house'' (ibid., 282-283).

Compared with such gestures, the polymorphemic verbs in Danish Sign Language are semantically, syntactically, and morphologically much more complex. Handle stems can, for instance, be used for an actor moving somewhere holding something, and there are many semantically different stems with very specific meanings. Syntactically, two different stems may co-occur (see III.8.6 Polymorphemic verbs and space) and a stem may occur in a construction where the stem and the sender locus represent two different referents. Morphologically, the stems in polymorphemic verbs can combine with a much larger and more stable inventory of different movement morphemes than the movements seen in gestures accompanying spoken English.[2]

Classification or lexical idiosyncrasy
The analysis of the stems of polymorphemic verbs in Danish Sign Language presented here describes the stems as much more lexically idiosyncratic than the analyses of classifiers in ASL presented by especially McDonald (1982) and Supalla (1986). Their analyses present the handshape units as classifying entities primarily by shape and other physical characteristics.

McDonald distinguishes two major form groups in ASL, one whose members denote 'x-type of object' (i.e. 'x-shaped object') and another whose members denote 'handle x-type of object'. She examines these two groups in relation to three movement patterns, Supalla's *contact, random,* and *linear* movement (Supalla 1978). She finds that the major difference between the two groups is that verbs with 'x-type of object' forms combine with *contact* to form stative verbs ('x-type of object be located at a location'), while verbs with 'handle x-type of object' forms are process verbs which have a linear movement with an abrupt endpoint. The latter forms predictably mean 'move x-type of object to a given or canonical location' (ibid., 148), whereas they cannot denote 'x-type of object be located somewhere' (ibid., 157). McDonald concludes:

> The class of forms which signals the location of a <u>particular shape</u> class of concrete objects seems to be less "active or event-oriented" than those which signal <u>the handling</u> of concrete objects. This impression is strengthened by behavior in constructions. The x-type of object forms tend to mean "a particular shaped object be located or extend." The second class of forms yields more "verby" meanings such as "put, take, etc." within combinations. (ibid., 158 – emphasis in the original)

But McDonald also finds that a few forms of the 'x-type of object' kind can combine with *linear* and *random* movement resulting in process verbs. Then, however, the forms can only be used for more specific objects than 'an x-shaped object', namely 'car, conveyance' instead of 'object with two right angle extensions', or 'person' instead of 'straight thinnish, longer than wide object' (ibid., 118ff., 58). Following Supalla, she calls the forms "frozen" classifiers. The "frozen" classifiers fall in an

---
2 Leer (ms.) gives examples of more differentiated gestures accompanying narration in spoken Tlingit.

intermediate group because they can be used in process verbs without denoting 'handle x-type of object'.

McDonald's 'x-type of object' forms correspond by and large to my two categories whole entity stems and extension stems. Like Liddell and Johnson (1987, see here III.8.4 Movement morphemes in polymorphemic verbs), she does not distinguish distribution morphemes from extension morphemes within the morphemes expressed by movement, and therefore, she does not distinguish whole entity stems and extension stems either. Her 'handle x-type of object' forms correspond to my category handle stems. As in ASL, handle stems in Danish Sign Language are primarily used in process verbs, but they can be used in verbs with *hold* only or *loc* only (see example (1) above).

Forms that can occur in both stative and process verbs (i.e. McDonald's "frozen" classifiers) are more central to my analysis of types of verb stems than they are to McDonald's classifier analysis. As the forms are not classifiers in my analysis, but verb stems, the difference between stems which can occur in both stative and process verbs and stems which can only occur in stative verbs is a question of lexical semantics. The stems that can occur in both kinds of verbs are among the most frequently used stems in polymorphemic verbs, in particular Index-Pm, 1-Pm, and V-Pm as described in III.8.3 Classifiers or verb stems in Danish Sign Language? It is not always possible to predict, on the basis of the stem's meaning only, whether a stem can be used in both kinds of verbs or only in one kind. There is, for instance, no reason that has to do with the shape of trees why Tree-Pm is not normally used in a verb of a falling tree or a tree lying on the ground; Long-thin-entity-Pm is used instead. Neither has this restriction anything to do with the fact that the stem's meaning is restricted to more specific objects than 'an x-shaped object'; it is purely lexically idiosyncratic.

Another argument against analysing whole entity stems as primarily denoting 'x-shaped objects' is that at least one form, 1-Pm, does not originate in a form describing 'x-shaped objects'. The most likely "iconic" explanation of 1-Pm is not its shape, but the use of the same handshape in the number sign ONE.

Finally, whether a stem can be used in process verbs or in stative verbs depends, besides on lexical idiosyncrasies, on the kind of entities in the motion event denoted by the verb, and not on whether the stem is a whole entity or a handle stem. Many whole entity stems can be used in process verbs denoting many different kinds of motion, while other whole entity stems can be used in process verbs only if they are used for typical motion of the entities in question, such as a glass falling off a table (Cylindrical-entity-Pm, Ill. 50). When asked how they would describe a fantasy world with, for instance, dancing glasses, signers use nonpolymorphemic verbs like DANCE or they indicate that they feel uncomfortable about answering the question. Conversely, a whole entity stem expressed by a manual articulator consisting of the lower arm and the hand bent at the wrist can be used in a process verb of a swan's majestic glide over the water. Thus, which types of verbs whole entity stems can occur in depends partly on lexical idiosyncrasies, and partly on the normal behaviour of the entities in the motion event.

As the examples show, there are some stems that have identical forms across the whole entity – handle boundary, e.g. Lumplike-entity-Pm and Handle-lumplike-entity-Pm, and Cylindrical-entity-Pm and Handle-cylindrical-entity-Pm. But while the whole entity stem Cylindrical-entity-Pm can be used for mugs as well as glasses, the handling of mugs is usually described by verbs with the stem Handle-handle-Pm, provided that the signer uses a polymorphemic verb at all, and not a nonpolymorphemic verb such as GIVE. It is the idiosyncrasies of individual stems, or classifiers, in ASL that make McDonald talk about "frozen" classifiers.

The picture that appears from the analysis of polymorphemic verbs in Danish Sign Language is that the stems of polymorphemic verbs semantically classify the entities in the motion events to different degrees. Some stems are selected on the basis of only physical characteristics of the entities in the motion events; and they can combine with different types of movement morphemes, provided that the resulting (predictable) meaning makes sense in some world. Other stems are idiosyncratic with respect to which entities in the motion events they can denote and with respect to the types of movement morphemes they can combine with. In one particular area, the motion and location of human beings, there are many different stems that can be used in verbs that denote motion events involving the same type of entity (i.e. a human being), but which describe different aspects of the events in which the entity takes part. The movement morpheme *move-line* can be used for the motion of a human being with all of the following stems (disregarding the motion of a human being by a means of transportation other than the feet): Index-Pm, V-Pm, 1-Pm, General-entity-Pm, Handle-three-dimensional-entity-Pm, Handle-handle-Pm (and other handle stems), Legs-Pm, and Feet-Pm, and the verbs with these stems all focus on different aspects of the motion. Therefore, the stems can hardly be said to classify the entity semantically.

8.6 Polymorphemic verbs and space

Backgrounded and foregrounded constructions
Example (1) is an excerpt from the basketball example of III.8.1 Introduction. It shows how the two hands interact in such a way that either they both move in the same way or one is held still (*hold*):

```
(1)    right:   AT GOAL /        DEFEND
       left:             1.p             1.p 1-Pm+(hold+c)+

       right:   1-Pm+(near-r.shoulder+ move-line+forward)+
       left:    (move-line+forward)+---------------------

       right:   (hold)--------------------+(move-line+
       left:    (move-arc+forward-of-r.hand)+(hold)-----
```

```
right:    into-l.hand) / ...
left:     ------------
```
```
At the goal, when I'm in the defence and I see someone moving
forward and I pursue him and overtake him and he bumps into me,
...
```

At the point in the example where both hands have been moved forward linearly, there are many possible continuations which all express different locative relations between the two referents, e.g. 1) the hands stop next to each other; 2) the right hand stops and the left hand moves ahead of the right hand and stops; 3) the right hand stops and the left hand moves ahead of and in line with ("overtakes") the right hand and stops (example (1)); 4) the right hand stops and the left hand moves into the right hand; and 5) the hands move into each other midway between their original paths. Possibilities 2, 3, and 4, of course, also have alternatives with the reverse distribution of strong and weak hand. All these possibilities are meaningful and acceptable.

If for a moment we think of the articulator of one of the verbs as expressing a locus in relation to the other verb, it becomes clear that the relation between the other hand and this "locus" is quite different from what we see with nonpolymorphemic verbs. The only possible relation between a nonpolymorphemic verb and a locus is agreement, which is expressed by a lexically specified relation between the articulator of the verb and the direction of the locus. In the above example, there are many possible relations between the articulators of the two polymorphemic verbs, none of them is lexically specified, and each of them expresses a different meaning. That is, a polymorphemic verb does not have the same function in relation to another polymorphemic verb as a nonpolymorphemic verb showing agreement in relation to a locus.

Talmy (1985) defines the Figure in a motion event as 'a moving or *conceptually movable* point whose path or site is at issue'; and the Ground as 'a reference-frame, or a reference-point stationary within a reference-frame, with respect to which the Figure's path or site is characterised' (1978, 61 – emphasis in the original). The notions of Figure and Ground are not only pertinent to moving entities in relation to stationary entities, but also to two stationary entities in relation to each other. The two sentences *The bike is near the house* and *The house is near the bike* are not synonymous.[1] Each expresses an asymmetric relationship, with the subject having the semantic function Figure and the prepositional object having the semantic function Ground.

In Danish Sign Language, the notions of Figure and Ground can be used to describe constructions where a polymorphemic verb occurs with a *hold*-morpheme simultaneously with another polymorphemic verb as in (1). One of the two players in

---

[1] Leech (1969, 275) argues that such sentences are 'cognitively synonymous', but 'answer different questions', i.e. he points out the difference in thematic relations between the two sentences. Talmy's definition of Figure includes a thematic notion as that item is defined as Figure whose path or site is 'at issue' (1985, 61).

the basketball situation is 'a moving point' whose path is conceived in relation to the other player. This relationship is expressed by the simultaneous use of the two polymorphemic verbs. The one that takes the *hold*-morpheme at any given moment serves the Ground function; it predicates something about the player who serves as a reference point with respect to which the Figure's path is characterised. For instance, in line 2, the Ground function is served by 1-Pm+(hold) articulated by the right hand, and the Figure function by 1-Pm+(move-arc+forward-of-r.hand) ('I overtake him') articulated by the left hand.

Talmy compares the relationship between Figure and Ground in the locative relations of objects with the relative location of events in time. A Figure event is situated in time in relation to a Ground event, as can be seen from the parallelism of *The fly was located (at a point) along the branch* and *The explosion took place (at a point) during the performance* (ibid., 632). Talmy further points out that Figure and Ground applied to events are 'very near, if not the same as, "assertion" and "presupposition" for propositions' (1978, 632). In the complex sentence *He exploded after he touched the button*, the button-touching event has a Ground function; it is presupposed and set up as a fixed, known reference point in relation to the explosion event which is asserted.

In the example from Danish Sign Language, the temporal and the locative uses of Figure and Ground blend. The signer describes not only the locative relation between the two basketball players, but also the relation in time between what they are doing: they move forward at the same time, one of them overtakes the other and stops short, and then the other person bumps into the stationary person. The meaning of the *hold*-segments is presupposed while motion is asserted by means of the motion segments.

Talmy's example with the bicycle and the house shows that some distributions of the semantic functions of Figure and Ground are more likely than others. It is more likely that we describe the position of a smaller, movable entity such as a bicycle in relation to a bigger, stationary entity such as a house than the other way round. In example (1) from Danish Sign Language, the two referents are equally likely to serve as Figure and as Ground from a semantic point of view; the example demonstrates that the two functions can switch back and forth between the constituents. The right hand and the left hand express two tokens of the stem 1-Pm and they alternately take a path motion morpheme and the morpheme *hold*, i.e. they "take turns" in expressing asserted and presupposed information.

At one moment, both hands move at the same time, which means that neither verb is backgrounded (lines 2-3). Still, there is a thematic difference. The signer starts by signing 1.p 1-Pm+(hold+c) with her left hand, which means that her left hand expresses the verbs that predicate something of 1.p, also when she signs 1-Pm+(move-line+forward) with both hands. With respect to information packaging, the construction is a mixture of the English *I am running next to him,* where *I* as the subject is thematic and it is implied that 'he' is running, and *We are running next to each other*, where neither actor is singled out, but it is asserted that both are running. The construction in (1) makes it possible to present one actor as the theme and, at the same time, assert the parallel actions of both actors.

In backgrounded constructions in Danish Sign Language, the semantic difference between location and motion, or state and nonstate, can only be inferred from the context or from real-world knowledge; in backgrounded verbs (or sections of verbs, see the discussion at the end of III.8.4 Movement morphemes in polymorphemic verbs), *hold* is neutral with respect to the state – nonstate distinction. The player in the situation described in (1) does not stop moving while the referent of 1.p overtakes him; that is, the verb 1-Pm+(*hold*) with the *hold*-morpheme (line 2 of the transcript) does not imply that the other person stopped moving. Correspondingly, the referent of 1.p is not stationary when her opponent moves into her (1-Pm+(*hold*) articulated with her left hand in line 3 of the transcript). The whole point of the signer's story is that you are not allowed to run when you try to stop an opponent.

Locative configurations and coherence
In example (1), the two polymorphemic verbs occur simultaneously to describe a locative relation between two referents, i.e. a locative configuration. Such a relationship can also be expressed by polymorphemic verbs occurring sequentially. An example of this is seen in (2), which is a description of the deaf children's amazement at seeing a Christmas tree at the school for the deaf in the 19th century:

```
(2)   right:    NEVER SEE CHRISTMAS-TREE BEFORE+deictic-tl /
      left:               CHRISTMAS-TREE

      right:    CANDLE  Short-thin-entity-Pm+(loc+distribution-
      left:             Short-thin-entity-Pm+(loc+distribution-

      right:    random+vertical) / PAPER FESTOON Tiny-entity-
      left:     random+vertical)   PAPER FESTOON Tiny-entity-

      right:    surface-Pm+(extension-vertical-cone)
      left:     surface-Pm+(extension-vertical-cone)

      right:    Look-Pm+(A:c+move-line+P:up-to-neutral)+
      left:

      right:    (move-line+P:up)+(hold) Thin-entity-surface--
      left:                             Short-thin-entity-Pm+

      right:    Pm+(extension-end-of-stick+tip-of-1.index)*
      left:     (hold+vertical+neutral)--------------------

      right:    DET+tip-of-1.index / GOLD STAR / Look-Pm+
      left:     ----------------------------------------

      right:    (A:c+hold+P:up) IMPRESSED GREATLY-SURPRISED /
      left:     ----------------------- GREATLY-SURPRISED
```

*Ill. 75

They had never seen a Christmas tree before. There were candles all over it, and paper festoons hanging from the top. They looked all over and saw at the top a gold star. They were greatly impressed.

The relationship between the candles, the festoons, the children's gaze direction, and the top of the tree is expressed spatially through the signer's use of the vertical dimension in the signing space; but the relation between, on the one hand, the candles, the festoons, the tree top, and the children's gaze direction and, on the other hand, the Christmas tree must be inferred. The use of space in the polymorphemic verbs resembles the use of loci with verbs showing agreement in that the signer's hands move in a general direction; they are not at the exact same positions in space in the different polymorphemic verbs. When the signer describes more detailed locative configurations as the part-whole relationship between the star at the top and the rest of the tree, she uses a backgrounded construction with the stem Short-thin-entity-Pm+(hold+vertical+neutral) (Ill. 75) and makes the relationship between the top of the tree and the star clear by maintaining the articulator of Short-thin-entity-Pm while signing the rest of the example except for the two-handed sign GREATLY-SURPRISED.

Example (2) demonstrates the double status of signs with extension stems. The construction in Ill. 75 is accompanied by the mouth pattern of the Danish noun *top* ('top') and followed by a pointing sign and a boundary. It might, therefore, be analysed as a noun in a nominal serving as the P or goal argument of the verb with Look-Pm. But verbs with Look-Pm can occur in foregrounded constructions with a backgrounded verb with a whole entity stem which does not occur in a noun. Look-Pm can even take a motion morpheme to indicate the motion of the entity observed, as in a clause meaning 'I saw him cross my path' or 'I followed him with my eyes as he crossed my path'. The construction in Ill. 75 can be analysed as indicating an entity in a certain state as well as an entity of a certain kind.

Example (1) demonstrates how a backgrounded polymorphemic verb can serve the Ground function in the expression of a locative configuration. The verb is backgrounded in relation to a verb having propositional value, in (1) another polymorphemic verb. In (2), the backgrounded verb Short-thin-entity-Pm+(hold+vertical+mid) and the foregrounded nonpolymorphemic verb IMPRESSED do not express a locative configuration, but a causal relationship; the children were impressed by the tree or the star at the top of the tree. And in (3) below, the backgrounded verb expresses discourse coherence rather than any semantic relation. Example (3) is from a signer's description of a collision of two ferries; the signer described how one of the ferries backed out of the harbour and turned around in a foggy area, and then she went on:[2]

---

2   As the two-handed stem Boat-Pm is expressed by two slightly curved hands held in the shape of

288   Verbs and Space

```
(3)  right:   Boat-Pm+(move+loc+neutral+orientation-front-
     left:    Boat-Pm+(move+loc+neutral+orientation-front-

     right:   facing-right)*/      PRON+emphatic+right# /
     left:    facing-right)+(hold)---------------------

     right:   SECOND FERRY Vessel-Pm+(right+move-line+right-
     left:    SECOND FERRY Vessel-Pm+(hold+neutral+orienta--

     right:   of-l.hand+orientation-front-facing-left) /
     left:    tion-front-facing-right)-----------------

     right:   PRON+where-r.hand-was BE-CALLED Romsø(M) /
     left:    -----------------------------------------

     right:   PRON+where-r.hand-was /
     left:    --------------------

     *Ill. 76a    #Ill. 76b
```

So the ferry came here, and the other ferry which came from the other side, it was called Romsø.

The signer makes the locative relationship between the two ferries explicit by using a polymorphemic verb with *hold* while signing another polymorphemic verb (lines 2-5). Boat-Pm+(hold) (left hand, line 2) and Vessel-Pm+(hold) (left hand, line 3-4) serve the Ground function, and the signs made with the right hand from PRON+emphatic+fr in the second line to the beginning of line 4 express the Figure. But the signer keeps her left hand in position, articulating the backgrounded verb with the stem Vessel-Pm, also while she signs the last clause, which is a statement about the name of the other ferry. There is a locative relation between the referents implied by the verbs with Vessel-Pm articulated simultaneously by the two hands. The relationship, however, between the backgrounded verb ("the first ferry in a certain position") and the proposition of PRON+where-r.hand-was BE-CALLED Romsø(M) / PRON+where-r.hand-was ("the second ferry's name") is not locative. Immediately afterwards, the signer describes the collision, and here she "revives" the backgrounded verb. What went in between was parenthetical information.[3]

In the following example, nouns related to polymorphemic verbs can also occur in backgrounded constructions. In this case, they have neither a locative nor a temporal function, but express coherence and discourse relevance. When a signer talked

---

a hull and Vessel-Pm by a flat hand with the little finger edge down as its unmarked orientation, it is not possible to distinguish a single hand "left over from" Boat-Pm (line 2) from an instance of Vessel-Pm.

3 In II.2 The frame of reference, I described an example where a change in the frame of reference contributed to marking part of the discourse as a digression from the main track of the monologue. In (3), the signer does not change the frame of reference when she gives parenthetical information. A digression makes a change possible, but the frame of reference is not necessarily changed in a digression. In the example in II.2, the change was in accordance with the convention of semantic affinity; in example (3) here, there is no convention that would make it appropriate to change the frame of reference.

about Christmas at the school for the deaf in the 19th century, she explained that the children stayed at the school and were given games such as Ludo for entertainment. The noun GAME is related to a polymorphemic verb with a handle stem. The signer used the sign GAME, signed 20 other signs in a digression about the children not going home for Christmas (and therefore, getting the games for entertainment during the Christmas holidays), and then signed GAME again. Ten seconds elapsed between her first and second use of GAME. During that time, she kept her left hand in the position of the manual articulator of GAME, signing two-handed signs with one hand (except for VACATION which is a two-handed sign that can be articulated with the same manual articulator as GAME). At the end of the digression, the hand was used in the second version of GAME. It might be claimed that the "left-over" manual articulator is only a phonetic or physiological phenomenon, but such an articulator reappears when the hand has been used to articulate a two-handed sign and it disappears the second it is no longer semantically or pragmatically relevant.

In example (2) of III.7 Pragmatic agreement (repeated here as (4)), the articulator of GOOD is maintained during the last clause:

```
(4)   PRON+fsl GOOD+fsl EXPLAIN+p.a.:fsl        /
                                       GOOD+fsl--
      PRON+fsr SO-SO+fsr /
      -----------------

      One group was good at exposing their ideas, whereas the other one
      wasn't really so good.
```

GOOD is not related to a polymorphemic verb, but the sign has a locus marker and thereby expresses a referent projection in the same way as the stem of a polymorphemic verb (see below). In this example, the backgrounded construction also shows discourse coherence and underlines the contrast between the two referents. In order to illuminate what a backgrounded polymorphemic verb as 1-Pm+(hold) in (1) and GOOD+fsl in (4) have in common, I now develop the concept of referent projection which is unique to signed languages.

Referent projections
A whole entity or handle stem of a polymorphemic verb in a backgrounded construction expresses a referent projection in the same way as a locus. A referent projection can be used for reference; it is not a pronoun in itself. A pronoun is either a symbol such as the first person pronoun 1.p or a sign, usually a pointing sign, that may fulfil its referring function by being directed at entities present in the context of utterance or at directions or points of loci. Also the manual articulator of a whole entity or handle stem of a polymorphemic verb can serve as the "place" that the index hand of a pronoun is pointing at when the pronoun is used to refer. The manual articu-

lator of a pronoun cannot serve as such a "place" for another pronoun. That is why the articulator of a whole entity or handle stem does not express a pronoun, but a referent projection. In (5), the signer refers to some gifts by pointing at the manual articulator of a verb with a handle stem meaning 'handed out':

```
(5)    right:   AFTERWARDS PRINCIPAL c+GIVE+neu GIFT /
       left:                                                    PRON+neu-

       right:   BIG CHILDREN / Handle-two-dimensional-entity-
       left:    --------------- Handle-two-dimensional-entity-

       right:   Pm+(c+move-line+distribution-line+fr) /
       left:    Pm+(c+move-line+distribution-line+fr)--

       right:   PRON+l.hand VARIOUS GAME /
       left:    ------------------ GAME

       Afterward the principal handed out gifts to the big children; the
       gifts were various games.
```

The signer uses the handle stem Handle-two-dimensional-entity-Pm (Ill. 73) in a two-handed version and maintains her left hand articulating a backgrounded verb (line 3 of the transcript). She then refers to the gifts by means of a pronoun whose articulator is directed at her left hand ('the gifts (that he was handing out)').

The similarity between the manual articulator of a polymorphemic verb and the direction or point in space of a locus demonstrated here shows one more reason why it is helpful to distinguish the locus marker and the locus (see also *Locus in Danish Sign Language* in I.6.4 The term *locus*). The locus marker is affixed to a sign, e.g. a pronoun. It is expressed in the way it influences the position or orientation of the hand(s) in the production of the sign. Correspondingly, what influences the orientation of the hand in PRON+l.hand in line 3 of example (5) is a marker for the stem of the verb with Handle-two-dimensional-entity-Pm (for simplicity transcribed as *l.hand*); the specific direction is determined only by where this manual articulator is in space. The pronoun can only be used to refer to the gifts if the manual articulator of the stem is conceived as expressing a projection of the cognitive entity, the referent 'gifts', into space. A pronoun can fulfil its referring function by taking a locus marker, but we can describe this as a parallel to the pronoun in (5): a pronoun fulfils the referring function by pointing at the expression of a referent projection, i.e. the locus's direction or point in space.

In (5), the pronoun is used to refer to the referent of the patient argument of the polymorphemic verb. But reference by means of the manual articulator of a polymorphemic verb can also have a more abstract semantic relation to the arguments of the backgrounded verb. In the following example, the signer explains that someone called an institution, but the lines were busy, so he had to wait:

```
(6)  right:  DIAL Handle-telephone-receiver-Pm+(down-
     left:

     right:  right+move-line+r.cheek)+(hold)--------------
     left:                                       / PRON+r.hand

     right:  WAIT  QUEUE /
     left:         QUEUE
```

He dialled (and held the receiver to his ear). There was a queue.

In the pronoun (line 2), the index hand points at the right hand representing the telephone receiver (the nonpolymorphemic verb TELEPHONE, which has the same manual articulator as the stem Handle-telephone-receiver-Pm, can be seen in Ill. 38). The pronoun does not refer to the telephone handle, however, but to what was said on the telephone.

The difference between pronouns and referent projections also appears from the fact that General-entity-Pm (see *Whole entity stems* in III.8.5 Categories of stems) cannot be used as a referent projection. The iconic origin of General-entity-Pm is a gesture pointing at a located entity or following the course of a moving entity, i.e. General-entity-Pm is related to PRON in that the manual articulator of both point at actual or imagined entities. In neither case does the manual articulator represent the referent; and by contrast to all other whole entity stems, it is not possible to point at the manual articulator in order to refer to the entity taking part in the motion denoted by a verb with General-entity-Pm.

The manual articulator of GOOD+fsl in (4) does not express a referent projection; it is not possible to refer to anything by means of a pronoun with an index hand pointing at the manual articulator of GOOD. The referent projection in (4) is the locus of the locus marker in GOOD. What GOOD+fsl shares with the polymorphemic verbs with whole entity and handle stems is that they include a referent projection. In the case of GOOD+fsl, it is the locus expressed through the locus marker in the way it influences the position of the hand in the production of GOOD+fsl; in the case of the polymorphemic verb, it is its stem expressed by the manual articulator.

A referent projection contributes to 'the apprehension of a linguistic object', i.e. the referent in question (Lehmann 1982, 233, quoted here in III.6.2 Agreement features, direction, and domain; see also Lehmann 1982, 249-250). Sometimes the referent is relevant as the Ground in a locative configuration (examples (1) and (2)); sometimes it is the reference point in a comparison (example (4)); and sometimes it contributes to discourse coherence (example (3)).

Referent projections are unique to signed languages. The manual articulators of polymorphemic verbs are visible and contribute to reference in the way they do by being visible: the receiver can see what the index hand of PRON is pointed at and thereby understand the reference. Directions or points of loci are not visible as such, but only through locus markers that affect the orientation of the hand(s) in modified signs. They depend on the receiver's visual memory for contributing to reference-tracking. In order for a direction from the signer or a point in space to express a referent projection, it must express a locus with all that it implies to be a locus (see in particular II.2-4 and II.7). Similarly, not just any manual articulator can express a referent projection; it has to be the manual articulator of the stem of a polymorphemic verb, or of a sign related to a polymorphemic verb. Unless the handshape by which Handle-two-dimensional-entity-Pm is expressed occurs as the expression of this stem in a polymorphemic verb, it cannot contribute to the apprehension of the referent.

Manual articulators of polymorphemic verbs express referent projections within the signing space. Sometimes such an articulator is used for a while and then disappears; but the signer can go on referring to the referent by a pronoun with an index hand directed at the point in space where the manual articulator was. Then the point serves the same function as the direction of a locus. That is, a locus that represents a specific referent as a consequence of the use of a polymorphemic verb can be thought of as expressed by a meaningful point in the signing space. Such points differ from the directions that are relevant to expressing agreement with nonpolymorphemic verbs. In the transcriptions, I therefore avoid using the same symbols for markers expressed by these points as for the locus markers in agreement. A polymorphemic verb may, however, take one of the locus markers seen with nonpolymorphemic verbs (see, for instance, the verb with Look-Pm in Ill. 25a), which is one symptom of the verb being closer to the nonpolymorphemic end of the continuum between polymorphemic and nonpolymorphemic verbs.

The sender locus vs. the signer's head and body
One of the ways in which the signer of example (1) of III.8.1 describes the interaction of the two basketball players involves her own body as an articulator in relation to a polymorphemic verb:

```
(7)   body:    rot.r.----------------------------------
      right:   1.p V-Pm+(loc+c) gesture Index-Pm+(right+move-

      body:             ----------------------neu----------------
      right:   line+into-signer's-body)+(orientation-change:

      body:    -----
      right:   fall) /

      I stand innocently, and he bumps into me and falls.
```

The signer's body "interacts" twice with the manual articulator of a polymorphemic verb in this example. First, V-Pm+(loc+c) is articulated close to the signer's body (Ill. 57). The verb by itself is ambiguous: it can mean either 'I/the holder of the point of view stand' or 'someone stands close to me/the holder of the point of view'. In (7), only the former meaning is possible, since the verb is preceded by the pronoun 1.p. In the last line of (7), the signer's body has the same function as the articulator of the polymorphemic verb with a *hold* morpheme in the last line of example (1) in this section. There the signer uses two polymorphemic verbs to describe one person moving into the other: 1-Pm+(move-line+into-l.hand) and 1-Pm+(hold). In (7), she uses the stem Index-Pm, because the stem 1-Pm cannot be used with *into* in relation to the signer's body, but the movement morphemes are identical: in (7), the articulator of the verb moves into the signer's body; in (1), it moves into the other hand. That is, the signer's body can serve the Ground function in the same way as a backgrounded verb with a whole entity stem in relation to a foregrounded polymorphemic verb. In such constructions, the articulator of the backgrounded verb as well as the signer's head and body express projections of referents.

There is a difference between stems of polymorphemic verbs expressing referent projections and loci expressing referent projections. The verb V-Pm+(loc) made in relation to the articulator of another polymorphemic verb means 's/he is standing in relation to another entity'. By contrast, V-Pm+(loc) made in relation to the direction or point of a locus means either 'he is standing there' (the locus represents the actor referent of V-Pm+(loc+(lokus-marker)) or 's/he is standing close to/on another entity or in a location' (the locus already represents another entity or location). The verb V-Pm+(loc+c) is ambiguous in the same way as V-Pm+(loc+(locus-marker-different-from-c]): 'I/the holder of the point of view is standing' or 's/he is standing close to me/the holder of the point of view'. That is, the area close to the signer's body can serve the same function as any other locus. That is what is meant by *the sender locus c*. But the signer's body can serve the same function as the articulator of a polymorphemic verb: in relation to Index-Pm+(right+move-line+into-signer's-body), the signer's body unambiguously represents a different entity. That is, we must distinguish the sender locus and the signer's head and body in relation to some polymorphemic verbs. In (7), c stands for the sender locus in V-Pm+(loc+c); but in Index-Pm+(right+move-line+into-signer's-body), the signer's body expresses a referent projection in the same way as the manual articulators of polymorphemic verbs.

We may say that the signer's head and body express a whole entity stem in some verbs of motion and location. While example (7) demonstrates a stative construction, the signer's head and body is used in the same way as the manual articulator of a whole entity stem in a motion verb, e.g. when the signer imitates a child looking out from a hideout represented by her hands.

The use of the signer's head and body with polymorphemic verbs is related to shifted reference, shifted attribution of expressive elements, and shifted locus (II.5), and to marking for a specific point of view in agreement verbs (III.6.3 The many uses of the c-form). The signer uses her own body and her own facial expression to represent the body or facial expression of a personifiable entity. Pronominal reference to a person other than the signer by means of the pronoun 1.p is only possible in reported speech; but shifted attribution of expressive elements, shifted locus, marking for a specific point of view, and the use of the signer's head and body to express a referent projection in constructions with polymorphemic verbs is possible also in nonquoted signing.

The use of the signer's head and body to express a whole entity stem and constructions with shifted attribution of expressive elements resembles mime, but there are important differences. When the signer's head and body are used to express a referent projection, her head and body represent one entity while at the same time her hand may represent another entity as the manual articulator of a verb. In example (7), the signer's body represents the signer in another situation than the context of utterance, while the articulator of the verb that she articulates with her right hand in Index-Pm+(right+move-line+into-signer's-body)+(orientation-change:fall) represents the other basketball player. The simultaneous use of the signer's head and body for one referent and her hand in a verb for another is impossible in mime. Moreover, the sender locus may be used for one referent while at the same time her face and body posture express another referent's feelings or attitude (see Ill. 25b).[5]

In III.6.3 The many uses of the *c*-form, I showed how the signer's body encodes agentivity in relation to agreement verbs, but in constructions where the signer's head and body represent one entity and the manual articulator of a polymorphemic verb another entity, the actor or agent is encoded with the manual articulator and the patient or backgrounded entity is encoded with the head and body. By contrast to constructions with two manual articulators representing two different entities, constructions with the signer's head and body expressing a referent projection and the hand representing another entity encode the point of view of the patient or spectator. Such constructions can be seen as an avenue to the development of marking for a specific point of view in agreement verbs where the sender locus can be used for a non-first person P/IO argument.

The distribution of the different constructions over generations of signers indicates, however, that the point-of-view marker only developed after the emergence of first person P/IO argument agreement (see III.6.3 The many uses of the *c*-form). While many elderly people do not use agreement verbs with first person P/IO agreement or the *c*-form for a non-first person P/IO argument (the point-of-view marker), they do use their head and body as referent projections in constructions with polymorphemic verbs also for a non-first person patient referent. Moreover, the use of the *c*-form as a first person P/IO agreement marker is much more widespread than the use of the same form as a point-of-view marker for a non-first person P/IO argument. That is, the point-of-view marker did not develop directly from constructions with polymorphemic verbs and the signer's head and body used as a referent projection, but only after the emergence of the first person P/IO agreement marker.

---

5 At a workshop in Hamburg, November 1987, Regina Leven presented a videotaped story in German Sign Language in which a signer described a situation where the protagonist was surrounded by mocking children. The signer held her body very rigid with her arms stretched along the sides of her body in a position imitating the frightened child in the middle of the group. At the same time, she moved her head and eyes from one side to the other while laughing. It was as if she meant to indicate simultaneously the frightened child by her body posture *and* the laughing children by her facial expression and her gaze indicating the circle of children. Danish deaf informants reject the example as impossible in Danish Sign Language, and I have never seen an example in Danish Sign Language of "separating" the facial expression and the body posture. Both are articulators of expressive elements and the expressive elements may be attributed to either the signer or another referent; they cannot be "distributed" to two referents.

The form of simultaneous verbs

Constructions with simultaneous polymorphemic verbs tend to be formally restricted so that they resemble two-handed signs in some ways. The two most frequent combinations of simultaneous polymorphemic verbs are: 1) one is a backgrounded verb with a *hold* morpheme, the other combines with a movement morpheme other than *hold*; and 2) both verbs combine with the same movement morpheme. Such combinations of polymorphemic verbs can be subsumed under the Symmetry Condition formulated by Battison (1978) as a morpheme structure constraint on two-handed signs in ASL:

> The Symmetry Condition states that (a) if both hands of a sign move independently during its articulation, then (b) both hands must be specified for the same location, the same handshape, the same movement (whether performed simultaneously or in alternation), and the specifications for orientation must be either symmetrical or identical.
> "Same location" in this case means either (a) the physically identical location – both hands are actually in the same area; or (b) the hands are in mirror-image locations on either side of the line of bilateral symmetry. (Battison 1978, 33)

But there are differences between constructions with two polymorphemic verbs and two-handed lexemes. Two-handed signs where one hand is active and the other is passive only have a very limited number of handshapes in the passive hand; constructions with simultaneous polymorphemic verbs allow other types of handshapes in the stationary hand, e.g. the handshape of 1-Pm (Ill. 59). Moreover, a stationary hand in a two-handed sign serves as a place of articulation for the activity of the other hand, i.e. there is some sort of contact between the hands during the sign production. That is not necessarily the case in a construction with two simultaneous polymorphemic verbs. Moreover, polymorphemic verbs have sequences of movements that are not allowed in nonpolymorphemic signs. In the basketball example, the signer describes the same situation twice, using the two constructions repeated here as (8) and (9):

```
(8)   right:   AT GOAL/       DEFEND                       1-Pm+
      left:                1.p         1.p 1-Pm+(hold+c)+(move-

      right:   (near-r.shoulder+move-line+forward)+(hold)----
      left:    line+forward)+---------------------(move-arc+

      right:   ------------------(move-line+into-1.hand) / ...
      left:    forward-of-r.hand)+(hold)------------------

      At the goal, when I'm in the defence and I see someone moving
      forward and I pursue him and overtake him and he bumps into me...


(9)   right:   IF 1.p SIMULTANEOUSLY 1+Pm+(right+move-line+
      left:                            1+Pm+(left+move-line+-

      right:   into-1.hand)...
      left:    into-r.hand)

      If we bump into each other both running...
```

The two verbs in (9) are expressed by the same handshape and the same, symmetrical movement, which makes the construction indistinguishable from a two-handed sign.[6] In (8), the two hands express locative configurations that cannot be expressed by a nonpolymorphemic verb in relation to another verb of the same kind or in relation to a locus.

Spatial morphemes
The question is now what locative relations can be expressed by polymorphemic verbs in constructions that involve another polymorphemic verb, a locus, or neither. In the description of the first verbs of the basketball example (see (8) here), we need to talk about spatial morphemes, even though the movement is not related to another polymorphemic verb or a locus. The forward movement of the hands is described as *forward* in relation to both the orientation of the articulators, which have inherent orientation determined by the stem, and in relation to the signer.

Some of the most commonly expressed locative relations are:

distance: Apart from *contact*, it is not yet clear how many distinct distances can be expressed. Absolute distance is inferred from contextual factors. In the basketball example, the signer uses the stem 1-Pm in verbs to describe two players in competition; she holds her hands about a hand's breadth apart. In other cases where the same stem is used for people going for a walk together, the hands are very close, but the distance between the walkers may be greater than the distance between two basketball players running toward a goal. Here, I concentrate on the expression of contact.[7]

In stative constructions with two polymorphemic verbs, *contact* is expressed by placing the hands close to each other. Some signers do use physical contact between the articulators in asymmetric constructions, especially with Tree-Pm and Ground-Pm in a backgrounded verb combined with some whole entity stems in a motion verb (for instance, in a sentence meaning 'The monkeys climbed the tree'). On the whole, however, signers avoid physical contact between the articulators of different stems and between all articulators in stative constructions (see *Contact between articulators* in III.8.5 Categories of stems in polymorphemic verbs).

In constructions with two polymorphemic verbs, where one verb is background-

---

6 Brennan describes the derivation of some signs from 'classifier forms' as simultaneous compounding in British Sign Language and states that the 'movement component of the sign articulated by the left hand is usually eliminated' (1990a, 211). Simultaneous compounds correspond to constructions with two simultaneous polymorphemic verbs in which one has the movement morpheme *hold*. Lexical forms corresponding to constructions with two simultaneous polymorphemic verbs in which both verbs have the same movement morpheme are seldom recognised as compounds.

7 Since distance concerns the relationship between two entities, both of which are represented by the stems of polymorphemic verbs or loci, there is a descriptive problem here: to which expression does the specification of distance belong? Often the distance information will appear from information about the articulators' positions in relation to the signer's body, but this information may be independently relevant. I have not solved these problems of morphological description and the transcription of spatial information with polymorphemic verbs should be regarded as ad hoc.

ed and the other verb includes a motion morpheme, the more commonly seen movements of the hand are toward, away from, or around the stationary hand. One hand's movement around the other stationary hand articulates *move-arc*, which can be expressed by arc movements of different sizes. The unmarked starting point of the articulator is near the signer, which is also the starting point when the signer identifies with one of the referents.

Just as physical proximity in the signing space implies contact, so movement of one hand toward another hand or in the direction of a locus implies that the motion described ends at the goal. What matters with movement morphemes expressing motion toward an entity is not the exact physical distance between the hands when the construction finishes. Unless the movement is marked (e.g. by being interrupted by an occurrence of *loc*, 'move to a certain point in relation to the other entity'), it implies motion all the way to the goal. This means that if a locus or the articulator of another polymorphemic verb is specified in relation to *move-line, move-arc*, or *loc* without a spatial morpheme such as *into*, the construction is understood as meaning 'move to and reach' in the case of *move-line* and *move-arc* and 'having contact with' or 'being in a certain position' in the case of *loc*. If *move-line* or *move-arc* combine with a manner morpheme, they do not necessarily denote motion to the goal. For instance, 1-Pm articulated by both hands can be combined with a manner morpheme expressing intensity and strain ('try to catch up with'). If the expression of manner disappears simultaneously with the moving hand approaching the hand articulating the *hold*-morpheme, the goal has been reached. Otherwise, the motion was not all the way to the goal.

into: is used for events in which two entities move into momentary contact ('bump into'). It may be expressed by physical contact between the hands or the hand and the signer's body as seen in the basketball example of III.8.1, or by one articulator being moved close to another articulator and then in the opposite direction ("rebound") without touching the other articulator.

enclosure: A few stems, Cylindrical-entity-Pm, Boat-Pm, and some extension stems with extension morphemes denoting containers, can be used in backgrounded constructions with, for instance, General-entity-Pm in a foregrounded verb to express enclosure ('Something is in or moves into the glass, boat, cave').

The spatial behaviour of polymorphemic verbs in relation to loci without another, simultaneous polymorphemic verb, differs somewhat from the situation when there is another polymorphemic verb. I have already pointed out that verbs with *loc* and a locus maker (including the marker of the sender locus) without another polymorphemic verb are ambiguous between 'two entities or an entity and a location are in contact in a particular way' and 'one entity is located somewhere'. That is, the locus may already represent another entity or a location, and the statement is about a particular relation between the first and the second referent; or the locus may represent one referent only. The difference between the manual articulators of polymorphemic verbs and the directions of loci in this respect is due to the difference in their visibility, mentioned in *Referent projections* above. The manual articulators unambiguously represent another referent. A polymorphemic verb with a morpheme expressed by movement away from the signer's body is also ambiguous between 'an entity moves from the holder of the point of view' and 'the holder of the point of view moves somewhere'. In the first interpretation, the sender locus represents another entity than the moving entity; in the second, it represents the starting point of the moving entity.

An entity's motion and location must also be determined in relation to the vertical dimension and two horizontal dimensions. There are two interpretations of the horizontal axes, either a 'quasi-deictic' interpretation with reference to an observer's field of vision or an interpretation in relationship to the inherent orientation of the entity (Leech 1969, 167-168).

In Danish Sign Language, the signer can take on another being's point of view and describe the scene as she would see it if she were in that being's position. To understand such a message, the receiver must "see" the description from the sender's point of view: what the receiver, if he is face to face with the sender, sees as 'to the right of' means 'to the left of'.[8]

Oléron (1978, 124-125) describes a source of some confusion in what he calls 'le langage gestuel des sourds' (L.G.S.) in France. The meanings 'in front of' and 'behind' can be expressed in three ways in L.G.S. One of them is by indicating the area either in front of or behind the signer's body; the other two ways make use of the relations between the two hands. In what Oléron calls *le code symbolique*, one hand is placed a little outside the body with the palm facing the signer, the other hand moves forward from the hand (i.e. away from the signer) for 'in front of', and back toward the signer for 'behind'. In the other expression, *le code mimique*, the hands are placed in such a way that the hand closer to the signer's body represents the entity that is 'in front of' the other entity. The two French "codes" are contradictory: in *le code symbolique*, the hand closest to the signer represents the entity 'behind' the other; in *le code mimique*, the hand closest to the signer represents the entity that is 'in front of' the other. In Danish Sign Language, a description in terms of *le code mimique* is very common, especially in narration. An alternative strategy was found in a study of some deaf children's description of drawings (Kjær Sørensen & Hansen 1976): the deaf children of deaf parents used a linearisation rule, i.e. they mentioned first the items that were closest to the picture's foreground.

In spoken languages, there are two ways of expressing locative relations. Clark (1973) describes the English use of *in front of* and *behind* in relation to entities

---

8 Lucas and Valli (1990) have found that in ASL a number of constructions with what I call polymorphemic verbs can be signed either at 'the general level' (i.e. chest level) or at eye level. The difference does not reflect a height difference in the situation described. Rather, eye level represents what Lucas and Valli call 'the signer's perspective' such that there is a difference between, for instance, (in Lucas and Valli's transcription) TWO-PEOPLE-BE-SEATED-IN-CAR (at the general level) and PERSON-BE-SEATED-WITH-BACK-TO-ME (at eye level). Within the two levels, height differences reflect height levels in the situations described. A train seen from a hill is described by a verb at waist level, but this is still 'the signer's perspective' and not 'the general level', since it appears from the context that the train was seen from above. It is still uncertain whether the height difference is used in a similar way in Danish Sign Language.

without an inherent orientation as based on 'the canonical encounter', i.e. the situation where two human beings are face to face. The relations of this situation are projected onto the situation in which there are two entities at different distances on a line from the observer's front. If the observer perceives the most distant entity as the equivalent of a human being in a face-to-face situation, the entity between the two is 'in front of' the entity farthest away. This strategy of expressing relations between entities without an inherent front and back is the 'ego-opposed' strategy (Hill 1975; Fillmore 1982, 41; see also here II.3.2 A comparison with time lines in spoken languages, and II.6.3 Person, place, and shifters). It contrasts with the 'ego-aligned' strategy, which is also found in some spoken languages, e.g. Hausa (Hill 1975). The 'ego-aligned' strategy is based on a perception of the observer and the entities as placed on a line with everyone facing the same way as the observer and the observer at the back end of the line. If the observer and the entities A and B are placed on a line with B farther from the observer than A, then the 'ego-opposed' strategy results in a description of A as *in front of* B (B is "facing" the observer) and the 'ego-aligned' strategy results in a description of A as *behind* B (B is "facing away from" the observer) (see Fig. 14).

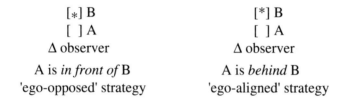

Fig. 14. The 'ego-opposed' and the 'ego-aligned' strategies of assigning front and back to entities without an inherent front-back orientation (The asterisk indicates which side is interpreted as B's "front".)

In signed languages, the hands may represent the referents, so the relationship between the three entities, the observer, A, and B, will become immediately clear from the way the hands are placed in relation to the signer's body: the hand representing A will be closer to the signer's body than the hand representing B. There is no need to impose an orientation on the entities whether they have an inherent orientation or not. Therefore, the signed language strategy can appropriately be described by Oléron's term *code mimique*. The strategy does not impose an orientation on entities without an inherent front-back orientation. What is at issue in signed languages, however, is whether the scene is described from the signer's point of view or from the receiver's point of view.

Spoken French uses an 'ego-opposed' strategy, which means that the relationship between the observer, A, and B depicted in Fig. 14 is described as *A est devant B* ('A is in front of B'). In what Oléron calls *le code symbolique* in L.G.S., the spoken French sentence *A est devant B* is translated into L.G.S. by means of a sign in which the strong hand is moved forward from the weak hand, i.e. away from the signer. This sign can be interpreted as rendering the French symbol meaning 'in front of' in accordance with the 'ego-aligned' strategy. If the direction away from the weak hand and from the signer represents 'in front of', the weak hand must be interpreted as "facing" away from the signer, i.e. the signer is at the back of a line consisting of the signer, the weak hand, and the strong hand with the strong hand at the front. The reason for the confusion in L.G.S. is, therefore, that the French words use the 'ego-opposed' strategy while the symbolic signs use the 'ego-aligned' strategy.

It may seem puzzling at first that the symbolic signs use the 'ego-aligned' strategy when the French words must be interpreted in accordance with the 'ego-opposed' strategy. The reason is probably that the 'ego-aligned' strategy is quite common in signing to express what can be called an internal point of view of a situation. When a native signer of Danish Sign Language is asked to describe a picture, she usually describes it as she sees it: the front of the picture is described as what is closest to the signer. This is the 'ego-opposed' strategy and what could be called the external point of view. But a description of a situation as a participant in the situation would see it, i.e. an internal point of view, is also quite common in signing: from an internal point of view, a person in a car or a queue is described with the car and the queue facing the same way as the signer. Such a description is 'ego-aligned' or rather 'alter-opposed' in the sense that the queue and the car are described as facing the receiver. The neutral, unmarked orientation of the articulator of stems with an inherent orientation is also with the side representing the front of the entity facing the receiver and its back turned to the signer (see below). When the French *A est devant B* ('A is in front of B') is translated by a sign in which the strong hand moves forward from the weak hand so that the strong hand represents the Figure A and the weak hand the Ground B, the relationship between A and B is described as seen from the receiver: the receiver, A, and B are on a line with A between the receiver and B. The choice in signing is thus between describing something as seen from the sender (corresponding to the 'ego-opposed' strategy) or from the receiver (the 'ego-aligned' or 'alter-opposed' strategy).

Leech (1969, 182) points out that in English prepositions there is a distinction between point of observation and point of orientation. The sentence *The cottage is behind the tree* implies that the tree is visible and that the cottage is hidden from view by it, while there is no such inference in *The cottage is beyond the tree*. That is, *behind* implies a point of observation, *beyond* merely a point of orientation. There is not an exact parallel to this in Danish Sign Language, but a difference between what is visible and what is hidden is relevant for the choice of stem: when an entity is behind something, hidden from the observer's view, the stem General-entity-Pm (with an index hand) is used of the hidden entity, and not any more special stem such as Animal-Pm or Car-Pm.

The articulators of some stems in polymorphemic verbs have an inherent orientation reflecting the orientation of the entity involved in the state or motion. As described in III.8.4 Movement morphemes in polymorphemic verbs, and III.8.5 Categories of stems in polymorphemic verbs, some of the stems with an inherent orientation also have a lexical neutral orientation, which determines whether the stem takes an orientation-changing morpheme to describe states of unusual orientations ('the car was lying upside down'). The inherent orientation denoted by some stems combined with the iconic expression of locative relations means that, in Danish Sign Language, there are no ambiguous sentences like the English *The man is in front of the car*. The sentence means either 'The man is ahead of the car's front' (inherent orientation) or 'The man is between the car and me' (observer's point of view). In Danish Sign Language, a backgrounded verb with the stem Car-Pm describes the car's orientation in relation to the holder of the point of view. When the verb with the stem V-Pm and the movement morpheme *loc* ('(the man) stands') is articulated in the signing space, it is necessarily related both to the articulator of the backgrounded verb (Car-Pm+(hold)) and to the signer. That is, the two verbs can express such meanings as 'The car is parked with its side to me and its front facing right in relation to me, and the man is ahead of the car's front (i.e. to the right of the car in relation to me)' (Ill. 77a) and 'The car is parked with its front toward me, and the man is ahead of the car's front (i.e. in front of the car in relation to me)' (Ill. 77b). In stative verbs, the orientation must be specified in relation to the three spatial axes, in nonstative verbs in relation to the direction of the movement, which must then be specified in its turn.

As mentioned earlier, there is a neutral use of stems with an inherent orientation in relation to the vertical and the horizontal axes: the stems are used with the side of the articulators representing the backside of the entities facing the signer at chest level ('ego-aligned' or 'alter-opposed' strategy). The stem V-Pm has an inherent orientation where the back of the hand represents the front of a human being, but V-Pm+(loc+right-of-l.hand+distance-neutral) (Ill. 77a) means that the man was standing next to the car, no matter his orientation in relation to the point of view.

Changes in the frame of reference

As polymorphemic verbs express motion by movement in the signing space, it might be expected that such verbs change the frame of reference. Example (10) from ASL shows what Padden (1988b, 185ff.) calls locus shifting in certain two-sentence sequences. To avoid confusion with the concept *shifted locus*, I prefer to talk about a change in the frame of reference imposed by a polymorphemic verb. One locus is expressed in the first pronoun ($_i$INDEX) and the initial position of the articulator of the verb ($_i$CL:V-WALK-TO$_j$); another locus is expressed by the final position of the articulator of the verb and in the second pronoun ($_j$INDEX), which is coreferential with the first pronoun. (Example (10) = Padden's example (43) (ibid., 188); in the original, the subscript on the second pronoun of the translation is left out by mistake.)

(10) MAN $_i$INDEX GET-UP, $_i$CL:V-WALK-TO$_j$. $_j$INDEX SEEM DEPRESSED.
      The man$_i$ got up and walked away. He$_i$ seemed depressed.

Examples from Danish Sign Language show that in this language, changes in the frame of reference as a result of polymorphemic verbs of motion depend on discourse factors as well as syntactic factors (see also Padden 1988b, 190, 1988a,

262-263). In a monologue where a signer explains how a neighbour helped her get her car started, the signer first uses the locus sideward-left of her neighbour; but when she uses a polymorphemic verb with Car-Pm (he drove his car around the corner), she switches to using the locus sideward-right for the man, i.e. there is a change in the frame of reference. A counterexample to this is an example from a monologue in which a signer says about a friend that he went over to inspect a hotel room, but found that he did not like it, so he came to her to ask her if they could change rooms. When the signer introduces her friend, she uses the locus forward-sideward-right for him. Then she uses a polymorphemic verb with V-Pm about his going to inspect the room. She uses the locus forward-sideward-left for the room, and the polymorphemic verb with V-Pm includes a locus marker for this locus. But when the signer explains that her friend did not like the room, she refers to him by PRON+fsr, i.e. she returns to using the locus forward-sideward-right for him. The frame of reference has not changed as a consequence of her using the polymorphemic verb describing the man's going to the room represented by the locus forward-sideward-left.[9]

The example shows that discourse factors influence whether a polymorphemic verb entails a change in the frame of reference or not. When the signer has said that her friend went to inspect the room, she introduces another man who is relevant to the hotel room and for that reason is represented by the same locus as the room (i.e. the locus forward-sideward-left). To keep the two men apart, her friend and the man associated with the hotel room, the signer keeps referring to her friend by means of the locus forward-sideward-right. Moreover, what she says about her friend is that he does not like the room, and this is true whether he is in the room or not. That is, there is no reason to associate him with the room at that point in the discourse.

When the signer goes on to saying that her friend came up to her, she uses a verb in which the articulator starts at a point outside her centre (*f*) and moves toward her, while at the end of the preceding sentence she refers to her friend by PRON+fsr. Here we see a change in the frame of reference which is motivated by a change in point of view. When the signer talks about the hotel room, she is not herself part of the story until the point where she says that her friend came to ask her if they could change rooms. At that point, she introduces herself by a verb with a marker for the sender locus (neu+APPROACH+c ('He came up to me')). She describes a new situation and introduces a new point of view, herself. From her point of view, her friend approached her, not from the side as would have been implied if the articulator had started on her right, but from whatever direction was appropriate in the given location (movement from the direction forward toward the signer is neutral). Moreover, the identity of the person approaching the signer was clear, since the preceding sentence was about this person. That is, the frame of reference depends at any given

---

9 Padden defines locus shifting as restricted to 'certain two-sentence sequences' (1988b, 187). The examples from Danish Sign Language do not fulfil this condition: in the hotel room example there are some sentences between the polymorphemic verb and the first following pronominal reference to the man; in the car example (with a change in the frame of reference), there is a sentence between the polymorphemic verb and the first pronominal reference to the man. A construction with a pronoun in the second clause as in the ASL example is, however, unlikely to appear in a natural context in Danish Sign Language.

moment on its use for reference-tracking and the need to distinguish referents and on the signer's wish to express a particular point of view.

Scale differences

The articulator of many handle stems represents a hand manipulating an entity iconically, while the articulator of whole entity stems represents an entity in its entirety. Apparently there is a difference in *scale* between verbs with the two kinds of stems (see Supalla 1982, 45-50; Schick 1990). Therefore, it might be expected that the signer's head and body could only be used to express a referent projection in constructions with polymorphemic verbs having handle stems whose articulator is the same scale as the signer's body. The movement of a verb with a whole entity stem can represent motion of a few inches, some yards, or thousands of miles, depending on the stem (Insect-Pm vs. Car-Pm vs. Aeroplane-Pm), and on contextual cues. Since the hand represents a hand in many handle stems, however, the movement of a verb with a handle stem might be expected to reflect the length of the motion described. These expectations are not fulfilled. It is indeed possible to use the signer's body to express a referent projection in relation to a verb with a whole entity stem. The whole entity stem Index-Pm in example (7) of the basketball player bumping into the signer is a case in point. Moreover, it is possible to use a verb with a handle stem of motion for a length which is disproportionate to the size of the articulator of the verb. A signer described the preparations for a birthday party and explained that she was going to borrow a friend's kitchen, but that she would bring everything herself. She used the verb Handle-three-dimensional-entity-Pm+(c+move-line+loc+fl) ('We would bring everything there'); the distance from the signer's body to the end position of the verb's movement represented a much larger distance.

The choice between a verb with a whole entity stem and a verb with a handle stem is determined by what the signer is talking about. That is, signers do not generally have a choice between describing something in one scale or the other.[10] Like handle stems, limb stems are iconically at "the body scale", and signers can choose to represent some situations by means of a verb with a limb stem rather than a verb with a whole entity stem. Animal-Pm, for instance, is a whole entity stem (Ill. 70) which can be used in a verb about a stalking cat; but if the signer wants to describe the cat's manner of stalking (e.g. like the king of the animals), she may use a verb with a limb stem iconically representing the cat's forelimbs and paws. Signers often switch back and forth between verbs with whole entity stems and verbs with handle stems or limb stems to describe different aspects of a motion event (see also Supalla 1990). Verbs with handle stems and limb stems are said to make the style more lively.

Point of view

The following example demonstrates the interaction of differences in scale, shifts in attribution of expressive elements, and spatial point of view, i.e. shifted locus in

---

10 Baker and Cokely (1980, 319-321) show how some stems (in their terminology: classifiers) in ASL can be used to describe a scale difference: columns seen from different distances appear like sticks or like solid cylinders. A similar possibility exists in Danish Sign Language.

polymorphemic verbs. A signer described how one of her friends, Ole, was skiing down a hill when he suddenly saw an old lady crossing the track. The signer first used a verb with a handle stem about her friend holding the ski poles in the position when he was about to set off (Ill. 78a). Then she switched to a verb with the stem V-Pm and a downward movement with small zigzags (Ill. 78b): a shift from "the body scale" (holding the ski sticks) to "the whole entity scale" (running down the slope described by a verb with V-Pm). The point of view remained that of Ole, as the movement of the verb with V-Pm started near the signer's body. Both verbs were accompanied by an intense facial expression and the signer's gaze was directed at a point somewhere forward and down. That is, both verbs were constructed with shifted attribution of expressive elements and an imitation of the non-first person's gaze direction (shifted locus) in spite of the scale difference. Then the signer signed UNFORTUNATE with her left hand in a construction with the verb with V-Pm backgrounded (i.e. the verb had the *hold* morpheme in this section). She went on to a rhetorical question (WHAT) and began an answer to this question: OLD WOMAN. While signing UNFORTUNATE / WHAT / OLD WOMAN ('But alas! What happened? An old woman ...'), she had eye contact with the receiver (the narrator's point of view). Then she used a verb with the whole entity stem Index-Pm to describe the woman's motion across the track (Ill. 78c). During this sign, the signer's face expressed worried caution and she stooped. That is, the expressive elements were shifted to the old woman (an old woman skiing cautiously), but the spatial morphemes of the verb were appropriate for Ole's point of view (the articulator of Index-Pm moved from right to left, i.e. '(An old woman) crossed the track' seen from Ole's point of view), which means the sender locus was shifted to Ole. Then the signer signed the name of her friend, OLE, followed by a verb with the handle stem used for the ski poles and the *hold* morpheme while opening her mouth as if screaming in terror ('Ole screamed out while rushing down') (Ill. 78d). The verb with the handle stem and the signer's face express both Ole's point of view and his emotions. The verb with the *hold* morpheme is backgrounded and expresses presupposed information (Ole was skiing); what is asserted is that Ole screamed.

In summary, the example shows:
— how the signer switches between focusing on her friend (the verb with the handle stem about holding the ski poles and the verb with the whole entity stem V-Pm) and focusing on the woman (the verb with the whole entity stem Index-Pm about the woman crossing the track);
— how she switches between Ole's point of view and the narrator's point of view;
— how she uses differences in scale (the verb with the handle stem and the verb with V-Pm of Ole) to describe Ole's actions in two ways with the verb with the handle stem making the style more lively.

The example also shows that the signer can shift the expressive elements to one referent while concurrently expressing the point of view of somebody else by shifting her locus to that referent. The woman's motion is described as seen from the top of the hill (a verb with Index-Pm from right to left), i.e. Ole's point of view, but the expressive elements, the signer's face and body posture, signal the woman's state. It seems that if an agent referent is shifted to the sender locus, the expressive elements should be attributed to that referent. In contrast, if a patient or spectator referent is shifted to the sender locus, the attribution of the expressive elements is ambiguous; they may be attributed either to the same referent as represented by the sender locus or to the agent referent.

On the basis of his analysis of locative expressions in spoken languages, Talmy (1988) distinguishes four 'imaging systems', i.e. 'complexes in language that organize the structuring and the "viewing" of conceptual material' (194). Two of the 'imaging systems' relate to the points made above about the skiing example. The second 'imaging system', "the deployment of perspective", is described thus: 'Given a structurally schematized scene, this system pertains to how one places one's "mental eyes" to look out upon that scene' (ibid., 194). This strategy is demonstrated by the expression of a specific point of view through shifted locus in Danish Sign Language. Talmy's third imaging system is "distribution of attention": 'Given a schematized scene and a vantage point from which to regard it, this system pertains to the allocation of attention that one can direct differentially over the aspects of the scene' (ibid., 194-195). Included here is the distinction between Figure and Ground. In the skiing example, the vantage point is with one of the two referents, namely the signer's friend; in the extract from the story, the signer's friend does not direct his attention differentially over the scene, but rather focuses on the woman only (the signer looks in the direction that Ole would look). Even though the narrator does not change the point of view to the old woman, she does shift the attention from Ole (the verbs with the handle stem and the verb with V-Pm starting at the narrator's position) to the old woman (the verb with Index-Pm and a movement from the right to the left). This double perspective – Ole is the vantage point, but the attention is shifted to different aspects of the scene – is possible because the narrator can both represent Ole's point of view by representing Ole and thereby direct the receiver's attention to Ole (the verbs with the handle stem and shifted attribution of expressive elements), and she can represent Ole's point of view by focusing on what Ole focuses on thereby directing the receiver's attention to the old woman as seen by Ole.

IV

Space in Danish Sign Language

'Spatial mapping' and 'spatialized syntax'
One of the major themes of this book has been the connection between locative relations and other kinds of semantic-pragmatic relations, in particular the semantic notions behind transitivity. In III.1 Localism and transitivity, it was pointed out that both a localist description of verb-argument relations and a description in terms of transitivity involve the notion of transfer, but that transitivity also involves, among other features, agentivity. Moreover, the difference between the nonpolymorphemic, transitive verb GIVE (Ill. 34) and the polymorphemic, locative verb with the stem Handle-flat-entity-Pm (Ill. 35) in Danish Sign Language demonstrates the communicative and cognitive need to distinguish standard events from processes with focus on details of location, motion, and manner. Here I further illuminate those points by a comparison of polymorphemic and nonpolymorphemic verbs.

Polymorphemic verbs can express spatially such different locative relations as distance, contact, and enclosure, while nonpolymorphemic verbs use space for expressing agreement. Poizner, Klima, and Bellugi (1987, Chapter 8) describe signers' use of space in descriptions of their living quarters and in signing about nonvisual subjects as two different uses of space, 'spatial mapping' and 'spatialized syntax':

> In ASL...descriptions of spatial array and layout use the same horizontal plane of signing space as do ASL nominal and pronominal reference and ASL verb agreement devices. But in spatial description the relations among spatial loci become significant because they represent actual spatial relations topologically. This significance of relations among loci for mapping stands in contrast to the arbitrary, abstract nature of loci established for the syntax and discourse of ASL. (ibid., 206)

That is, Poizner, Klima, and Bellugi find an absolute difference between 'relations among spatial loci' in 'spatial description' and 'the arbitrary, abstract nature of loci established for the syntax and discourse' in ASL. My analysis of Danish Sign Language does not confirm an absolute distinction in that language. In Danish Sign Language, the choice of loci in the frame of reference is not arbitrary, but reflects semantic and pragmatic factors such as canonical location, possession, comparison, geographical location, and empathy (II.2 The frame of reference).

Still, it is true that the movement morphemes and spatial morphemes of polymorphemic verbs differ significantly from the lexically specified movement and the spatially expressed morphemes of nonpolymorphemic verbs. While a prototypical nonpolymorphemic verb has a lexically specified movement, can be modified for distribution, and take at most two spatially expressed morphemes in the form of locus markers that express agreement, a prototypical polymorphemic verb does not have a lexically specified movement. Rather, it can take a number of morphemes that express motion, the state of being located, manner, distribution, and locative relations.

But there are also striking similarities between the two types of verbs. For instance, Liddell (1980, 97) points out that for ASL there is a certain margin in the manifestation of a locus in an agreement verb. He further says that this is not true of what he calls locative predicates. With these there is 'always a physical-locative relationship between the two classifiers' (ibid., 98). Terminology apart, Liddell's last generalisation is also true of Danish Sign Language. But from that it cannot be inferred that there is no margin with respect to the manifestation of loci in polymorphemic verbs. Locative configurations can be expressed by polymorphemic verbs in a sequence, and the only requirement is that they make use of directions from the signer which can easily be identified as the same or different in the signing space, just as in the case of signs showing agreement. That is, there is also a margin in the manifestation of locative relations in polymorphemic verbs.

When polymorphemic verbs are used to describe locative relations that are not easily identifiable on the basis of the spatial morphology of sequential signs and the signs' lexical meanings (e.g. the part-whole relationship between the top of the Christmas tree and the star in example (2) of III.8.6 Polymorphemic verbs and space), a backgrounded construction can be used, i.e. a construction where the articulators as referent projections clearly show the intended locative relation. But otherwise the position and movement in space of the articulator of a polymorphemic verb is as little or as much restricted as the position and movement of the articulator of a nonpolymorphemic verb.

Localism and transitivity
In III.1 Localism and transitivity, it was pointed out that the parallelism between constructions with expressions of motion and location, on the one hand, and transitive verbs, on the other, could be analysed as evidence that transitive constructions basically express locative transfer (the localist hypothesis) or that transitive constructions with locative arguments are metaphorical extensions of true transitive constructions (the transitivist hypothesis). The parallelism between the constructions with nonpolymorphemic and polymorphemic verbs in Danish Sign Language might be taken as evidence for the localist theory. Such a conclusion would, however, be guilty of the iconicity fallacy. The fact that space is used to express transitive relations as well as locative relations does not mean that transitive constructions are calqued on locative constructions. Again and again it has turned out that space is used to express not only locative relations, but other kinds of semantic and pragmatic notions in Danish Sign Language as well. The choice of loci reflects locative relations, but also other kinds of semantic affinity and the signer's attitude to the referents such as empathy and contrast. Backgrounded verbs can express locative configurations, but also discourse coherence. Pragmatic agreement can be agreement with a locative argument, but also with other semantic arguments, in particular agents and patients. It can be used to underline mental distance, parallel focus, and comparison, and to focus the relationship between an advice or an order and the receiver.

Space is used to express both locative and nonlocative relations. The formal and functional differences between polymorphemic and nonpolymorphemic verbs demonstrate that neither can be reduced to the other. There is rather a continuum between using space to express locative notions and using space to express other kinds of semantic and pragmatic notions.

The signer's head and body and the sender locus
Signed languages also have another "unusual" means of expression, i.e. the signer's head and body. In III.6.3 The many uses of the *c*-form, it was pointed out that the notion of agentivity (including agent and experiencer) plays a part in the spatial morphology of agreement verbs. Once it is recognised that many verbs encode the agent/experiencer in the signer's body at the lexical level, the agreement patterns of verbs showing semantic agreement form a coherent system. In polymorphemic verbs, the signer's body may serve the same function at the morphological level. The verb with the stem Handle-flat-entity-Pm (Ill. 35) can be used in relation to two non-first person loci only if it is used either in a clause meaning, 'Somebody saw somebody else transfer a flat entity to a third party' or if the referents are present in the context of utterance. Otherwise, the sender locus is shifted to either the agent argument's referent in a clause meaning '(The holder of the point of view) handed (a tray) to her' (Ill. 35), or the recipient argument's referent in a clause meaning '(The holder of the point of view) was handed (a tray)'.

Still, there is a difference between nonpolymorphemic and polymorphemic verbs in terms of agentivity. Even in varieties of Danish Sign Language that do not include agreement with a first person P/IO argument (i.e. the sender locus is bound to express agentivity in agreement verbs), polymorphemic verbs may occur in constructions where the signer's head and body serve as a referent projection of the goal, patient, or recipient. An example of this would be a clause meaning 'Somebody bumped into him' with a verb in which the articulator of the stem Index-Pm is moved into contact with the signer's own body. Constructions like the one in the skiing example of III.8.6 are also very common: the spectator is encoded in the signer, and the actor is encoded in the manual articulator of a polymorphemic verb with Index-Pm about the old woman crossing the track in front of the holder of the point of view (Ill. 78c). That is, in relation to polymorphemic verbs the signer's head and body and the sender locus are freer to be used for other semantic notions than agent and experiencer compared with the sender locus in relation to agreement verbs.

Process and event verbs
Process verbs describe dynamic situations which are extended in time, while event verbs describe dynamic situations which are momentary (Lyons 1977, 483). The definitions leave open the question of how much time distinguishes *extended in time* from *momentary*. In signed languages, the movement of the hand(s) in space is always extended in time, but that does not mean that the verbs always denote processes. The sign c+GIVE+fr denotes an event even though the movement of the hand is 'extended' in time. By contrast, Handle-flat-entity-Pm can be used in a process verb. As described in III.8.4 Movement morphemes in polymorphemic verbs, *move-line*

and *move-arc* may denote motion to a point, i.e. Handle-flat-entity-Pm+(c+move-line+loc+rightward) (Ill. 35) denotes a process with an end point, while c+GIVE+fr (Ill. 34) denotes an event. With the former verb and not with the latter, it is possible to use a particular mouth pattern (protruding, extended lips) denoting a process that runs smoothly, without problems. The two verbs belong to different points on the continuum between nonpolymorphemic and polymorphemic verbs. But a verb of motion with only *move-line* or *move-arc*, possibly combined with *loc*, (e.g. Handle-flat-entity-Pm+(c+move-line+loc+rightward)) is closer to a double agreement verb that shows agreement with two arguments[1] (e.g. c+GIVE+fr) than to a verb with, for instance, an *analogue*-kind of movement morpheme or with more than one movement morpheme denoting motion.

Hopper and Thompson (1980) find that transitivity correlates highly with punctuality ('the absence of a clear transitional phase between onset and completion' (ibid., 286; see also DeLancey 1987, 60; Taylor 1989, 207, 216)). In this sense the nonpolymorphemic event verb GIVE is higher on the transitivity scale than the polymorphemic process verb with the handle stem. The verb with the handle stem and the motion morphemes *move-line* and *loc* is a process verb, but describes a bounded situation (Talmy 1988, 178-180); in this capacity, it is higher on the transitivity scale than most process verbs with the *analogue*-type of motion morpheme, which often describe unbounded situations.

Lyons links the occurrence of transitive verbs like *kill* in many languages with an interest on the part of human beings 'in the results of our purposive actions and in the effects that our actions have upon patients' (Lyons 1977, 491; see also III.1 Localism and transitivity). Such verbs not only emphasise the results of our purposive actions and their effects, but also denote standard events and are used to describe hosts of real-world situations that may differ in numerous ways. In the same way, many verbs related to polymorphemic verbs, but closer to the nonpolymorphemic end of the continuum denote events and bounded processes of standard value. The movement morphemes *move-line* and *move-arc* can denote bounded processes and can be used to describe motion of many different kinds. Compared to them, the *analogue*-type of movement morphemes and the complex sequences of many movement morphemes, as in the description of a defence in basketball, are much more limited in the kinds of situations they can be used to describe. They denote much more specific types of motion, even though they are also standardised.

Polymorphemic and nonpolymorphemic verbs
Some researchers claim that, except possibly for some 'frozen' forms, all verbs are polymorphemic, some as a result of metaphorical extension as when thought, sight, and sound in verbs of perception are represented by the classifier for long thin object in ASL (Gee & Kegl 1982; see also Kegl & Schley 1986 and other works by Kegl;

---

[1] A similar parallelism exists between polymorphemic verbs with the morpheme *loc* and verbs showing pragmatic agreement.

McDonald 1982, 1983). Kegl, in particular, finds that all verb signs are morphologically complex and that this complexity plays a part at the syntactic level. Others distinguish polymorphemic and nonpolymorphemic verbs in semantic terms (GIVE can be used for all kinds of entities, not just flat entities (see Supalla 1978, 42; McDonald 1983, 39; Johnson & Liddell 1984, 183; Kegl & Schley 1986, 428-429)) or describe the difference syntactically as a difference between verbs agreeing with syntactic arguments and verbs taking locative markers (Padden 1988b; works by Liddell and Liddell & Johnson).

In Danish Sign Language, there is no absolute boundary between the nonpolymorphemic and the polymorphemic verbs and, therefore, no absolute boundary between 'spatialized syntax' and 'spatial mapping'.[2] Nonpolymorphemic verbs reflect their common origin with polymorphemic verbs when the description of the agreement pattern of agreement verbs only becomes coherent if the sender locus is seen as encoding agentivity (agents and experiencers), i.e. if we include a level of meaningful representation in the description of the lexical structure of agreement verbs. But by contrast to the articulators of polymorphemic verbs, the stems of nonpolymorphemic verbs cannot serve as referent projections and cannot combine with all the movement morphemes that may occur in polymorphemic verbs.

The continuum between nonpolymorphemic verbs and different kinds of polymorphemic verbs has at one end plain verbs and verbs that can be modified for agreement, and at the other polymorphemic verbs with especially the *analogue*-type of movement morphemes. Polymorphemic verbs with only the movement morphemes *move-line* and *move-arc* are in between. The continuum reflects a number of features:

— The closer to the nonpolymorphemic end a verb is, the more likely the signer is to have eye contact with the receiver; and the closer the verb is to the polymorphemic end of the continuum, the more likely the signer is to look in the direction of a referent projection;
— The closer a verb is to the nonpolymorphemic end of the continuum, the more likely it is to be accompanied by the mouth pattern of a Danish verb;
— The closer the verb is to the polymorphemic end of the continuum, the more likely it is to include more than one movement morpheme or an *analogue*-type of movement morpheme;
— The closer a construction is to the polymorphemic end of the continuum, the more likely it is that the hands articulate two stems of polymorphemic verbs.

There is, however, a factor that interferes with these tendencies, namely the difference between narrative and non-narrative discourse pointed out by Ahlgren and

---

2 Poizner, Klima, and Bellugi (1987, Chapter 8) found a hemisphere distinction between 'spatial mapping' and 'spatialized syntax' in deaf aphasics. It might seem to speak in favour of a rigid separation of the two uses of space in signing. Their data for 'spatial mapping' were, however, the patients' descriptions of their living quarters, a use of polymorphemic verbs that requires much use of backgrounded constructions to describe precise locative configuration. It is possible that the communicative task that the patients were asked to perform required cognitive skills beyond their capacity.

Bergman (1990; see also Bergman & Dahl in press, and the end of III.8.4 Movement morphemes in polymorphemic verbs). Ahlgren and Bergman found a lexical difference between narrative and non-narrative discourse. They do not specify the verbs which only occur in narrative discourse, but their example indicates that they are verbs closer to the polymorphemic end of the continuum. Other verbs can also occur in narrative contexts and may then have some of the form features typical of this end of the continuum (especially the mouth pattern and the gaze behaviour), without taking on other of the form features. The interaction of particular discourse types with the verb continuum requires further research. It highlights the fact that the relation between prototypical unanalysable lexical verbs and prototypical polymorphemic verbs is multidimensional and that nonprototypical verbs of either kind can deviate from the prototypes along several dimensions.

To conclude the discussion of the localist and the transitivist point of view, the data from Danish Sign Language do not support the view that there is a sharp boundary between locative constructions and other kinds of syntactic constructions. Neither do they support one theory above the other. The continuum between polymorphemic and nonpolymorphemic verbs demonstrates that both types of verbs can be seen as denoting some kind of transfer, but also that the morphosyntax of Danish Sign Language is influenced by other semantic-pragmatic factors than locative relations. These include in particular the distinction between events and processes, the distinction between bounded and unbounded processes, standardisation in the description of situations without attention to details of transfer, agentivity, point of view, focus on the relationship between the predicate and the topic, and other kinds of semantic affinity than locative relations.

Syntactic and morphological analysis
An area that has been touched upon in the course of this book and that requires further research is the syntactic analysis of the clause constituents. Agreement verbs may agree with semantically unambiguous arguments, but the pattern is "disturbed" by the use of the c-form, the marker for the sender locus, as a point-of-view marker. Because the c-form is used to express a specific point of view, it is tempting to see it as a subject marker. But such an analysis disregards the fact that topicality, what the clause is about, is expressed in pragmatic agreement, which involves locus markers other than the c-form. Moreover, an analysis of syntactic arguments in Danish Sign Language must include constituent order and the relationship between clauses with a transitive verb such as ANALYSE and its use in the clause PRON+fr ANALYSE which is ambiguous between 'He analyses (something)' and 'He is analysed'. Another factor is discourse type, as it seems that the ratio of nominals per verb differs significantly between different discourse types, with narrative discourse having many verbs per nominal. It is possible that different kinds of discourse require different kinds of syntactic analysis.

This study has also revealed a need for further analysis of what I describe as the distribution of information over signs at the end of III.8.4 Movement morphemes in polymorphemic verbs. It seems that much information which is usually part of the grammar of spoken languages can show up in several places of the clause or in different places, depending on sign type and possibly other factors of the clause. Just to mention two examples, the proform can carry agreement and other types of modification with a plain sign, and modifications for distribution can apparently occur with signs having different syntactic functions.

The category of locus
In linguistic research, the expression of a grammatical category and its meaning and pragmatic funtion should be kept apart. Tense is a grammatical category which can be expressed by a paradigm of affixes and which may cover meanings such as time in relation to the deictic now, the "time" of timeless utterances (definitions, generic utterances), factivity, and the difference between "stage directions" and utterances that are part of the play in children's role-playing. The category has members such as *present, past,* and *future.* In signed language research, it is often difficult to keep apart the expression of a category and its meaning and pragmatic function. For example, Lillo-Martin and Klima feel a need to make the distinction between form and semantics explicit when they say, 'To keep things clear, it is necessary to point out that, in our terminology, an R-index is part of the vocabulary of *semantics* in ASL as well as in the other languages of the world. On the other hand, an R-locus in ASL is part of the vocabulary of *form*.' (1990, 196 – emphasis in the original). Lillo-Martin and Klima here distinguish *form* and *semantics*, but do not talk about a category.

For Danish Sign Language, I distinguish *locus* as the name of a category from its members, individual loci, and their expression which are directions from the signer's body or points or areas within the signing space as well as the area close to and, with some agreement verbs, on the signer's body. Moreover, I distinguish individual loci and locus markers. A locus marker is a morpheme that is expressed in the way it influences the position and/or orientation of the hand(s) in the production of the sign. Its meaning is the meaning of the locus and the meaning the locus has acquired through association with a specific referent in the discourse. A locus can only be expressed through a locus marker, but it can be thought of as a direction or a point in space that serves as a projection of a referent into space.

The category of locus in Danish Sign Language serves many semantic and pragmatic functions. The 'R-indexing' function of loci, i.e. their reference-tracking function, is the function they fulfil by virtue of the directions or points expressing loci being referent projections. But the category of locus has other semantic and pragmatic functions. It intertwines with the category of person in the pronouns, such that 1.p is the first person pronoun and PRON is the non-first person pronoun, which can distinguish different non-first person referents through loci. The category of locus also expresses time relations (II.3 Time lines) and semantic affinity between referents as shown by the conventions for choosing loci in the frame of reference (II.2 The frame of reference). Moreover, the category of locus expresses pragmatic notions such as high referentiality, empathy, mental distance, comparison, and point of view, and it contributes to establishing discourse coherence and to underlining the relation between a predicate and its topic. Only referents with high referentiality are represented by loci (II.4 Loci and referentiality). The conventions for choosing loci reflect the attitude of the holder of the point of view to the individual referents: referents with which the holder of the point of view empathises are represented by loci close to the signer in contrast to the loci expressed by directions forward, away from the signer. The side-to-side dimension is used for referents of equal importance (II.2 The frame of reference). In pragmatic agreement, locus markers are used to focus the relationship between the clause or predicate and the topic in order to signal contrast, mental distance, and persuasion (III.7 Pragmatic agreement). Finally, in marking for a specific point of view in agreement verbs and in shifted locus, one member of the category of locus, the sender locus, is used to express a specific point of view (III.6.3 The many uses of the *c*-form, and III.8.6 Polymorphemic verbs and space). To fulfil these semantic and pragmatic functions the category of locus is expressed in locus markers in pronouns and determiners, the proform, and as agreement markers and the point-of-view marker in nonpolymorphemic verbs.

Referent projections
I have described loci, the stems of polymorphemic verbs, and the signer's head and body as referent projections. They share some functions, in particular the referential indexing function; but they also differ in ways that make it impossible to reduce them to one. A polymorphemic verb with *loc* and a locus marker is ambiguous between a meaning where it predicates something of the referent represented by the locus and a meaning where it predicates something of another referent in relation to the referent represented by the locus. The same ambiguity is not present when a polymorphemic verb with *loc* is made in relation to the manual articulator of another polymorphemic verb; it can only have the second meaning.

With respect to the spatial morphology of agreement verbs, there is only a lexical difference between the signer's body and the area close to the signer's body; some verbs have contact forms when they show first person P/IO argument agreement. In others, the articulator does not make contact with the signer's body. With polymorphemic verbs, the signer's head and body function in the same way as stems of polymorphemic verbs, i.e. they express meaning unambiguously. The area close to the signer's body, however, expresses the same ambiguity as the directions and points of loci (the verb in Ill. 57 may mean either 'I stand like this' or 'Someone stands close to me'). When the signer's body is used as a referent projection in a backgrounded construction, the expressive elements must be attributed to the same referent. By contrast, when the sender locus is used for another referent than the sender, it may represent the patient or goal referent or the spectator, while the signer's face and body posture express the agent referent's feelings or attitude.

The referential indexing function contributes to what Lehmann describes as keeping the linguistic object, or referent, constant as part of the apprehension of the object (see III.6.2 Agreement features, direction, and domain, and III.8.6 Polymorphemic verbs and space). The means by which signed languages are expressed permit each of the three types of referent projections – stems of polymorphemic verbs, loci, and the signer's head and body – to be present throughout the production of whole predicates and clauses: loci in the form of locus markers in the proform or in pragmatic agreement, and the manual articulators of polymorphemic verbs and the signer's head and body in backgrounded constructions. Their presence enhances the possibility of their contributing to keeping the linguistic object constant.

There is, however, a difference in this respect between the directions of non-first person loci and the stems of polymorphemic verbs, on one side, and on the other, the signer's head and body and the sender locus. The signer's head and body and the sender locus are ambiguous between representing the signer or narrator and a non-first person animate referent. When they represent a non-first person referent, they partly counteract the function of keeping the linguistic object constant as the referent may be represented alternately by a locus different from c or the stem of a polymorphemic verb and by the signer's head and body or the sender locus. However, the signer's gaze, imitating the referent's gaze, and her facial expression and body posture may help to sustain the constancy of the linguistic object. What is gained by the switch from one type of referent projection to the other is the possibility of expressing a specific point of view.

The signer's identification with a referent can be expressed to varying degrees and in different ways. The highest degree of identification is only seen in reported speech without reference to the signer; here the first person pronoun 1.p may refer to the quoted sender, and the sender locus and the expressive elements are shifted to the quoted sender.

Shifted attribution of expressive elements is expressed by the signer's face and head and body posture, as distinct from her head and body orientation. In reported speech, the expressive elements are attributed to the quoted sender, but in nonquoted signing the expressive elements may be attributed to the referent that is represented by the sender locus or to a different referent. That is, it is possible to shift the sender locus to one referent and the expressive elements to another referent. When the signer's head and body are used in a backgrounded construction in relation to a foregrounded polymorphemic verb, the attributive elements must, however, be attributed to the same referent as is represented by the signer's head and body.

Finally, shifted locus means that the signer uses another locus than c for herself or, more often, that the sender locus is used for a referent other than the signer. Shifted locus is a way of singling out a referent different from the signer as the holder of the point of view. The use of the sender locus marker in the A argument cell of agreement verbs is, however, hardly a way of signalling a specific point of view, but rather a result of the encoding of agentivity in the sender locus in many nonpolymorphemic verbs. Identification with another referent to some degree is seen in the signer's use of the marker of the sender locus in the P/IO or goal argument cell of an agreement verb with a non-first person P/IO or goal argument. Shifted locus can also be seen in body and head orientation and gaze direction imitative of the referent's head or body orientation or gaze direction. The sender locus and the signer's head and body are moreover often used for another referent in polymorphemic verbs where the spatial morphology implies that the sender locus or the signer's head and body represent the holder of the point of view.

Linguistic differentiation
In the introduction, I mentioned that signed languages underdifferentiate compared with spoken languages by not distinguishing three or more persons in the pronoun. The analysis of how space is used in Danish Sign Language has shown that there are also areas with a very high degree of differentiation in this language, in particular the stems of polymorphemic verbs, the continuum between polymorphemic and nonpolymorphemic verbs, and the many degrees of identification of the sender with one of the referents. It might be claimed that Danish Sign Language underdifferentiates in its means of expression by using space for so many different functions, but there are formal differences in the uses of space: agreement verbs take agreement markers for semantic agreement and agreement markers for pragmatic agreement in different cells; polymorphemic verbs take spatial morphemes which nonpolymorphemic verbs cannot take; the distribution of the point-of-view marker differs from the distribution of the neutral marker; and so on. The analysis has shown that Danish Sign Language profits from its "unusual" means of expression in its structure. What I have described as referent projections depends totally on the means of expression of signed languages. But otherwise, the semantic-pragmatic functions that the articulatory means of Danish Sign Language serve are well-known from spoken languages.

Appendix A
Signed Language in Denmark

Denmark has about 5 million inhabitants, of whom about 3000 make up the deaf population that uses Danish Sign Language as its primary language. Apart from a few more or less geographically bounded minority languages (Greenlandic, Faroese, and German), Denmark has been linguistically fairly homogeneous for a long period. This means that the majority of deaf Danes come from Danish-speaking families. In recent years, however, Denmark has received an increasing number of immigrants and refugees, which is also reflected in the makeup of the current deaf population.

The first school for deaf children was founded in 1807 by P. A. Castberg, who had visited schools for deaf children in Germany and France. He preferred the sign-based teaching of the French school to the oralism of the Germans and introduced signing into the teaching of deaf children in Denmark. This teaching method continued until the late 1860's when it became more and more common to separate the children into groups according to whether or not they were expected to learn to talk. Children who were expected to learn to talk were taught in spoken Danish; the other children were taught by means of signs. In 1880, the two different teaching methods were confirmed by a law, and the children were sent to different schools: one for deaf children who were expected to learn to talk (the oral teaching method) and one for deaf children who were not expected to learn to talk (the sign-based teaching method). There was furthermore a school for children who had lost their hearing after they had acquired Danish (again, the oral teaching method). In 1880, an international conference of teachers of deaf children in Milan recommended exclusive use of the oralist method, and in Denmark, the recommendation meant that signed language was used even less than before and that deaf teachers and deaf assistants at the schools were dismissed

Since the early 1970's, signed language has spread more and more in the teaching of deaf children in Denmark. Today, the idea of bilingual education is widely accepted and bilingualism in Danish Sign Language and Danish is the official aim of all schools for deaf children as well as of the parents' association (Hansen 1987; Klim et al. 1991). According to a regulation issued by the Ministry of Education, Danish Sign Language, starting in 1992, is a part of the curriculum for all deaf children (Tegnsprog 1991), and in recent years, there has been an increase in the number of deaf teachers of deaf children. There are several kindergartens with groups of deaf children using signed language. The basic school training takes place in schools for the deaf or in special sections for deaf and hard-of-hearing students in schools for hearing children. For vocational and more advanced training, deaf students attend courses with hearing students and are provided with signed language interpreters. For adults, there is a "folk high school" which offers noncredit courses in general and special subjects. Every fortnight, a government-supported organisation distributes videorecorded signed news and background information to all adult deaf users of signed language, free of charge. One of the two Danish TV channels broadcasts signed children's programmes regularly.

Deaf people have a legal right to interpreters only when questioned by the police, in a courtroom, and in consultations with a doctor in a hospital; but local authorities usually provide deaf people with an interpreter for one educational programme, for medical examinations, and for meetings at their (hearing) children's schools. Deaf children and adults have a right to certain technical equipment free of charge, e.g. a hearing aid, a video-recorder, and a telecommunications device for use with the telephone.

The first deaf club was founded in 1866, and there are now eighteen deaf clubs all over the country. The National Association of the Deaf has about 2000 members.

The Ministry of Education started a two-year programme for signed language interpreters in 1986 and, in 1990, a 25-week programme primarily in signed language training for teachers of deaf children. Besides these programmes, shorter courses (nine levels of one week each) exist for parents of deaf children, social workers, kindergarten teachers, and others who are professionally involved with deaf persons. Most of the teaching of signed language is handled by The Centre for Total Communication, an organisation which was founded in 1972 with the aim of spreading information about deaf people and their means of communication. The schools for the deaf also offer courses in Danish Sign Language to parents and professionals.

In some countries, signed language has been given official recognition as deaf people's language. That is not the case in Denmark, and probably never will be, as no language is given official recognition in Denmark. The only way a language is "officially recognised" in Denmark is through specific laws making it part of the curriculum in the schools, the language of the courtrooms, the language of exams in higher education, and the like.

There are two comprehensive books on the history of the teaching of deaf children in Denmark and the history of deaf culture in Denmark, both in Danish: Holm et al. 1983, and Widell 1988.

Appendix B
Guide to the transcriptions

The transcription is based on English glosses for manual signs of Danish Sign Language, supplemented with symbols for nonmanual signals and for modifications of signs. There are a number of alternatives to this tradition of notating signed languages. Phonological analyses of manual signs have resulted in notations of individual signs by means of symbols (Bergman 1977; Stokoe 1978; Brennan, Colville & Lawson 1984); analyses of manual signs as composed of a number of meaningful units have led to two-dimensional notations of a tree-like kind (Kegl 1985, 1986, 1990); and there are various attempts at expressing a linguistic analysis in notational icons or symbols, also on a computer (see the articles in Prillwitz & Vollhaber 1990). The most serious drawback of transcription based on glosses from a spoken language is the risk that it obscures the linguistic structure of the signed language. If a sign is transcribed as GIVE, we tend as readers of the gloss to understand the sign in terms of the English word with respect to word class, meaning, and syntax. Moreover, we tend to see the sign as morphologically simple, but it is a question of debate whether a sign such as GIVE is morphologically simple or complex (see III.6.3 The many uses of the *c*-form, III.8 Polymorphemic verbs, and works by Kegl). The greatest advantage of a transcription based on glosses is that it is fairly intelligible without much training.

The glosses are chosen according to two criteria. If a sign is usually accompanied by the mouth pattern of a Danish word, or if there is an obvious Danish equivalent of the sign in the sense that signers will give the sign as an equivalent of the Danish word, this word is used in transcriptions in Danish. For the transcriptions in English, I have chosen the most obvious English translation of the Danish word, e.g. BIL in a transcription with Danish glosses, CAR in a transcription with English glosses. If a sign does not have a standard mouth pattern corresponding to a Danish word, I have chosen a gloss that is not used for any other sign and that has a mnemonic value, i.e. it is chosen for its meaning. An example is VERY-CURIOUS: the sign is not accompanied by a Danish mouth pattern, and there is already a standard equivalent of the Danish word *nysgerrig* ('curious'). The gloss VERY-CURIOUS does not really cover the meaning of the sign which includes an aspect of 'be eager to', but the gloss is sufficiently close to the sign's meaning to have a mnemonic value.

As signed languages are expressed by a number of simultaneous articulators, the notation makes use of a "score" with horizontal lines where each line represents the activities of an articulator (see the list in Fig. 15). The vertical dimension represents simultaneous activities of the articulators. The number of lines for each articulator can be increased when the articulator is focused in the analysis. It is, for instance, possible to separate out different types of head movements in different lines.

```
body_____
head_____
face_____
eye muscles_____
gaze direction_____
dominant hand_____
nondominant hand_____
mouth_____
```

Fig. 15. The "score" of the transcription system

In the transcriptions used for illustration in this book, I do not use all the lines. Other lines than the line or lines representing the manual signs are only included when the activities of these articulators are relevant to the points made in the text or to a general understanding of the meaning of the example. In some cases a configuration of nonmanual signals is reduced to a single symbol, e.g. *neg* (for negation), and its scope is represented by a line above the glosses for the manual signs.

Manual signs

The manual signs are notated on two lines, with the upper line representing the activities of the signer's dominant hand (in all cases here, the right hand) and the lower line representing the activities of the non-dominant hand. Two-handed signs are either notated as one gloss in the line of the dominant hand or, if the activities of the non-dominant hand are relevant in other parts of the example, as the same gloss in both lines.

`NOT-YET`	If several words are needed for one manual sign, the words are connected by hyphens.
`           DEAF`	A dotted line indicates that the articulator of a manual sign is
`PRON+fr-----`	maintained in the final position of the sign during the other activities of the transcription until the end of the dotted line.
`gesture`	A manual "sign" which native signers regard as a gesture, and not a symbol of Danish Sign Language. The notation `gesture` covers several different gestures.
`Vibely(M)`	The notation of a Mouth-Hand System version of a word or a name (see I.6.2).
`1.p`	A gloss for the first person pronoun (see II.6.3).
`PRON`	A gloss for the nonfirst person pronoun (see II.6.1).
`DET`	A gloss for the determiner (see II.6.1).
`/`	A manually and/or nonmanually marked clause or major constituent boundary. Nonmanual markers are movements of the head and body, eye blink, and changes in facial expression;

	manual markers are especially a prolonged final segment of a sign.
`TRAVEL^GONE`	`^` indicates a compound.
`THIRTY+sl..` `PRON+sl`	Two full stops between the glosses for two signs indicate that either the orientation or the handshape of the second sign is assimilated to the orientation or the handshape of the first sign. This is only notated in the examples when assimilation is discussed in the text.

Modifications of signs are indicated before and after the gloss for the sign with a + between the sign gloss and the symbols of the modifications and between each modification.

`c+ANSWER+fr`	Locus markers are indicated by letter symbols for loci (see I.6.4).
	Agreement with an A argument is notated by a locus symbol before the gloss and P/IO argument agreement by a symbol after the gloss.
`EXPLAIN+p.a.:fsl`	Pragmatic agreement of agreement verbs is notated by `p.a.` before the locus symbol to distinguish pragmatic agreement from semantic agreement with these verbs. With other signs, pragmatic agreement is notated by a locus symbol after the gloss without `p.a.`
`+pl.`	Plural of nouns.
`+pron.`	A pronominalized form of a number sign.
`+multiple`	A modification for distribution (see III.5).
`+redupl.`	Reduplication without displacement of the hand.
`+alt.`	A one-handed sign is made with two hands and the two hands move alternatingly, a special kind of reduplication.
`[+]`	The sign is modified in a way as yet undescribed or not discussed in this book.

The notations of *polymorphemic verbs* consist of a symbol for the stem, e.g. `Car-Pm` (see III.8.5), followed by notations for the morphemes expressed through movement and space (see III.8.4 and III.8.6). One unit of simultaneous morphemes appear within parentheses, e.g. `Car-Pm+(loc+right)`. With a sequence of morphemes expressed through movement (each within parentheses with its simultaneous morphemes expressed spatially), the spatial morpheme indicating the final position of the manual articulator in relation to one movement morpheme is relevant also to the following movement unit, but it is not repeated in the notation. The transcription of the morphemes of polymorphemic verbs is preliminary.

Nonmanual articulators
The behaviour of the individual nonmanual articulators is notated in the lines below and above the lines with the notation for the manual articulators, but only to the extent that this behaviour is relevant to what the example is meant to exemplify here. The behaviour of an articulator goes on until the end of the dotted line following the symbol or until a different symbol is notated.

Symbols of *nonmanual configurations* are underlined and the length of the line indicates the formal and functional scope of the configuration. The formal scope is usually identical with the functional scope, but the signals of the configuration may fade off before its functional scope finishes:

<u> ? </u>	A question configuration. There are several such configurations, but the difference in meaning is not yet clear.
<u> neg </u>	Negation.
<u> t </u>	Topicalization before or, in rare cases, after the clause.
<u> squint </u>	Contraction of the muscles of the eyelids. Indicates that the sender expects the receiver to know the referent, but invites him to signal if it is the case.

Mouth patterns are notated below the line of the nondominant hand:

`stop`	The closest possible translation equivalent in English of a Danish word.
`a`	As close as possible a rendition of a soundless mouth pattern in
`tongue out`	the Latin alphabet, or a description of the mouth pattern.

Gaze directions and *eye behaviour* are notated in the line above the dominant hand:

`+`	Eye contact with the receiver.
`fr`	The symbols used to notate the modifications for loci of manual signs are also used for eye gaze in the direction of a locus.
`*`	The signer imitates the eye gaze of a referent.
`#`	The sender looks away from the receiver without looking in the direction of a locus or imitating the eye gaze of a receiver.
`v`	Eye blink, which is one of the most pervasive signals of a clause or major constituent boundary.

The line above the symbols of eye behaviour is used for the notation of *facial expression* and nonmanual configurations (see above):

`frigthened`	The facial expressions of emotions and attitudes are described in English words.

The movements of the *head* and the *body* are notated in the lines above the line for the facial expression. Most of the notations are immediately understandable.

rot.   Signals that the surface plane of the head or body faces the direction indicated (rot. stands for *rotation*) (e.g. rot.r., i.e. the head or the body faces right).

left   Sideways movement of the body or head without rotation.

References

Ahlgren, Inger. 1984a. Deictic pronouns in Swedish and Swedish sign language. *Scandinavian Working Papers on Bilingualism 3*, 11-19.
Ahlgren, Inger. 1984b. Persondeixis i svenska och i teckenspråk. *Forskning om Teckenspråk XIV*. Stockholm: Stockholms Universitet, Institutionen för lingvistik. 38-51.
Ahlgren, Inger. 1990. Deictic pronouns in Swedish and Swedish Sign Language. In S. Fischer & P. Siple (eds.), 167-174.
Ahlgren, Inger, & Brita Bergman. 1990. Preliminaries on narrative discourse in Swedish Sign Language. In S. Prillwitz & T. Vollhaber (eds.), 257-263.
Allan, Keith. 1977. Classifiers. *Language 53(2)*, 285-311.
Allen, Barbara J., & Donald G. Frantz. 1978. Verb agreement in Southern Tiwa. In J. J. Jaeger et al. (eds.), *Proceedings of the Fourth Annual Meeting of the Berkeley Linguistics Society*. Berkeley, CA: Berkeley Linguistics Society, University of California. 11-17.
Amith, Jonathan D. 1988. The use of directionals with verbs in the Nahuatl of Ameyaltepec, Guerrero. In J. K. Josserand & K. Dakin (eds.), *Smoke and Mist: Mesoamerican Studies in Memory of Thelma D. Sullivan* (BAR International Series 402). 395-421.
Anderson, Arthur J. O., & Charles E. Dibble. 1975. Fray Bernardino de Sahagún: *Florentine Codex: General History of the Things of New Spain: Book 12: The Conquest of Mexico*. Santa Fe, New Mexico: The School of American Research and the University of Utah.
Anderson, Lloyd B. 1982. Universals of aspect and parts of speech: Parallels between signed and spoken languages. In P. Hopper (ed.), *Tense – 3Aspect: Between Semantics and Pragmatics*. Amsterdam: John Benjamins. 91-114.
Anderson, Stephen R., & Edward L. Keenan. 1985. Deixis. In T. Shopen (ed.), 259-308.
Ashton, E. O. 1944. *Swahili Grammar*. London: Longman.
Baker, Charlotte. 1977. Regulators and turn-taking in American Sign Language. In L. Friedman (ed.), 215-236.
Baker, Charlotte, & Dennis Cokely. 1980. *American Sign Language: A Teacher's Resource Text on Grammar and Culture*. Silver Spring, MD: TJ Publishers.
Baker, Charlotte, & Carol A. Padden. 1978. Focusing on the nonmanual components of American Sign Language. In P. Siple (ed.), 27- 57.
Banfield, Ann. 1973. Narrative style and the grammar of direct and indirect speech. *Foundations of Language 10*, 1-39.
Barlow, Michael, & Charles A. Ferguson (eds.). 1988. *Agreement in Natural Language: Approaches, Theories, Descriptions*. Stanford: CSLI.
Barron, Roger. 1982. Das Phänomen Klassifikatorischer Verben. In H. Seiler & C. Lehmann (eds.), *Apprehension: Das sprachliche Erfassen von Gegenständen, Teil I: Bereich und Ordnung der Phänomene*. Tübingen: Gunter Narr. 133-146.
Battison, Robbin. 1978. *Lexical Borrowing in American Sign Language*. Silver Spring, MD: Linstok Press.
Bellugi, Ursula, & Edward S. Klima. 1982. From gesture to sign: Deixis in a visual-gestural language. In R. J. Jarvella & W. Klein (eds.), 297-313.
Bellugi, Ursula, & Don Newkirk. 1981. Formal devices for creating new signs in American Sign Language. *Sign Language Studies 30*, 1-35.
Benveniste, Emile. 1974. Le langage et l'expérience humaine. In E. Benveniste: *Problèmes de linguistique générale II*. Paris: Gallimard. 67-78.

Berenz, Norine, & Lucinda Ferreira Brito. 1990. Pronouns in BCSL and ASL. In W. Edmondson & F. Karlsson (eds.), 26-36.
Bergman, Brita. 1977. *Tecknad svenska*. Lund: LiberLäromedel. (English translation. 1979. *Signed Swedish*. Stockholm: National Swedish Board of Education.)
Bergman, Brita. 1983. Verbs and adjectives: Morphological processes in Swedish Sign Language. In J. Kyle & B. Woll (eds.), 3-9.
Bergman, Brita, & Östen Dahl. In press. Ideophones in sign language? The place of reduplication in the tense-aspect system of Swedish Sign Language. In C. Bache, H. Basbøll, & C. E. Lindberg (eds.), *Tense – Aspect – Modality: New Data – New Approaches*. The Hague: Mouton.
Birch-Rasmussen, Signe. 1982. *Mundhåndsystemet* (with summaries in English, German, and French). København: Døves Center for Total Kommunikation.
Bloomfield, Leonard. 1935. *Language*. London: George Allen & Unwin.
Bos, Heleen. 1990. Person and location marking in SLN: Some implications of a spatially expressed syntactic system. In S. Prillwitz & T. Vollhaber (eds.), 231-246.
Boyes Braem, Penny. 1981. Features of the Handshape in American Sign Language, Ph.D. Dissertation, University of California, Berkeley.
Boyes Braem, Penny, Marie-Louise Fournier, Françoise Rickli, Serena Corazza, Maria-Luisa Franchi, & Virginia Volterra. 1990. A comparison of techniques for expressing semantic roles and locatives in two different sign languages. In W. Edmondson & F. Karlsson (eds.), 114-120.
Brennan, Mary. 1983. Marking time in British Sign Language. In J. Kyle & B. Woll (eds.), 10-31.
Brennan, Mary. 1990a. Productive morphology in British Sign Language: Focus on the role of metaphor. In S. Prillwitz & T. Vollhaber (eds.), 205-228.
Brennan, Mary. 1990b. *Word Formation in BSL*. Stockholm: University of Stockholm.
Brennan, Mary, Martin D. Colville, & Lillian K. Lawson. 1984. *Words in Hand* (second edition). Edinburgh: Moray House College.
Brentari, Diane. 1988. Backwards verbs in ASL: Agreement re-opened. CLS 24(2): *Papers from the Parasession on Agreement in Grammatical Theory*, 16-27. Chicago: Chicago Linguistic Society.
Brentari, Diane. 1992. Review article: Phonological representation in American Sign Language. *Language 68(2)*, 59-74.
Bresnan, Joan, & Sam A. Mchombo. 1987. Topic, pronoun, and agreement in Chichewa. *Language 63(4)*, 741-782.
Bruner, Jerome. 1983. *Child's Talk: Learning to Use Language*. Oxford: Oxford University Press.
Bybee, Joan. 1985a. Diagrammatic iconicity in stem-inflection relations. In J. Haiman (ed.), 11-47.
Bybee, Joan. 1985b. *Morphology: A Study of the Relation Between Meaning and Form*. Amsterdam: John Benjamins.
Bybee, Joan L., & Carol Lynn Moder. 1983. Morphological classes as natural categories. *Language 59(1)*, 251-270.
Cameracanna, Emanuela, & Serena Corazza. 1989. Time lines in Italian Sign Language (L.I.S.). Presented at the Deaf Way conference, Washington, D.C., July.
Castberg, P.A. 1809-1811. *Om Tegn- eller Gebærde-Sproget med Hensyn paa dets Brug af Døvstumme og dets Anvendelighed ved deres Undervisning 1-3*. København.
Chafe, Wallace L. 1976. Givenness, contrastiveness, definiteness, subjects, topics, and point of view. In C. Li (ed.), 25-55.
Chao, Yuen Ren. 1968. *A Grammar of Spoken Chinese*. Berkeley, CA: University of California Press.

Christensen, Dorrit. 1989. Ikke "bare" tunghør. In B. Hansen (ed.), 97-99.
Chung, Sandra, & Alan Timberlake. 1985. Tense, aspect, and mood. In T. Shopen (ed.), 203-258.
Clark, Herbert. 1973. Space, time, semantics, and the child. In T. E. Moore (ed.), 27-63.
Cogen, Cathy. 1977. On three aspects of time expression in American Sign Language. In L. Friedman (ed.), 197-214.
Collins-Ahlgren, Marianne. 1990. Word formation processes in New Zealand Sign Language. In S. Fischer & P. Siple (eds.), 279-312.
Comrie, Bernard. 1976. *Aspect: An Introduction to the Study of Verbal Aspect and Related Problems.* Cambridge: Cambridge University Press.
Comrie, Bernard. 1981. *Language Universals and Linguistic Typology: Syntax and Morphology.* Oxford: Basil Blackwell.
Corazza, Serena. 1990. The morphology of classifier handshapes in Italian Sign Language (LIS). In C. Lucas (ed.), 71-82.
Corbett, Greville G. 1988. Agreement: A partial specification based on Slavonic data. In M. Barlow & C. Ferguson (eds.), 23-53.
Corbett, Greville G. 1991. *Gender.* Cambridge: Cambridge University Press.
Coulmas, Florian (ed.). 1986. *Direct and Indirect Speech.* Berlin: Mouton de Gruyter.
Coulter, Geoffrey R. 1983. A conjoined analysis of American Sign Language relative clauses. *Discourse Processes 6,* 305-318.
Coulter, Geoffrey R. 1990. Emphatic stress in ASL. In S. Fischer & P. Siple (eds.), 109-125.
Craig, Colette. 1986. Introduction. In C. Craig (ed.), 1-10.
Craig, Colette (ed.). 1986. *Noun Classes and Categorization: Proceedings of a Symposium on Categorization and Noun Classification* (Eugene, Oregon, October 1983). Amsterdam: John Benjamins.
Creider, Chet A. 1986. Constituent-gap dependencies in Norwegian: An acceptability study. In D. Sankoff (ed.), *Diversity and Diachrony.* Amsterdam: John Benjamins. 415-424.
Croft, William. 1988. Agreement vs. case marking and direct objects. In M. Barlow & C. Ferguson (eds.), 159-179.
Dahl, Östen. 1981. On the definition of the telic-atelic (bounded-nonbounded) distinction. In P. J. Tedeschi & A. Zaenen (eds.), 79-90.
Dahl, Östen. 1985. *Tense and aspect systems.* Oxford: Basil Blackwell.
DeLancey, Scott. 1987. Transitivity in grammar and cognition. In R. S. Tomlin (ed.), *Coherence and Grounding in Discourse.* Amsterdam: John Benjamins. 53-68.
DeMatteo, Asa. 1977. Visual imagery and visual analogues in American Sign Language. In L. Friedman (ed.), 109-136.
Denny, J. Peter. 1986. The semantic role of noun classifiers. In C. Craig (ed.), 297-308.
DeRoeck, Marijke. In press. A functional typology of speech reports. In E. Engberg-Pedersen, L. Falster Jakobsen, & L. Schack Rasmussen (eds.), *Function and Expression in Functional Grammar.* Berlin: Mouton de Gruyter.
Deuchar, Margaret. 1984. *British Sign Language.* London: Routledge & Kegan Paul.
Dik, Simon C. 1989. *The Theory of Functional Grammar. Part I: The Structure of the Clause.* Dordrecht: Foris Publication.
Dik, Simon, Maria E. Hoffmann, Jan R. de Jong, Sie Ing Djiang, Harry Stroomer, & Lourens de Vries. 1981. On the typology of focus phenomena. In T. Hoekstra, H. van der Hulst, M. Moortgat (eds.), *Perspectives on Functional Grammar.* Dordrecht: Foris Publications. 41-74.

Dixon, R. M. W. 1986. Noun classes and noun classification in typological perspective. In C. Craig (ed.), 105-112.

Dressler, Wolfgang. 1968. *Studien zur verbalen Pluralität: Iterativum, Distributivum, Intensivum in der allgemeinen Grammatik, im Lateinischen und Hethitischen.* Wien: Herman Böhlau.

Ebbinghaus, Horst, & Jens Hessmann. 1990. German words in German Sign Language: Theoretical considerations prompted by an empirical finding. In S. Prillwitz & T. Vollhaber (eds.), 97-112.

Ebert, Karen. 1986. Reported speech in some languages of Nepal. In F. Coulmas (ed.), 145-159.

Edge, VickiLee, & Leora Herrmann. 1977. Verbs and the determination of subject in American Sign Language. In L. Friedman (ed.), 137-179.

Edmondson, William. 1990a. A non-concatenative account of classifier morphology in signed and spoken languages. In S. Prillwitz & T. Vollhaber (eds.), 187-202.

Edmondson, William. 1990b. Segments in signed languages: Do they exist and does it matter? in W. Edmondson & F. Karlson (eds.), 66-74.

Edmondson, W. H., & F. Karlsson (eds.). 1990. *SLR '87: Papers from The Fourth International Symposium on Sign Language Research.* Hamburg: SIGNUM-Press.

Ellenberger, Ruth, & Marcia Steyaert. 1978. A child's representation of action in American Sign Language. In P. Siple (ed.), 261-269.

Engberg-Pedersen, Elisabeth. 1981. Classifiers i dansk tegnsprog. In *Skrifter om Anvendt og Matematisk Lingvistik 8*. København: Institut for Anvendt og Matematisk Lingvistik, Københavns Universitet. 101-111.

Engberg-Pedersen, Elisabeth. 1985. Proformer i dansk tegnsprog. In B. Hansen (ed.), *Tegnsprogsforskning og tegnsprogsbrug.* København: Døves Center for Total Kommunikation. 32-54.

Engberg-Pedersen, Elisabeth. 1988. Skift i brug af hænderne og fastholdelse af tegn (working paper).

Engberg-Pedersen, Elisabeth. 1989. Tegnmodifikation, i samarbejde med Anne Skov Hårdell og Sussi Toft. In B. Hansen (ed.), *Tegn på tegnsprog: Holdninger og kultur.* København: Døves Center for Total Kommunikation. 54-65.

Engberg-Pedersen, Elisabeth. 1990. Pragmatics of nonmanual behaviour in Danish Sign Language. In W. Edmondson & F. Karlsson (eds.), 121-128.

Engberg-Pedersen, Elisabeth. (Forthcoming). Speech Reports in Danish Sign Language.

Engberg-Pedersen, Elisabeth, & Britta Hansen. 1986. Thirty signs from Danish Sign Language. In B. Tervoort (ed.), 209-212.

Engberg-Pedersen, Elisabeth, Britta Hansen, & Ruth Kjær Sørensen. 1981. *Døves tegnsprog: Træk af dansk tegnsprogs grammatik.* Århus: Arkona.

Engberg-Pedersen, Elisabeth, & Annegrethe Pedersen. 1985a. Proforms in Danish Sign Language: Their use in figurative signing. In W. Stokoe & V. Volterra (eds.), 202-209.

Engberg-Pedersen, Elisabeth, & Annegrethe Pedersen. 1985b. *30 tegn fra døves tegnsprog.* København: Døves Center for Total Kommunikation.

Faltz, Leonard M. 1978. On indirect objects in universal syntax. In D. Farkas, W. M. Jacobsen, & K. W. Todrys (eds.), *Papers from the Fourteenth Regional Meeting.* Chicago: Chicago Linguistic Society. 76-87.

Faustrup, Ole. 1980. "Du behøver ikke at bruge tegn til mig...". In B. Hansen (ed.), *Døve børn: Sprog, kultur, identitet.* Døves Center for Total Kommunikation, København. 76-78.

Ferguson, Charles A., & Michael Barlow. 1988. Introduction. In M. Barlow & C. Ferguson (eds.), 1-22.

Ferreira Brito, Lucinda. 1985. A comparative study of signs for time and space in São Paulo and Urubu-Kaapor Sign Language. Presented at the III. International Symposium on Sign Language Research, Rome, June 22-26, 1983. (The handout for the presentation is published in W. Stokoe & V. Volterra 1985, 262-268).
Fillmore, Charles J. 1972. "How to know whether you're coming or going". In K. Hyldgaard-Jensen (ed.), *Linguistik 1971*. Frankfurt: Athenäum. 369-379.
Fillmore, Charles J. 1981. Pragmatics and the description of discourse. In P. Cole (ed.), *Radical Pragmatics*. New York: Academic Press. 143-166.
Fillmore, Charles J. 1982. Towards a descriptive framework for spatial deixis. In R. J. Jarvella & W. Klein (eds.), 31-59.
Fischer, Susan. 1973. Two processes of reduplication in American Sign Language. *Foundations of Language 9*, 469-480.
Fischer, Susan. 1975. Influences on word order change in ASL. In C. N. Li (ed.), *Word Order and Word Order Change*. Austin, Texas: University of Texas Press. 1-25.
Fischer, Susan, & Bonnie Gough. 1978. Verbs in American Sign Language. *Sign Language Studies 18*, 17-48. (Reprinted in W. Stokoe (ed.) 1980, 149-179.)
Fischer, Susan, & Wynne Janis. 1990. Verb sandwiches in American Sign Language. In S. Prillwitz & T. Vollhaber (eds.), 279-293.
Fischer, Susan, & Patricia Siple (eds.) 1990. *Theoretical Issues in Sign Language Research, Volume 1: Linguistics*. Chicago: Chicago University Press.
Foley, William A., & Robert D. Van Valin. 1984. *Functional Syntax and Universal Grammar*. Cambridge: Cambridge University Press.
Fortescue, Michael. 1990. Aspect and superaspect in Koyukon: An application of the functional grammar model to a polysynthetic language. In L. Falster Jakobsen (ed.), *Functional Grammar in Denmark*. Copenhagen: University of Copenhagen, Department of English. 100-105.
Fortescue, Michael. Forthcoming. Polysynthetic morphology. In R. E. Asher et al. (eds.), *The Encyclopedia of Language and Linguistics*. Pergamon Press.
Friedman, Lynn A. 1975. Space, time, and person reference in American Sign Language. *Language 51(4)*, 940-961.
Friedman, Lynn A. 1976. The manifestation of subject, object, and topic in the American Sign Language. In C. Li (ed.), 125-148.
Friedman, Lynn A. 1977. Formational properties of American Sign Language. In L. Friedman (ed.), 13-56.
Friedman, Lynn A. (ed.). 1977. *On the Other Hand: New Perspectives on American Sign Language*. New York: Academic Press.
Frishberg, Nancy. 1975. Arbitrariness and iconicity: Historical change in American Sign Language. *Language 51(3)*, 696-719.
Frishberg, Nancy. 1985. Dominance relations and discourse structures. In W. Stokoe & V. Volterra (eds.), 79-90.
Gee, James Paul, & Wendy Goodhart. 1988. American Sign Language and the human biological capacity for language. In M. Strong (ed.), *Language Learning and Deafness*. Cambridge: Cambridge University Press. 47-74.
Gee, James Paul, & Judy Anne Kegl. 1982. Semantic perspicuity and the locative hypothesis: Implications for acquisition. *Journal of Education 164*, 185-209.
Givón, Talmy. 1976. Topic, pronoun and grammatical agreement. In C. Li (ed.), 149-188.

Givón, Talmy 1978. Definiteness and referentiality. In J. Greenberg, C. Ferguson, & E. Moravcsik (eds.) (1978b), 291-330.

Givón, Talmy. 1984a. The pragmatics of referentiality. In D. Schiffrin (ed.), *Meaning, Form, and Use in Context: Linguistic Applications,* GURT '84. Washington D.C.: Georgetown University Press. 120-138.

Givón, T. 1984b. *Syntax: A Functional-typological Introduction: Volume I.* Amsterdam: John Benjamins.

Givón, T. 1990. *Syntax: A Functional-typological Introduction: Volume II.* Amsterdam: John Benjamins.

Goldsmith, John. 1989. Qu'est-ce qu'une phonologie d'une langage des signes? Version préliminaire d'une communication présentée au colloque "Langue des signes et culture québécoises" à l'Université du Québec à Montréal, 16 mai.

Gragg, Gene B. 1972. Semi-indirect discourse and related nightmares. In P. M. Peranteau, J. N. Levi & G. C. Phares (eds.), *Papers from the Eighth Regional Meeting, Chicago Linguistic Society,* 75-82.

Greenberg, Joseph H. 1966. Some universals of grammar with particular reference to the order of meaningful elements. In J. H. Greenberg (ed.), *Universals of Language* (second edition). Cambridge, MA.: MIT Press. 73-113.

Greenberg, Joseph H. 1985. Some iconic relationships among place, time, and discourse deixis. In J. Haiman (ed.) (1985a), 271- 287.

Greenberg, Joseph H., Charles A. Ferguson, & Edith A. Moravcsik (eds.). 1978a. *Universals of Human Language, Vol. 3: Word Structure.* Stanford, CA: Stanford University Press.

Greenberg, Joseph H., Charles A. Furguson, & Edith A. Moravcsik (eds.). 1978b. *Universals of Human Language, Vol. 4: Syntax.* Stanford, CA: Stanford University Press.

Gruber, Jeffrey S. 1976. *Lexical Structures in Syntax and Semantics.* Amsterdam: North-Holland Publishing Company.

Haiman, John. 1978. Conditionals are topics. *Language 54(3),* 564-589.

Haiman, John (ed.). 1985a. *Iconicity in Syntax.* Amsterdam: John Benjamins.

Haiman, John. 1985b. *Natural Syntax: Iconicity and Erosion.* Cambridge: Cambridge University Press.

Hansen, Britta. 1986. Sign language varieties and the T.V. medium: Phases in the process of developing a variety of Danish Sign Language used for T.V. presenting. In B. Tervoort (ed.), 147-153.

Hansen, Britta. 1987. Sign language and bilingualism: A focus on an experimental approach to the teaching of deaf children in Denmark. In J. Kyle (ed.), *Sign and School.* Clevedon: Multilingual Matters. 81-88.

Hansen, Britta (ed.). 1989. *Tegn på tegnsprog: Holdninger og kultur.* København: Døves Center for Total Kommunikation.

Hill, Clifford Alden. 1975. Variation in the use of 'front' and 'back' by bilingual speakers. In C. Cogen, H. Thompson, & J. Wright (eds.), *Proceedings of the First Annual Meeting of the Berkeley Linguistics Society.* Berkeley, CA: Berkeley Linguistics Society, University of California. 196-206.

Hoijer, Harry. 1945. Classificatory verb stems in the Apachean languages. *IJAL 11,* 13-23.

Holm, Asger, Sven Gudman, Jan William Rasmussen, & Palle Vestberg Rasmussen. 1983. *Døveundervisning i Danmark 1807-1982: med et tillæg om voksne døve.* København: Døveforsorgens Historiske Selskab.

Hopper, Paul J., & Sandra A. Thompson. 1980. Transitivity in grammar and discourse. *Language 56(2)*, 251-299.

Hopper, Paul J., & Sandra A. Thompson. 1984. The discourse basis for lexical categories in universal grammar. *Language 60(4)*, 703-752.

Hopper, Paul J., & Sandra A. Thompson. 1985. The iconicity of the universal categories of "noun" and "verb". In J. Haiman (ed.) (1985a). 151-183.

Jackendoff, Ray. 1983. *Semantics and Cognition*. Cambridge, Mass.: The MIT Press.

Jacobowitz, E. Lynn, & William C. Stokoe. 1988. Signs of tense in ASL verbs. *Sign Language Studies 60*, 331-340.

Jahn, Manfred. 1992. Contextualizing represented speech and thought. *Journal of Pragmatics 17(4)*, 347-367.

Jakobson, Roman. 1971. Shifters, verbal categories, and the Russian verb. In R. Jakobson, *Selected Writings II: Word and Language*. The Hague: Mouton. 130-147.

Jarvella, R.J., & W. Klein (eds.). 1982. *Speech, Place, and Action*. New York: John Wiley & Sons.

Jespersen, Otto. 1924. *The Philosophy of Grammar*. London: George Allen & Unwin.

Johnson, Robert E., & Scott K. Liddell. 1984. Structural diversity in the American Sign Language lexicon. In D. Tosten, V. Mishra, & J. Drogo (eds.), *Papers from the Parasession on Lexical Semantics*. Chicago: Chicago Linguistic Society. 173-186.

Kakumasu, Jim. 1968. Urubú Sign Language. *IJAL XXXIV*, 275-281.

Kantor, Rebecca. 1980. The acquisition of classifiers in American Sign Language. *Sign Language Studies 28*, 193-208.

Keenan, Edward L. 1976. Towards a universal definition of "subject of". In Li (ed.), 303-333.

Kegl, Judy Anne. 1985. Causative marking and the construal of agency in ASL. In W. H. Eilfort, P. D. Kroeber, K. L. Peterson (eds.), *CLS 21: Part 2*. Chicago: Chicago Linguistic Society. 120-137.

Kegl, Judy. 1986. Clitics in American Sign Language. In H. Borer (ed.), *Syntax and Semantics, Vol. 19: The Syntax of Pronominal Clitics*. New York: Academic Press. 285-309.

Kegl, Judy. 1990. Predicate argument structure and verb-class organization in the ASL lexicon. In C. Lucas (ed.), 146-175.

Kegl, Judy, & Sara Schley. 1986. When is a classifier no longer a classifier? In V. Nikiforidou, M. VanClay, M. Niepokuj, & D. Feder (eds.), *Proceedings of the Twelfth Annual Meeting of the Berkely Linguistics Society*. Berkeley, CA: Berkeley Linguistics Society. 425-441.

Kegl, Judy, & Ronnie Bring Wilbur. 1976. When does structure stop and style begin? Syntax, morphology, and phonology vs. stylistic variation in American Sign Language. In *CLS 12*. Chicago: University of Chicago. 376-396.

Kjær Sørensen, Ruth, & Britta Hansen. 1976. *Tegnsprog: En undersøgelse af 44 døve børns tegnsprogskommunikation*. København: Statens Skole for Døve. (A short version in English has been published (1976) as *The Sign Language of Deaf Children in Denmark*. Copenhagen: Døves Center for Total Kommunikation.)

Klim, Susanne, Glenn Andersen, Orla Bryld Mortensen, Erik Dyhr, & Torben Pedersen. 1991. *Døve børn er børn: Bonaventuras model for døve børns vilkår i tiden 1900-2000*. København: Bonaventura.

Klima, Eward S., & Ursula Bellugi. 1979. *The Signs of Language*, with R. Battison, P. Boyes Braem, S. Fischer, N. Frishberg, H. Lane, E. M. Lentz, D. Newkirk, E. Newport, C. C. Pedersen, P. Siple. Cambridge, MA: Harvard University Press.

Kuno, Susumu & Etsuko Kaburaki. 1977. Empathy and syntax. *Linguistic Inquiry Vol. 8, No. 4*, 627-672.

Kuschel, Rolf. 1974. *A Lexicon of Signs From a Polynesian Outliner Island: A Description of 217 Signs as Developed and Used by Kagobar, the Only Deaf-Mute of Rennell Island.* Københavns Universitet.

Kyle, Jim, & Bencie Woll (eds.). 1983. *Language in Sign: An International Perspective on Sign Language.* London: Croom Helm.

Lakoff, George. 1986. Classifiers as a reflection of mind. In C. Craig (ed.), 13-51.

Lakoff, George. 1987. *Women, Fire, and Dangerous Things: What Categories Reveal about the Mind.* Chicago: The University of Chicago Press.

Lakoff, George, & Mark Johnson. 1980. *Metaphors We Live By.* Chicago: The University of Chicago Press.

Landar, Herbert. 1967. Ten'a classificatory verbs. *IJAL XXXIII(4)*, 263-268.

Leech, Geoffrey N. 1969. *Towards a Semantic Description of English.* London: Longmans.

Leer, Jeff. Ms. Report on the Tlingit gestural system (unpublished manuscript).

Lehmann, Christian. 1982. Universal and typological aspects of agreement. In H. Seiler & F. J. Stachowski (eds.), *Apprehension: Das sprachliche Erfassen von Gegenständen. Teil II: Die Techniken und ihr Zusammenhang in Einzelsprachen.* Tübingen: Gunter Narr. 201-267.

Lehmann, Christian. 1988. On the function of agreement. In M. Barlow & C. Ferguson (eds.), 55-65.

Lentz, Ella. 1986. Teaching role shifting. In C. A. Padden (ed.), 58-69.

Li, Charles N. (ed.). 1976. *Subject and Topic.* New York: Academic Press.

Li, Charles N. & Sandra A. Thompson. 1976. Subject and topic: A new typology of language. In C. Li (ed.), 457-489.

Liddell, Scott K. 1978. Nonmanual signals and relative clauses in American Sign Language. In P. Siple (ed.), 59-90.

Liddell, Scott K. 1980. *American Sign Language Syntax.* The Hague: Mouton.

Liddell, Scott K. 1984a. THINK and BELIEVE: Sequentiality in American Sign Language. *Language 60(2)*, 372-399.

Liddell, Scott K. 1984b. Unrealized-inceptive aspect in American Sign Language: Feature insertion in syllabic frames. In *Papers from the 20th Regional Meeting of the Chicago Linguistic Society.* Chicago: University of Chicago Press. 257-270.

Liddell, Scott K. 1990a. Four functions of a locus: Reexamining the structure of space in ASL. In C. Lucas (ed.), 176-198.

Liddell, Scott K. 1990b. Structures for representing handshape and local movement at the phonemic level. In S. Fischer & P. Siple (eds.), 37-65.

Liddell, Scott K., & Robert E. Johnson. 1986. American Sign Language compound formation processes, lexicalization and phonological remnants. *Natural Language and Linguistic Theory 4*, 445-513.

Liddell, Scott K., & Robert E. Johnson. 1987. An analysis of spatial-locative predicates in American Sign Language. Paper presented at the Fourth International Symposium on Sign Language Research, July, Lappeenranta, Finland.

Liddell, Scott K., & Robert E. Johnson. 1989. ASL: The phonological base. *Sign Language Studies 64*, 195-277.

Lillo-Martin, Diane. 1986. Two kinds of null arguments in American Sign Language. *Natural Language and Linguistic Theory 4*, 415-444.

Lillo-Martin, Diane, & Edward S. Klima. 1990. Pointing out differences: ASL pronouns in syntactic theory. In S. Fischer & P. Siple (eds.), 191-210.

Lucas, Ceil (ed.). 1989. *The Sociolinguistics of the Deaf Community.* San Diego, CA: Academic Press.

Lucas, Ceil (ed.). 1990. *Sign Language Research: Theoretical Issues*. Washington, D.C.: Gallaudet University Press.

Lucas, Ceil, & Clayton Valli. 1989. Language contact in the American deaf community. In Lucas (ed.), 11-40.

Lucas, Ceil, & Clayton Valli. 1990. From signer's perspective: A comparative sign language study. In W. Edmondson & F. Karlsson (eds.), 129-152.

Lyon, Shirley. 1967. Tlahuitoltepec Mixe clause structure. *IJAL 33*, 25-33.

Lyons, John. 1968. *Introduction to Theoretical Linguistics*. Cambridge: Cambridge University Press.

Lyons, John. 1975. Deixis as the source of reference. In E. L. Keenan (ed.), *Formal Semantics and Natural Language*. Cambridge: Cambridge University Press. 61-83.

Lyons, John. 1977. *Semantics. Vol. I-II*. Cambridge: Cambridge University Press.

Mallinson, Graham, & Barry J. Blake. 1981. *Language Typology: Crosslinguistic Studies in Syntax*. Amsterdam: North Holland Publishing Company.

Mandel, Mark. 1977. Iconic devices in American Sign Language. In L. Friedman (ed.), 57-107.

Matthews, P. H. 1974. *Morphology: An Introduction to the Theory of Word-structure*. Cambridge: Cambridge University Press.

McDonald, Betsy H. 1982. Aspects of the American Sign Language predicate system. Ph.D. Dissertation, University of Buffalo.

McDonald, Betsy. 1983. Levels of analysis in sign language research. In J. Kyle & B. Woll (eds.), 32-40.

McIntire, Marina L. 1982. Constituent order and location. *Sign Language Studies 37*, 345-386.

McNeill, David, & Elena Levy. 1982. Conceptual representations in language activity and gesture. In R. J. Jarvella & W. Klein (eds.), 271-295.

Meier, Richard P. 1990. Person deixis in American Sign Language. In S. Fischer & P. Siple (eds.), 175-190.

Mithun, Marianne. 1986. The convergence of noun classification systems. In C. Craig (ed.), 379-397.

Moore, Timothy E. (ed.). 1973. *Cognitive Development and the Acquisition of Language*. New York: Academic Press.

Moravcsik, Edith A. 1978a. Agreement. In J. Greenberg, C. Ferguson, & E. Moravcsik (eds.) (1978b). 331-374.

Moravcsik, Edith A. 1978b. Reduplicative constructions. In J. Greenberg, C. Ferguson, & E. Moravcsik (eds.) (1978a), 297-334.

Moravcsik, Edith A.. 1988. Agreement and markedness. In M. Barlow & C. Ferguson (eds.), 89-106.

Mourelatos, Alexander P. D. 1981. Events, processes, and states. In P. Tedeschi & A. Zaenen (eds.), 191-212.

Munro, Pamela, & Lynn Gordon. 1982. Syntactic relations in western Muskogean: A typological perspective. *Language 58(1)*, 81-115.

Nelfelt, Kerstin. 1986. *Referentiell användning av mimik i svenskt teckenspråk*. (Gothenburg Papers in Theoretical Linguistics S8.). Gothenburg: University of Gothenburg.

Newport, Elissa L. 1982. Task specificity in language learning? Evidence from speech perception and American Sign Language. In E. Wanner & L. R. Gleitman (eds.), *Language Acquisition: The State of the Art*. Cambridge: Cambridge University Press. 450-486.

Newport, Elissa L., & Richard P. Meier. 1985. The acquisition of American Sign Language. In D. I.

Slobin (ed.), *The Crosslinguistic Study of Language Acquisition. Vol. 1: The Data*. Hillsdale, N.J.: Lawrence Erlbaum. 881-938.

Newport, Elissa L., & Ted Supalla. 1980. Clues from the acquisition of signed and spoken language. In U. Bellugi & M. Studdert-Kennedy (eds.), *Signed and Spoken Language: Biological Constraints on Linguistic Form*. Weinheim: Verlag Chemie. 187-211.

Nichols, Johanna. 1985. The directionality of agreement. In M. Niepokuj et al. (eds.), *Proceedings of the Eleventh Annual Meeting of the Berkeley Linguistics Society 1985*. Berkeley, CA: University of California, Berkeley Linguistics Society. 273-286.

Oléron, Pierre. 1978. *Le langage gestuel des sourds: Syntaxe et communication*. Paris: Centre National de la Recherche Scientifique.

Osherson, D. N., & E. E. Smith. 1981. On the adequacy of prototype theory as a theory of concepts. *Cognition 9*, 35-58.

Padden, Carol A. 1981. Some arguments for syntactic patterning in American Sign Language. *Sign Language Studies 32*, 239-259.

Padden, Carol A. 1986. Verbs and role-shifting in ASL. In C. Padden (ed.), 44-57.

Padden, Carol A. 1988a. Grammatical theory and signed languages. In F. J. Newmeyer (ed.), *The Cambridge Survey of Linguistics. Vol. II: Linguistic Theory: Extensions and Applications*. Cambridge: Cambridge University Press. 250-266.

Padden, Carol A. 1988b. *Interaction of Morphology and Syntax in American Sign Language*. New York: Garland Publishing. (1983 Ph.D. Dissertation, University of California. Interaction of morphology and syntax.)

Padden, Carol A. 1990. The relation between space and grammar in ASL verb morphology. In C. Lucas (ed.), 118-132.

Padden, Carol A. (ed.). 1986. *Proceedings of the Fourth National Symposium on Sign Language Research and Teaching*. Silver Spring, MD: National Association of the Deaf.

Padden, Carol A., & Tom Humphries. 1988. *Deaf in America: Voices from a Culture*. Cambridge, MA: Harvard University Press.

Padden, Carol A. & David M. Perlmutter. 1987. American Sign Language and the architecture of phonological theory. *Natural Language and Linguistic Theory 5*, 335-375.

Perlmutter, David M. 1978. Impersonal passives and the unaccusative hypothesis. *Berkeley Linguistics Society 4*, 157-189.

Petitto, Laura A. 1983. From gesture to symbol: The acquisition of personal pronouns in American Sign Language. (Qualifying paper, Harvard University.)

Petitto, Laura A. 1985. From gesture to symbol: The relation of form to meaning in ASL personal pronoun acquisition. In W. Stokoe & V. Volterra (eds.), 55-63.

Petitto, Laura A. 1987. On the autonomy of language and gesture: Evidence from the acquisition of personal pronouns in American Sign Language. *Cognition 27*, 1-52.

Pimiä, Päivi. 1990. Semantic features of some mouth patterns of Finnish Sign Language. In S. Prillwitz & T. Vollhaber (eds.), 115-118.

Pizzuto, Elena. 1986. The verb system of Italian Sign Language. In B. Tervoort (ed.), 17-31.

Pizzuto, Elena, & Malinda Williams. 1979. The acquisition of the possessive forms in American Sign Language. In B. Frøkjær-Jensen: *The Sciences of Deaf Signing, Proceedings from a seminar in Recent Developments in Language and Cognition: Sign Language Research*. Copenhagen: University of Copenhagen. 97-110.

Pizzuto, Elena, Enza Giuranna, & Giuseppe Gambino. 1990. Manual and nonmanual morphology in Italian Sign Language: Grammatical constraints and discourse processes. In C. Lucas (ed.), 83-102.

Poizner, Howard, Edward S. Klima & Ursula Bellugi. 1987. *What the Hands Reveal about the Brain.* Cambridge, MA: MIT Press.
Prillwitz, Siegmund, & Tomas Vollhaber (eds.). 1990. *Current Trends in European Sign Language Research: Proceedings of the Third European Congress on Sign Language Research.* Hamburg: SIGNUM-Press.
Prince, Ellen F. 1981. Toward a taxonomy of given-new information. In P. Cole (ed.), *Radical Pragmatics.* New York: Academic Press. 223-255.
Ravnholt, Ole, & Elisabeth Engberg-Pedersen. 1986. Børn og dig og mig – Børns deiktiske brug af pronominer i talesprog og tegnsprog. In *Skrifter om Anvendt og Matematisk Lingvistik 12.* København: Københavns Universitet, Institut for Anvendt og Matematisk Lingvistik. 5-27.
Rosch, Eleanor. 1977. Human categorization. In N. Warren (ed.), *Studies in Cross-Cultural Psychology, Vol. 1.* London: Academic Press. 1-49.
Rudzka-Ostyn, Brygida (ed.). 1988. *Topics in Cognitive Linguistics.* Amsterdam: John Benjamins.
Sandler, Wendy. 1990b. Temporal aspects and ASL phonology. In S. Fischer & P. Siple (eds.), 7-35.
Sandler, Wendy. 1990a. *Phonological representation of the sign: Linearity and nonlinearity in American Sign Language.* Dordrecht: Foris.
Sapir, Edward. 1921(1970). *Language: An Introduction to the Study of Speech.* London: Rupert Hart-Davis.
Schachter, Paul. 1977. Reference-related and role-related properties of subjects. In P. Cole & J. M. Sadock (eds.), *Syntax and Semantics, Vol. 8: Grammatical Relations.* New York: Academic Press. 279-306.
Schermer, Trude. 1985. Analysis of natural discourse of deaf adults in the Netherlands: Observations on Dutch Sign Language. In W. Stokoe & V. Volterra (eds.), 281-288.
Schermer, Trude M. 1990. *In Search of a Language: Influences from Spoken Dutch on Sign Language of the Netherlands.* Delft: Eburon.
Schermer, Trude, & Corline Koolhof. 1990. The reality of time-lines: Aspects of tense in SLN. In S. Prillwitz & T. Vollhaber (eds.), 295-305.
Schick, Brenda S. 1990. Classifier predicates in American Sign Language. *International Journal of Sign Linguistics Vol. 1, No. 1,* 15-40.
Schröder, Odd-Inge. 1985. A problem in phonological description. In W. Stokoe & V. Volterra (eds.), 194-198.
Shopen, Timothy (ed.). 1985. *Language Typology and Syntactic Description, Vol. III: Grammatical Categories and the Lexicon.* Cambridge: Cambridge University Press.
Siple, Patricia (ed.). 1978. *Understanding Language Through Sign Language Research.* New York: Academic Press.
Slobin, Dan I. 1981. The origins of grammatical encoding of events. In W. Deutsch (ed.), *The Child's Construction of Language.* London: Academic Press. 185-199.
Smith, Wayne H. 1989. The morphological characteristics of verbs in Taiwan Sign Language, Ph.D. Dissertation, Indiana University.
Stokoe, William C. 1960. Sign language structure: An outline of the visual communication system of the American deaf. *Studies in Linguistics Occasional Papers, No. 8.*
Stokoe, William C. 1978. *Sign Language Structure: The First Linguistic Analysis of American Sign Language* (second edition). Silver Spring, MD: Linstok Press.
Stokoe, William C. (ed.). 1980. *Sign and Culture: A Reader for Students of American Sign Language.* Silver Spring, MD: Linstok Press.
Stokoe, William C. 1991. Semantic phonology. *Sign Language Studies 71,* 107-114.

Stokoe, William C., H. Russell Bernard, & Carol Padden. 1976. An elite group in Deaf society. *Sign Language Studies 12*, 189-210. (Reprinted in W. Stokoe (ed.) 1980, 295-317.)

Stokoe, William, & Virginia Volterra. (eds.). 1985. *SLR' 83: Proceedings of the III. International Symposium on Sign Language Research.* Silver Spring, MD: Linstok Press & Roma: Istituto di Psicologia CNR.

Supalla, Ted. 1978. Morphology of verbs of motion and location in American Sign Language. In F. Caccamise (eds.), *American Sign Language in a Bilingual, Bicultural Context: Proceedings of the National Symposium on Sign Language Research and Teaching.* Silver Spring, MD: National Association of the Deaf. 27-45.

Supalla, Ted. 1982. Structure and acquisition of verbs of motion and location in American Sign Language. Ph.D. dissertation, University of California, San Diego.

Supalla, Ted. 1986. The classifier system in American Sign Language. In C. Craig (ed.), 181-214.

Supalla, Ted. 1990. Serial verbs of motion in ASL. In S. Fischer & P. Siple (eds.), 127-152.

Supalla, Ted, & Elissa L. Newport. 1978. How many seats in a chair? The derivation of nouns and verbs in American Sign Language. In P. Siple (ed.), 91-132.

Suwanarat, Manfa, Charles Reilly, Anucha Ratanasint, Lloyd Anderson, Vilaiporn Rungsrithong, Soontorn Yen-Klao, Warunee Buathong, & Owen Wrigley. 1986. *The Thai Sign Language Dictionary: Book One.* Bangkok: National Association of the Deaf in Thailand & International Human Assistance Programs/Thailand.

Talmy, Leonard 1978. Figure and ground in complex sentences. In J. Greenberg, C. Ferguson, & E. Moravcsik (eds.) (1978b). 625-649.

Talmy, Leonard. 1985. Lexicalization patterns: Semantic structure in lexical forms. In T. Shopen (ed.), 57-149.

Talmy, Leonard. 1988. The relation of grammar to cognition. In B. Rudzka-Ostyn (ed.), 165-205.

Tannen, Deborah. 1986. Introducing constructed dialogue in Greek and American conversational and literary narrative. In F. Coulmas (ed.), 311-332.

Taylor, John R. 1989. *Linguistic Categorization: Prototypes in Linguistic Theory.* Oxford: Clarendon Press.

Tedeschi, Philip J., & Annie Zaenen (eds.). 1981. *Syntax and Semantics, Vol. 14: Tense and Aspect.* New York: Academic Press.

Tegnsprog: Undervisningsvejledning for Folkeskolen. 1991. København: Undervisningsministeriet.

Tervoort, Bernard T. (ed.). 1986. *Signs of Life: Proceedings of the Second European Congress on Sign Language Research.* Amsterdam: The Dutch Foundation for the Deaf and Hearing Impaired Child, The Institute of General Linguistics of the University of Amsterdam, & The Dutch Council of the Deaf.

Thompson, Chad, Melissa Axelrod, & Eliza Jones. 1983. *Koyukon Language Curriculum: Scope and Sequence.* Nenana, Alaska: Yukon Koyukuk School District.

Thompson, Henry. 1977. The lack of subordination in American Sign Language. In L. Friedman (ed.), 181-195.

Toft, Sussi, & Britta Hansen. 1988. Vurdering af 8 døve børns tegnsprog. In R. Kjær Sørensen et al., *To-sproget døveundervisning 3.* København: Skolen på Kastelsvej. 178-194.

Traugott, Elizabeth Closs. 1978. On the expression of spatio-temporal relations in language. In J. Greenberg, C. Ferguson, & E. Moravcsik (eds.) (1978a), 369-400.

Vikkelsø, Anne. 1989. Integration. In B. Hansen (ed.), 91-96.

Vogt-Svendsen, Marit. 1983. Lip movements in Norwegian Sign Language. In J. Kyle & B. Woll (eds.), 85-96.

Vogt-Svendsen, Marit. 1984. Word-pictures in Norwegian Sign Language (NSL) – A preliminary analysis. *Working Papers in Linguistics 2*. Dragvoll: Department of Linguistics, University of Trondheim. 112-141.

Vourc'h, Agnès, Rachild Benelhocine, & Michel Girod. 1989. Time-lines in L.S.F. Presented at the conference The Deaf Way, Washington, D.C., July.

Wallin, Lars. 1987. *Non-manual Anaphoric Reference in Swedish Sign Language*. Stockholm: University of Stockholm.

Wallin, Lars. 1990. Polymorphemic predicates in Swedish Sign Language. In C. Lucas (ed.), 133-148.

Washabaugh, William. 1986. *Five Fingers for Survival*. Ann Arbor: Karoma.

Widell, Jonna. 1988. *Den danske døvekultur, bind I-II*. København: Danske Døves Landsforbund.

Wilbur, Ronnie Bring. 1987. *American Sign Language and Sign Systems*. Baltimore, MD: University Park Press.

Wilbur, Ronnie B. 1990. Why syllables? What the notion means for ASL research. In S. Fischer & P. Siple (eds.), 81-108.

Wilbur, Ronnie B., Mark E. Bernstein, & Rebecca Kantor. 1985. The semantic domain of classifiers in American Sign Language. *Sign Language Studies 46*, 1-38.

Winston, Elizabeth A. 1989. Timelines in ASL. Presented at the conference The Deaf Way, Washington, D.C., July.

Woodward, James. 1983. Review of *American Sign Language Syntax* by Scott K. Liddell. *Language 59(1)*, 221-224.

Woodward, James, & Harry Markowicz. 1980. Pidgin Sign Languages. In W. Stokoe (ed.), 55-79.

Zimmer, June. 1989. Toward a description of register variation in American Sign Language. In C. Lucas (ed.), 253-272.

Zimmer, June, & Cynthia Patschke. 1990. A class of determiners in ASL. In C. Lucas (ed.), 201-210.

Zwicky, Arnold M., & Geoffrey K. Pullum. 1983. Cliticization vs. inflection: English n't. *Language 59(3)*, 502-513.

Subject Index

A

A argument 50, 51-52, 58, 59, 153, 154, 168, 189, 190, 193, 194, 196, 198, 202, 205, 212
agentivity, agency 21, 148, 205-208, 213-226, 293, 311, 313
agreement 16, 20-21, 22, 63-64, 152, 156, 159-161, 165, 167-168, 169, 173-176, 177-194, 199, 200-208, 241-242, 284, 313
agreement marker 174, 177-183, 188, 294
agreement omission 21, 152, 194, 200-204
agreement verbs 154, 157, 159-160, 162, 181-182, 311, 316
anaphora 54, 71, 79, 104-105, 130, 140, 141, 143, 177-179
anaphoric time line 80-81, 85-86, 93, 94
animacy, animateness 101-102, 212-213
apprehension of a linguistic object 187-189, 291, 317
aspect 62-63, 151, 266
aspectual model (phonology) 37-38
assimilation 176-177, 223-224

B

backgrounding 22, 277, 283-286, 287, 293, 294, 296-297, 301, 310, 316
backward verb 58-59
base form 20, 35, 39, 59, 194-195, 203-204
body shift 106, 109, 135, 136-137, 199

C

c-form 135, 194-208, 292-294, 311, 314, 316-317
calendar plane 80-81, 83, 88-89, 95
canonical encounter 92-93, 299
canonical location 73, 141
case 173, 174-176
cherology 36
classificatory verb 21, 236-240, 251-253
classifier 21, 157, 159-161, 202, 234-236, 239, 241-245, 250, 281-283, 296
clitic 176-177, 180, 199, 221-223
coherence 286-289
comparison 74, 99, 142

configuration 22, 69, 286-289, 296
conflation 21, 240-241
contact signing 31-32
cross-reference 178, 222

D

Deaf/deaf 30
deaf community 30-32
defective agreement paradigm 193-194, 206
deictic time line 80-81, 83, 84-85, 93-94
deixis 54, 71, 117-119, 127, 130, 131-132, 133, 140, 141, 143, 188, 207, 208-209
derivation 761-64, 65, 252
determiner 20, 119-122, 128-130
discourse value 20, 69, 99-101
distribution 20, 152, 156, 158, 160, 165-172, 255, 263-264, 273
double agreement verb 57-58, 155, 163, 168, 174, 191-192, 193, 194, 203, 206, 214, 215-217

E

ego-aligned strategy 93, 96, 137-138, 299-300
ego-opposed strategy 93, 94, 96, 137, 299-300
empathy 75, 310
emphasis 126, 128-130, 217-218
event verbs 149-150, 311-312
extension 264-265, 268, 269
extension stem 279, 287
eye blink 42

F

Figure 240-241, 284-285, 305
foregrounding 22, 283-286, 293
frame of reference 69, 71-79, 133, 140-142, 301-303
free indirect style 114-116
fuzzy set theory 26-27

G

gaze direction 42, 109-110, 135, 137, 163-164, 232, 271, 313
gender 97, 117, 142-143, 166, 174, 183, 184, 189, 220, 225
gesture 280-281
goal 148, 189, 190, 206
grammaticality 22, 25-30
Ground 240-241, 284-285, 287, 305

H

handle stem 207, 251, 275-278, 279, 280, 289-292, 303, 304
handshape 37, 47-48, 206, 244-245, 252-253
head and body orientation 42, 110, 111, 163-164, see also body shift
head and body posture 42, 110, 111, 294
hold (phonology) 46-47, 162

I

iconicity 18, 22, 23-25, 74, 131-132, 141, 162-163, 172, 206-207, 255-258, 268, 272, 273, 278, 298-301, 303, 310
ideophone 64, 166
incorporation of pronoun 173, 177-183
indefinite number of members of a category 14, 20, 134, 185
inflecting languages 60-61
inflection 60-64, 65, 84, 252
information-packaging 20, 128
IO argument 50, 51-52, 58, 154, 189, 190-193, 204, 212, 294

L

lexicalization 281-283, 312-314
limb stem 278-279
localism 17, 147-148, 149-150, 310-311
location 16-17, 21, 69, 90, 95-96, 118-119, 132, 153, 158, 159, 161, 192, 199, 209-211, 244, 246-251, 258-259, 286-289, 296-301, 305, 309
locus 14, 18-19, 22, 24-25, 51, 52-57, 69, 71-79, 82-84, 87-88, 97-102, 106, 108-110, 112-113, 129, 140-143, 159-160, 175, 184-186, 284, 290, 293, 311, 315-316

locus marker 50, 51, 54, 56-57, 78, 169, 185-186, 290
locus symbols (transcription) 56-57

M

manner 261-263
manual alphabets 43-44
metaphor 90, 95-96, 131-132, 206, 310, 312
mime 115, 293-294
mixed agreement pattern 163, 192
mixed time line 80-81, 88, 93, 94
modification 39-41, 53, 60-65, 84, 151
Motion 240-241
motion 21, 230-231, 244-245, 246-251, 259-262, 286
mouth pattern 41-42, 231-232, 272, 313
Mouth-Hand System 44-45
movement (morphology) 160, 229-232, 244-245, 252-253, 254-270, 313
movement (phonology) 37, 46-47, 162

N

name sign 45
narrative discourse 115-116, 272, 313-314
neutral locus marker 155, 195, 200
neutral space 37, 163
nonmanual articulation 23-24, 41-42, 230
number 165-167, 170, 171, 175

O

object 22, 157, 159, 160, 190-191
ordinal locus 129, 159-160
orientation (phonology) 37, 48-52

P

P argument 50, 51-52, 58, 153, 154, 189, 190-193, 204, 212, 294
p-morph 50, 56, 176, 177, 183
parameter model (phonology) 36-37, 38, 55
particle 123, 128
person; first person, non-first person 14, 20, 131-139, 166, 175, 184-186, 188, 192-194, 207-213, 294
phonetic description of signs 36, 55-56, 83

Subject Index 343

"phonology" 36
place of articulation 37, 48-52, 162, 205, 224-225
plain sign 160, 162-164, 223, 313
point of view; marking for a specific point of view 18, 20, 75, 76, 78-79, 91-93, 95, 104, 112-116, 152, 156, 197-200, 202-205, 208-213, 293, 303-305, 314
polymorphemic verbs 18, 21, 22, 53, 160-161, 207, 227-305
polymorphemic verbs vs. nonpolymorphemic verbs 160-161, 234, 266, 284, 295-296, 309-310, 311-314
polysynthetic 253-254
possession 72, 142
pragmatic agreement 21, 155, 156, 160, 164, 169, 214-226, 310
process verbs 149-150, 311-312
proform 20, 124-125, 273
pronoun 20, 104-105, 111, 117-122, 128-131, 177-183, 221-223, 244-245, 289-291, 293, see also person
prototype 25-30, 64, 65, 97, 163, 314

R

R-indexing, referential indexing 14, 79, 136, 315
reciprocal verb 59, 168, 195, 216
reduplication 39, 40, 77, 85-86, 151, 165, 167, 170, 171, 255
reference check 42, 121, 128
reference-tracking 19, 20, 54, 79, 142-143, 291, 315
referent projection 18, 22, 54, 140, 289-292, 316-318
referentiality 20, 97-102
regular verbs 58-59
reported speech 104-111, 113-116, 135, 136-137
represented speech or thought 113-116
role shifting 103

S

SASS 279
s-morph 50
segmentation 61, 229-232, 257-258

semantic affinity 71-72, 133, 140, 141
semantic agreement 21, 154, 156, 159, 160, 189-194, 199-208, 214-217, 218-219
sender locus, see c-form
sentence intertwining (Danish) 25-26, 28-29
sequence line 80-81, 86-88, 95
sequentiality 38, 45-50, 232, 270-273
serial verbs 127, 271, 273
shifted attribution of expressive elements 18, 20, 69-70, 101, 102, 103-116, 139, 293-294, 303-305, 317
shifted locus 18, 20, 69-70, 78, 101-102, 103-116, 198, 199, 271, 293, 301, 303-305, 317-318
shifted reference 18, 20, 69-70, 103-116, 136, 293, 317
shifter 104, 131, 133, 134, 189
sign-supported Danish 31-32
signing space 37, 53, 77-78
simultaneity 38, 232, 257-258, 270-272, 295-296
single agreement verb 57-58, 155, 163, 191-192, 193, 194, 203
source 147-148, 189, 190, 206
'spatial mapping' 16-18, 309-310, 313
spatial morphology 20, 39, 40, 95, 160, 162, 169, 254-255, 296-301
'spatialized syntax' 16-18, 309-310, 313
squint (squinted eyes) 23, 42
strong hand 36, 55, 125, 284
subject 22-24, 157, 159, 160, 175, 190, 208

T

telecity 63, 171-172
tense 56, 63, 80, 84, 90
thematic value 97, 99-101, 102
Theme 147
time lines 20, 53, 54, 69, 80-96
topic 153-154, 174, 208, 220-221, 226, 314
topicalization 42, 121, 123, 180
transcription 16, 56-57, 57-58, 59, 78, 321-325
transitivity 18, 148-150, 158, 163, 310-311, 312

V

variation 22, 30-33, 64-65, 192-194, 199-200, 204-205, 217, 294
verb root 194, 244-245
verb sandwich 271, 273

W

weak hand 36, 124-125, 284
whole entity stem 251, 273-275, 280, 289-292, 293, 303, 304

Name Index

A

Abildgaard, E. 5, 6
Ahlgren, I. 5, 103, 115, 137, 138, 272, 313, 314
Albertsen, K. 5
Allan, K. 21, 235, 236, 239, 241, 243, 244
Allen, B. J. 212
Amith, J. D. 209, 210
Anderson, A. J. O. 210
Anderson, L. B. 151, 166
Anderson, S. R. 90, 92
Ashton, E. O. 147, 167, 224, 226
Axelrod, M. 236, 239

B

Baker, C. 24, 30, 31, 42, 74, 103, 130, 135, 235, 265, 303
Banfield, A. 105, 114, 115
Barlow, M. 183, 184, 189
Barron, R. 239, 240
Battison, R. 36, 43, 295
Bellugi, U. 16, 23, 24, 36, 39, 60, 61, 62, 63, 103, 109, 151, 165, 173, 199, 235, 244, 265, 309, 313
Benelhocine, R. 81
Benveniste, E. 92
Berenz, N. 137, 138
Bergman, B. 5, 23, 37, 60, 61, 64, 115, 151, 166, 272, 314, 321
Bergmann, A. 5
Bergmann, R. 5
Bernard, H. R. 31
Bernstein, M. E. 235, 265
Birch-Rasmussen, S. 44
Blake, B. J. 212
Bloomfield, L. 178, 253
Boas, F. 178
Bos, H. 241
Boyes Braem, P. 6, 192, 206, 246
Brennan, M. 36, 81, 84, 173, 206, 235, 296, 321
Brentari, D. 36, 59

Bresnan, J. 176, 179, 180
Bruner, J. 73, 132
Brøndum, J. 5
Bybee, J. L. 25, 61, 63, 166, 167, 170

C

Cameracanna, E. 81
Canger, U. 5, 209, 210
Castberg, P. A. 13
Chafe, W. L. 220
Chao, Y. R. 153
Christensen, D. 32
Chung, S. 172
Clark, H. 94, 298
Cogen, C. 81
Cokely, D. 24, 30, 31, 74, 103, 130, 235, 265, 303
Collins-Ahlgren, M. 235
Colville, M. D. 36, 173, 235, 321
Comrie, B. 50, 171, 208, 212, 226
Corazza, S. 81, 235, 280
Corbett, G. G. 23, 173, 175, 183, 184, 185
Coulmas, F. 104, 113
Coulter, G. R. 36, 42
Craig, C. 246
Creider, C. A. 26, 28
Cristensen, D. 32
Croft, W. 191, 226

D

Dahl, Ö. 25, 27, 60, 61, 64, 115, 151, 166, 272, 314
DeLancey, S. 29, 149, 312
DeMatteo, A. 23, 255, 256
Denny, J. P. 250
DeRoeck, M. 113
Deuchar, M. 173
Dibble, C. E. 210
Dik, S. 151, 220, 221
Dixon, R. M. W. 242, 243
Dressler, W. 170

E

Ebbinghaus, H. 42
Ebert, K. 105
Edge, V. 173
Edmondson, W. 38, 241
Ellenberger, R. 235
Engberg-Pedersen, E. 23, 32, 36, 42, 43, 60, 81, 105, 138, 151, 173, 235

F

Faltz, L. M. 190
Faustrup, O. 32
Ferguson, C. A. 183, 184, 189
Ferreira Brito, L. 81, 137, 138
Fillmore, C. J. 92, 93, 105, 114, 115, 137, 208, 209, 291
Fischer, S. 60, 103, 116, 148, 151, 154, 161, 173, 271, 273
Foley, W. A. 142, 143
Fortescue, M. 5, 243, 253, 262
Frantz, D. G. 212
Frederiksen, L. 5
Friedman, L. A. 36, 81, 103, 125, 148, 154, 161
Frishberg, N. 23, 36, 234

G

Gambino, G. 103
Gee, J. P. 148, 149, 157, 158, 160, 235, 312
Girod, M. 81
Giuranna, E. 103
Givón, T. 54, 97, 122, 176, 188, 190
Goldsmith, J. 83
Goodhart, W. 148, 157, 158, 160
Gordon, L. 225
Gough, B. 60, 148, 151, 161, 173
Gragg, G. B. 105
Greenberg, J. H. 14, 117, 130, 131, 132
Gruber, J. S. 147, 273

H

Haiman, J. 24, 170
Hansen, B. 5, 32, 33, 42, 43, 81, 173, 235, 298, 319

Herrmann, L. 173
Hessmann, J. 42
Hill, C. A. 93, 299
Hoffmeister, R. 138
Hoijer, H. 237
Holm, A. 320
Hopper, P. J. 25, 97, 118, 148, 312
Humphries, T. 30
Hårdell, A. S. 5

J

Jackendoff, R. 90
Jacobowitz, E. L. 54, 56, 60, 82, 83, 84
Jahn, M. 104, 105, 114
Jakobson, R. 104, 131
Janis, W. 103, 116, 271, 273
Jespersen, O. 104, 131
Johnson, M. 90, 92, 149
Johnson, R. E. 5, 22, 35, 38, 45-52, 56, 57, 58, 59, 61, 157, 159, 160, 169, 176, 194, 215, 216, 253, 258, 266, 267, 269, 270, 280, 282, 313, 351
Jones, E. 236, 239

K

Kaburaki, E. 212
Kakumasu, J. 81
Kantor, R. 235, 265
Keenan, E. L. 90, 92
Kegl, J. A. 148, 149, 157, 158, 173, 181, 199, 223, 235, 244, 312, 313, 321
Kjær Sørensen, R. 32, 42, 43, 81, 173, 298
Klim, S. 319
Klima, E. S. 14, 16, 23, 24, 36, 39, 60, 61, 62, 63, 69, 78, 79, 103, 106, 109, 120, 136, 137, 151, 165, 173, 184, 185, 199, 244, 265, 309, 313, 315
Koolhof, C. 81, 84
Kuno, S. 212
Kuschel, R. 81

L

Lakoff, G. 27, 90, 92, 118, 132, 149
Landar, H. 239
Lawson, L. K. 36, 173, 235, 321

Leech, G. N. 284, 300
Leer, J. 281
Lehmann, C. 18, 174, 176-181, 183, 187, 188, 189, 193, 217, 222, 241, 242, 291, 317, 355
Lentz, E. 103
Leven, R. 294
Levy, E. 280
Li, C. N. 153
Liddell, S. K. 5, 16, 17, 22, 35, 38, 42, 45-52, 54, 56, 57, 58, 59, 60, 61, 103, 129, 154, 157, 158, 159, 160, 169, 176, 181, 190, 194, 215, 216, 235, 253, 258, 266, 267, 269, 270, 280, 282, 309, 313, 351
Lillo-Martin, D. 14, 69, 78, 79, 103, 106, 109, 120, 136, 137, 173, 181, 184, 185, 315
Lucas, C. 32, 235, 298
Lyon, S. 175, 212
Lyons, J. 17, 61, 71, 117, 118, 119, 122, 127, 131, 141, 142, 143, 147, 149, 311, 312

M
Mallinson, G. 212
Mandel, M. 23, 24, 103, 130, 267, 268
Markowicz, H. 64
Matthews, P. H. 61, 62
McDonald, B. H. 235, 244, 245, 246, 251, 258, 265, 274, 281, 282, 283, 313
Mchombo, S. A. 176, 179, 180
McIntire, M. L. 6, 235
McNeill, D. 280
Meier, R. P. 24, 106, 130, 135, 136, 139
Mithun, M. 242, 243
Moder, C. L. 25
Moravcsik, E. A. 170, 176, 180, 183, 186, 188, 190
Munro, P. 225

N
Nelfelt, K. 103
Newkirk, D. 235
Newport, E. L. 24, 36, 60, 128, 130, 235, 256
Nichols, J. 224
Nielsen, G. K. 6
Nielsen, J. R. 5

Nielsen, K. 5

O
Oléron, P. 298, 299
Orlof, H. 6
Osherson, D. N. 26, 27

P
Padden, C. A. 16, 30, 31, 36, 42, 59, 60, 69, 76, 78, 103, 119, 135, 151, 152, 157, 158, 159, 160, 161, 165, 184, 185, 190, 193, 194, 221, 222, 223, 235, 301, 302, 313
Patschke, C. 119, 120
Pedersen, A. 5, 32, 235
Pedersen, I. 5
Peirce, C. S. 131
Perlmutter, D. M. 36, 151
Petersen, B. 5
Petitto, L. A. 138, 139
Pimiä, P. 42
Pizzuto, E. 103, 138, 157, 173, 193, 194
Poizner, H. 16, 309, 313
Prillwitz, S. 321
Prince, E. F. 128
Pullum, G. K. 176, 177

R
Ravnholt, O. 138
Rischel, J. 6
Rosch, E. 25

S
Sandler, W. 38, 46, 151
Sapir, E. 60, 253
Schachter, P. 174
Schermer, T. 42, 81, 84
Schick, B. S. 235, 266, 268, 269, 303
Schley, S. 148, 157, 312, 313
Schröder, O.-I. 42
Slobin, D. I. 149
Smith, E. E. 26, 27
Smith, W. H. 26, 157, 181, 193, 221, 235
Spang-Hanssen, H. 6

Stokoe, W. C. 13, 31, 36, 37, 38, 39, 45, 54, 55, 56, 60, 82, 83, 84, 321
Supalla, T. 36, 60, 69, 126, 128, 235, 241, 243, 244, 245, 246, 250, 251, 256, 258, 261, 265, 266-268, 269, 271, 274, 279, 281, 303, 313
Suwanarat, M. 235

T

Talmy, L. 21, 240, 241, 251, 253, 284, 285, 305, 312
Tannen, D. 105, 111
Taylor, J. R. 25, 29, 30, 149, 312
Thompson, C. 236, 239
Thompson, H. 103
Thompson, S. A.
 25, 97, 118, 148, 153, 312
Timberlake, A. 172
Toft, S. 5, 235
Traugott, E. C. 80, 90-95

V

Valli, C. 32, 235, 298
Van Valin, R. D. 142, 143
Vikkelsø, A. 32
Vogt-Svendsen, M. 42
Vollhaber, T. 6, 321
Vourc'h, A. 81

W

Wallin, L. 103, 235
Washabaugh, W. 14
Widell, J. 30, 320
Wilbur, R. B. 13, 23, 24, 36, 38, 39, 130, 138, 154, 173, 192, 235, 244, 246, 265
Williams, M. 138
Winston, E. A. 81, 86
Woodward, J. 31, 64
Woolf, V. 114

Z

Zimmer, J. 119, 120, 217
Zwicky, A. M. 176, 177

Index of Signs in the Illustrations

The signs are only represented by their gloss without regard to the forms in the illustrations

1-Pm Ills 56, 58, 59
ALL-RIGHT Ill. 5a
ANALYSE Ill. 37
Animal-Pm Ill. 70
ANSWER Ills 1, 12a, 12b
APRIL Ill. 22
Arm-Pm Ill. 74
BAD Ills 4b, 7
BECKON Ills 9a, 9b
BEFORE Ill. 20
Boat-Pm Ills 76a, 76b
Car-Pm Ills 68, 77a, 77b
CAT Ill. 27, 28
CLASS Ill. 37
COMFORT Ills 48a, 48b, 48c
Cylindrical-entity-Pm Ill. 50
DANGEROUS Ill. 3a
DAY Ill. 5b
DECEIVE Ills 14a, 14b
DET (determiner) Ills 20, 22, 27
DISCUSS Ills 16a, 16b, 21, 54
DRIVE-CAR Ill. 72
EXPLAIN Ills 13a, 13b, 33, 45a, 45b, 46, 53
FINISH Ill. 37
FIX Ill. 26
General-entity(B)-Pm Ills 24, 67c
GIVE Ills 6a, 6b, 34
GIVE-KEY Ill. 40
GO-TO Ill. 8
GREATLY-DISAPPOINTED Ill. 39
GROUP Ill. 21
Group-Pm Ill. 64
Handle-cylindrical-entity-Pm Ill. 50
Handle-flat-entity-Pm Ill. 35
Handle-hand-Pm Ill. 58
Handle-handle-Pm Ill. 67a
Handle-large-cylindrical-entity-Pm Ill. 65
Handle-three-dimensional-entity-Pm Ill. 71
Handle-two-dimensional-entity-Pm Ill. 73
HAPPY Ill. 2b
IF Ill. 41

IN-TROUBLE Ill. 29
Index-Pm Ills 62, 72, 78c
INVITE Ills 15a, 15b
JANUARY Ill. 20
JUMP Ill. 43
LEAVE Ill. 63
Legs-Pm Ill. 60
Look-Pm Ills 25a, 25b
MARCH Ill. 22
Mass-Pm Ill. 69
MONDAY Ills 19a, 19b
MONTH Ill. 20
MOVE-PERSON Ill. 50
OF-COURSE Ill. 10
OUT Ill. 11b
PAY Ills 51, 52
PROFORM Ill. 29
PRON (non-first person pronoun) Ills 28, 31, 42, 76b
READ Ill. 17
REPAIR Ill. 26
SECOND Ills 30, 37
SEND Ill. 32
Short-thin-entity-Pm Ill. 75
SLEEP Ill. 27
STRANGE Ill. 3b
STRING Ill. 67b, 67c
SUGGEST Ill. 42
SUMMER Ill. 4a
TALK-WITH-EACH-OTHER Ill. 44
TEACH Ills 49a, 49b
TEASE Ill. 47
TELEPHONE Ill. 38
Thin-entity-surface-Pm Ill. 75
THINK Ill. 2a
THIRTY Ill. 36
TO-TOWN Ill. 11a
TYPE Ill. 18
V-Pm Ills 57, 61, 66a, 66b, 77a, 77b, 78b
WEEK Ill. 23
WHO Ill. 55

List of figures

Fig. 1. The seven feature bundles of a segment in Liddell and Johnson's model
Fig. 2a. Representation of the feature matrix of the sign GOOD (ASL)
Fig. 2b. Representation of autosegmental attachment of feature bundles of the sign GOOD
Fig. 3. A simplified notation of the form of ANSWER in Ill. 1 ('he$_i$ answers me')
Fig. 4. The side-to-side dimension and the diagonal dimensions
Fig. 5. Time lines in Danish Sign Language
Fig. 6. Tense
Fig. 7. Sequencing
Fig. 8. Two classifications of verbs in ASL
Fig. 9. Classification of verbs in Danish Sign Language
Fig. 10. Base forms, agreement forms, forms marked for a specific point of view, and forms with agreement omission
Fig. 11. Number of movement units in some polymorphemic verbs of example (1)
Fig. 12. Examples of verbs with the classificatory stems for 'compact object' in Koyukon
Fig. 13. Classifications of movement morphemes in ASL
Fig. 14. The 'ego-opposed' and the 'ego-aligned' strategies of assigning front and back to entities without an inherent front-back orientation
Fig. 15. The "score" of the transcription system

Summary in Danish / Resumé på dansk

Afhandlingen tager udgangspunkt i et udtrykstræk i dansk tegnsprog, nemlig sprogets udnyttelse af det tredimensionale rum på diskursniveau og morfosyntaktisk. Det tredimensionale rum er en del af tegnsprogs udtryksside, og afhandlingen søger dels at belyse, hvordan dette udtrykstræk påvirker strukturen i tegnsprog, dels at vise, at de semantisk-pragmatiske fænomener, som udtrykkes gennem rummet, er de samme, som er grammatikaliseret i mange sprog, hvis udtrykssubstans primært er lyd.

Afhandlingens to hoveddele er Del II og III. Inden disse afsnit introducerer Del I problemstillingen ved en kort beskrivelse og eksemplificering af det, der er blevet kaldt 'spatial mapping', dvs. udnyttelse af rummet i tegnsprog til at gengive lokativiske relationer, over for 'spatialized syntax', dvs. brugen af rummet til at udtrykke relationerne mellem verbalet og dets led inden for sætningen.

I 'I.5 Characterisation of the data' diskuteres først tegnsprogs ikonicitet som et metodeproblem. Både informanter og lingvister forledes let til at antage, at tegnsprog er mere ikoniske, end de er. Desuden diskuteres validiteten af grammatikalitetsbedømmelser ud fra en mindre undersøgelse af sætningsknude på dansk. Der peges på, at lingvister ofte bruger grammatikalitetsbedømmelser til at vurdere den grammatiske acceptabilitet af sætninger, der afviger på ganske bestemte måder fra en prototype, og da grænserne for en kategori opbygget omkring en prototype netop ikke er faste, sætter man informanterne i en umulig situation, når man beder dem tage stilling til eksempler i grænseområderne. Desuden kan tegnsprogsbrugere finde sådanne vurderinger specielt vanskelige, fordi tegnsprog ikke har nogen skriftsprogstradition og ikke nogen stærk standardisering. Endelig er mange af de fænomener, rummet bruges til at udtrykke, stærkt kontekstafhængige, hvad der også bidrager til at vanskeliggøre grammatikalitetsvurderinger. I slutningen af I.5 beskrives endelig de data, afhandlingens analyser bygger på.

Afsnittet 'I.6 Form analysis of signs' omfatter dels en kort introduktion til tegnsprogs udtryksmidler og analysen af tegn på det, der svarer til fonologisk niveau i lydsprog, dels introduceres en særlig model til beskrivelse af enkelttegn, Liddell og Johnsons model. Denne model er specielt velegnet til analyse af verber, der udnytter rummet til at udtrykke relationerne mellem verbalet og dets led ved hjælp af kongruens. Modellen giver også anledning til en diskussion af kategorien *locus*. Da et tegns manuelle artikulator befinder sig forskellige steder i rummet i forhold til tegnerens krop i forskellige verber med samme semantiske relation til et nominal, kan locus ikke være et fysisk punkt i rummet i forhold til tegneren, som påstået i nogle beskrivelser af amerikansk tegnsprog (ASL). Derfor tales om retninger ud fra tegneren snarere end punkter i rummet i forbindelse med verber, der viser kongruens. I andre sammenhænge, nemlig i forbindelse med tidslinjer og den gruppe verber, der betegnes som polymorfemiske, udtrykkes loci snarere ved punkter eller områder inden for tegnrummet.

Locus bruges altså om en kategori, hvis udtryk er retninger ud fra tegneren eller punkter og områder i tegnrummet, og hvis indhold nærmere præciseres i de følgende afsnit. Loci kan ikke ses i sig selv, men kun gennem den måde, de påvirker udførelsen af et tegn, der har en locusmarkør.

I Del I beskrives også nogle verbetyper formelt, og tegnsprogs morfologiske type diskuteres. Det er blevet hævdet, at tegnsprog er stærkt flekterende sprog, idet mange tegn kan ændres på systematisk måde. Der er imidlertid sjældent tale om bøjning i den forstand, at alle tegn af en bestemt ordklasse ændres på samme måde obligatorisk i en bestemt grammatisk kontekst. Snarere er det sådan, at sandsynligheden for, at et tegn modificeres på en bestemt måde øges i bestemte sproglige kontekster og afhængig af semantiske og formelle træk ved tegnet.

I 'II Discourse and Space' beskrives først fænomenet referenceramme i tegnsprog. En referenceramme er de loci, en tegner anvender til referentielle formål i en bestemt diskurs eller en bestemt sekvens af et diskursforløb. Det drejer sig dels om deiktiske, dels om anaforiske loci. De deiktiske loci styres naturligvis af referenternes position i forhold til tegneren i samtalesituationen. Men anaforiske loci vælges heller ikke arbitrært; valget af dem, og dermed opbygningen af referencerammen, er styret af en række semantisk-pragmatiske konventioner. Loci vælges under indflydelse af ikonicitet (rummet afspejler lokativiske relationer mellem referenterne), sammenligning (hvor to referenter modstilles ved at blive knyttet til loci til højre og venstre i forhold til tegneren), semantisk beslægtethed mellem referenterne, herunder konventionen om, at 'ejendel følger ejer' (dvs. ejendel knyttes til samme locus som ejer), og referentens kanoniske sted (en referent knyttes til samme locus som en stedreferent, som den første referent typisk er forbundet med (en mand med sin arbejdsplads, den by, han bor i, osv.)). Det vises også, at ændringer i referencerammen kan signalere forskellige diskursniveauer, fx et indskud i forhold til en fortløbende fortælling. Konventionerne for valg af loci udtrykker også tegnerens holdning (empati eller mangel på samme) til referenterne. Hvis tegneren kun taler om én referent, vælges locus til højre eller til venstre. Hvis tegneren taler om to referenter og identificerer sig mere med den ene end med den anden, vælges locus frem lidt til højre eller venstre for midten om den ene referent og tættere på tegneren oftest i modsat side om den anden referent. Hvis tegneren identificerer sig lige meget eller lige lidt med de to referenter, vælges loci skråt til siderne. Der er altså en kontrast mellem dimensionerne diagonalt i tegnrummet og en dimension parallelt med tegnerens kropsplan.

Konklusionen her er, at det rum, der udnyttes i referencerammen, er semantisk og pragmatisk "ladet", før tegneren overhovedet begynder, og at referenter kan tilføres betydning gennem de loci, de knyttes til. Dette vises også gennem en analyse af tidslinjer i dansk tegnsprog ('I.3 Time lines'). Tidslinjer er bestemte loci, der forholder sig sådan til hinanden, at et locus udtrykt ved ét punkt i tegnrummet repræsenterer et tidligere eller senere tidspunkt end et locus udtrykt ved et andet punkt afhængig af tidslinje.

I 'II.4 Loci and referentiality' vises det, at ikke alle referenter knyttes til loci. Jo højere et nominals referentialitet, des større sandsynlighed for, at referenten knyttes til et locus. Begrebet referentialitet kendes også fra lydsprog, og i det indgår, at referenten er konkret og specifik og har høj tematisk relevans eller høj generel relevans for deltagerne i samtalen. Animathed spiller en mindre rolle i dansk tegnsprog, idet såvel animate referenter som stedreferenter i reglen knyttes til loci, hvis de også har høj tematisk værdi eller høj generel relevans. Dog er der animate referenter med høj tematisk værdi, som ikke knyttes til loci. Dette forhold skal ses i lyset af et andet træk ved tegnsprog, det fænomen, som jeg kalder 'shifted locus', og som gennemgås i afsnit II.5 ('II.5 Shifted reference, shifted attribution of expressive elements, and shifted locus').

Referenceskift, er det forhold, at pronominel reference i citeret tale afspejler den citerede senders synsvinkel. Der er kun delvis referenceskift i citeret tale i dansk tegnsprog, idet en tegner kun kan henvise pronominelt til sig selv ved en pegning mod sig selv uanset den oprindelige ordlyd af citatet. Et andet fænomen er 'shifted attribution of expressive elements'. Det betyder, at tegnerens mimik og kropsholdning skal tolkes som udtryk for en omtalt persons (eller andet kognitivt væsens) holdninger og følelser. Dette fænomen sammenlignes med træk i talesprog, der viser *style indirect libre*, hvor såvel en persons tanker som vedkommendes ytringer kan gengives med de emotionelle udtryk, som vedkommende selv ville bruge, men med den *shifter*-brug (pronominer, tempus, stedsadverbier), som er udtryk for den egentlige sender. I mange kontekster bruges desuden locusskift, dvs. det forhold, at tegneren bruger senderlocus om en anden referent end sig selv, og at tegneren bruger et andet locus om sig selv end senderlocus. Senderlocus er det locus, der udtrykkes ved området tæt på tegneres krop. Den referent, som senderlocus bruges om, betegnes som synsvinkelholderen.

De tre fænomener, referenceskift, skift i tillæggelse af ekspressive elementer og locusskift, hænger sådan sammen, at alle tre følges ad i citeret tale (med de begrænsninger i pronomenbrugen, der er nævnt ovenfor). Men de to sidste fænomener kan forekomme sammen eller uafhængigt af hinanden uden referenceskift i andre kontekster end citeret tale.

I afsnit 'II.6 Pointing signs' beskrives først fem typer pegetegn, et pronomen, en bestemmer, en partikel, et verbum og en proform. Proformen er et pegetegn, der forekommer sammen med tegn af den type, der ikke kan modificeres i rummet; proformen er så bærer af modifikation, der udtrykkes rumligt. Pronominet og bestemmeren findes i flere former med mere eller mindre fonetisk vægt, som afspejler træk som senderens forventning om modtagerens kendskab til referenten, referentens forudsigelighed for modtageren og kontrast. Til sidst analyseres de pronominelle pegetegn for trækket *person*, dvs. findes der personlige pronominer på tegnsprog? Kun en pegning mod sender selv kan analyseres som et symbol med shifterfunktion og betydningen første person. I pronominerne skelnes der altså kun mellem første person og ikke-første person i dansk tegnsprog.

I konklusionen på Del II sammenlignes loci's funktion i dansk tegnsprog med de mekanismer i lydsprog, som bruges til at holde styr på referenterne ('reference-tracking mechanisms'), og her specielt naturligt genus. Substantiver i dansk tegnsprog har ikke inhærent locus på samme måde som substantiver i lydsprog kan have inhærent genus. Da loci ikke vælges arbitrært i tegnrummet, afspejler de i et vist omfang semantiske træk ved referenterne på samme måde som naturligt genus. Loci kan også sammenlignes med demonstrativer brugt anaforisk i lydsprog til at holde styr på referenterne. Demonstrativerne afhænger af modtagerens erindring om diskursforløbet for at opfylde deres funktion, mens loci afhænger af modtagerens visuelle hukommelse og erindring om diskursforløbet samt semantisk-pragmatiske træk ved referenten.

I bogens anden hoveddel, 'III Verbs and Space', analyseres især verbernes rumlige modifikation i lyset af to teorier om ledrelationen i sætninger, den lokativiske teori, hvor relationen mellem verbalet og dets argumenter analyseres som semantisk overførsle fra et udgangspunkt til et mål, og transitivitetsteori, hvor vægten i højere grad lægges på bl.a. agentivitet og punktualitet. Transitive sætninger kan også ses som standardiserede måder at beskrive lokativisk komplekse begivenhedsforløb. I dansk tegnsprog er der to hovedtyper af verber, polymofemiske verber og ikke-polymorfemiske verber.

De ikke-polymorfemiske verber kan tage tre forskellige typer rumlig modifikation ('III.2 Different types of modifications: An overview'). Den første type er distributionsmodifikationer, som ikke blot forekommer ved verber, men også ved andre prædikative tegn og ved hele sætninger eller konjunktioner ('III.5 Modifications for distribution'). Denne type modifikation består i reglen af reduplikation af tegnet samtidig med en rumlig bevægelse af hånden/hænderne, og den udtrykker, at indholdet af prædikatet eller hele sætningen er fordelt over enheder eller steder eller over punkter eller perioder i tid. Den næste type modifikation er kongruens. Kongruens betyder, at et tegn modificeres for en eller to referenters locus. Der findes to typer kongruens, semantisk kongruens, hvor bestemte verber, de såkaldte kongruensverber, kongruerer med et eller to semantisk bestemte led med hensyn til locus, og pragmatisk kongruens, hvor et prædikat kongruerer med et topik. Den tredje form for rumlig modifkation er synsvinkelmarkering, hvor et kongruensverbum forsynes med en markør for senderlocus i stedet for en kongruensmarkør.

I forbindelse med diskussionen af kongruens vises det, at locusmarkørerne på verbet ikke kan være inkorporerede pronominer ('III.6 Semantic agreement and marking for a specific point of view', 'III.6.1 Alternative descriptions'). Kongruens i dansk tegnsprog er utypisk ved, at det styrende led kan være ufuldstændigt specificeret for kongruenstrækkene (person og locus), og ved at kongruenstrækket locus har et måske ubestemmeligt antal underkategorier. Kongruens i dansk tegnsprog kan imidlertid meget enkelt tolkes ind i Lehmanns (1982) teori om kongruens i lydsprog og belyser rigtigheden af denne. Lehmann påpeger, at kongruens bidrager til at fastholde den sproglige genstand eller referenten (dvs. endnu engang den 'reference-tracking', som blev omtalt ovenfor) og sammenligner kongruens i naturlige sprog med differentierende referentielle indices i formelle sprog. Det er netop denne funktion, loci opfylder. Lehmann hævder ganske vist, at deiksis ikke bidrager til at holde referenten konstant, og loci bygger på deiksis, men i modsætning til udtryk brugt deiktisk i lydsprog er tegn med locusmarkører ikke shifters i tegnsprog, og derfor kan loci, på linje med nominalklassifikation i lydsprog, bidrage til at holde referenten konstant.

Kongruensverberne kan deles i to hovedtyper, enkeltkongruens- og dobbeltkongruensverber. Det vises, at nogle defektive paradigmer inden for hver hovedtype såvel som det usædvanlige forhold, at verberne fortrinsvis kongruerer med P-led frem for A-led, belyses af udviklingstendenser i dansk tegnsprog. Ældre døve er mere utilbøjelige til at bruge locusmarkører i verbet for A-leddet end yngre døve. Der tegner sig således en udvikling fra den ældre til den yngre generations sprog mod stigende brug af A-ledskongruens. Denne tendens forklares i afsnit 'III.6.3 The many uses of the *c*-form' ud fra en analyse af de mange funktioner, som opfyldes af locusmarkøren for senderlocus, betegnet *c*. Senderens "krop" bruges til at udtrykke agentivitet (inklusiv 'experiencer') i tegnenes subleksikale struktur. Desuden bruges senderlocus til at udtrykke kongruens med første person i yngre tegneres sprog. Derigennem udvikles muligheden for at bruge senderlocus til at udtrykke synsvinkel, dvs. det forhold, at locusmarkøren for senderlocus kan indsættes på P-leddets plads i nogle kongruensverber, uanset om P-leddet har første persons reference eller ej. Denne udvikling af en synsvinkelmarkør fra en enhed med første persons reference sammenlignes med brugen af retningsaffikser i dialekter af nahuatl og i aztekisk.

Semantisk kongruens er semantisk entydig i dansk tegnsprog, mens pragmatisk kongruens er semantisk flertydig ('III.7 Pragmatic agreement'). De former af et kongruensverbum, der viser pragmatisk kongruens, er forskellige fra de former, der viser semantisk kongruens, og pragmatisk kongruens rammer hele prædikatet, ikke kun verbalet. Forskellen på semantisk og pragmatisk kongruens afhænger af forskelle i sætningernes opbygning. Pragmatisk kongruens bruges til at fokusere relationen mellem prædikatet og topik, bl.a. i udtryk for psykisk afstand, kontrast, parallelfokus og en sætnings eller et prædikats relevans for modtageren i overtalelse og ordrer.

De manuelle artikulatorer i polymorfemiske verber ('III.8 Polymorphemic verbs') beskrives i adskillige tegnsprog som classifiers og en parallel til klassifikatoriske verber i athabaskiske sprog. I afsnit 'III.8.2 Predicate classifiers and classificatory verbs in spoken languages' vises det med det athabaskiske sprog koyukon som eksempel, at de klassifikatoriske verber ikke er classifiers, men verbalstammer, og i 'III.8.3 Classifiers or verb stems in Danish Sign Language?' bruges tre stammer, som alle kan bruges om menneskers stilstand og bevægelse, til at vise, at der er tale om netop stammer med hver deres leksikale semantiske egenart. De polymorfemiske verber analyseres således som bestående af en stamme (udtrykt ved verbets manuelle artikulator), som obligatorisk kombineres med et eller flere morfemer udtrykt ved bevægelse, hvortil knyttes et eller flere rumligt udtrykte morfemer.

I afsnit 'III.8.4 Movement morphemes in polymorphemic verbs' diskuteres det først, om bevægelsesenhederne i polymorfemiske verber er analoge helheder eller kan analyseres som morfemer, og det vises, at en sekvens af bevægelser kan analyseres som enheder af genkommende bevægelser med en fast betydning, at det i reglen er muligt at specificere en bevægelsesenheds distribution både i relation til andre bevægelsesenheder og i relation til stammer, og at tegnere selv bryder komplekse bevægelser ned i sekventielle strenge af bevægelser og integrerer strenge af bevægelsesenheder i komplekse bevægelser uafhængigt af ikonicitet. Derpå følger en gennemgang af en række bevægelsesmorfemer (dvs. morfemer udtrykt ved bevægelse) i dansk tegnsprog delt op i hovedgrupperne *location, motion, manner, distribution, extension* og *aspect* med diskussioner af afgrænsningsproblemerne. I 'III.8.5 Categories of stems in polymorphemic verbs' følger en gennemgang af forskellige typer stammer, hvor inddelingen bygger på en kombination af semantiske og morfologiske kriterier (hvilke bevægelsesmorfemer kan de kombineres med?).

I afsnittet 'III.8.6 Polymorphemic verbs and space' vises det, hvordan de polymorfemiske verber kan udnytte rummet på helt andre måder end de ikke-polymorfemiske verber til at beskrive lokativiske forhold. En særlig mulighed i forbindelse med polymorfemiske verber er, at tegneren fastholder en stamme med en bestemt rumlig placering med den ene hånd, samtidig med at hun udfører et prædikat, en sætning eller et forløb af sætninger med den anden hånd. Den "fastholdte" stamme beskrives som 'a backgrounded construction', og det vises, at dens funktion kan være at udtrykke lokativiske forhold ('locative configurations') og tekstkohærens. Denne mulighed bygger på udtryksforhold i tegnsprog, som er udelukket i talesprog. Det fører videre i en diskussion af kategorien referentprojektion, som er helt særegen for tegnsprog. En referentprojektion er en form, som repræsenterer referenten i forskellige sammenhænge. Bl.a. kan man henvise til en referent ved en pronominel pegning mod en referentprojektions udtryk. Der findes tre typer af referentprojektioner, loci, stammer i polymorfemiske verber og tegnerens krop.

I gennemgangen af forskellige rumlige morfemer i polymorfemiske verber vises det bl.a., at de lokativiske forhold mellem en iagttager og to genstande kan beskrives umiddelbart ved hjælp af tegnerens to hænder. I lydsprog skelnes der mellem to strategier til at udtrykke lokativiske relationer mellem enheder uden inhærent orientering, 'the ego-opposed strategy' og 'the ego-aligned strategy', som hver især tillægger genstandene forskellig orientering i forhold til taleren. I tegnsprog kan der opstå misforståelser, når det er uklart, om tegneren beskriver en situation set fra sin egen synsvinkel eller set fra modtagerens synsvinkel. Tegnsprog peger derved på, at 'the ego-aligned strategy' i lydsprog kan tolkes som en 'alter-opposed strategy', dvs. som en beskrivelse af enhederne sådan, som de ses fra modtagerens side snarere end fra senderens.

'Locus shifting' er en term, der er blevet brugt i tegnsprogsforskningen til at beskrive det fænomen, at en referents locus ændres som følge af et bevægelsesverbum. I dansk tegnsprog er 'locus shifting' ikke syntaktisk, men pragmatisk bestemt. Dvs. 'locus shifting' forekommer eller forekommer ikke afhængig af behovet for at fastholde referenters identitet eller vise synsvinkelskift.

Tegnerens krop kan som nævnt bruges som referentprojektion, og det vises, at det er nødvendigt at skelne mellem tegnerens krop og senderlocus. Desuden sættes brugen af tegnerens krop som referentprojektion i sammenhæng med kodningen af agentivitet i senderlocus i kongruensverbers subleksikale struktur. Til sidst i afsnit 'III.8.6 Polymorphemic verbs and space' diskuteres forskelle i målestok eller skala, dvs. forskellen på referentprojektionen tegnerens krop og referentprojektioner, som består af stammer i polymorfemiske verber, hvor hånden repræsenterer hele referenten. Ved et eksempel vises det, hvordan skift i målestok kan bruges til at gøre en stil mere levende, og hvordan skift i målestok, skift i tillæggelse af ekspressive træk og locusskift virker sammen om at udtrykke synsvinkel og skiftende fokus på forskellige referenter i en situation.

I konklusionen, Del IV, vises det, at der ikke er nogen absolut forskel mellem ikke-polymorfemiske og polymorfemiske verber. Der er tale om et kontinuum med ekstremer. Rummet bruges til at udtrykke såvel lokativiske forhold som andre semantiske og pragmatiske forhold, og den ene funktion kan ikke ses som primær i forhold til de andre. Kongruensverberne viser, at agentivitet spiller lige så stor en rolle som lokativiske relationer, og rummet bruges også til at udtrykke synsvinkel, fokus på relationen mellem et topikalt led og prædikatet og semantisk beslægtethed i valget af loci og referentialitet. Mange par af ikke-polymorfemiske verber og beslægtede polymorfemiske verber kan analyseres som udtryk for modsætningen mellem 'event'-verber og proces-verber, hvor 'event'-verberne typisk er transitive.

I konklusionen sammenfattes også kategorien locus's status, og der peges på nogle områder i sammenhæng med udnyttelsen af rummet, som bør uddybes, især en analyse af sætningens led med henblik på at fastlægge deres syntaktiske status (subjekt, objekt; topic, comment) og en analyse af sammenhængen mellem kontinuet mellem ikke-polymorfemiske og polymorfemiske verber og forskellige diskurstyper.

I Appendix A beskrives ganske kort dansk tegnsprogs status og udvikling i den danske døvegruppe og det danske samfund. Appendix B er en vejledning til forståelse af de transskriberede eksempler i bogen.

Illustrations

Illustrations 361

initial   final

Ill. 1: fr+ANSWER+c

Ill. 2a: THINK   Ill. 2b: HAPPY

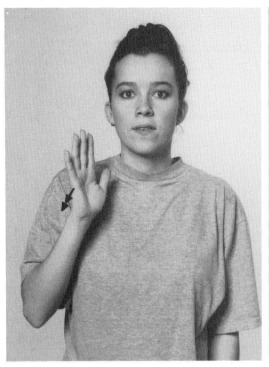

Ill. 3a: DANGEROUS   Ill. 3b: STRANGE

Ill. 4a: SUMMER   Ill. 4b: BAD

Illustrations 363

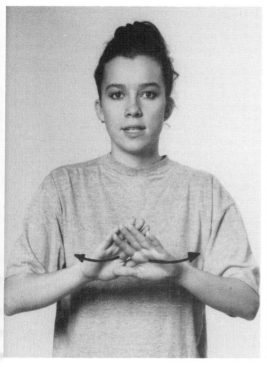 

Ill. 5a: ALL-RIGHT   Ill. 5b: DAY

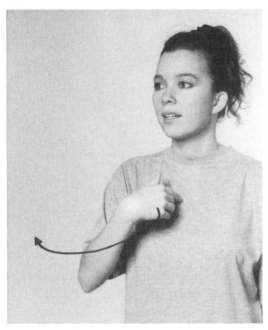 

initial   final

Ill. 6a: c+GIVE+multiple+fr
I give to many/all of them

initial   final

Ill. 6b: c+GIVE+fr
I give to him

initial

medial

Ill. 7: BAD+intensive

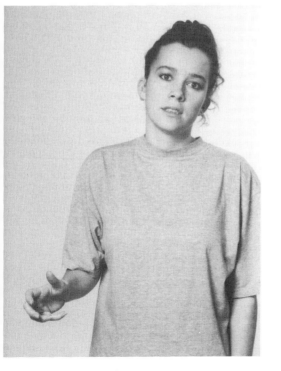

final

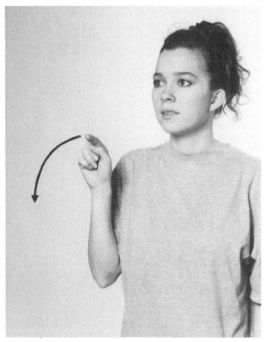
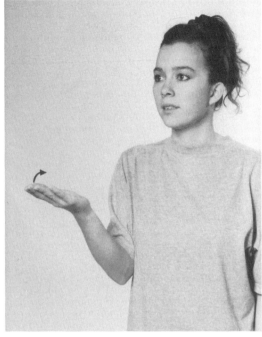

Ill. 8: GO-TO (base form)Ill. 9a: BECKON (base form)

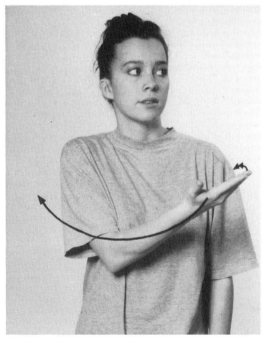
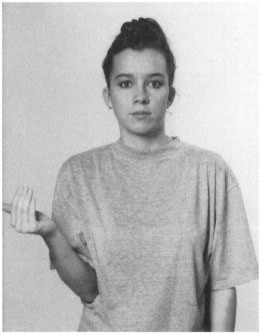

initialfinal

Ill. 9b: BECKON+multiple
beckon many/all of them

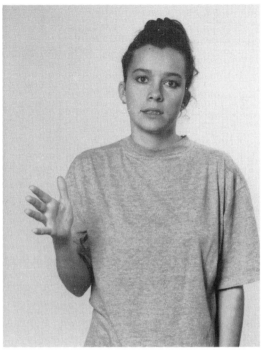

initial final

Ill. 10: OF-COURSE

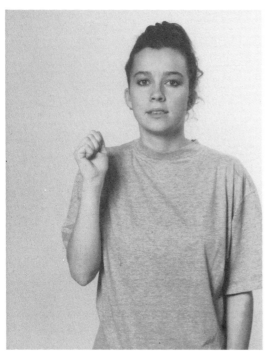 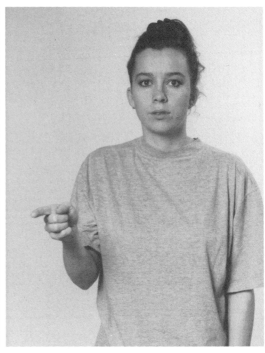

initial   final

Ill. 11a: TO-TOWN

initial   final

Ill. 11b: OUT

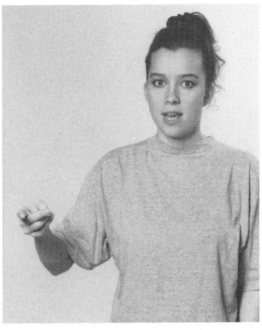

      initial   final

Ill. 12a: c+ANSWER+fr
I answer him_i

      initial   final

Ill. 12b: fr+ANSWER+fl
he_i answers him_j

 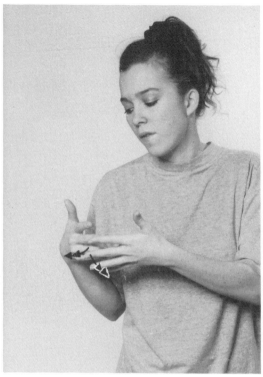

Ill. 13a: c+EXPLAIN+fr
         (neutral level)
         I explained it to him

Ill. 13b: c+EXPLAIN+frd
         (low level)
         I explained it to him

Illustrations 371

initial   final

Ill. 14a: DECEIVE+fsr
(someone) deceives him

 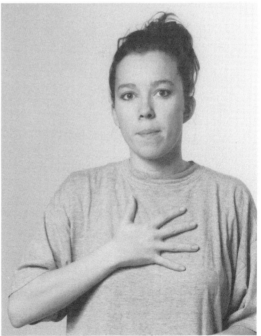

initial   final

Ill. 14b: DECEIVE+c
(someone) deceives me

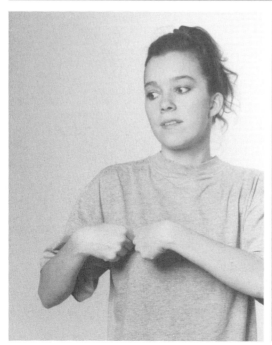
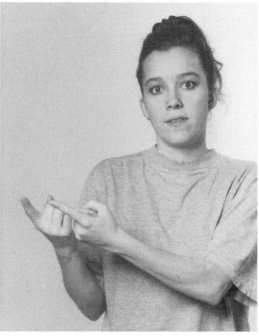

initial   final

Ill. 15a: fr+INVITE+c
he$_i$ invites me

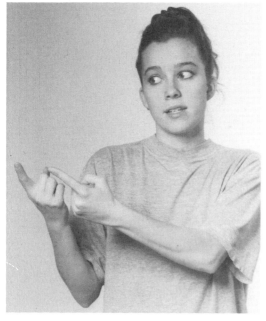
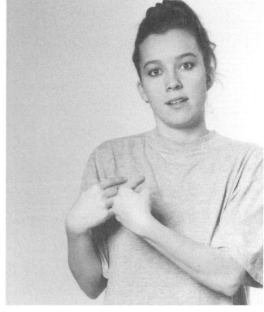

initial   final

Ill. 15b: c+INVITE+fr
I invite him

Illustrations 373

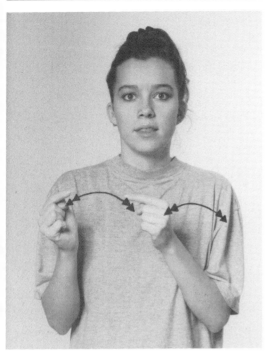

Ill. 16a: DISCUSS (base form)

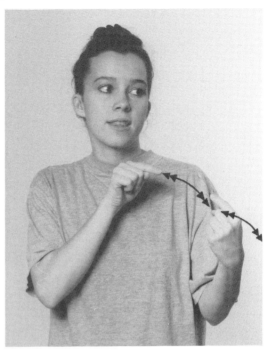

Ill. 16b: c+fs1+DISCUSS
he$_j$ and I discuss

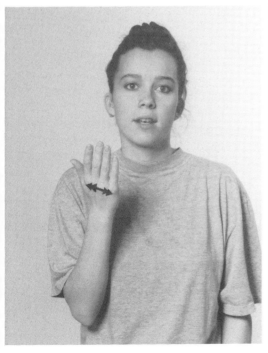

Ill. 17: READ (base form)

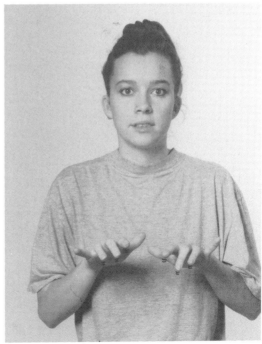

Ill. 18: TYPE (base form)

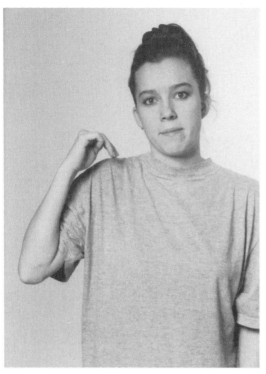 

Ill. 19a: 'last Monday' Ill. 19b: 'next Monday'
(movement not shown)   (movement not shown)

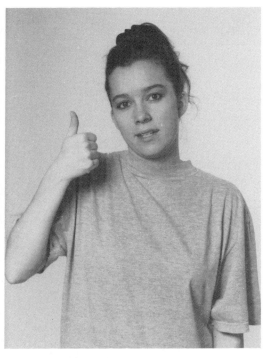

Ill. 20a: JANUARY+deictic-tl-before...
(movement not shown)

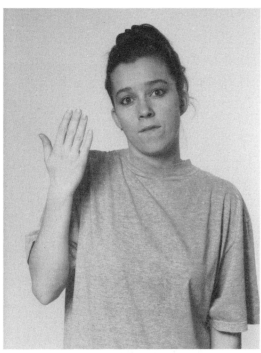

Ill. 20b: ...BEFORE+deictic-tl...
(movement not shown)

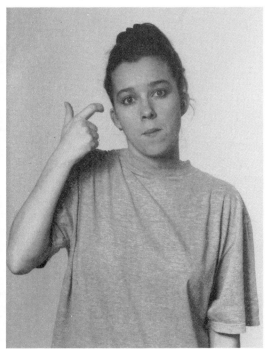

Ill.20c:...MONTH+deictic-tl-before...
(movement not shown)

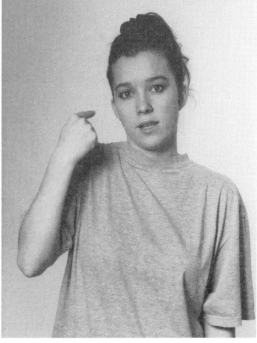

Ill.20d:...DET+deictic-tl-before...
(movement not shown)

 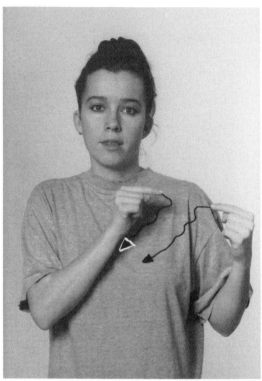

Ill. 21a: GROUP+pl.+anaph.-tl-before ...

Ill. 21b: ...DISCUSS+multiple+anaph.-tl-before

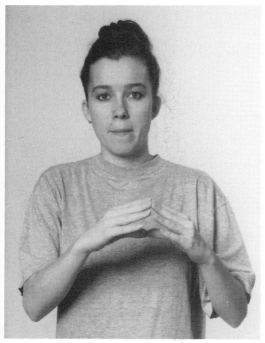
(MARCH (movement not shown))

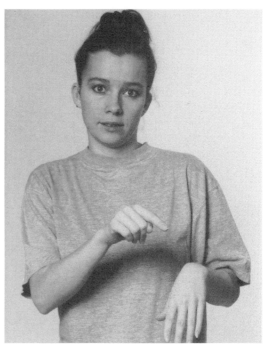
(DET (movement not shown))

(APRIL (movement not shown))

(DET (movement not shown))

Ill. 22: 'end of March, beginning of April'

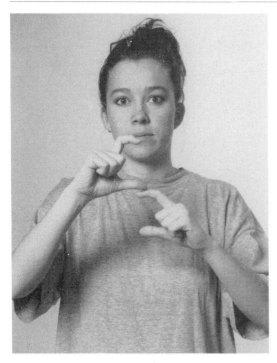

Ill. 23: 'one week earlier'

 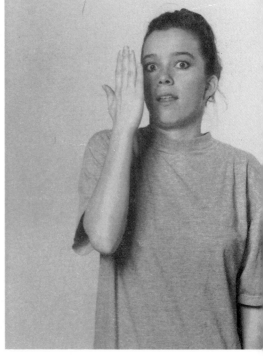

initial   final

Ill. 24: '(Suddenly Christmas) came up'

Illustrations 379

Ill.25a: She looked at him arrogantly. (woman's point of view)

Ill.25b: She looked at him arrogantly. (man's point of view)

(REPAIR+fsld) (movement not shown)

(FIX+fsld) (movement not shown)

```
Ill. 26: gaze: +----------Vfsld-v+----
        REPAIR+fsld FIX+fsld /
        He repaired and fixed (the dishwasher).
```

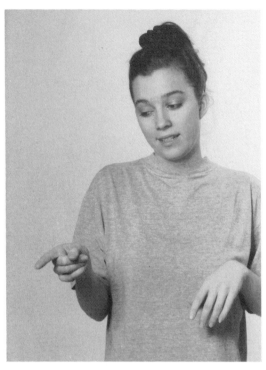

(DET+fsrd)(movement not shown)

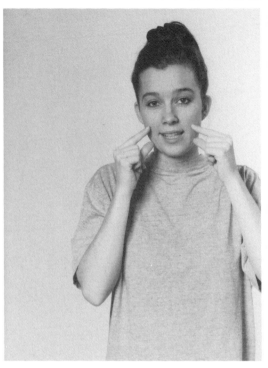

(CAT) (movement not shown)

(SLEEP) (movement not shown)

Ill. 27: _____t
DET+fsrd CAT / SLEEP /
The cat, it's asleep.

(PRON+fsrd) (movement not shown)   (CAT) (movement not shown)

Ill. 28:   _____t
        PRON+fsrd / CAT /
        That's a cat.

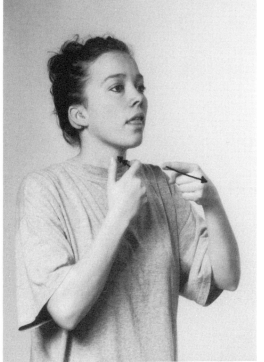

Ill. 29:
IN-TROUBLE
PROFORM+multiple+mixed-tl
(I'll) run into trouble again
and again.

Ill. 30: SECOND+redupl.
(movement not shown)
(My) second (child)...

Ill. 31: _____squint
PRON+emphatic+1.index
...she (is called
Charlotte)...

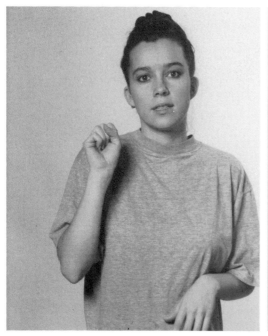

initial   final

Ill. 32: c+SEND+fr
She was sent to (the nursery school).

Ill. 33:
c+EXPLAIN+sl
(I) told (her grandmother)...

initial   final

Ill. 34: c+GIVE+fr
I gave to him

 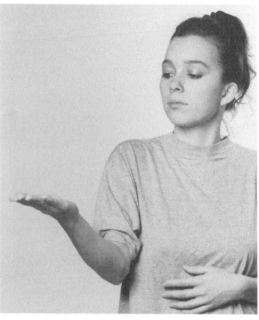

initial   final

Ill. 35: Handle-flat-entity-Pm+(c+move-line+loc+rightward)
I handed it to him on a tray.

initial   final

Ill. 36:
THIRTY+multiple
Everyone (who works shorter hours works) thirty (hours a week).

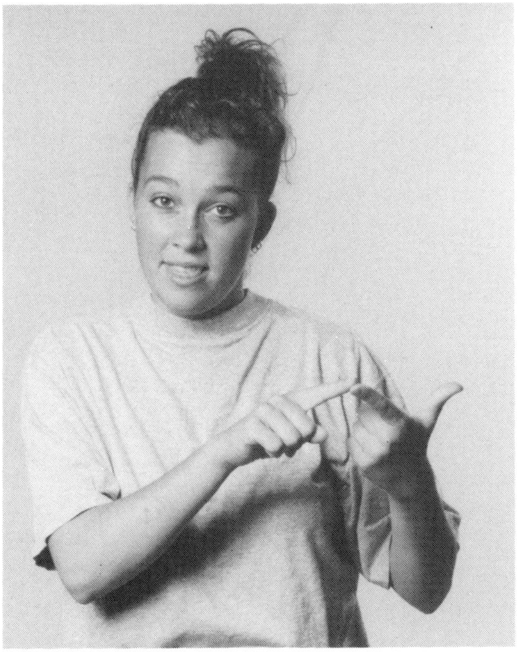

(SECOND+fsl) (movement not shown)

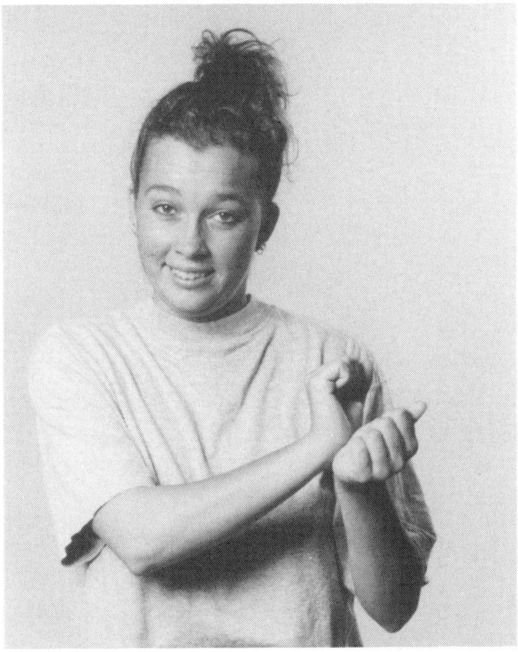

(CLASS+fsl) (movement not shown)

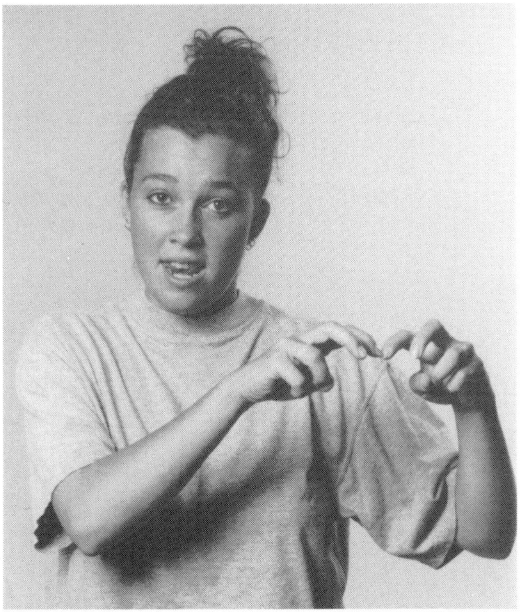

(ANALYSE+fsl) (movement not shown)

(FINISH+fsl) (movement not shown)

Ill. 37: ______________________________________ t

SECOND+fsl CLASS+fsl ANALYSE+fsl FINISH+fsl
When grade two had finished analysing...
or When grade two had been analysed...

 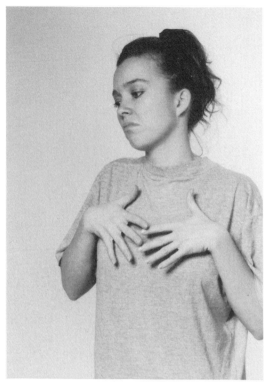

Ill. 38: TELEPHONE (intrans.)

Ill. 39: GREATLY-DISAPPOINTED (movement not shown) (gaze and body and head rotation indicate the locus of the cause of the disappointment)

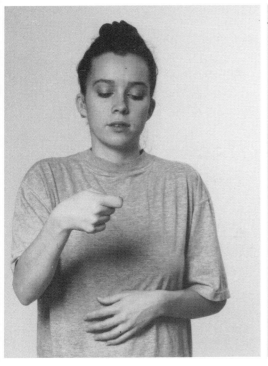

initial

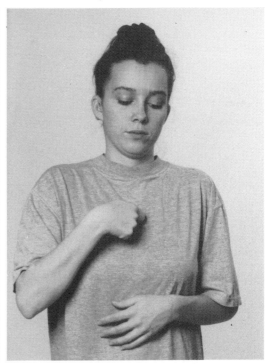

medial

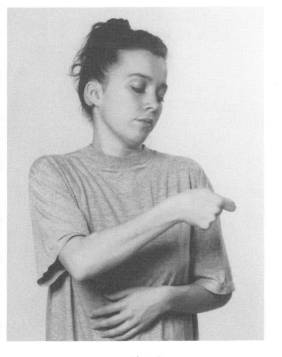

final

Ill. 40:
neu+GIVE-KEY+multiple+c+sl
Then we all got (keys).

388 Illustrations

Ill. 41:

                cond
IF+multiple+deictic-loci

If anyone of you (wants to participate,...)

Ill. 42:

[PRON SUGGEST]+multiple /

(The sequence of signs is repeated an indefinite number of times while the hands move rightward.)

They all made different suggestions.

(PRON (movement not shown))

(SUGGEST (movement not shown))

Illustrations 389

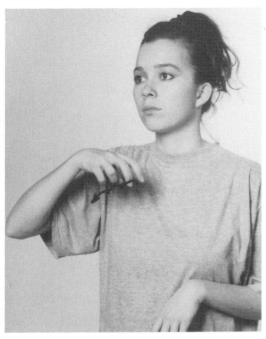

Ill. 43: JUMP+multiple+mixed-tl /
Then they skip them as
they go along.

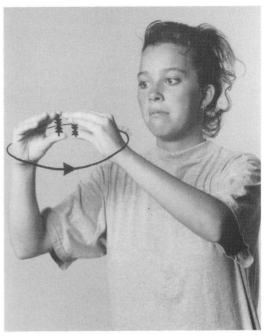

Ill. 44: TALK-WITH-EACH-OTHER+
group+p.a.:fsr
They'll all just sit
talking with each other.

Ill. 45a: EXPLAIN (base form)

Ill.45b: f1+EXPLAIN+c
(Dan) explained it to me.

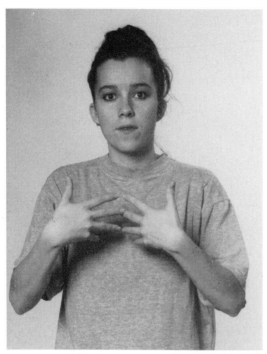 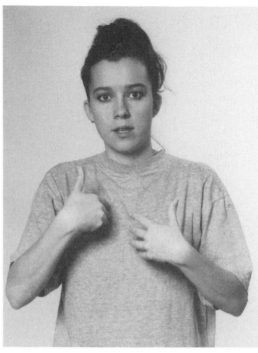

(neu+EXPLAIN+c)(movement not shown)   (..1.p)
         Ill. 46: neu+EXPLAIN+c..1.p
                 (Annegrethe) will explain it to me...

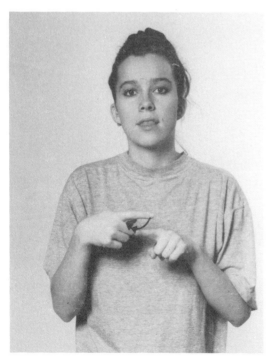

Ill. 47: c+TEASE+neu
        (...the blind there
        often) teased (us).

Ill. 48a: COMFORT+c /
...he should be comforted.

Ill. 48b: COMFORT (base form)

Ill.48c: COMFORT+fsrd /
(...his mother)
comforted him.

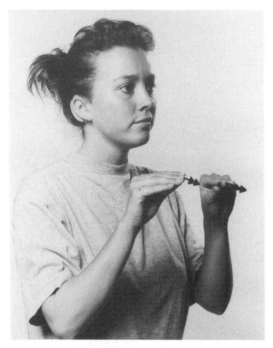

Ill. 49a: TEACH (base form)

initial final

Ill. 49b: _____affirm_____
neu+TEACH[+]+c
(The participants) have already learnt (the B-proform).

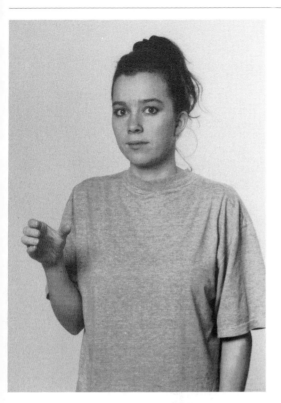

Ill. 50: articulator of MOVE-PERSON,
Handle-cylindrical-entity-Pm,
Cylindrical-entity-Pm

              initial   final

Ill. 51: semantic agreement form of PAY: c+PAY+fr

              initial   final

Ill. 52: pragmatic agreement form of PAY: PAY+p.a.:fr

Ill. 53:
pragmatic agreement form of
EXPLAIN: EXPLAIN+p.a.:fsl

Ill. 54:
pragmatic agreement form of
DISCUSS: DISCUSS+p.a.:fsl

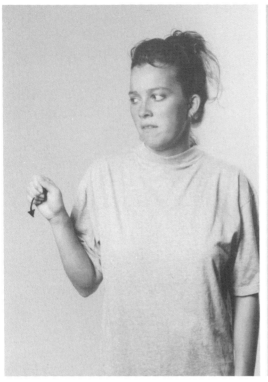

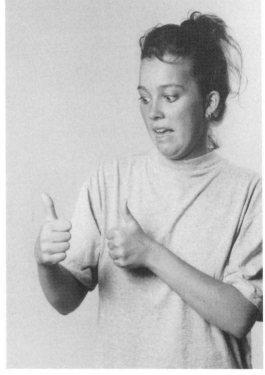

Ill. 55: WHO+deictic-locus /
Who is that?

Ill. 56:
1-Pm+(hold+c)+ 1-Pm+(near-
r.shoulder+move-line+forward) (move-line+
forward)--------------------

(initial position)

...I see someone moving forward
and I pursue him...

Ill. 57:
V-Pm+(loc+c)
I stand (innocently...)

```
              initial                           final
Ill. 58:  ................Handle-hand-Pm+(c+move-line+1.hand+closing)
          1-Pm+(hold+left)------------------------------------------
          ...he finally caught him...
```

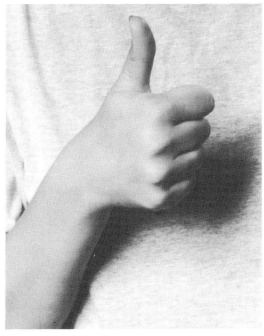 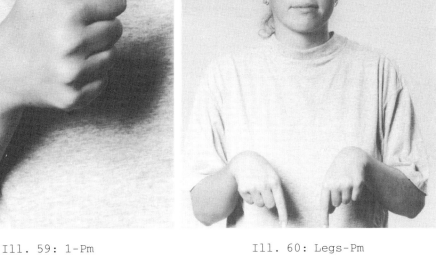

Ill. 59: 1-Pm   Ill. 60: Legs-Pm

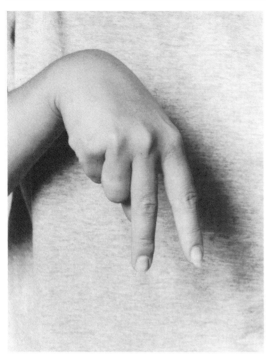

Ill. 61: V-Pm   Ill. 62: Index-Pm

 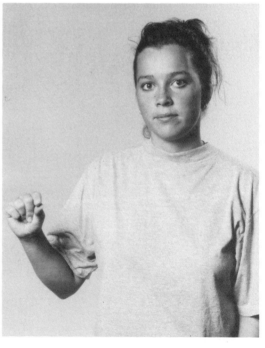

initial   final

Ill. 63: LEAVE

Illustrations 399

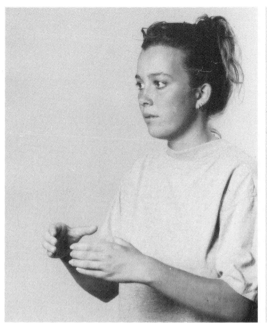

Ill. 64:
Group-Pm, Pillar-Pm,
Medium-sized-cylindrical-
entity-Pm, Handle-medium-
sized-cylindrical-entity-Pm

Ill. 65:
Handle-large-cylindrical-entity-
Pm+(at-a-loss)
What should we do with
(the children)??

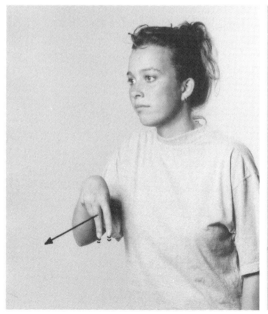

Ill. 66a:
V-Pm+(c+move-line+forward)
go somewhere, walk straight

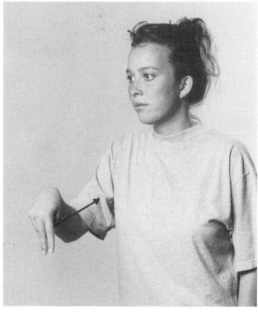

Ill. 66b:
V-Pm+(distribution-line+neu)
many/they stand in a line

400 Illustrations

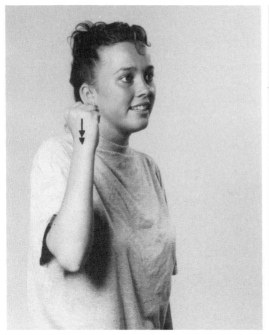

Ill. 67a:
Handle-handle-Pm+(over-
r.shoulder+resolutely)
(Eight people...) walked in
holding (a string...)

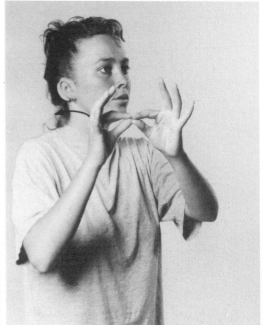

Ill. 67b:
STRING+over-r.shoulder-per-
STRING+over-r.shoulder-per-

pendicular-to-body-surface
pendicular-to-body-surface

(Eight people...walked in
holding) a string...

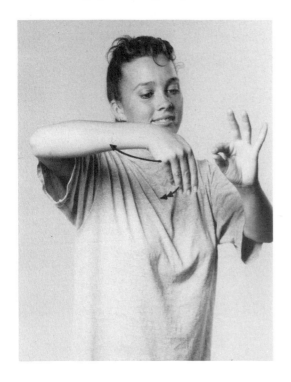

Ill. 67c:
STRING+over-r.shoulder-per-
STRING+over-r.shoulder-per-

pendicular-to-body-surface /
pendicular-to-body-surface--

General-entity(B)-Pm+(loc+
----
distribution-line+over-
----
r.shoulder-perpendicular-
----
to-body-surface)

(...holding) a string with
various things...

Illustrations 401

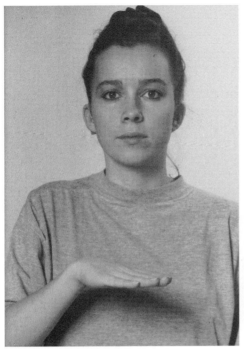

Ill. 68: Car-Pm

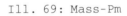

Ill. 69: Mass-Pm

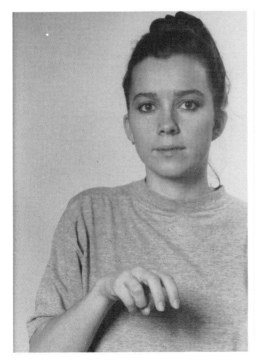

Ill. 70: Animal-Pm

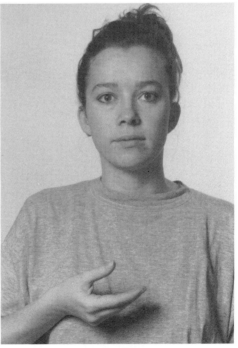

Ill. 71: Handle-three-dimensional-entity-Pm

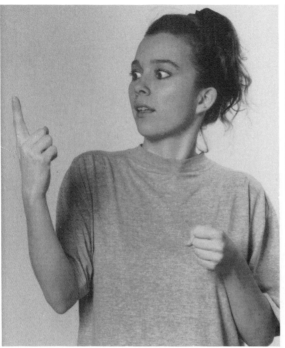

Ill. 72:
Someone is sitting in a car while seeing somebody else approaching. (movement not shown)

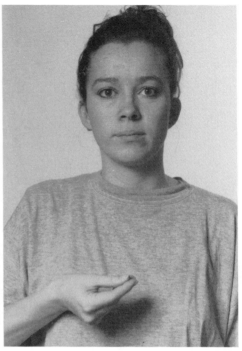

Ill. 73: Handle-two-dimensional-entity-Pm

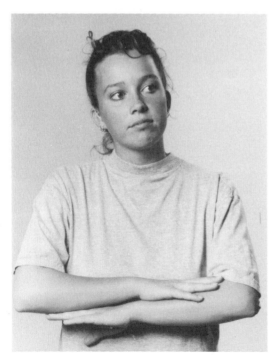

Ill. 74: Arm-Pm+(analogue-wait)

                    initial   final

Ill. 75:
Thin-entity-surface-Pm+(extension-end-of-stick+tip-of-1.index)
Short-thin-entity-Pm+(hold+vertical+neutral)------------------
(They...saw at) the top (a gold star).

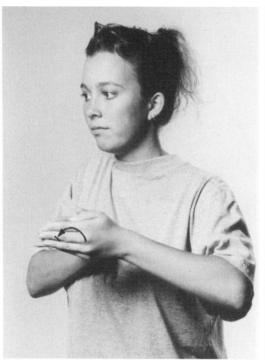 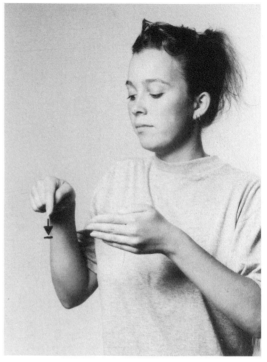

Ill. 76a:
Boat-Pm+(move+loc+neutral+
Boat-Pm+(move+loc+neutral+

orientation-front-facing-right)
orientation-front-facing-right)

So the ferry came here...

Ill. 76b:
Boat-Pm+(move+loc+neutral+
Boat-Pm+(move+loc+neutral+

orientation-front-facing-
orientation-front-facing-

right) / PRON+emphatic+right
right)+(hold)---------------

Literally: ...and this one, (the other ferry...)

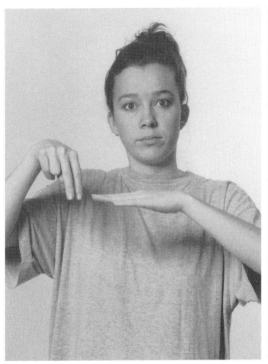 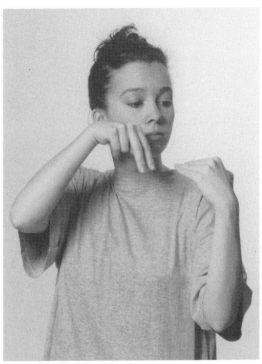

Ill. 77a:
The car is parked with its side to me and its front facing right in relation to me, and the man is ahead of the car's front.

Ill. 77b:
The car is parked with its front towards me, and the man is ahead of the car's front.

Ill. 78a: He was ready to set off.
(movement not shown)

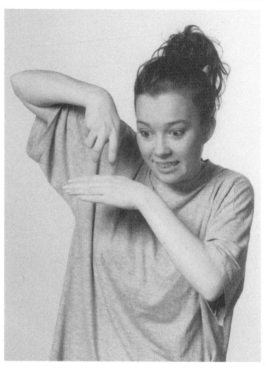

Ill. 78b: He skied downhill.
(movement not shown)

Ill. 78c: (An old woman) crossed the track.
(movement not shown)

Ill. 78b: (Ole) screamed out while rushing down.
(movement not shown)